Wild Rover

the advEntuRes of

a mEntal deFectiVe

Gary Dennis

a memoir

First Published June 2015

Trysofta Productions
Box 300872
Albany
Auckland
New Zealand

Email: gary@trysoftaproductions.com

Website: www.trysoftaproductions.com

Typeset in Times New Roman 11 pt

Cover design by JD photography & design, Auckland, NZ.

ISBN: 978-09864566 1 9

For my Darling Lorene

from

your Mad Irishman

Thank you for teaching me the value of persistence

and

With thanks to my parents, Rosie and Skipper, who nicknamed me
Wild Rover and endowed me with a sense of adventure greater than
any of us could ever have imagined.

2017

For Corina,

Dare your Genius

Sam

x x

In memory of Dr. Lewis Jones D.C.

The life of every man is a diary in which he means to write one story, but writes another and his humblest hour is when he compares the volume as it is with what he vowed to make it.

J.M. Barrie
(Peter Pan)

Dear Reader

It's taken me a lifetime of adventure and a world of pain to learn how to live and love without condition, but the essence of it came to me one day when revenge handed me the opportunity to crucify my best friend. I realized in that moment that life is not determined by fate, but rather our faith in the bigger hand that is playing our game. That while we are being played we have a choice; to become like the petty thieves and pirates who would see to our undoing, or confront ourselves and through courage and daring find a better way to end our story. Idealistic I know, but I have since discovered that it is the difference between a life well lived and one that is wasted on false Gods and missed opportunities.

I started my journey around the world as a philosopher and a seeker of truth guided by the ultimate question that haunts most parents; 'what do I tell my children?' On my quest I have climbed from the pits of despair to the pinnacles of success and then fallen all the way down again. Unexpectedly, I would find the answer to my question by going through hell. I might still be there now, if it had not been for her brown eyes and her tropical smile that whispered "what if?" but ultimately it was her courage that saved me.

My story then is a long one and a busy one. I have written it for my children so that they will know what really happened. I have changed the names of some of the characters for the sake of their children to save undue publicity.

I do hope that you enjoy!

Book One

1

THE END

This is how my adventure started.

A dark cloud descended on me one day when I was fourteen. It blew on before it had any chance to impact on my consciousness or give clue to what lay ahead. A few weeks later it blew in again and left within me a dread that I am yet to forget. The visits became more frequent and the periods much longer until a week ran into a fortnight and then settled for months at a time. The unwanted visitor, squatting in my head and taking a dump over every thought I might dare to have that might save me. This went on for years. The only way to end it I thought, was … well, to end it!

Harry Byrnes is an ancient pub half way up the Howth Road close to where I lived at the time. It's funny how Irish stories always seem to revolve around a pub. Back in those days it was a pirates' den. A magnet for teenage iniquity. A place to which I had never belonged. My first and only visit was planned to be a swan song to all that was wrong with the world. That and the need to swallow Dutch Courage. Because I had never driven a car into a granite wall before I needed a bit of a helping hand. It was finding the courage to swallow Dutch Courage that presented the greater challenge.

I wasn't a drinker. I'd failed the test when I was fourteen years old on a twelve pack of beer that I had been unable to hold down. The experience created in me an instant allergy to beer. Life gave me a second chance the following year when my best friend and I shared a large bottle of Bacardi Rum with Coke as a chaser. We woke up defeated in a field a day later and swore to never touch the drink thereafter.

I'd heard somewhere after, that it was "important to pace yourself." Downing a half bottle of Bacardi in less than an hour had been my original downfall! Shy of Bacardi I sat at the bar and ordered vodka. I was amazed at how much it tasted like lemonade when you mixed the mixer in with the alcohol instead of drinking it as a chaser. A new innovation in drinking. I felt nothing, so tried another and then one more shortly thereafter in an effort to get into the rhythm of what was going on around me. The measures seemed petty in comparison to the whole mouthfuls that I was historically used to, but I did not complain. In fact I actually started enjoying the buzz. Driving into the granite was going to be a lot easier than I had imagined

I could have stayed all night, but decided after eight shorts that I had courage enough. Any more might ruin my focus. I had a date with a railway bridge and as a stickler for punctuality, I did not want to be late. To make sure I got there I had lavished my car with extra drink of the octane type. Behind the driver's seat I'd stashed a plastic gallon container full of petrol whose lid was stuffed with a soaked cotton rag. Behind the passenger seat and in the boot were matching cocktails. I was tanked and ready to burn.

The desired "ending" was five hundred meters downhill from the pub, but I took off in the opposite direction. I had been raised with the firm belief that you sometimes had to *make a good run at it,* if you were to reach your objective. The fact that I was driving an old rust bucket made my theory more relative. It would take her a good mile and a half at least to get her up to the necessary impact speed.

When I reached the correct distance I made a u-turn without spilling a drop. I undid my seat belt and pulled over to the side of the road to say a quiet prayer for my parents. I had not left a note. It would look like an unfortunate accident. Messy, but final, with no guilt attached. They had done their best. What more could a favorite son ask for.

I did not idle too long because I did not want to waste petrol. It is amazing the thoughts that can run through a screwed up brain. First gear, then second. I was doing sixty before I knew it. I'd had the car serviced especially for the occasion. I sailed past Harry's at the estimated seventy I would need with the downhill stretch still to go. I was easily going to make it. The headlines would read how I'd gone out in a blaze of glory.

Then suddenly everything started to slow down. I'd heard talk about how your life flashes before you "movie-like" just as it ends. I'd never imagined that my insignificant existence was even worth the credits. But there it was for all that it was worth. What surprised me most was the regret. Not for the things that I had done, but rather, the pot of gold that stood undiscovered at the end of the rainbow. This of course was followed immediately by the usual blinding flash of light.

When I came too, I found that I had missed the bridge and was sitting in the car park of the local squash club a hundred yards down the road. Not a burn nor a singe mark in sight. However, one of the petrol containers had tipped over and spilled on the floor of the car. The smell from the fumes was so nauseating that the first thing I did was open the door and throw up on my shoes as I abandoned the car.

'How the fuck did I get here?' I questioned as I came to my senses and took stock of the situation. No red-hot metal, no billowing smoke, no charred remains. Just a half drunk idiot who had failed to end his miserable life, but found himself instead staggering aimlessly around an empty car park.

'Maybe you were afraid,' came a reply. Don't ask me from where. Certainly not from any of the voices in my head. They were too numbed from the near miss with the bridge to have anything to do with this madness.

They say God sometimes speaks when we are open to hearing. He sounded like Anthony Hopkins!

'I'm not afraid of dying,' I shouted in frustration. 'Do you think I'd go to all this trouble and not finish the job!' I screamed and whirled around in all directions looking for a body upon which to vent my spleen. There was no reply. 'I'll show you!' I shouted, looking up at the stars, angry at the thought that I had been cheated of my objective by a Prick who never had the balls to show himself.

I climbed back into the car and started the engine. The voice, I decided, was nothing more than a psychedelic mixture of vodka and petrol fumes. I rolled down all of the windows to clear my head. I was sick and tired of other people who thought they knew better, having a say in what I was doing.

First gear out of the car park, then second as I turned left on to the main road and headed back for the bridge. I'd have to go all the way back to the starting line again before making the second attempt.

'I'm not afraid of dying,' I muttered to no one in particular as I passed under the bridge.

'Who said anything about dying?' "Tony Hopkins" replied from the back of the car.

'What?' I looked in the rear view mirror, but the Bastard was still hiding.

'I did not say anything about being afraid to die!' The voice echoed, everywhere and nowhere.

'Then what the hell are you on about?' I was tired of the riddles.

'Has it ever occurred to you that you've been afraid to live?'

The next part of the conversation about me *not* being afraid to live, went something like this.

'I left school when I was fourteen, qualified in construction and joinery at eighteen, had my own sub contract business with several employees and a combined income that the Tax Man would have hung me for had he known half of what I was earning. While the rest of my friends were still riding pushbikes and going on camping holidays in the freezing rain a few miles down the east coast of Ireland, I had a car, a hang glider and a sailing boat and I had just spent the previous summer driving around Europe with my girlfriend. On top of this I had an opportunity to go to the United States and study to be a *Doctor* of Chiropractic. Afraid to live ... I don't think so!

'Really?' came the voice.

'Really!' For someone who was *All Seeing*, he had clearly missed a thing or two.

'Then why are you so miserable?'

It was like a slap in the face. The fact that it was prefaced by the 'f' word only accentuated my true pain that much more. I had it all, but I had nothing. Living my life the way I had been taught to do by those who thought they knew better had failed me miserably. As good as it might have seemed, my life was like climbing a mountain of somebody else's choice burdened with a back pack with all sorts of stuff that I did not want to carry.

My teenage years as a consequence had descended into a fog of depression and such unrelenting loneliness that by the time I reached nineteen I had grown hopeless. *The All seeing Bastard*, in one foul swoop, had gotten right to the heart of the matter. I was so stunned by the realization that I didn't have an answer to his question.

As I came out the far side of the bridge, I was distracted by a new sign board that was brightly lit on the opposite side of the road. It was a beach scene advertising the joys of living in Australia. In the background were a gang of happy people playing happy beach-ball to a backdrop of a happy, sun-drenched turquoise sea. In the foreground was a handsome guy at a massive charcoal BBQ with beer in one hand and a set of tongs in the other. The BBQ was decked out with steaks and kebabs and all sorts of delicious looking seafood. He was placing the biggest shrimp I had ever seen on the barbie, but his eyes were fixed directly on mine.

"Hurry up mate. I'm just putting some shrimp on for ya!" stated the caption below the poster. It was another world. So singularly inviting that for an instant, I forgot my misery and the mission that I was on.

'What if?' Tony interjected.

'Wha...?'

'What if you chose to be brave instead of scared, to follow your heart instead of your head, to start living the life of which you have dreamed, instead of waiting for some imaginary life to show up before you choose to be happy?'

'Wha...?'

'If you are not afraid of living, then what if you were to go to Australia instead of driving into granite?'

I realized then, that my entire existence up to that point could be classed as a near life experience. I don't know what happened to make me miss the bridge, but it had taken a close shave with death to see the light.

'What if?'

Tony faded into silence after that, but the billboard was like the writing on the wall. I decided then to go home and rethink my story. Say nothing to nobody about anything. The big bang was deferred, but not cancelled. Going to Australia would mean breaking my parent's hearts, but it was a better alternative than crushing their souls.

A month later, it occurred to me at 30,000 feet as I flew across the world's oceans, that I was travelling in the footsteps of the greatest adventurers before me; Saint Brendan, Magellan, Columbus and Cook. While they had no charts at the time, they had a compass and an inner confidence that could be relied upon to guide them. I had nothing, other than the false beliefs and dubious indoctrination of others which had almost cost me my life.

I knew I needed a reference, something to guide me, a singular truth that could be relied upon to check my journey and make sure that I was staying on course. It finally came to me in the form of a question as I departed Hawaii on the final leg of my journey.

What do I tell my children?

2

"The injustice and unfairness of it all!"

Before going any further, this story is not a trauma drama or pity party about how hard I had it in the past. It's not a rags to riches story. Nor is it about happy endings. It's much more important than that. It's more of an 'after story' about the journey I made 'after' taking responsibility for my own life. If it was a 'before story' I could point the finger of blame in various directions and state with the strongest of convictions that it was somebody else's fault that my head was so twisted as a teenager. A long list could easily be constructed to include parental control, school bullying, economic recession, born on the wrong side of the tracks, butt ugly or low self-esteem and the injustice and unfairness of it all. I could give you a bunch of statistics and facts to back up my argument. The news is full of it, psychologists make a fortune out of it and the psychos use it as an excuse for going off the rails. The truth is that there is always some other poor bugger out there who is worse off than you.

We don't go around blaming people when we are successful, so why should we give anyone a hard time for the spectacular ways in which we are *bound* to fail? History is abundant with thousands of successes that have been born of poverty, deprivation and bad starts. As Winston Churchill once said: "if you are going through hell ... keep going. You will eventually come out the far side."

Being down, for whatever reason, does not have to mean out. It doesn't have to mean THE END of your story. For me it was just the beginning of many new beginnings yet to come.

3

"Globalfornacteduptedness"

One of the things you learn as an adventurer is that the world isn't flat and that there aren't any dragons on the horizon. Nowadays, we know this to be the case, but a few hundred years ago we dared not venture too close to the edge of the world. The thinking was so ingrained that the great explorers often had to recruit their crews from jails and force them into service to make up the numbers necessary to sail their ships.

So what has this all got to do with me shagging off to Australia? Well, it's not the threat of dragons on the horizon that stops you from breaking out. It is mostly the dragons in your head. You have to push back the horizon of your imagination first, if you are ever to push back the boundaries of your reality. This can be hard though when you have monsters guarding the perimeter.

The early excitement of the adventure to Australia carried me over the fence. I hit the ground running, got myself a job as a bar tender at The Menzies Hotel in Sydney and met some friendly people just like I'd seen on the poster. But after a few months, when the novelty wore off and I had settled into a routine, the monsters caught up and began to haunt me with a vengeance.

By day I was Mr Happy Go Lucky "top of the morning to ya," nothing was too much trouble. By night I lay in my room, alone and terrified, my mind a living hell. For someone who the year before had no fear of throwing himself off the side of a cliff into thin air strapped to a flimsy hang glider, there was nothing more terrifying to me than losing the light of day.

Being a health care professional now I could give you a diagnosis of my condition. Something along the lines of acute agoraphobia, or social deprivation syndrome or paranoia. Personally, I think 'Globalfornacteduptedness' (fucked in the head) has a certain ring to it! You'd think someone like this would be incapable of carrying out a normal life, but by day I was a different animal.

I finally lied my way into the post of Senior Trades Instructor in the rehabilitation department of the Royal South Sydney hospital. They specialised in brain damage and the treatment of injuries caused in industrial accidents and motor vehicle accidents. There is no way they would normally let a 'fruit and nut case' work in a place like this. However, people with Globalfornacteduptedness are like chameleons and very good at disguising themselves to appear far more normal than the average person. In spite of my success though, I knew as I made my way home every night in the fading light, that monsters the size of Godzilla were waiting for me in the shadows.

This went on for months.

There comes a day though, when you finally hit rock bottom, when you want out, no matter the cost. As much as it appealed to me to walk out on the balcony and take a flying leap, neither suicide (nor drugs) were an option. My only alternative was to call Godzilla's bluff. Inspired by the poster under the bridge, I decided to go out and build a better life. I did not have a clue how I was going to do it, but my first step was to get out of the room.

Tossing Godzilla and his mates to one side I finally struck out one night, determined to meet someone (anyone) I could talk to, that might break the inertia of fear that *I had allowed* to enslave my mind. That they might be strangers did not matter. All I knew was that I needed allies and the more I could muster the stronger I would become.

Going on the defensive, for they now knew that their very existence was at stake, Godzilla and company roared and stomped and threatened me with painful destruction. This may all sound a bit melodramatic to a normal person like yourself, but for me, the inner war had just begun.

As luck would have it I met a one-armed gay guy in a bar also seeking salvation. A machine had taken a fancy to his right arm and he had come off second best, just below the elbow. Feeling less than whole, he had become a recluse for over a year and this was the first time he had ventured out. By the time he had finished telling me about how he had become detached from his arm (and the difficulty he was having masturbating with the opposite hand) I felt somewhat better about losing my mind. He drank beer and I drank lemonade and we played pool and shot the shit and drank some more. When we parted company outside the bar in the early hours, Godzilla was nowhere to be found.

The following night I did not go home from work, but walked the streets around Circular Key and the Rocks in search of another invalid with a story. There were none to be found, but as long as I kept moving on a nightly basis, I managed to stay one step ahead of the posse of demons that tried to drag me back to my room. Again, this all might sound like it's a bit over the top, but to me it was a matter of life and death. I was a dead man walking so long as the monsters ruled my head.

It wasn't easy. There were many nights of terror, but when a man is committed the Gods join in and with the bit of luck that they brought me, I managed to finally shake off the Wild Things and build a life for myself outside the cave.

As it turned out, working at the hospital was also my salvation. While I may have been missing part of my mind, there were some there who were missing parts of their brains or arms or legs or any bodily part that comes off when the laws of nature conspire with bad luck. It took a year, but I managed to climb out of the hole that I had allowed myself to fall into. Wouldn't you know it though, just as I was starting to feel confident again, I received the strangest of phone calls that was to change my fate forever.

4

"Trust me!"

'Have you made a decision yet?'

'I'm still thinking about it,' I lied over the crackling long distance line. My younger brother had gone to America to study Chiropractic at the same time that I departed for Sydney. Worn out from the academic demands of the first year, he was miserable with home sickness and wanted me to join him for company. Having no High school diploma, I had no yardstick by which to gauge my intelligence other than he was my kid brother and as such, I was smarter than him ... shaky ground upon which to plan a future! However, I found his tales of academic woe so discouraging that I had pretty much decided not to be a Chiropractor when suddenly, our conversation took a different slant.

'Who is starting from overseas this year?' I hoped to dilute his mood by giving him new friends to look forward to before I told him I wasn't coming.

'There are two coming from France, three from Japan, a guy from Australia and I hear there is one from England as well. Oh yeah, and one of the Kiwis here said that there is a girl coming up from New Zealand.'

'She will be your wife!'

'What did you just say?' I was shocked by the statement, but equally confused. The voice was no longer that of my brother.

'I said there were two from France, three from Japan, a ...'

'No, no! I interrupted. 'After that, what did you say after that?'

'A girl from New Zealand?' he was bewildered my tone of urgency.

'Trust me!'

It was the voice again. The one from the car park in Ireland after my close shave with the bridge. Tony Hopkins was back on the scene.

'Are you all right?' my brother asked.

I was so dumbfounded I hung up.

I remember my father telling me that the first time he laid eyes on my mother at a dance that he knew she was the one for him. That it had been the single most important moment of his life and he knew, without the shadow of a doubt, that they would spend the rest of their lives together. We have all seen it in the movies and read about it enough to know that not only is it possible, but for many, it is the one factor that people rely on to choose their mate. Now here I was listening to a voice telling me to *'trust it'* without a shred of evidence, visual, logical or otherwise to back it up. What if she was ugly? Then I remembered an old story that goes something like this ...

In his quest to find a better world, an adventurer became lost in heavy fog and stumbled over the edge of a cliff. Miraculously, his fall was broken by a tree stump jutting out from the side of the rocks. The freezing weather however was such that he would still die if he remained latched to the security of the tree.

'Help!' he cried out, terrified that his quest might end before finding his true Nirvana. 'Help,' he called repeatedly long into the night, until his voice became a rasp for all that could have been and he began to slip slowly away. He was not a religious man, but his desperation was great and his pride no longer mattered. 'God, *please* help me,' he whimpered one last time.

'I have come to save you,' a voice suddenly answered from the edge of the precipice.

'Dear God yes!' the man cried out. 'Please, hurry for I am almost frozen.'

'Do not despair. I am the answer to your prayers. It won't be long before you are back on the road again,' the voice encouraged. 'But you will have to be brave if I am to save you.'

'I am!' the man replied. He had faced many dangers on his quest and somehow, always managed to get through. 'I will do anything. Please help me,' he begged.

'Do you believe in me?' came the unexpected reply.

'Yes I do!' declared the man, even though he could not see where the voice was coming from.

'Do you have faith in me?'

'Without doubt!' His conviction was true, for in his hour of need he felt that he had found God and his prayers had truly been answered.

'Let go!' the voice instructed.

'What?' replied the man, for below was certain oblivion.

'If you believe in me and have faith in me and know that I will save you … then let go.'

'But Lord I will die.'

'Let go!'

Like the guy on the cliff, I was suddenly stuck between the proverbial rock and a hard place. In his case he chose to hold on to the only security that he had in the hope that a more sane solution showed up. The following morning, when the fog had lifted, his frozen body was discovered by two natives on a narrow pathway just four feet below the tree stump that he had staked his life on. The pathway led to a beautiful valley where the Land he had dreamed of lay waiting.

Disenchanted by the undertones of my brother's take on how tough college was and the limitations of my aforementioned lack of intelligence, the sane choice for me was to hold onto the security of what I knew.

The alternative? To listen to "Tony" and 'trust him' and continue my adventure to America. To a guy who was just starting to get his head back in order, this verged on madness. The odds weren't just stacked against me. They were so left field that I was likely to fall off the edge. Insanity really, until I realized that listening to the *voice* a year before had saved my life … all that I had to do was let go.

5

"Dorkus"

When a push comes to a shove sometimes you have to jump and build your wings on the way down. That's what I did when I went to America. The fact that my brother had paved the way was a deception that I relied upon heavily. I kept telling myself that if he could do it then so could I. After all, Chiropractic wasn't rocket science!

The first hurdle was getting a High School diploma. This was a requirement for entry into college to study the two year science diploma necessary to qualify for acceptance to College. If successful, then I faced a further four years of study before final graduation. Six years of hard slog and all because of a girl I had yet to meet!

I'd love to tell you that I was confident, but the truth is I wasn't. Not in any way shape or form. If Sydney Harbor was big then, I was out of my depth in America, where a simple Paddy like me was just about treading water.

You can imagine then, how I felt going in to take my first exam. This wasn't just a matter of a high school diploma or my future as a Chiropractor. It was 'make or break' for the girl across the room that I had yet to meet. My palms were sweaty, my mouth suddenly dry. I had shortness of breath from the hyperventilation caused by my racing heart. Before entering the confines of the exam hall I had dry wretched once, been to the bathroom twice and had to stop myself from making a bee line for the emergency exit. I'd have sooner faced a firing squad.

After all of the drama though ... the exam didn't seem so bad, but whatever confidence I may have felt afterwards soon disappeared when my brother told me that the exam was nothing compared to the three hundred and sixty 'ball busters' I would have to pass over the next six years to get through College. Six weeks later, my High School Diploma arrived in the mail!

Two things of great significance happened shortly after that.

The first ... as promised by Tony ... was that I met the love of my life. I'd like to brag that having travelled all that distance on a wing and a prayer, it was the most romantic encounter that a guy could ever imagine or hope for. That in a stadium full of well hung studs, she had eyes only for me and that our hearts, from the opposite sides of the world, were bound together 'as one' the moment our souls connected.

The truth is that I bumped in to herself and her roommate in the Fresh Veggie section of Ingles supermarket.

There was no thunder bolt. No cherubs shooting arrows of love from the side lines. No ground shaking cataclysmic revelation. Our eyes didn't lock ... they bounced ... hers out of disinterest ... mine for fear that they might reveal my secret. She was more interested in the price of broccoli than this poor idiot who had listened to a voice that said *'trust me!'*

The best description that I could give you of her is that she was way out of my league. That and the fact that she was madly in love and pining for her boyfriend whom she just had left behind in New Zealand.

While the Gods may have been taking the piss out of me behind my back, they had also conspired that the two of us were the only students to enroll that term. It was inevitable then, that in taking the same classes together, that we soon became friends. Well, she was friends with me that is. I was her *'man in waiting'* who very quickly came to adore the ground that she walked upon. In my desperation, I was prepared to take anything as a sign of affection and soon found that it was not all one sided when, after a few months of carrying her school bag she finally acknowledged her fondness of me with the pet name of 'Dorkus.' I'm not saying that she was the greatest judge of character that ever walked the planet, (especially when she herself was pining for some idiot in NZ) but her keen observation of a guy who was by in large, mostly faking it, made me want to be a better man.

As our friendship developed, so did our ambitions. She wanted to become a Specialist in children's health and open the first Centre in New Zealand with a focus on *Holistic* Family Health care ... whatever that meant.

Me, I was still wrestling with the idea of becoming a Doctor of Chiropractic *and* the voices that echoed around my head. Whatever about my head though, somewhere in the recesses of my heart I had discovered the pilot light of ambition to be a writer. The match had yet to be struck, the fire had yet to be fueled, but there wasn't a day go by that the *Muse* did not whisper inspirations of some sort between the margins of my lecture notes. In my chemistry folder (the most boring subject in the world) I had half a novel written about three best friends who were fighter pilots during the second world war. In the back of my Psychology folder I had two thirds of a *self help* book written on the deep dark world of Godzilla and the Black Dog and how to tame depression. Did I talk about it? No, they were the scribblings of a mental defective who was listening to another kind of voice that he had yet to come to terms with, but it was better than listening to Anthony Hopkins who had come up short on delivering his promise.

The second thing to happen was that the exchange rate doubled, which effectively halved our savings for college fees. This represented a major challenge. Neither of us came from a wealthy background and our original budgets were already stretched (we worked illegally two nights a week to subsidize our living expenses). To overcome the hurdle, we finally devised an accelerated study program of tripling up on classes that would save us a small fortune. This involved travelling a distance of one hundred and twenty miles a day between three different colleges. We managed this by car pooling with a maniac who had a five liter Thunderbird and an *Escort* radar detector that allowed us to cruise at nail biting speeds in excess of a hundred miles an hour on a daily basis.

What I remember mostly about this time is the physical exhaustion and sleeping in class on a regular basis because we also had to increase our work load to four nights a week at the restaurants to make ends meet. There was very little time for love other than pining for someone … who was pining for someone else … which was a complete waste of pining altogether!

This went on and on and on and on for almost six months until I was out of my head with distraction. Finally ... I decided to do something about it.

6

"My mind is distracted and diffused"

We had stopped in to a shopping mall on the way back from college one night and quickly became separated when I was too embarrassed to accompany her in to a lingerie shop. A half an hour later, I found her outside a gift shop glued to a computerized machine that wrote *Poetry* for a dollar a paragraph. In an attempt to find the right words to send to her long distance *beau*, she already had fifteen sheets of paper in her hand. There were another six or seven scrunched up in a waste paper basket on the floor. Minding my own business (I was being completely ignored *as usual*) I reached into the basket and retrieved one of the sheets. I didn't know which was more hopeless. Her dying devotion to some guy she was never going to see again, or the fact that she was relying on some heart-less machine to make a connection.

Being one who hails from the land of saints and scholars where a single word can be a sacred devotion, or a rapier that cuts to the bone, the words on the piece of paper were nothing more than verbal diarrhea. I could tell she was thinking the same thing by the disappointed look on her face after the machine suckered her for another dollar.

My resolve to tell her how I felt though suddenly paled in significance to her enduring commitment to the Eejit overseas.

After six months of wasted desperation, I finally realized that it was time to throw in the towel.

'You can do better than this,' I ventured, crumbling the piece of paper I held in my hand.

'What?' She was oblivious to my observation.

'I said that you can do better than this crap machine that spits out shite like this!' I threw the paper back into the basket.

'I'm not very good with words.' Her embarrassment at being caught out gave me permission to share in her intimacy.

'It's easy.' I found it hard to believe that a straight A student should have such problems with something so simple. 'My mind is distracted and diffused.'

'Your what?'

'Write this down.' I handed her a pen.

'My mind is distracted and diffused,
My thoughts are many miles away,
They lie with you when you are asleep
And kiss you when you start your day!'

She hesitated for a moment, during which I thought I had been caught out, but when she asked me to repeat one of my all-time favorite verses from Simon and Garfunkel, I knew that I had gotten away with it. After that, all I had to do was look in to her eyes and tell her how I felt about her every moment of every single day. The words flew out of me like butterflies and fluttered around her in a halo of crimson that accentuated her beauty so much that my heart ached for the losing of her. Then they danced their merry dance onto the page as traitors to my soul, which she duly sealed in an envelope to send to her boyfriend ... B$%#@&d!

My only consolation was the friends that we made, who were mostly among the small group of international students. One in particular, also from New Zealand, was this handsome-looking bugger by the name of Scotty. Tall and broad of shoulder, he had the classic chiseled features of an adventure hero. His wit and sense of humor was as sharp as his looks and it wasn't long before we started hanging out like brothers. He proved his mettle early on at a welcome dinner for new students when he picked up this stunning brunette who melted into his arms the second the music started. 'Some guys have all the luck,' I thought and gave him the thumbs up in admiration of his conquest as I saw them leave together arm in arm later that night.

Imagine my mortification two days later when I went around to his place and found her there. Not only did Angel have a Kiwi accent, but she and Scotty were married! She took it well and being an equal to his sense of humor, it sealed her friendship as a sister for the future.

Our routine by then was pretty much set. School, work, study, exams, sleep, school, work, study, exams, sleep for months on end. Every now and then there was a bit of a party or the dollar movies, but it was mostly heads down and bums up and counting the days and our dollars till we got through the science diploma and into Chiropractic College. My trepidation at taking exams slowly receded. I had passed so many tests by this time that it had become more of a technique than brains that got me through. With nine subjects on the go at any one semester, there weren't enough hours in the day to learn everything, so I had devised a method of memorization and topic recognition that pretty had much insured a passing grade. While I still had sleepless nights before every test, which in some cases was twice a week, the *ball busters* that my brother described never gave me a squeaky voice … until!

'Have you heard the news? If there was an anxiety in Darling's voice that bordered on concern, then *my* response verged on the edge of hysterics.

'They have made physics a requirement!'

'Noooooooooo!'

'Yes!'

'F%$#&%!'

So far so good, is what I recorded in my diary at that time. It had been eighteen months since I'd faced off with the granite wall under the bridge and a year since dragging my sorry ass out of a darkened flat in Sydney. I was alive and striving along with a new group of friends towards a future that looked brighter. From a scholastic point of view, the 'Faker' who had been treading water just six months before, was doing swimmingly in keeping up with his peers. My elevation from Dorkus to 'Poet Laureate' may not have been the promise that had brought me to America, but that was okay. In my eyes, it was enough for me to be Darling's confidant and protector. However, with physics as a requirement, all of this was suddenly a fragile and tentative existence tainted by memories of the past.

I was a complete idiot at math. Before travelling to America I had made specific inquiries about math and physics being a requirement and had received reassurances to the contrary. My highest grade ever in my previous academic life had been a C minus!

Delaying entry as a strategy to allow for a brain transplant and sole focus on physics might get me through, but this wasn't an option. If I didn't pass the science diploma at the same time as Darling, then she would go on to Chiropractic College before me and all would be lost.

Talk about being screwed. There was no court of appeal. No back date clause. To top it all off, even if I wanted to subject myself to such humiliation, I also found that in a State that was bigger than the size of New Zealand and Ireland combined, there were no college physics 101 courses available that would complete in time for the new term in College. Well, none that is except one.

The University of South Carolina had an honors physics program on 'Trajectories and Ballistics.' It was way more than we needed, but guaranteed our acceptance to Chiro College. The only requirement for entry was that you had to have physics 101!

7

'Nothing gives greater confidence than ignorance!'

'Read the sign,' the professor pointed to the back wall of his
office when I visited in the hope of gaining entry to his program.
'Nothing gives greater confidence than ignorance,' he stated out
loud just to make his point. Beside the sign was a shield with a coat
of arms. On the opposite wall hung a large painting of two knights
locked in mortal combat. Without invitation to enter, I had to make
my appeal from his doorway. He had long shaggy hair, a shaggy
beard, shaggy dress and an impatient manner that let me know that
with no physics background, I had 'shag all' hope of getting onto
the course.

'I'd be grateful for the opportunity to at least give it a go.' I
tried not to sound like I was begging. As a former Auckland
University student with brains to burn and transfer credits to show
it, Darling had managed to persuade him to make an exception and
give her a place. Knowing that we were heading in the same
direction, I pressed this point home in the hope that the professor
might overlook my total lack of knowledge on the subject.

'This is one of the toughest courses in the university,' he
explained, the same way he had done with every other schmuck
before me who thought that they could talk their way on to the
program. 'Of the twelve thousand students enrolled in this

university, twenty three will start the course. Maybe eight will finish. Of those, one will be further groomed to go and work for NASA. This isn't just any physics program. It's rocket science!

'I know but ...!

'There are no buts. You are not the first. You won't be the last,' he frowned. 'Now I'd be grateful if you could please close the door. I have a busy schedule and I need to get some preparation done.' With that he turned his back to me, reached across his desk to a small stereo that was playing opera and wound up the volume to drown out any chance of further appeal.

Shit out of luck I did as he bid, but not as he expected. Stepping in to his tiny room, I slammed the door behind me and in the grip of passion stood over him with my fist clenched to my chest.

'The New Zealand girl,' I stared him straight in the eyes. 'She is the reason I'm doing all of this,' I tapped my heart with my fist. 'I'm not asking for any favors. I just need the chance, that's all. If I fail, it won't be your fault.'

'Again, the answer is no. If I make an exception for you, then I will have to make it for everyone. Now leave my room immediately ... or I will call security!'

'Please,' I was finally begging.

'Leave,' he demanded and reached for the phone.

I was at the end of the long corridor before I began to realize how intimidating I must have been standing over the poor guy in the confines of his little room. As I descended the stairs to the car park, I cursed each step. All was lost ... or so it seemed.

'Hey!'

I'd reached the bottom of the stairwell before I heard the echo overhead.

'You, down there!' Leaning over the balustrade four flights above was the face of the professor. 'What's your name?'

I thought for sure that he was going to report me. 'Look, I'm really sorry!' I began to climb the stairs to make an act of contrition.

'I don't want an apology. I want your name!' he was adamant.

'Please, don't report me!' I was panting by the time I reached him. 'You'll never see me again, honestly. I'll walk out the door and never come back!'

'I need to know your name,' he repeated, but in a more conciliatory tone. 'How else am I going to register you for the course?'

'No way!'

'Yes ... way,' he half smiled and led us back to his office. He made a point of closing the door after we entered the room. 'I'm making an exception here. Absolutely no-one is to know about this. Do you understand?'

I nodded resolutely. 'What made you change your mind?' I was smiling like the Cheshire Cat.

He ignored my question by shuffling some papers around his disorganized desk. He had his back to me, in a half-hearted attempt to hide what he was doing, but I saw him turn a photo stand of a pretty girl and himself arm in arm, and point it towards the wall. When he turned to me, he had the trace of a bittersweet memory on his face.

'Are you sure she is worth all this trouble?'

'I don't know.' I decided to be honest. 'She doesn't even notice me.'

'Oh, you poor bastard,' he sighed, shaking his head knowingly as he gazed in the direction of the photo. For a moment he hesitated, as if he had changed his mind, then he handed me the registration slip.

'You won't regret this,' I promised.

'No ... but you probably will,' he avoided any eye contact. 'I don't take prisoners.'

As I walked away from his office, the volume increase on his stereo echoed his warning.

It was the 'Nutcracker' by Pyotr Ilyich Tchaikovsky

8

Genius

1% inspiration ... 99% perspiration

If there was one word that best described me up to that moment it was Dorkus. Not because Darling had nicknamed me so, but because in truth, why call a spade by any other name? You can fool some of the people all of the time, but this Faker was just about to have his cover blown. I realized, within fifteen minutes of starting the first physics class, why it was called rocket science. The professor might as well have been an alien.!

The empathy he had displayed in allowing me to join the course vanished the second we started. I'm not just talking about me. Nobody was safe, not even Darling, whom he bawled out in our second class because he couldn't understand her *funny accent*. The attrition rate was so high that within the first three days there were five casualties. His teaching method was the equivalent of academic bullying. I almost came to grief in the third week.

'What is there not to understand?' he yelled in exasperation when I asked for clarification on the hieroglyphics that shone from an overhead projector onto the white board. It was a theorem on velocity and trajectory and I just wasn't getting it. 'Is there anyone else who has a problem with this?' he demanded.

When none of the blank faces that surrounded me dared to volunteer, I became the sole focus of his abomination.

'Rant, rant, rave, rave, cosine this, tangent that, square root multiplied by inverse thrust, subtracted from C multiplied D times the horizon on and on and on and on!' he recounted in a babble that was something close to the speed of sound. 'Do you get it now?'

'No!' I gritted my teeth. After three weeks of humiliation I'd had enough and was just about to tell him, but then the bastard suddenly went ballistic.

'Rant, rant, rave, rave!' he screamed. 'Cosine this, tangent that, square root multiplied by inverse *fucking* thrust, subtracted from C multiplied D times the horizon! What is there not to understand?' he cried in a demented voice. With that, he grabbed the thousand dollar overhead projector and launched it off the top of the bench. It made a perfect arc as it sailed through the air to the far side of the room where it disintegrated into a thousand pieces against the concrete wall.

'I got it. I got it!' I cried in utter disbelief, no longer wishing to throttle him. Watching the projector flying through space had been the perfect *Eureka* moment of understanding. Not just the *now* simple equation that he had scribbled on the board, but my perception of the entire course.

There is a big difference between being a rocket scientist and an astronaut. I may not have been going on to NASA, but this Space Cadet was suddenly going places he had never gone before. I knew there and then that if I could crack that equation, then my thick head was going to be able to crack anything else he chose to slam against the wall.

'Bring it on Motherf$#@%r!'

And he did. By the time mid-term exams came around Darling and I were sweating off the same amount of kilos for physics study as for the eight other subjects in our combined workload. Based on my mid-term result of a B+ I assumed that I had physics mastered and backed off in favor of a number of the other subjects that were becoming shaky from neglect. It was to be a big mistake.

'Shiiiiiit!' is the best word to describe my opening impression of the final physics exam. The first page had six questions on topics, none of which I recognized. Of the twelve questions on the next two pages only seven looked familiar. There were three more pages to go. I scanned the room to see how my fellow study group were doing and could see by the way that they were shaking their heads that they were about as far up the creek as me.

'Did you call me?' The professor was standing right in front of me. By now we had developed a mutual (grudging) respect for each other ... him for my grim determination to hang on, me for the fact that the bastard also happened to be a genius.

'I'm screwed,' I whispered and shook my head as I calculated the cost of failure. Not just the months of setback, but with Darling now writing studiously across the room, it might as well have been a *Dear John* she was completing.

'Bit of a ball buster isn't it?' He smiled, as if somehow he had been talking to my brother. I was already starting to get the headache.

'Please tell me that there is a retake on this exam,' I half begged. It was a contingency I had never had to consider before and I could sense some of my classmates were listening in on the conversation for the very same reason.

'No retake,' he announced out loud. A low-level chattering bounced off the walls. 'You won't need to,' he added in a mollifying tone. 'Go to the extra credit questions on the back page.'

Not expecting much of a reprieve, I turned to the last page of the exam as instructed.

Question: 1

You are in a bush clearing in the African Jungle. Your left ankle is attached to a hoop in the ground by a three foot metal chain. You are upwind of a rhino which has just caught your scent. Beside you, on a mat on the ground, are the parts of a disassembled AK 47 assault rifle. Describe in specific detail your assembly of the weapon and dispatch of the rhino before it charges and kills you. (20 points)

'You're joking me! Right?' I noticed half a dozen students looking hopefully in my direction.

'Have you ever heard me make a joke before?' The professor shook his head.

'No. Not at all, but ...!'

'No buts then,' he cut me off. 'Don't waste your time. Rhinos are very territorial. If you are to have any hope of surviving I'd do the extra credit questions first. Then go back and do the main exam.'

'I'm going to need more paper!' I was suddenly hopeful of rising to the challenge. There was enough adrenalin in the first question alone to fill at least four pages.

Answer 1

I thought it important to give some context as to my purpose in Africa and so began by giving some back story.

I had come to Africa as part of an animal conservation group to save the White Rhino from extinction. My unique qualification for this mission was that I had kissed the Blarney Stone on three separate occasions. As such, my powers of persuasion put me in the position as chief negotiator with the local Warlord who was killing the rhino and selling their horns on the black market. Unfortunately, in a moment of heated exchange over animal rights, we had come to blows and as a show of power to demonstrate who was the better man, he decided to teach me a lesson for breaking his nose. Hence the reason for my present predicament!

Rhinos have very poor eyesight that is compensated for by an acute sense of smell. I knew it was only a matter of time before he discovered me. If I was to have any chance at all, I needed to have the weapon assembled before he made his charge. The first thing I did was check the magazine of the AK. To my great relief I found it was fully loaded. I knew from the research on hunting these two ton behemoths that 9.35 mm bullets are pretty useless against their thick hide, but if I could get the weapon to work then I had a different plan in my mind.

As a conservationist, I know very little about guns, but my one bit of luck was that whoever had disassembled the rifle had unwittingly done so in a systematic fashion and laid each part out in order of re-assembly on the mat. All I had to do was to put it back together in reverse. This is a whole lot harder when you are shiiiiiitting yourself!

By now my nemesis had gotten the measure of me and was sending warning signals in the form of snorts and foot stomping on the ground that was between us. He had yet to break in to a full blown charge, but when he did!

'Keep the focus, keep the focus,' I repeated over and over to myself as the adrenalin coursed through my veins. The desire to run was almost overwhelming. 'Come on, come on!' I screamed through clenched teeth. The firing pin which was the second to last component in the assembly refused to snap into place because of my shaking hands.

At one hundred yards the rhino decided that I needed to be taught a lesson. To the roar and chants of the Warlord and his cronies from the safety of a baobab tree on the sidelines, it broke from a trot into a full blown ground quaking attack.

'Snap!' At ninety yards the firing pin finally found its place. By sixty I had inserted the magazine, cocked the firing mechanism, taken off the safety catch, set the rifle to single shot and, at point blank range, pointed the muzzle into the chain link that was closest to my ankle.

"BAM" the link exploded and like a matador, I just managed to sidestep the beast's horn as he thundered past, but not before he left a gash in my right shoulder. Knowing that I faced certain death if I tried to outrun him, I snapped the firing mechanism to automatic and dropped to one knee to steady myself as he turned for his next attack. I had twenty-nine rounds left in the magazine to persuade him differently.

'Come on!' I roared and laid down a chatter of fire across the ground in front of his head before he had a chance to line up on me. In spite of my braced position the recoil of the weapon threw me off balance, but the dust it kicked up had the desired effect. The rhino swerved off track and slowed down, shaking its head violently as if flicking off a swarm of flies.

'Run!' a disembodied voice screamed in my head and, needing no further prompt, my legs stood up and took it upon themselves to carry me across the clearing in the direction of a river that promised safety. I was halfway there before I felt the rumble of hooves behind me. A rhino doesn't roar on the attack. It snorts. My senses were so attuned by now that I could tell as each exhalation grew closer, that this one was really pissed off. All of this for the love of a girl who had nicknamed me Dorkus!

'Turn!' my brain screamed, knowing that we were not going to make the final hundred yards to the river. Using my shoulders as a lever, it finally managed to wrestle my legs around to face the oncoming juggernaut.

Bam, bam, bam, bam, bam the AK rattled again from my hip and the magazine emptied itself in a hail of lead that exploded into the dirt in line with the rhino's charge.

This time, to my great surprise, and relief, the animal halted. Something had happened. A greater force had prevailed and silenced all in the jungle, including the Warlord. Sensing an opportunity to make a truce with my predator, I slowly unlocked the firing pin from the empty weapon and threw it on the ground in front of him as a peace offering. He snorted at it once, then flicked his head towards the river. I was free to go.

This did not stop my original captors from shooting me in the heart as I backed away, but if I was to go out dying, then at least I had remained true to my original mission in Africa.

'Yala, yala, yala I cried and struck the air above my head with my right fist to honor the rhino as I reached the safety of the riverbank. I threw the AK into the murky depths and without further hesitation, I dived into the water and swam to freedom.

I was on a roll. It had only taken me three and a bit pages and ten minutes to sort out the rhino. I knew that if I could get through the remaining three extra credit questions in less than an hour, then I'd have two left to tackle the physics.

Question 2:

You are a solo yachtsman in the middle of the Atlantic Ocean. You develop an acute pain in the lower right abdomen. The first aid book diagnoses it as an inflamed appendix, which, if not removed immediately, will kill you. You have a full emergency surgical kit on board. Describe in detail how you remove your own appendix. (20 points)

Answer:

The details to this are so thoroughly nauseating that I won't go into them for fear of making you sick on the spot. However, I will tell you that I had so much adrenalin coursing through my veins from question one, that it got me through the toughest part, which was to make the three inch *self incision* in my groin necessary to find the wayward organ. I'm proud to say that once in, it was a textbook procedure that would have immediately qualified me for medical school had I chosen to be a medical doctor instead.

It was strange, but after finishing the extra credit questions I felt *unexpectedly* better about completing the rest of the paper (which is what I think the nutty professor had intended in the first place). I kept my head down and ploughed on through with a renewed sense of possibility and to a greater or lesser degree, managed to finish every question within the allotted three hours.

Two weeks later, when I got the result, I found that I had scored a 'C' on the final exam which was enough to pass the entire course. Written as a comment on the back of the last extra credit answer page was the following.

"Congratulations! Not only were you the first student to NOT kill the rhino to save your own hide, but I loved the fact that one of the bullets from your second burst of fire ricocheted off its horn and killed the Warlord instead. Such irony! On top of this I also loved that the leaderless gang, being of superstitious nature, saw it as an act of God and immediately disbanded, leaving the rhino population to flourish. What an ending!

As a result of your answer I am a born-again conservationist and have decided to never again use that question for extra credit in my exams.

Well done!'

Holy Shit. I was in. It might have been by the skin of a rhino's chinny chin chin, but I was in … and so was Darling!

9

"All is fair in love and war"

'There goes Harley.'

'What do you mean?' I'd hitched a ride home from clinic with a senior student that I barely knew who was just about to graduate. We had come to a t-junction and were turning left when a huge white *Caprice* cut the corner and almost collided with us. The car belonged to my best friend Scotty. Angel was driving and had misjudged the corner because of her short sightedness.

'The school bike!'

'Sorry?' I was slow to catch on, but I could tell by the tone of his voice that it was not a very endearing description.

'Haven't you heard?' he answered, not knowing that it was two of my best friends that he was talking about.

My dumb confusion was sufficient for him to continue.

'Tollison and some of the other studs. They have been vying for bragging rights to see who would be the first to bang her.'

I shook my head, as the realization slowly sank in.

'Don't you get it? *School bike*. Harley? Apparently she grunts when you ride her!' He laughed as much to mock my failure to understand as he did the shock on my face at the unconfirmed rumor that was going around the school. If it had been any other couple I might have understood his play on words, but I was devastated. This was my family that he was talking about. I was relieved that my house was just around the next bend for it took all of my self-control not to smack the guy up the side of the head for being such an asshole.

It's amazing how you can be so close to someone yet be the last to find out what was really going on. I wasn't just shocked when it finally dawned on me. I was raging. "For rich or for poor, in sickness and in health, what God brings together let no man pull asunder." I wanted to kill Tollison for defiling their relationship.

Chiropractic College was tough from the get-go. The people who found it the hardest, regardless of age or maturity, were quite often the married couples, one supporting the other and having to spend long times apart. I did not know the bastard other than he worked with Angel in the same bar at night, but I knew of his reputation with women.

This was personal. Tollison had a flash sports car that he used as bait. I wanted to go around to his house that night and torch it. Instead I sat on the stoop at the back of my house and raged against Southern mentality, the confederate flag, racism and lack of honor among my fellow students. In a country that celebrates the ideals of freedom and hope and loyalty and trust, I felt that a terrible sacrilege had been committed.

I had known that they were stressed. We all were. All of the international students maintained an accelerated program that shaved an entire year off the curriculum. At six days a week, with only a three week break for summer holidays, the pace was unforgiving of anyone who weakened. What little time there might have been for romance was overshadowed by the relentless grind of living hand to mouth and the eternal toil of keeping on the straight and narrow path to graduation. You grinned and bore it and made light of it when it got too much. I'd had no idea that Scotty and Angel had been so miserable.

'I have Angel over here,' Darling confirmed when I called her to see if she'd had any idea about what was going on. 'Go and find Scotty and see that he is okay,' she advised when I asked what I should do. 'Make sure he doesn't do anything stupid.'

'What? Like burn the bastard's car?'

'Don't!'

'I won't,' I reassured.

'It's bad enough as it is. You are his best friend. Don't let him make it any worse.'

I found him at home watching TV. Too proud to admit to me that anything was wrong I kept him company by staring at the box and making muted one way conversation during the commercials until it was time for me to go to work.

'Come on,' I coaxed and dragged his sorry ass along to the Steak House where I worked to keep an eye on him. Not that I had anything to worry about. He was too shellshocked to be of harm to anyone. He ignored the food that I brought him and spent the entire shift watching MTV on the screen over the bar. My biggest worry was what he might do during the witching hours after midnight when dogs bark at the moon and men do crazy things. I had zero experience of matters of the heart, but sensed that if he did come clean about the pressure cooker of emotion that was building inside him, that it might explode and cause disastrous consequences.

Ten minutes before quitting time I had an inspiration.

'Let's go get wild! I slung my work bag over my shoulder and steered him roughly out to my car before he could brook any refusal. Accompanied by Meat Loaf, I drove like a Bat out of Hell for the Milliken research center on the edge of town that was surrounded by three thousand acres of park like grounds with a lake in the center.

'I don't drink,' he stated lamely after I dragged him out of the car and handed him one of two bottles of wine from my bag that I had 'borrowed' from the cellar in the restaurant.

'You do now!' I shouted above the blaring music on my stereo. 'Come on, I'll race you!' I pushed his bottle up to his lips. 'Yeehar!' I cried to lead the charge.

His misery lightened, he rose to the challenge and we threw our heads back and gulped our way through the bottles. Soon after, we were babbling along with the music. We spread our arms like wings and pretended to dive bomb the ducks that were sleeping by the lakeshore until our legs gave out and we ended up on our backs on the grass staring up at the stars.

'I'm hungry.'

'I'm starving,' Scotty replied reminding us both that he had not eaten all day.

'Do you wanna go to *Tracers* and pick up some meat?' I boldly suggested. Tracers was a local night club otherwise known as the "Meat Market" where it was reputed that any guy with half decent looks could score a hussy if he wasn't too fussy.

'Yeah let's do it!' He replied with equal bravado, but made no effort to move.

'Come on man,' I shook him after I'd struggled to my knees. 'All is fair in love and war. It will do us the world of good.' I echoed the drought filled wasteland that was my own love life.

'Nah, I can't.'

'You can,' I pushed. 'You are the Man. You can have any girl you want!'

'I can't!' he stated again in a lament filled apology, as if he was somehow letting me down.

'Thank God!' I thought and dropped down on the grass beside him. It wasn't my style either.

The stars above us started to spin. I held on to the ground with my left hand and grabbed his shoulder with my right to try and stop us being swallowed by the Milky Way. 'Hang on man!' I yelled as the first wave of French Chablis washed through our veins. 'How you doing?' There was a roaring, like surf, breaking in my head.

'Fucked up,' he whispered and held his hand to his face to cover the tears that ran down his cheeks. I knew then, when I heard him sobbing, that he was going to be okay.

10

The three most significant things

that happened after that.

(1)

It was a measure of their fortitude and underlying devotion to each other that not only did Scotty and Angel reunite, but a number of months later fell pregnant. While the drama that preceded had rocked all of our boats, the new life they bore was the catalyst needed to put the past behind them. A home birth was elected for and when Angel got bigger (20 kgs!) and was no longer able to work, Scotty got a job working nightshift in a toilet factory that paid by volume rather than the hour. The money was good, with lots of overtime. So much so that when Scotty could not make it, yours truly became the surrogate father to Angel and resident *clown* at the antenatal classes for first time parents. If humor is an antidote to nervousness, then I knew I had gone too far during our second class when one of the mothers-to-be wet her pants at one of my wisecracks! Not long after I assumed the honorary role of Godfather, babysitter and nappy changer and in many ways their daughter heralded the turning point of our time at college.

We were now over halfway through our degree. The biggest battles had been fought and won. As veterans we had stopped talking about how tired we were, or the next exam or the next dollar that had to be scraped. More and more we became invigorated by the subject of the future, about the real world, life and possibilities beyond graduation where my brother was about to step up to the plate and Scotty and Angel were not far behind. Our workload had not changed, but the realization that we were going to make it through meant that we could finally let our guard down and begin to enjoy the journey

(2)

After three years of hard academic slog we had acquired the elevated status of Resident Doctors in the college Health Center. Through clinical application, our lives had become the appliance of science as we experienced what it is like to change someone else's life just by using our hands. I was finally convinced that the *Son of God* was a Chiropractor when my very first patient yelled *Jesus Christ* after I adjusted him. I wasn't exactly making wine out of water, but when the same patient credited his recovery to me as "making a silk purse out of a sow's ear," I knew that I was on the right track.

(3)

If the upside was that we were getting close to graduation then the downside was that so were all of our friends including Scotty and Angel who went back home to New Zealand. As they went on their merry way, the dearly departed left our lives a little more lonely. As their numbers diminished, Darling and I were drawn closer together so that the strings of our social lives shrank and gradually entwined. Not that it mattered any more. The voice that so many years before had predicted our destiny had long grown silent.

I now had a girlfriend and had finally resolved to finish out my last year marking time by passing exams and making plans for the future that was Ireland. Then one day, I got the proverbial 'slap upside the head' that awakened in me a distant longing.

'I need help to move my clinic.' Vince was the head of the x-ray department in the health center. We had become friends after I did a small construction job at his house for which I traded my time for the opportunity to observe him treating patients in his private clinic. The experience was so valuable that I brought Darling along so that we could practice on each other under his supervision. Helping him move would cement the arrangement for the year ahead so I readily agreed. We pulled a couple of all-nighters and ended up celebrating the completion of the job when Darling rocked up unexpectedly with a thermos of coffee and a basket full of home baked scones that were still warm. It was a nice gesture that Vince and I really appreciated. A shared camaraderie between the three of us that I thought nothing more of until after she had departed.

'She did that for you,' Vince stated.

'What do you mean?'

'The scones and jam. She did it for you,' he repeated, smiling at my feigned disbelief.

'Nah. I got a girlfriend, remember. It was for you. She really appreciates the extra instruction you give us.'

'I'm telling you man. She likes you,' he teased.

'Don't be silly, we are just friends!' I was shocked that he would allude to something that had gone completely over my head. I had become so fixated over the years in my role as her friend and protector that the suggestion seemed ludicrous. This was further reinforced by her now legendary commitment to the 'idiot' overseas.

Call me old fashioned, call me chivalrous call *me* the *idiot*, but so long as she had feelings for someone else, then I would honor and support them. Constrained by this highfalutin idea, my every moment with her had been a stumbling, feigning, twisting contortion of a dance that completely avoided any form of display, real or imaginary, that she might have associated with or considered affection. To have acted any differently would have been incongruous to my loyalty and a betrayal of the unique trust that she had invested in me. Not to mention my girlfriend!

If my devotion was like a one way street where I had done all of the maintenance, then as far as Vince was concerned, she had done a u turn without me noticing. Scones and jam though were hardly proof. The fact that she had commandeered one of my favorite jerseys months before and worn it every day to school meant nothing either. And if she had taken to having afternoon tea at my house so often that it left me at a loose end on the days that it didn't happen ... so what? We were friends. It was the sort of thing we had done for the past three years.

What did occur to me though, as I drove home from Vince's, was that I was tired of this dance. Tired of not being able to show how my heart soared every time we met. Tired of all the friendly hugs when I wanted to embrace and hold her cheek to cheek, and heart to heart and slow dance into the early hours of the morning. Tired of wanting to hold *her* hand instead of my girlfriend's when we went to the movies. Tired of the vulnerability that all of the international students shared and the superficial life of detachment that we were forced to lead in order to survive. Tired of being tired, because in truth, I hadn't slept for months for the fever inside had been reignited and wracked every part of my being for the want of her.

11

'Do you f%$k on first dates?'

There was no fallback position in to which I could retreat and, so exposed, felt the full force of fate turn against me. I contained the fever with cold showers and long walks alone and any excuse I could find not to be around her. If my girlfriend had served as a foil to Darling's distraction in the past, then my fondness for her soon became blunted by the guilt of a deceitful mind. For a simple gesture or sign of affection I'd have thrown caution to the wind and taken my chances in telling Darling how I felt, even if I ended up looking like a Dorkus! But none had ever been forthcoming. She held rigid to the dance of friendship that we had always played. Platonic to the point of being puritan.

As an act of desperation, I chose to go back to Ireland to seek salvation in the hope that a good dose of the 'ould sod' might cure me. The inspiration came from Cheryl, a clinic intern and friend with a broken ankle who needed someone to drive her car north to New York for the Christmas holiday. From there I could catch an affordable flight across the Atlantic.

My compass set, I found comfort in the plans that we made and was further fortified when she suggested that we detour to Iowa to visit Palmer College where the founders of Chiropractic had established the profession. This was a once in a lifetime opportunity to step back in history and walk the hallowed halls of our forefathers. Not only that, but we had friends there who promised to 'show us a good time,' the anticipation of which acted like a balm to my aggravated soul.

'Would you mind if I invited someone else along?' Cheryl asked, three weeks before we departed.

'Not at all, the more the merrier,' I declared. I was in such high spirits about making my escape that nothing could upset me.

Later that night I was awoken by a knock on my bedroom window.

'I can't believe we are going to Palmer!' Darling called. She had been on the way home from work and dropped in for a cup of tea which she knew this sucker would make her at any hour of the day.

'It's one a.m.!' I almost shouted, as I stumbled to the door to let her in; my exasperation hiding my shock at how my plans to escape had so easily been undone. I cursed my dear friend Cheryl under my breath as I put on the kettle. My tickets home were non-refundable.

'I know, but it's a road trip. We are going on a road trip!' Darling said unknowing of my true intentions for getting away. In the three years we had lived in the USA she had been home only once to NZ and never out of state. By the time we finished our tea her excitement was infectious enough to dilute my resolve *not* to be around her. Realizing there was no point in fighting it, I decided on one last indulgence knowing that my return home would bring me to my senses.

We finally hit the road with a single cassette tape of Kevin Bloody Wilson, the crudest rudest Australian you ever heard. 'Do you fuck on first dates,' melted our inhibitions along with the miles as we sang over and over for most of the fourteen glorious hours it took to drive north. By the time we got to Iowa we were high as kites on the relief of being free of the constraints of college and the intimacies of shared friendship in such tight quarters. The feeling flowed on into the early part of the morning, when, reunited with our friends, we partied in a cheap and cheerful Chinese restaurant just around the corner from their house.

'Oh my God, it's snowing!' Cheryl shouted just as we were about to leave. It was nothing to the surprise I got when Darling took me by the hand and dragged me outside. That's what I said!

She took me by the hand. My left hand. The one that is attached directly to my heart! It was the first time that we had ever made contact in such a non-platonic fashion. Squeal, dance, joy, prance, in that single moment of intimacy we made love with our footsteps in the fallen snow. The anomaly though was corrected the second she let go and reverted back to our *normal* routine. So much so, that I fell asleep later that night not sure if it had ever happened.

There were eighteen inches of snow on the ground the following morning. It took us an hour to dig out the car and twenty-one more to drive to New York; a distance that normally took nine.

The magic of the Big Apple was like Disney compared to Spartanburg. For the next two days we toured all the sights and stuffed ourselves with roasted chestnuts, pretzels, hotdogs, China town, Little Italy and Cheryl's mother's good old fashioned homemade Italian cooking when we arrived home each night exhausted. After a year without family, the goodwill extended by Cheryl's family was intoxicating.

On our second night I couldn't sleep and snuck downstairs in the darkness to the kitchen to make some tea.

'I miss my husband. That is why I can't sleep,' Nan announced from the shadows of the kitchen. She scared the shit out of me. She was Cheryl's twenty-thousand-year-old, four-foot-nothing grandmother who ruled the family from her equally ancient armchair in the kitchen of her parents' house. 'What's your excuse?' she asked me.

'Too much gnocchi I think,' I rubbed my stomach that was still stuffed from home cooking.

'Too much gnocchi and not enough nookey! That's what my Al used to say,' she laughed as she raised herself up and switched on a small lamp beside her chair. 'We were married for sixty years!' You could tell by the tone of her voice that she was proud of the achievement. She invited me to sit down next to her and without my asking, she launched into stories of the old country. How she and Al had first met, how poor they had been, the decision to leave Italy, the Statue of Liberty, their new life, her children. 'He was a good man,' she said, her crooked hand sweeping beyond the room to acknowledge the abundance that was her extended family. I felt honored that she had marked the time by telling me her story. It was three a.m. before I decided to try sleeping.

'You should tell her how you feel,' she said nodding in the direction of Darling's room upstairs when I stood up and wished her good night. She smiled at the surprise on my face.

'It's complicated.' There was no point in denying her keen observation. It felt like a load off just to share confidences.

'She loves you!' she nodded without doubt. 'Nothing could be so obvious,' she smiled when I shrugged my confusion.

My mind was no clearer the following morning when we gathered to say our goodbyes.

'Nan is sleeping,' Cheryl's mother explained when I sought to thank and bid her farewell. 'She never sleeps!' she added in a surprised tone as she ushered us out towards the car. When nobody was looking, she pulled me to one side and whispered out of earshot. 'I have a message from Nan. She says that you have to tell her!' She nodded in Darling's direction and gave me a wink of encouragement. I was mortified that in her enthusiasm she might have been overheard.

Our departure for the airport was a subdued affair over-shadowed by heavy rain and three hearts that knew that the unique bond of friendship that had been forged by our adventure together was soon to be broken by obligation. Mine to my family in Ireland. Darling's by her need to return south to work over the Christmas holidays. Our somber mood was further magnified by navigating the cheerless sea of humanity we faced upon reaching the airport and the quick goodbyes we'd had to make with Cheryl outside the terminal because of her broken ankle.

'Here, hold my hand so that we don't get separated!' I said without thinking and, swopping my suitcase to my right, I extended my left which Darling grabbed without hesitation. We were halfway across the first terminal before it occurred to me that we were, in fact, holding hands for the second time and well in to the Departure area when I realized that somewhere along the way, our fingers had become entwined like lovers. Rather than separate when we reached the check in desks, I used my right and she her left "as one" to fill out forms and rummage through each other's pockets for passports and tickets. It felt perfectly normal, as if we had always been together like this. From there we made our way to the Domestic terminal where I had lots of time to see her off before making my way to International.

'You can't go in there if you are not booked on the flight,' an attendant pointed to the invisible line that separated passenger from well-wishers at the departure gate.

Suddenly we were there. That awkward place where the value of a life shared is only realized in a goodbye and words are never good enough to express it. I thought at least that we might try. To move to a more private space and acknowledge the significance of our holding hands and "tell her" as Nan had advised, but she made no attempt. She turned instead and without warning she embraced me. It wasn't the type of hug that I was used to. It was heart to heart, cheek to cheek. A long held soul to soul. The sign that I had been looking for, for so long that it should have led to the inevitable kiss and happy ever after. But it didn't. She turned instead and without a word, walked away and never looked back.

12

Life is what happens when

you are busy making other plans

    Visits home were always like a double-edged sword that cut to the quick in the bittersweet detachment that was required to enjoy them. Knowing that my time with my family was to be short, the lack of emotion needed to sustain myself overseas was now engaged in making sure that while we reconnected, I did not become vulnerable to the pull of home. This detachment worked both ways and, belonging to a typical Irish family that rarely showed outer signs of affection, it always left one with a sense that while loved, you were living in limbo until the day when you could return home and settle for good. It was a difficult dance often laced with regret, where you were more of a spectator than a participant. The intensity of each visit was only ever shown by the tears that my mother shed on my arrival at the airport and later by my father on departure. Yet it was these tears for which I lived. They cleansed my soul and that let me know where I belonged. In the shortness of my stay they dissolved the distraction that was Darling and helped to bring me to my senses. (Which had been the objective of my visit home in the first place!) With this in mind I further determined to get a grip on my future by forming a partnership with my brother who had just taken over the only Chiropractic center on the north side of Dublin city. Unbound by the constraints of college and glowing in his new title of 'Doctor', he was fast becoming known as the convivial Chiropractor around town We were a gnarly mismatch tainted by sibling rivalry and polarized viewpoints, but wholly suited by our grudging affection for each other. That, and the desire to make money. I had significant debt that would be pending straight after graduation. A busy practice was the best sort of remedy for the affliction.

The die now cast, I was set to return to my final year with a plan that would keep me on the straight and narrow. By chance, as my parents drove me to the airport, we were caught in a traffic jam that stopped us right under the granite bridge where my planned ending so many years before had in fact been the beginning of a new life. Beside it the poster board had a new advertisement stating boldly that 'Guinness was good for me!' Not that I needed it, but it served nicely as a metaphor for the last time I had been under the bridge. While I had never spoken to my parents about my original reason for leaving, it was obvious that the lens through which I viewed life had changed. In the darkness I had found light. In desperation I had found inspiration and from that a metamorphosis had occurred that would shortly see me transform from Dorkus to Doctor of Chiropractic. All I had to do was survive the last year.

'This is your Alamo!' my father stated, sensing my reluctance to let go of his handshake as he farewelled me at the airport. He was referring to the only defeat the Americans had ever suffered in battle against the Mexicans a century before. 'If you can make it through this year you'll make it through anything!' he said half patting me on the shoulder, half pushing me through our mutual tears in the direction of the departure gate.

On my return to America I was determined to hit the ground running and make the best of my last year. With my emotions in lock down I redoubled my dedication to my girlfriend and focused on raising my grade point average. I was rewarded within the first month for my efforts with a 97% best ever student score in Chiropractic adjusting technic. To maintain my focus when I wasn't busy with study or clinic I took up racket ball and worked extra nights to save for another trip home half way through the year to reinforce my commitment. It was a good plan that had the desired effect so long as I stayed busy and avoided Darling.

In truth though, my mind was fallow of the vital inspiration and motivation that had sustained me through the early years. Within a month of my return I had taped on the wall beside my bed a piece of A4 paper with the days ticked and weeks crossed off as I counted down to graduation. Like a convict in a penal colony, each day became a slow trudge through the sludge of a routine that was based at best on survival and mostly staying sane during the long wait. On top of this the weather was atrocious and unfriendly and soon began to resonate a deep seated longing to get the hell out of the place.

Six weeks after my return, it all came to a head one day when Darling started a bitching session about "everything and nothing" as we walked out of the clinic after seeing patients. We did it all of the time to blow off steam, but in my waning attempt at being hyper-focused on the future, I was determined not to be swayed from my faltering course of self-conceited optimism. Fortified by my recent trip home and my supposed plans for the future, I gave Darling a verbal broadside to fend off the malevolence she uttered that was a mirror to my own heart. By the time I had finished my outburst, both barrels were smoking. The devastated look on her face told me that I had caught her off-guard, her tears a sign that I had shown no quarter. If ever I had a voice inside of me, it was now busy telling me what an idiot I was as I watched her walk away in tears. In all of the time that we had known each other there had never been a cross word between us. Quite the opposite. While there had never been a romantic moment either, our feelings ran deep in how we cared for each other as friends.

I blew off work that night. I needed time to think. To howl at my demons and bark at the moon and justify the injustice that I had perpetrated against my best friend. If I admired her for her dignity and grace in self-preservation, then I resented her equally for making it so hard for me to show how I felt. I cursed her for the road trip that we had made and the intimacies that we had shared and the touch of her hand that had left my heart with nothing but frustrated hope as she withdrew again on my return from Ireland. However I might have justified it though, in the end she did not deserve the berating that I had given her. Contrary to my role as president of the Honors Council and her honorary best friend, I had been uncouth and cruel in my choice of words. A self-conceited cad and a bounder! I finally realized that my father, for all of his prudishness, was intuitively aware that besides making it to graduation, there was an altogether different struggle going on in my heart. That without knowing it perhaps Darling was to be my "Alamo."

If life is what happens when you are busy making plans, then I knew as the next morning dawned, that all of the plans that I had made to secure my future were in fact hollow without her. For a sign or a signal I would never have made such commitments nor surrounded myself with the false wall of mirrors that I had constructed for my own self-protection. She wasn't the prude. I was. I could have thrown my hat in the ring with all of the other guys over the years who had been contenders for her affection. I'd chosen instead to stay safe by being her *friend* rather than run the gauntlet of rejection that they had all eventually suffered.

To make restitution for my sins I ordered enough roses to cost me almost an entire week's wages. I could have gotten away with buying her a box of her favorite chocolates, but I didn't. Roses were more than a peace offering that left a question mark over the muted silence that had been our secret connection. I was finally doing what Cheryl's grandmother had advised me to do.

It was time to face the enemy.

13

'The platonic dance of avoidance'

'Eet's dun!' the florist reported in her long Southern drawl by phone as arranged, straight after she had made the delivery.

'How'd she take it?' I was shaking in my boots.

'Guud, ah reckon. She smaaled when she dun saw yor card. She's very purdy. Y'all dun tha raght thang,' the florist twanged in reassurance, having been privy to my reasons for the delivery. On the inside of the card I had written the most powerful single word universally known to every man regarding any sort of negotiations of recompense when dealing with a woman … "SORRY!" From that moment of delivery the clock started ticking. In the twenty-four hours since my outburst she had neither looked at me in class nor acknowledged my presence. The longer she held out, I figured the deeper the shit I was in. If it took another 24 hours to chill out then I reckoned we would be okay. Any longer and I'd have to carry someone else's school bag.

Five minutes later the phone rang. I answered as if it was just another day, but hoping my voice didn't sound like my legs were jumping for joy because she had called so soon.

'Thanks,' came her gentle reply. A long silence then, followed by a deep sigh of relief from both sides that all was not lost between us.

'I've just put the kettle on,' I said by way of invitation.

'I'll pick up the chocolate chips,' she replied.

'Cool.' A good sign, chocolate chip cookies were my favorite.

What wasn't part of the plan was that a minute after I put down the phone a fellow student dropped in unexpectedly in an agitated state. There had been a 'serious incident' connected to one of the students in the college that was likely to 'unfairly implicate' him and, as President of the Honors Council he needed my immediate advice on how he should handle the matter. Any other time this would not have been a problem, but the next half hour or so was likely to decide my own fate. Try as I might to reassure and get rid of him, his pressing concern (soap opera) was such that when Darling arrived shortly thereafter, I was practically pulling my hair out with distraction.

'Not a good time?' she could see from my body language that the guy (practically in tears at this stage) had me cornered. 'I can come back,' she offered.

'Would you mind?' he appealed, totally self-absorbed, before I had a chance to answer.

'Okay,' Darling nodded, but I could see that she was disappointed.

'Hang on!' I halted her in her tracks. The last thing I needed was this moment of reconnection between us totally ruined. I dashed into my bedroom and returned a moment later. It wasn't how I had planned it, but I knew somehow that this next step was important. Taking her by the elbow, I led her out of the house to the front verandah and, as calmly as my racing heart would allow, I handed her an envelope.

'This is for you.'

'What is it?

I stopped her from opening the card by laying my hand on the back of hers. It was the most exquisitely embarrassing intimate moment we had ever shared.

'Read it at home,' I gently instructed, nodding back to the guy inside who didn't need to see what was going on. My tone was apologetic, sorry in advance for crossing the line and fucking up what had, up to then, been such a great friendship.

'Okay.' There was hesitancy in her voice, as if she knew what was inside and wanted to hand it back before it was too late. *What you don't know won't hurt you; that sort of thing.* But she didn't.

'I'm such a dork!' I berated myself as I went back inside to face the other "dork" that had totally ruined the moment. The forlorn look on his face for a greater sympathy than his case deserved was the final straw.

'I quit!'

'Excuse me?' he replied horrified.

'I quit!' I repeated, letting him know in no uncertain terms that it was time to take his problems somewhere else. I was tired of being Mr. Goody Two Shoes President of the Honors Council, always having to be on my best behavior. 'Some guy screws your friend's girlfriend. In the heat of the moment you and your friend go out and give him a hiding to teach him a lesson. It was outside of school grounds so it is covered by civil law. He has not pressed charges, so you have nothing to worry about,' I stated, noting the relief on his dumb face while at the same time I raged inside at the injustice that I felt. If Scotty and I had gone out and hammered Tollison for the very same reason we would have faced expulsion and immediate deportation.

'Of course, why didn't I think of that?' he practically jumped out of his seat for joy. Without a word of thanks (which was typical of most of the cases that I'd had to deal with in the past) he made his departure just as quickly as he had arrived. Left alone with my thoughts, I sat on the chair on the front porch and berated myself for being such an idiot and an unromantic prat. In hindsight, I'd had ample opportunity to show my feelings, but had hid instead behind the highfaluting uppity notion of what it meant to be chivalrous when in fact I had been too scared all along to make a move. On the inside of the card I had written the following.

'So you see I have come to doubt
All that I once held as true
I stand alone without belief
The only truth I know is you'

It was the second verse of the Simon and Garfunkel song that I had originally plagiarized so many years before in the mall to tell her how I felt when she was writing poetry to her old Beau. There was no turning back now that I had given her the card. It wasn't an "I like you" or "I think that you are cute" or "let's be friends with benefits and keep each other company until we qualify and then go our separate ways." It was a declaration of intent that went way beyond graduation and carried the elevated status of *growing old together*.

A half hour later the phone rang.

'Can I come over? I have something for you,' Darling said without explanation. Ten minutes later she pulled into my driveway. Still dazed by my own stupidity I could hardly look at her when she handed me a sealed careworn envelope. I removed the vaguely familiar card from within and studied the front page. On the inside was the first verse of the Simon and Garfunkel song that I had quoted to her all of those years before in the shopping mall.

'I never sent it. I didn't know why until an hour ago,' she shrugged.

You would think that after such a cataclysmic realization that two hearts, finally unbound, would have come together in a passionate embrace soon to be consummated by nature's only recourse. But we didn't. We stood instead, like a couple of possums at a crossroads startled by a headlight that had suddenly appeared out of nowhere.

'What do we do now?' I finally had the gumption to question.

'Cup of tea?' she suggested.

So used had we become to the platonic dance of avoidance, that it took another sixteen hour road trip, a turquoise beach, balmy sunsets and a half bottle of blue label Smirnoff to finally throw off the shackles that had constrained us. The guy who said that Heaven was in the back seat of his Cadillac has never camped under the stars in the Florida Keys. For a few brief days of sweet surrender and unfettered bliss, we lived in a state of grace, the effects of which bound us together when we returned to college.

Any relationship though, that is serious about moving forward, has its kiss and tell. A time of revelation to phone a friend, buy a vowel, or rattle the skeletons in the closet. A time to forget about the snake between the sheets and reveal the python you forgot to mention that you keep under your bed. A time of reassurance, that you are in fact mad and that the other person feels just as truly, madly, deeply insane about you, before you both dive into the deep end of true commitment. That at least was what I had expected. More importantly, I needed to be able to tell Darling about Godzilla and Anthony Hopkins who still had a habit of showing up from time to time.

As the clock counted down our final days in college, I kept thinking 'tomorrow' we will have this conversation, tomorrow all will be revealed. Instead, our fate together was sealed just before graduation when we scored the highest mark possible in anatomy and physiology with not one, but three (to be sure, to be sure, to be sure) positive blue stick pregnancy test kits!

Holy Shit!!

One day you are a nobody in the pits of despair, the next you are standing on a stage being conferred with the degree of Doctor of Chiropractic *and* a soon-to-be parent. Of the two I don't know which was the greater miracle, but this Dorkus had made a metamorphosis from Faker to something greater and managed to muddle his way through and change his story. If I could do it, then perhaps my fate lay in teaching others to find the courage to do the same?

Little did I know that it was really just the beginning of our own education.

Book Two

1

"Living the Dream"

If ours was a match made in heaven then there was hell to pay for the plans gone astray, cultural sway, family expectations and the Hollywood illusions about what love was supposed to look like. It's amazing how an unexpected baby, moving country and becoming partner in a busy Chiropractic practice can accentuate all of the baggage two people can "suddenly" accumulate by the time they reach their mid-twenties. 'Fighting your corner' might be a better way to describe it! In truth though, our love was like a rough diamond that needed polishing and sparks flew on a regular basis when the pressure became too much. Some things however are worth fighting for and our friendship held fast through the hard days when on working on *yourself* was the key to success and a cup of tea together at the end of each day the antidote to most problems. Little did we know that we would eventually get to meet the very tea maker who produced our favourite tea ... but I'm getting ahead of myself.

So much so, that you had better fast forward and picture this.

A big house on twelve acres, on a big hill with a million dollar view out to the Coromandel Peninsula and Great Barrier Island on the east coast of New Zealand. Everything about this house is big. The bedrooms, the furniture, the designer kitchen, the round dining table that seats ten people. In the garden next to the house is a paved patio with a BBQ and a table big enough to seat a large party. Beside that, a double garage with a brand new Nissan Patrol and a sporty Mazda. Upstairs is a loft with a double bedroom for guests and a large office. In the house are a girl and a guy. The girl is gorgeous. They have two young children. Poppit is six years old and her brother Jack is two. The guy doesn't have to work much so he plays a lot of golf, takes the kids to the beach on a regular basis and is developing his skills in writing. On weekends when things are quiet, they go to the city and stay in a five star hotel and have fun. In the winter when life is miserable and wet and the days are dreary, they fly off to a tropical island in the Pacific and spend a month in the sun.

Does this sound like living the dream?

Well that's us. A far cry from 1984, ten years before, when I started my journey from under the bridge.

After graduation we went back to Ireland to practice with my brother in what grew into the busiest Chiropractic center in Europe. It was a blast, practicing six days a week, fifty weeks a year, living the high life after four years in College, but it was majorly stressful and after three and a half years we began to question the direction that we had taken. Our school debts were paid off and we had made some money, but we were time poor and began to feel that the exchange rate wasn't worth it. Finally our lives were rocked by a number of near-death experiences that were to change our course.

If bad things come in 3's then the first was the loss of a family friend to "the big C". The impact was minimal until the wife of our next door neighbour, who was the same age as Darling, left two young children behind after falling prey to a devastating illness that devoured her six weeks after her diagnosis. The final straw was a young patient by the name of Patrick. At fifteen years of age, he was on his second kidney transplant, but still dying by degrees. His parents had heard through the grapevine that my brother and I were miracle workers, (which wasn't true) but when you are desperate you will believe and do anything to save the life of your child. It still brings me to tears to think about Patrick, for there is nothing sadder than the eyes of a mother who knows that she is fighting a losing battle.

These experiences made us realise that for us at least, there were some things in life more important than money. When we began then to seriously think about returning to New Zealand the opportunity was presented by a fellow Chiropractor. Lewis had a beautiful wife and three great kids all living the dream by the beach, until cancer decided differently. He chose a non-medical route to recovery which included de-stressing by selling his practice, and his misfortune became our ticket to returning down under.

Our new practice was rural, the lifestyle laid-back. Being reunited with our New Zealand family including Scotty and Angel and their three children was an opportunity for pause and reflection.

It might sound like a breeze, but interestingly, after ten years of working our asses off I found it very difficult to wind down and learn to play again. I read some books and attended a bunch of seminars, but soon realised that the world in fact was doing the opposite. The property market was going off, 'Rich Dad Poor Dad' was on the New York Times best seller list and "I want it all" by Queen was the new mantra for success. A group of colleagues in Auckland had started the *Rhino Club* based on the book Rhinoceros Success by Scott Alexander. I liked the philosophy. The idea of being a "damn the torpedoes, three ton, *thick skinned* rhino," dedicated to *charging hard* to advance the success of the Chiropractic profession in New Zealand really appealed. It reminded me of my time in University when I faced off against the rhino in my final Physics exam in order to win Darling's heart. However, when I found out that some of the members were charging like wounded bulls instead to line their own pockets, I decided that I did not want to belong.

Tempered by our own experiences, we had already chosen to take *the road less travelled* and found ourselves venturing down a different path.

Lewis by now had made a miraculous recovery and to celebrate, he was writing about his experience in an effort to help others facing the same challenge. I loved the idea and after one of many lengthy discussions on his early manuscript, I decided to dust off the Self Help book that I had started in college. I had not experienced depression in years, so thought I might be able to shed some light on the nightmare that depression can be and share some of the principles that I believed were the key to 'living your dream.'

'Why don't you call it "The Power of Story",' Lew suggested when I outlined some of my ideas in an attempt to come up with a working title. 'It's not the situation, but the story that we tell about the situation that determines our success or our failure.'

I was impressed by how much he had picked up from my outline. I wanted to write about balancing out the seven areas of life – spiritual, mental, physical, family, social, career and financial. 'The Power of

Story' not only covered these, but was the foundation for my ultimate objective. If you want to future proof your family against the highs and lows of life then you have to make sure that each individual is honoured and encouraged to tell their own unique story. Ultimately I wanted it to be something a parent could share with their children to save them going through what I had experienced as a teenager.

While the book was aimed at family, the principles were universal and could be applied in corporate leadership to help future proof any company against the highs and lows (booms and busts) of the economy and ultimately the economy itself. Eventually the idea became an obsession and it wasn't long before I had three hundred pages of research on the seven areas of life plastered over the walls of my writing room above the garage. When I say that I was "living the dream" I was literally dreaming about this stuff. I had a notebook beside my bed for ideas that would pop in to my head and wake me during the night. I had notebooks in my practice, notebooks in my gym bag, a notebook in Darling's handbag so that I could dictate to her as we drove to Auckland. I had notebooks everywhere including the toilet. It was as if my Muse had verbal diarrhoea!

And then the most bizarre *out of this world* thing happened.

2

"The Christening"

Sleep deprivation had become a problem. My son was cutting his molars and I found myself playing musical beds every night. Between that and my *Muse* who just wouldn't shut up, it left me ragged and constantly trying to catch up. One particular night I gave into the urge and, dropping my head onto folded arms on my writing table, I surrendered to the calling. The last thing I remembered was falling into a deep dream knowing that I'd surface sooner or later with another idea on the Power of Story. But that's not what happened. In my dream I dreamt that I was dreaming (two dreams in parallel) and found myself on a small country road back in Ireland. You could tell by the wind that a storm had just passed. The ground underfoot was sodden. I was startled from behind by the sound of footsteps and laboured breathing and when I turned around there was a girl half walking, half running towards me. Her hair was saturated and her clothes were plastered to her skin as if she had been caught in the storm. She had a shawl over one shoulder and to my horror, I heard the cries of a baby hidden within.

'What happened to you? Where have you come from? Who has turned you out in this weather? Where is the father?' I demanded.

She told me that her name was Kate and started to tell me her story, but before she had a chance to finish I was awoken from the first dream by a sound so loud that the entire writing room shook. I thought it must be a hurricane. In my dream, I ran outside into the garden and looked up to see, not a hurricane, but an R.A.F. Spitfire diving time and time again across the roof. It was so close that I could see the pilot who stared back at me with a look of fierce determination. Painted on the cowling in front of the cockpit was a large green shamrock. The first thing that came to mind was that he must be part of the Kate's story, but it was too bizarre. What the hell was an Irish shamrock doing on an RAF spitfire? (The Irish and the Brits were still enemies back in those days.) I felt though that the two were connected, and I tried to return to Kate in my other dream to ask her for an explanation.

Darn and damnation, I was awakened instead by the sound of the phone clanging loudly on the writing desk beside my ear. It was six thirty in the morning and the sun had just broken the horizon.

'Hello,' I answered hoarsely, rubbing sleep from my eyes. After all of the excitement my throat was parched.

'I've got bad news.'

'Can't play golf today?' I joked, recognising Lew's voice on the other end of the line.

'No, the cancer is back.'

'Fuck!' followed by a long silence. 'I'll come down straight away,' I reassured. However, when I put down the receiver, I was further shocked to find thirty three pages of handwritten notes about Kate's story scribbled on pages that were strewn all over the table and the floor. Printed in large bold across what looked like the first page was "The Christening." I was too disturbed by Lew's news to give the pages any real attention so gathered them up and placed them in the top drawer of my writing desk where I promptly forgot about them.

My arrival at Lew's was greeted by a whistling kettle and a prolonged hug. Lew was so distracted by his recent diagnosis that I struggled to make small talk as we sat in the lounge and sipped our tea,

'What's this? In a moment of silent desperation I picked up a lined sheet of A4 paper off the coffee table. "Bucket List" was the heading and below it were several lines of unreadable scribble which I recognised as Lew's writing. Not familiar with the term I thought it might be something to do with gardening and offered to help in any way that I could.

'It's a list of all of the things that I want to do before I die,' Lew replied. Then, looking me straight in the eye he said, 'don't wait for cancer before you make one of your own!' It was like the shadow of death crossing over me. I went home that afternoon and working through several sheets of paper, I finally came up with my own Bucket List.

The following day I had a commitment to travel overseas. When I returned several weeks later I received a message that Lew was in hospital. The cancer this time was far more aggressive. As a last resort Lew had chosen to do chemotherapy.

Hospitals scare the bejesus out of me at the best of times. Not because I'm a Chiropractor, but because I'm human and don't like having to give up control of my body to masked strangers with very sharp knives. My visit coincided with Lew going through a bout of uncontrollable shakes and profuse sweating. I don't know if this was due to the medication that he was on, but it was like his body was possessed by an evil spirit. I sat beside his bed and gave him my hand to hold onto as wave after wave wracked and tore at his being.

'Did you make your bucket list?' was the first thing he said when the episode finally passed.

'Yes,' I was surprised that he would be concerned with such a thing. 'Actually I have it in my wallet.' I had followed his original instructions about keeping the list on me at all times.

'Show me!' he demanded. There was an urgency in his voice, as if somehow he knew that his time was running out.

'Here.' With trepidation I handed him the list. I felt like an errant school boy showing his father his end of year report. Failure was not an option.

The first two items on the list were as follows.

1.   Wealth creation.
2.   Security for my family.

It was a long list which ended with:

19.   Write a book that helps people.
20.   Sail around the world.
21.   Make a movie.

'This is not living the dream!' Lewis admonished. He had to place the list on his lap because the shakes were starting to come back.

'You said write down the list as it comes into your head!' I was trying not to show my disappointment.

'You remember those deep meaningful conversations we used to have about "living the dream" and "daring our genius"?' Lewis reminded me of several long beach walks where we had discussed our philosophies on life. 'Well this isn't it!' He gritted his teeth as he lay back and tensed his body to try to resist the shakes. 'The big house and the big car and the big holidays ... all you are doing is being safe and secure just like me and everyone else.' He let out a gasp of disappointment as a convulsion crushed his lungs. 'Do you really want to live the dream?' His eyes bored into my soul again.

'Yes,' I nodded.

'Then do the last three items on the list first. Write the book you have been talking about for the last two years. Sail around the world with Darling and the kids and make that damn movie. If you do that then you will be living the dream. Promise me that you will do it!'

I promised, without hesitation. Anything to stop the violence that ravaged his body. 'I promise!' I reassured again to make sure that he heard me through his convulsions. He squeezed my hand to seal the deal.

Darling knew nothing of my bucket list. It was something I had done on the spur of emotion. An exercise like one of the many I had done in the back of all of the self-help books and seminars that I had attended. 'Are you buckin' mad?' I could hear my father say at the thought of me turning my list upside down and starting from the bottom. 'After all the hard work and all you have been through and the sacrifices that you have made. Are you out of your buckin' mind?'

As it turned out I wasn't. At least not completely.

'You're mad!' Darling said when I broached the idea over a bottle of Merlot that evening, but I could tell that she was intrigued. We had been back in NZ almost three years by now. Three years of non-struggle and living off the fat of the lamb. Three years of chilling out and supposedly living the dream. Three years, as Lewis had pointed out, of being just like everybody else. If death defines life, then here we were having another near-death experience. Not our own, but close enough to put your life under the microscope and realise that in reality, we had just been running with the herd.

On page 120 of my 1986 diary I had written "The year of Discontent?" Property prices had doubled and business was booming. Everybody had more than they ever had before and yet ... enough just wasn't enough. When Scotty and Angel announced that they were off to the far side of the world to work for my brother in Ireland – the penny finally dropped. Over the previous three years Scotty had built up the busiest Chiropractic center in New Zealand. The burgeoning lifestyle that they had embraced had become too hard to sustain and he had become disillusioned and wanted out. Not just Scotty, but many of the people we knew seemed to be on the move for greener pastures. We began to realise that we too had a yearning for something different.

'Let's do it,' Darling announced the following morning.

'You're mad!' I dared not believe that she might be game enough to give it a try.

'Which end of a yacht is the bow?'

'The sharp end!' I knew then that she was serious.

3

D.G.U.T.D.J.

It's one thing to talk about having a bucket list. It's an entirely different story actually following one. With no experience, and not too sure where to start, we decided that the first thing to do was get the book on 'The Power of Story' written. We didn't expect this to happen overnight, but while doing so we could also research what it was going to take to sail around the world. We were in way over our heads on both counts, but since *nothing gives greater confidence than ignorance*, we forged ahead with determined hearts.

So, a week after making my promise to Lewis, I entered the "Cave" at five in the morning determined that I wasn't going to leave until I had at least ten pages of the first chapter written. I had an outline stapled to the wall above my writing desk that covered the twenty-one chapters I expected it to take. At the bottom of the stairs was a sign that basically said "F#&k off." I sat down, cleared my mind, opened my heart, and did my best to put my fears to one side before picking up a new pen and launching into a frenzy of writing longhand. When I finally came up for air nine hours later my brain was frazzled.!

'How'd it go?' Darling greeted when I stumbled through the kitchen door in a state of exhaustion.

'Amazing!' I had been a spectator more than a writer as my pen scribbled over forty pages of wisdom. 'I've written about stuff that I didn't even know I knew. It's like the walls were talking to me,' I referred to the hundreds of pages of research that I had pasted to the walls of the cave. 'It has a life of its own!'

'I want to read it.' Darling was immediately curious.

'It's in the front drawer of my writing desk.' I needed some fresh air to clear my head so headed off for a walk on the beach. She was up in the "Cave" before I reached the end of our driveway.

As I walked along the water line, I said a prayer for Lewis and gave thanks to my lucky stars for his influence on the path that we had chosen. It was almost two hours before I made it back home.

'Well, what do you think?' Darling had a thick sheaf of pages beside her on the sofa.

'I love the opening scene of the storm and the girl with her baby and the car almost running them down. What's a Spitfire?'

'There's no Spitfire in *The Power of Story*.' I picked up the pages to see what the hell she was talking about and was stunned by the title on the top of the first page. "The Christening." 'Where did you get these?' Then it dawned on me. She had discovered the papers that I had stashed in the same drawer after the dream that I'd forgotten about. 'This isn't *The Power of Story*.' I sat down beside her, unsure of how to explain their source.

'It's brilliant, you have to finish it!'

'But I don't even know how it ends,' I mumbled, unable to recall what I had written in the notes. 'I'm supposed to be writing a book that helps people. How's a book without an ending going to help anyone?'

'You will work it out,' she ended the conversation by promptly handing me a yachting magazine that she had bought that morning. 'There's a pretty 50 footer on page forty,' she winked.

If nothing gives greater confidence than ignorance, then said confidence is easily shaken, especially by those who are closest to you. I don't know about pioneers or adventurers, but I was soon to discover that writers by nature are needy for approval, in particular when they first start putting pen to paper.

I had no formal education in writing or literature and was anxious to have my course "checked" by some form of authority to make sure that I was on the right track. By this stage I had managed to cobble together the first six chapters of The Christening so I sought the advice of a school teacher friend who had a particular interest in all things literary.

'Your opinion on this would mean a lot to me,' I said as I handed him a freshly printed draft. It didn't occur to me to tell him that I had in fact staked my entire future on these words. What I had asked for in my ignorance was a written summary and any suggestions that he thought might be worthwhile. In essence; that he grade the paper in the same way he might an exam and red mark anything that needed attention. In my ignorance I knew that there was room for improvement, but overall I had expected the equivalent of a B.

A week later I found the pages stuffed in the letter box at the end of our long driveway. Attached by paper clip to the coffee stained front page was a scrap piece of paper with the immortal words written in bold.

D.G.U.T.D.J.

I had to call him to find out what it meant.

'Don't give up the day job!' was his terse reply. I could lie and tell you that I wasn't upset. That I didn't walk around in a daze for days after as if I'd been upper cut by Mohammed Ali. My course had been checked by a 'well meaning' torpedo. Blown out of the water before I'd had a chance to even get out of the harbour. A week is a long time to spend treading the waters of self-pity. However, I was soon to find my way again when I saw T.V. footage of the massive ketch Steinlager and her crew battling their way through a storm in the Southern Ocean as part of the round the world Whitbread Trophy. One of the crew was reading the latest best-selling novel below deck while off watch. Curious to know what great ocean warriors read to strengthen their resolve, I went out and bought the book the next day. To my astonishment I found that it was crap of the highest order. I mean total shit! Just as suddenly, I knew in my heart that I could do better and it was 'game on' again. I realised then that to follow *my* dream, I was going to have to stop being needy and *harden up* if I was to sail against the fickle winds of opinion.

It was a valuable lesson, but because I am Irish, it was also one that I would have to relearn over and over again. Let me tell you ... the learning curve was steeper than we could ever have imagined.

4

E.D.V.I.N.A

The 'Yachting' magazine that Darling handed me was one of a regular collection that we had begun to make of every magazine in NZ that had a decent marine brokerage section. Pictures were circled, inquiries made and lists drawn up until we had narrowed down the most amount of boats we could view in the least amount of marinas around Auckland on our precious weekends.

"Tyre kickers" is the derogatory name that yacht brokers give to dreamers who waste their time. In the early days we were no exception. We simply didn't have a clue what we were doing. Later on however, as experience was gained and we began to follow the worldly advice of adventurers whom had gone before us, 'tyre kicking' became my preferred method of venting my frustration caused by the brokers who wasted our time. A year had passed since we had made our fateful decision. Having exhausted all of the marinas in Auckland we found ourselves travelling further and further afield to view fewer and fewer options. Sometimes an entire weekend was spent travelling to see just one boat only to be disappointed yet again because the broker had failed to read the exacting list of requirements I had given that would have rendered the trip unnecessary in the first place.

Each disappointment contributed to a growing frustration that narrowed the window of opportunity I depended on to keeping

Darling's commitment up as much as my own. There is a certain tension to living close to the edge that can only be sustained by constant positive reinforcement of movement in the direction of your chosen challenge. One's enthusiasm as a consequence is directly proportional to how quickly you can makes things happen, the dwindling of which is also affected by the frustrations due to lack of progress. There are only so many times you can step up to the Start Line and go "ready, steady ..... STOP!" before your courage turns to jelly and finally dissolves.

By now we had gone through the gut-wrenching process of selling our beautiful house, had a contract on our practice and the kids were being home schooled. Darling and I had taken all the sailing courses we possibly could take without joining the fricken Navy and we were renting accommodation month to month in anticipation of making the big jump onto a boat that was nowhere to be found.

Finally, finally after eighteen long months of riding the emotional rollercoaster, the fateful call came through.

'I've found your boat!' was the first thing the broker said when my secretary handed me the phone during a busy day in practice. By now I had narrowed it down to just two brokers that I trusted. This guy wasn't one of them, but when he mentioned that he was connected to the agency where my *brothers in arms* worked and that the listing was exclusive to him, I decided to make an exception.

'Are you sure?' I asked, referring to the long list of requirements that the two other brokers used to filter all potential leads.

'This is the one!' he said mentioning the price which was more than within our budget. 'It's first come first served. I already have two other interested parties coming next weekend,' he added, playing on my emotions. We had lost a deal through hesitation some months before, so after such a long wait, I was determined not to let it happen again.

'How about Wednesday morning?' he inquired which was only two days later. It was a hassle. We'd have to cancel all of my patients, get the kids minded and make a six hour round trip to Whangarei basin to view the boat. The cost of doing all of this repeatedly over the last eighteen months had amounted to thousands of dollars down the drain. This was compounded by the fact that we had a family commitment the following weekend that we couldn't cancel and so with reluctance that was motivated by the fear of missing out again, I agreed to making the journey.

The first page of the 2 page list of requirements was prioritized in the following order:

1. 55 feet
2. Steel
3. 3 cabins, a good size saloon and a decent head (toilet and shower)
4. Galley to include three burner stove and oven
5. Sufficient refrigeration for three weeks of fresh food and a freezer capable of storing ice cream and making ice for vodka tonics!
6. Roller furling head sails.
7. 85 Hp engine
8. Generator for 240 volt power / recharging
9. 6 man life raft
10. Center cockpit (preferably) with a decent steering wheel and a storm dodger capable of withstanding any weight of water that crashed over the bow in rough weather.
11. Radar
12. G.P.S
13. 6 man dinghy with outboard
14. Etc

There were a further 126 items in total on another check list of requirements by NZ Coastguard for meeting the Category One safety standards for going offshore. This list was equally important because the more the boat met these requirements, the less had to be spent after purchase to bring it up to standard.

Our hearts were in our mouths as we made the final turn into the entrance to the marina. Having exhausted all avenues we knew that this was probably the last boat on offer that season. If all went well we would have just enough time to get it ready.

'Great to see you!' the Broker said shaking our hands enthusiastically and without further ado, led us down to where the boat was moored. As we walked along the floating pontoon my imagination ran ahead eagerly ticking off each boat in comparison to the mental picture of what I had in mind. If it was indeed the right boat then I would see it before he pointed it out.

'Well, what do you think?' he asked as he stopped well short of the boat my imagination had settled on. He had his hand held out as if to present the star attraction, his head nodding with the broadest of smiles. 'This is the one,' he said. It was forty feet long, wooden, aft cockpit with a tiller handle for steering, there were no furling head sails, no radar and it had an outboard engine hanging off the back!

'You're joking me, right?' I replied as I looked at Darling to see if her reaction was the same. 'Please tell me that you are joking,' I repeated as I saw her shoulders slump in the same realisation.

'No,' he replied as if I was the one making fun. 'It's such an incredible deal!' he said pointing to the price sheet he had in his hand.

'It's fuckin' wooden!' I half shouted in disbelief at having been duped yet again.

'But the price,' he stated with incredulity, as if I was missing the point. 'It's the best deal in the North Island.'

'It's a piece of shit!' I shot back, pointing at Darling. 'I have a wife and two children. I can't take them offshore in that!'

'Couldn't you use it to get experience and then trade up?' he answered in an attempt to explain his twisted sense of logic. It was then I decided to push him off the marina into the harbour.

'Don't!' Darling said jumping between us. 'It's bad enough as it is,' she added pushing me back when I tried to force my way through. 'Walk to the end of the marina and count to ten,' she ordered and pushed me again to make sure that I did. 'And you had better get out of here before he gets back,' she stated flatly to the broker.

'Wanker!' I shouted after him as he fled with his tail between his legs. 'One, two, three, fucker, five, six, wanker, seven, eight, nine... all Brokers are boloxes!'

The dream that had started with the bravest of intentions had ended literally in tears of frustration that were magnified by a bitter wind that blew across the marina. We had virtually cut all ties, such was our commitment to the idea of leaving at the end of this season. What to do from here?

'Are you having a bad day?' came a voice from over my shoulder when I returned to apologize to Darling for my behaviour. I turned to find the smiling face of a balding man sitting in the center cockpit of a forty-eight foot ketch. He had a careworn face and an air of grace that personified someone who had managed to remain optimistic in spite of all that life had thrown at him.

'You could say that,' I answered sensing that he somehow understood my feelings of disappointment.

'They should be called "heart breakers" not yacht brokers,' he stated, letting me know that he had been privy to my outburst. 'I'm Val,' he said leaning over the side of the boat and extending his hand to Darling. 'How about a nice cup of consolation coffee?' he smiled

73

and nodded to a stainless steel mug on the cockpit table with a bottle of rum beside it.

It wasn't long before he had us laughing at his own stories of past frustrations connected to buying his boat. 'There's luck involved, but it's worth the wait no matter how long it takes!' he stated with affection as he patted a beautifully varnished teak hand rail beside him.

'I think our luck has run out somehow. This is the end of our second season searching and we have seen every boat in New Zealand!' My frustration though was beginning to mellow with the rum.

'It took me forty years of hard work to be sitting here today,' he stated in a grandfatherly tone to appease my disappointment. 'I retired last year and I'm hoping for a few good winters with my wife in the Pacific. You still have your whole life ahead of you!'

It was just what we had needed. Someone older and wiser to salve our disenchantment and help us to appreciate more the luck that we already had. When we parted company an hour or so later I was in a far more pensive mood.

'Are you still brooding?' Darling teased as we made our way silently to the car.

'No, it's Val's boat,' I replied. He had given me a tour above and below deck before we departed. 'Did you notice that of all the boats that we have looked at, his boat comes the closest to matching the list of requirements we have made.

'It's only forty-eight feet long,' Darling replied reminding me that we weren't supposed to consider anything under fifty-five feet, 'and it's got two masts!'

'I know, but it would still do the job.' I stated, prepared to compromise on the length. In the big scheme of things two masts were not that big a deal either.

'It's not for sale.' Darling stated the obvious. I could tell though that she was edgy about the size.

'I know, but I was just saying.' It wasn't so much that I had to have the last word, but if she had been for sale I would have bought her on the spot.

'Every Dream Is Viable Inspiring New Adventure!' she said.

'What?'

'The name of Val's boat. Edvina!' she replied. 'Every dream is viable inspiring new adventures. Why don't we go live in the islands?

5

"Titty basket"

Our move to Vanuatu was the second prize, the compromise, if we failed to find a boat. It is a chain of islands five hundred miles west of Fiji and a thousand miles due north of New Zealand. The northern islands were the staging post for the Second World War up into Guadalcanal where the famous American novelist Michener wrote 'Tales of the South Pacific' about his experiences during the war.

'Only the newlywed and the nearly dead go there!' a travel agent advised when we had first made inquiries about the place. I'd originally set my sights on Western Samoa in an attempt to emulate Robert Louis Stevenson who had once lived there, but our research had proved it unviable. Vanuatu offered a larger population which would make it easier to be self-sufficient through opening a small clinic.

The travel agent's description could not have been further from the truth other than to serve as a deterrent which helped to preserve the island's unspoilt nature from the hordes of tourists that normally frequented Fiji. I'm not a snob, I'm just saying it as it was – paradise, but it took a bit of getting used to.

I wouldn't describe myself as a 'type A' personality, but the speed at which we had lived and worked all of our life up to that point made it hard to transition to doing almost nothing on a daily basis. 'Nothing' meant I wrote from 6.00 am till 1.00pm most days. Darling practiced three mornings a week and I did the alternate three afternoons, all of which were busy, but for me it was the equivalent of sleeping on the job. The rest of each day was mostly for play which included swimming, snorkelling, diving, canoeing, golf, running, tennis, sunbathing, sweating, losing weight (10kgs) socialising, visiting the market, playing with the kids, tropical sunsets and too many sundowners sitting under coconut trees.

To help us to integrate better with the locals we learned Bislama which is also known as Pidgin English. A woman's bra is known as a 'titty basket' and a condom is known as 'rubba blong fuk fuk' which were first introduced by the Americans during the war. The contrast to our former life in the so called 'real world' was the closest thing I have ever come to being blissed! I say the closest because I was almost there, a breath away, but for an itch that I just could not scratch that left me pissed.

There were two problems.

The first were the slums. Two streets back from every corner, the locals lived a third-world existence that bordered on poverty and deprivation caused by ignorance and good old colonialism. On the one hand, it made us more grateful for our privileged life, but there were days when it was hard to reconcile the disparity and double standards where our co-existence often required a blind eye.

That second problem was the persistent thought of 'the boat.' The harder you have worked on an idea, the harder it is to surrender, to give up and walk away. You'd think that a tropical island would have been far enough to go, but when I discovered that it was a major stop-off and replenishing point for the majority of cruising boats that sail around the world, my obsession was reignited. With this knowledge came an entirely new learning curve as I worked the boats from one end of the harbour to the other, gleaning information and advice from willing crews that were happy to share their experience for a home-cooked meal and a decent shower. We met all walks of life from all sorts of places, in all sorts of boats in all sorts of sizes, which expanded our horizons to what was truly possible. Whatever advice they may have had about sailing around the world, the message was always the same – "DO IT NOW." With this in mind my obsession became a fever that infected any other thoughts of what it might mean to be happy.

'Why don't you go and do one of those adventure courses to get it out of your system?' Justin suggested one afternoon when I appeared particularly distracted. Justin was a professional skipper who chartered his trimaran for sailing trips on Port Vila harbour. As a friend, he swapped outings with my family on his boat in return for Chiropractic care.

'That would be like using a pop gun to bring down an elephant!' I didn't want to do some Outward Bound leadership program where they take you to an isolated place and have you navigate your way back to *confidence* in a controlled environment where there is no downside. I was tired of playing it safe, of treading water in the shallow end of life. I wanted to strike out and lose sight of shore. To swim in the deep end where the wild things roar! To grab life by the horns and stick a cattle prod up its arse and find out who was the better man. I have since learned to be very careful for what you wish for because my prayers were going to be answered.

'Check these out,' Justin handed me a sheaf of badly-printed faxes a few weeks later when he arrived for one of his treatments. 'I have a friend who is a retired yacht broker living in the Bay of Islands in New Zealand. He still keeps an eye on the market and dabbles a bit when a good deal comes along. I wrote and gave him an idea of what you were looking for.'

On each sheet was the familiar layout of a broker's specifications and badly smudged photographs of the yachts that were available. There were seven boats in total, six over fifty feet, five of which we had already seen. The sixth was a forty-five foot ketch with a bowsprit that made it a shade over forty-eight feet. It had the best layout and a long list of extras that came close to matching my requirements, but like the other yachts, it was eighty-five thousand dollars more than we could afford. I wrote back to the broker and explained our position and asked him what he had available within our budget. 'Nothing!' was the long and short of his answer. We'd either have to reduce our requirements to a forty-footer or pretty much shelve the idea all together. It had been a long shot, but I knew the market so well that it was pretty much the answer that I had expected.

The days on the island were measured less by time and more by the number of pages that I had written about Kate's story. The six chapters that I had staked my life on had grown to twenty-one which now amounted to three hundred and sixty pages. In this idyllic environment the writing at first was easy, but turned into hard won graft that stretched over twelve months before I had the first draft finished. There were multiple frustrations to be endured including a computer that kept crashing, a printer that kept jamming and my brain which seemed unable to engage my hands to type what was in my head. My biggest challenge though was reconciling the pilot in the Spitfire with Kate and her baby. She had told me her story as best she could in the short time that we were together in my dream, but to be honest, I was having a hard time believing her. It was too big, of blockbuster proportions which pitched the chap as not only one of the youngest pilots, but also the top scoring fighter ace in the RAF during the Second World War. I knew all of the names of the top scoring pilots, and to the best of my recollection, none of them were Irish. However, for the sake of the story I decided that if he was Irish, then I might as well call him Paddy. Little did I know that this name was closer to the truth than I could ever have imagined and would come back to haunt me at a later date.

6

"Wage Peace"

If progress in life can sometimes be measured by a series of coincidences, then ours was about to coincide with a bizarre number, all taking place in the same week. After eighteen months I finished the first draft of 'The Christening' around the same time that I realized just how hard it is to write a novel. While I'd come to believe that it was a good story, my writing lacked the necessary skills needed to convey the sense of drama, adventure, joy and adversity that Kate and Paddy had gone through. It was a good first attempt, but I knew in my heart that the writer, like a good wine, was going to have to mature if he was to have any chance of making it a best seller. Having finished the first draft, I was now at a loose end and most days, like too rich a dinner, was starting to repeat as said focus became more distracted, not just by boat fever, but the reality of island fever as well.

'You gotta get off the rock every so often, or you start going a little crazy,' was the sage advice given by a longtime resident when we first set foot on the island. He'd been on the rock for over twenty years which we were beginning to discover … was a hell of a long time. We had started out with a twenty-year plan, but were quickly revising it when, among other things, we discovered that most foreign residents only last five and send their children off to boarding school the day they turn twelve. We happened to like having our children around, which created the beginnings of an enormous social void that our daughter Poppit would have to face the following year when all of the children her age left to go overseas. Along with the overwhelming desire to 'try again' for a boat, this realization was the beginning of the end of our time in the islands. That, and two separate e-mails from opposite sides of the world.

The first was the boat, the 'genuine article' my trusted broker had finally found in Auckland. "Wage Peace" was sixty feet of prancing steel that ticked off most of the items on my list, including her name, which I felt was synonymous with the essence of our journey. Better still, we actually knew her, having admired her from a distance when looking at other boats *and* the vendor was highly motivated.

The second was an e-mail from Muscat, the capital city of the Sultanate of Oman in the Middle East. It coincided with a conversation we'd had the previous week with Poppit's teacher.

'We have a really good friend looking for a Chiropractor to partner in opening a clinic in Oman,' was her reply when I shared the route of our possible voyage around the world. Somewhere along the way we were going to have to stop and work to replenish our kitty. Europe had seemed like the best option at the time, until Rashard Aziz Al Abdesalam came into our lives. As it turned out, it wasn't just any Chiropractic center, but rather the very first Chiropractic center to open in the Sultanate. The most bizarre of all of these coincidences was that our next door neighbor had lived in Muscat for several years and raved about the place.

'In a heartbeat,' he replied when we questioned if he would go back again. 'Of all the countries in the Middle East it is the best. This is a unique opportunity,' he encouraged.

'We could sail around the world, open the center, have an adventure somewhere completely different and then continue on around a couple of years later,' Darling suggested as an alternative to working in Ireland or the UK. The idea appealed and would give Poppit and Jack, our six year old son, a completely different perspective on life. 'If the boat doesn't work out then we can still go to Oman and spend a few years,' she added, surprising me with her enthusiasm and resonating the fact that we weren't ready yet to return to the settled confines of living a so called *normal* life on the mainland

No matter how hard we had tried two years before, we could not get it together, now suddenly, the dots seemed to be joining themselves. So we packed our container once more, bade our farewells and headed back to NZ to buy 'the boat' and keep my promise to Lewis.

7

'A high maintenance bitch!'

"Wage Peace" was everything I had dreamed of in a boat. She was long and sleek with tons of room below decks, without looking frumpy, she maintained lines that made her look fast standing still. Her extra size was made for the confidence that Darling needed, including a washing machine and a galley fridge and freezer twice the size of the one we had on our wish list. So confidant was I in her pedigree that I almost paid a deposit to secure the sale before having a consultant surveyor look over her. Almost.

'Vigilance is the key to finding the right boat, vigilance in maintaining her properly is essential to you surviving the storm, and vigilance at sea is what will save you from ever having to face the storm in the first place,' was the advice given to me by an old sea dog named Captain Keith when I asked him why he had named his boat "Vigilant." So impressed was I by how he thumped his knee to drive the point home, that it was he whom I invited to perform the necessary survey.

'Well, what do you think?' I inquired with enthusiasm after Keith had conducted a critical eye over my new mistress.

'She's a thoroughbred with real pedigree,' he stated. 'In the right conditions she will fly,' he affirmed, echoing my similar assessment of not only fast passage making but possible broken records as well. But there was a "but" in his voice, a hesitancy in the way he slowly shook his head, that echoed the previously mentioned vigilance. That and a desire to let me down gently.

'You don't want her,' he stated flatly, looking at Darling. 'In the wrong conditions, she will be a "*high maintenance bitch*" that will probably kill you ... and your children. I'm sorry,' he apologized for being the one to disappointment her. 'What you want is a boat that will look after you in a storm. A boat that will give as good as it gets and fight back long after you have run out of the will to live. This is not the boat,' he stated.

Whatever about Darling, my own disappointment could only be measured by the deep long bottomless sigh that left me dazed and inconsolable for weeks after.

'There are plenty more fish in the sea,' didn't resonate with me when Darling tried to cheer me up. There are only so many cruising boats in New Zealand and judging by the latest brokerage listings I was sure we had already seen all of them. We had three months to find 'the right boat' and get it ready in time for the Pacific cruising season. Once started, we had six months before the annual Hurricane season rolled around to either return to New Zealand, or set off around the world ahead of the weather.

'We need those six months.' I knew that every day would be vital to either gaining the experience necessary to make a circumnavigation, or scare the shit out of ourselves sufficiently to be content to forever return as dedicated Land Lubbers.

'We have come too far to give up now,' she stated bravely knowing full well the mountain we had to re-climb.

'Okay, but New Year's Eve is the line in the sand. Any later and it will be too late!' I was adamant. I was tired of the emotional rollercoaster ride of false starts, multiple disappointments and the chasing of tales that always led to the graveyard of broken dreams where all of the headstones were marked *dead end* or *dead in the water* or even *dip shit*. 'New Year's Eve, otherwise we are going to Oman.'

As we burned rubber along the same highways that we had driven so many times before we no longer needed a road map or directions to find marinas and boats that we had visited and revisited. We were now on first name terms with many of the managers who had become our eyes and ears on the ground and were proving more reliable than our two trusted brokers for news of anything that might be coming on the market.

If every dream is a compromise, then our wish list was getting shorter, wider, dumpier and frumpier by the day as we compared each boat to the original racehorse we'd had to put down. When I found myself considering an old fishing trawler that had been classified as a 'motor sailor' I knew the search was over.

'Looks like it's Oman,' I sighed to Darling as we drove back to our rental house in Auckland from Tauranga. We had spent the month of November and early December looking at the last of the dregs of what was available. With two weeks to Christmas, the line in the sand had been pretty much crossed. The second prize, the new compromise, now beckoned from the deserts of Oman.

It was time to set a different course.

8

'Missionaries, Mercenaries and Misfits!'

If everything that we did to make the boat happen led to frustration, then the opposite was the case for Oman. The barrage of correspondence that Rashard sent in answer to each inquiry became an affirmation that was to lay the foundation for a very different kind of future. Nothing was too much trouble. His answers were educated and articulate, objective and accommodating, but most of all enthusiastic that we visit and see for ourselves the potential that existed. As the dots started to reconnect in a different direction, lo and behold, Emirates airlines offered a special one week return deal for two to Dubai. When Rashard offered to take care of our expenses in Oman we figured that we were starting to sing off the same hymn sheet with many of the values that we shared.

As such, we were greeted on arrival by a 'family man' with a wife, three sons and a daughter. As head of training for Air Traffic Control in Oman, he also had interests in IT, graphic design, construction, and a new venture in high end furniture made from the same wrought iron that he manufactured for his security business.

'My motivation to open a clinic is based on my desire to set a good example for my children, and provide service for my people, as laid out in the Holy Koran,' Rashard explained as he drove us around

Muscat. 'If I can do this, then *Inshallah* (God willing) it will make me a better Muslim.' His wife Salwa nodded to confirm their commitment.

Our research on the ground was revealing in the way it not only mirrored the good press we had been given, but proved that of all the Arab states, Oman was the most 'normal' in lifestyle. Like the search for the boat, we had a check list that covered security, income potential, sustainability, personal freedom, lifestyle, cultural exchange and the opportunity to socially integrate. What we found was, that short of going to the Mosque on Saturdays, Darling could work, drive her own car, wear Kiwi clothes and take the kids to the beach without having to worry about cultural extremes or the threat of religious zealots breathing down her neck. We could also live among the locals in a normal suburb where it was safe for the kids to play on the streets, ride their bikes and go to the movies instead of a 'secure compound' where you lived in lockdown as required in some of the other countries.

'There are three types of people who live in the Middle East; Missionaries, Mercenaries and Misfits! Which one are you?' A wiry old expatriate lawyer with a tired smile questioned us when we sought his advice on doing business in Oman. Our answer was that we didn't see ourselves as any of the three and eventually settled on the idea of being Pioneers. It sounds kind of corny, but Chiropractic is still a relatively young profession that is yet to make its impact worldwide. Some of our professors in College had trained under the original founders. We saw ourselves breaking new ground, opening things up and heralding a new era of health in Oman and the Middle East.

Short on demographics or 'real' statistics, we stood on street corners and several roundabouts in the Central Business District and Consular areas and counted the number of BMW's, Mercedes and 'high end' cars that passed by per hour. It didn't take long to establish that 'lots' was the answer and that, combined with several up-market shopping malls in the same area, was sufficient to convince us that there was enough wealth to sustain a clinic.

Was the money important? Absolutely. The very success of the practice and thus the funds we needed to make the second part of our voyage, depended upon it. There would be no fallback position, no corporate bail-outs and no insurance policies that covered failure. It would be swim or sink in a land of quicksands that was thousands of miles from home and did not have a lifeboat or ambulance service. Profit therefore was vital to the success of the venture. However, we were determined not to measure our success in terms of dollars and cents. There is a very fine line between being a Pioneer and a Crusader and we wanted to make sure that line wasn't blurred by the egotistical adoration of 'False Gods' that led to carnal pursuits. In other words, we were not interested in f*&%$#g anyone to get what we wanted.

As pioneers for our profession, our children would be witness to the mark that we made. It was important therefore that we walked our talk. I know this sounds highfaluting, idealistic and perhaps even egotistic, but we felt that we were being given an opportunity not just to talk about it, but to show our kids how to make the world a better place. As a consequence, our discussions with Rashard were less about what we were willing to do and more about what we were determined not to do. It was to be a service, not a business, a source of profit, but not a cash cow that milked the patients for everything that they were worth. Its success would be based on it *not* being the first Chiropractic Center in Oman, but more importantly, by not being the last!

'If we can make it work, then there is likely to be the potential to encourage other Chiropractors to open more clinics in the future.' More Chiropractors meant more people being served and ultimately more profit. It would be a win win for everyone concerned.

'Inshallah,' Rashard repeated several times over dinner on our last night as we laid out our terms for a business partnership. When he agreed, without reservation, to giving us full control over the practice, we committed to returning and making it happen.

'When?' he asked for commitment.

'It all depends on this f$#&%n' boat,' I replied, sharing the frustrations of our unsuccessful search to date. 'If we don't find a boat then we will be back at the beginning of the year, say February or March.'

'If you do?'

'Then it is more likely to be eighteen months, or as long as it takes to sail here from New Zealand!'

Regardless of the time frame, he was impressed by our determination and agreed to hold out for our arrival rather than find someone else. We parted at the airport as friends, not just excited by the prospect of working together, but also by a sense that the dots were somewhat 'Divine' in their connection and that 'Inshallah', we would return.

9

'The only surprises you will get are good ones!'

'Happy New Year!' we cheered in unison at the allotted time. We were sharing the occasion with some close friends in their beach house north of Auckland. On the outside I was cheery, but on the inside I was weary. We had returned from the Middle East to face two last-minute disappointments from our brokers who, likewise, had given up on the idea of ever finding us a boat.

'Look out Oman!' Darling shouted above the din of celebration. In spite of the potential that it offered for the future, we were quietly disenchanted. Deep down inside I felt that in some way I had failed to keep my promise to Lewis. The liberal application of cheap champagne though served as an antidote for the blues. We toasted the new Millennium and honored absent friends with a resolution to making a great success of our New Year's adventure in the Middle East.

The following morning as a consequence, wasn't so cheery! The marina was the last place I wanted to go, but the need for a strong coffee outweighed our other New Year's resolution, and that was to stay away from boats! Because of the crowds, we were obliged to sit outside, so I made a point of positioning myself with my back to the yachts that were moored there.

'Are you catching flies?' I joked at Darling's slack jawed expression after she had finished a yawn. I had already finished my coffee and was just about to go back inside and order a second round.

'Look!' She pointed behind me, her eyes wide with astonishment. Sitting on the end of the marina was a forty-eight foot ketch.

'So?' I glanced back momentarily. Having given up on the idea of a boat, my mind was now a million miles away in Muscat wrestling with the vagaries of opening a new practice.

'Look at the stern!' she said. My gaze followed her finger to rest on the sign that held her gaze at the blunt end of a boat ... EDVINA - FOR SALE

'Holy ...t!' we both replied in unison. It was the ketch we had been on eighteen months before when I had almost assaulted the broker for wasting our time. It was like being struck with a bolt of lightning. Within an hour we had tracked down Val the owner. By lunchtime we were sitting on the boat talking like old friends, grateful for the fact that there was no broker involved. All thoughts of our resolution to go to Oman were suddenly thrown out the window.

'The only surprises you will get on this boat are good ones!' Val stated as I ticked off the list of required essentials that had changed significantly from our research with yachties in Vanuatu. Bad luck for Val, a heart attack the previous year had ended his dream of retiring to the Pacific. Good luck for us, Edvina was as close as you could get to being fully equipped for going to sea. Within a week we had organized a sea trial that proved her worthiness. A survey by Captain Keith a few days later confirmed she was indeed the boat we had been looking for all along. The last obstacle to be hurdled was the price.

'Two hundred and eighty five thousand dollars,' was the reply that winded and stopped me in my tracks. When I recovered, I didn't have the heart to tell Val there and then, but I'm sure my stunned look must have registered that there was no way we could afford her. All of my guesstimations had been based on the fact that the market price in boats had fallen significantly in the last year. I had figured an asking price of two hundred and forty thousand. If we took the brokers fees out and ten percent for negotiations and we met somewhere in the middle then we were talking somewhere around two hundred and five thousand. It was more than our original budget of two hundred thousand maximum, but I wasn't going to let an extra five thousand sink the deal. Eighty five thousand however was so far removed from what we could afford that to make an offer I felt would be an insult to Val and his wife

I waited a week before I called him. A week to calm down and recover my equilibrium; to refocus on the task that was Oman. We had been shaken, but not stirred to action. Pipped at the post, but not as disappointed as I thought we would. A year before I would have given my left testicle for this opportunity, but after a week, I felt strangely detached.

'Val, I'm sorry to disappoint, but I'm not going to make you an offer.' I explained about our budget and apologized to him and his wife, to whom we felt a great affinity, for wasting their time. I knew that as the vendor, this had been just as big an emotional rollercoaster for them as it had been for us.

'Okay, I will talk to the boss and see what she thinks.'

'Look Val I'm really sorry,' I stated, sensing that he might waste their time and ours by trying to negotiate us to a figure that was still way outside our budget. 'I've heard about too many disasters that have been caused by cruisers spending too much on their boat and not keeping enough in reserve for the voyage. We really can't afford to go beyond our budget.'

'I understand,' he replied and being the gentleman that he was, rang off wishing us well for our trip to Oman.

It was over. Finally, three weeks past the line in the sand, the Fat Lady had sung and ended our dream of sailing around the world for good. I didn't feel so bad second time around. In fact it was more like a weight had been lifted off our shoulders. I was left with no doubt that we had genuinely given it our best shot and that Lewis would understand.

The following week was filled with the logistics of shifting our lives once again to the northern hemisphere. Because Oman was still a relatively closed country to Westerners, the bureaucracy and number of phone calls we had to dial and receive to make this big step was enormous. We were just about to book our tickets a week later, when I received a phone call out of the blue.

10

"Ready steady ... stop!"

'Daddy, Val's on the phone!' Poppit called out.

'Who?' I was so engrossed in writing an e-mail to Rashard that I failed to register the name.

'You know, Val,' followed by a pregnant pause ... '*Edvina*!' she remonstrated as if I was an idiot (you can decide that for yourself). Then suddenly my brain clicked into gear and she handed me the phone.

'Hi, Val?' I wondered why he would be calling.

'I spoke to the boss,' he declared in a matter of fact tone, as if I should have been expecting to hear from him. 'You have yourself a deal!' There was no argument for extra value, or alternate figure or conditions, or suggested compromises. 'If you are still interested that is?'

'Holy sh..!' would be the best way to describe my response to an offer that I had *not* made. He'd just dropped the price by eighty five thousand dollars without making any demands. 'Are you serious?!' My mind went into overdrive trying to calculate if we still had time to make the necessary preparations for the upcoming cruising season. The fact that I had just been about to commit to Oman by pressing the send button on my e-mail to Rashard was enough to default to another pregnant pause. (This time it felt like triplets!) In the end though I could not deliver.

'I can't do it Val. It's too big a hit. I'd feel like we were taking advantage of you.' I tried to explain, without raising the issue of his health. It felt like kicking a man when he was down.

'You can,' he encouraged quietly. 'Go out there and live the dream for me with your wife and children. It's the only thing I'd ask you to do in return.'

'I can't Val. Not this way. If you hold out another few months you are bound to find someone who can pay you what she is worth.' It's not that I didn't want it. My brain had now finished making the calculations and we still had time to make the preparations. I just did not want it this way. It seemed so unfair that we would gain from the terrible loss he would be making at his stage in life.

'Another couple of months and she will miss the cruising season. Then I will have to wait for another year to come around. I'm tired,' he finally sighed.

'Val, you have caught me off guard here. I'll have to talk to my "Boss" and get back to you.'

It had been "ready steady ... stop" too many times. In our minds we had already walked away from the starting line to do the long jump to Oman. To "Go" meant having to return to the cleats and hunker down and start yet again.

There is only so long that you can live on the edge. The boundaries of my imagination that I had worked so hard to push back were turning in on themselves and pushing back in again. On top of this, the flame of obsession that had burned inside had been dulled by the facts, the figures, the dangers and the down side. This truly was the deep end where there were storms and pirates and sharks. We really could get eaten alive out there!

I realized at that moment that I was scared. That this wasn't a *We* decision. It was up to me. It had been my crazy idea in the first place. The starting gun was finally in my hand. All I had to do was pull the trigger and shout 'Go!' My problem was that it felt like the gun was pointed at my head!

'I always leave it up to the numbers. I find it keeps the emotion out of it,' Captain Keith recommended when I sought his wise counsel. 'Put all of the figures on the table and compare the upside to the downside. What you are looking for is a reason to commit, or a reason to quit,' he advised

It was too logical for me. I am by nature more intuitive. While I had proven my math ability in the past, I didn't want this decision about the lives of my family to boil down to some facts or figures on paper. Worst case scenario I was going to have to live with the consequences of this decision. What I needed was a sign ... something Divine, to let me know I was doing the right thing.

Finally, one morning early, I made up my mind - or rather ... my mind was made up for me.

'This is bullshit!' I had been in that halfway slumber between awake and sleep, ruminating over my dilemma. It was the voice again, but this time it wasn't Anthony Hopkins. In his place was my good mate Lewis sitting at the end of my bed. 'You've forgotten what it is to really adventure,' he said and reminded me of Scotty and Angel whose big O.E. was to swop Auckland suburbia for Dublin suburbia working for my brother, only to find more of the same, under a different name called security. Their big adventure had been reduced to one week escapes every three or four months on Ryanair 'one dollar specials' to obscure destinations in Europe. When they had soon grown tired of working for my brother they opted instead for the antithesis of adventure in the form of moving to the U.K.. There they had settled for the long delayed gratification of "living the dream" in return for 'profit sharing' in a new partnership with another Chiropractor.

'When the novelty wears off, Oman won't be any different!' Lewis stated. 'You have a promise to keep and it's not just to me. It's to yourself. Think of all of the people who have encouraged you along the way. Do you know why they do that ... because it's scary!' he answered without waiting for my reply. 'If you are not scared, then it ain't courage. Isn't that what you told me Eddy Rickenbacker the famous First World War fighter ace used to say?' And then he was gone.

It wasn't the sign that I'd been looking for ... that would come later, but it was enough to make me keep digging. For what I wasn't sure, but Lewis suddenly showing up was surreal enough to let me know that there was something I had overlooked, something that was missing from the equation.

'Val, I need a favor!' I wanted to sit on Edvina alone to see where my intuition took me. I started by sitting on the stern rail (the blunt end). In front of me was the aft cabin, then the center cockpit with the binnacle and steering wheel, throttle lever and gear stick, winches and

93

ropes of all sorts that led to the fifty-three-foot high mast just past center of the boat. After a while nothing came to me, so I swopped ends for the bow (sharp end). Looking back towards the stern I could see the for'ard hatch, for'ard cabin, more winches and ropes, the life raft and a four man dinghy that was draped across the cabin roof. Again nothing came to me but the pungent smell of the river on which we were moored and a grumble in my stomach to remind me that I had skipped breakfast that morning. What I was looking for was something that could not be crossed off Captain Keith's check list nor rationalized by the logical mind.

Having looked everywhere else I turned my attention to the contents of the three drawers under the chart table. The first was filled with cruising manuals, several folded charts and a sextant. The second had instruction books and user manuals on every piece of equipment on board, including the main engine and the generator. The third contained three thick binders detailing an extensive inventory of spare parts and a wad of paperwork connected to the history of Edvina. I had previously scanned them all before, but the immensity of information had been too much to absorb. Perhaps a detailed reading might give me the inspiration that I was looking for?

Three hours later I stood up slowly from the confined space of the navigation table to stretch and find caffeine. In doing so, I knocked the third of the manuals I had yet to read onto the cabin floor. An envelope dropped out of the back of the manual and landed at my feet.

The first thing to grab my attention was the Vanuatu postage stamp on the front. The second was more like a slap in the face and a better wakeup call than any coffee I might have had. The address was in my own hand writing! On the back was my name and address in Vanuatu. The date was the middle of the previous year.

I hesitated, (because it was still Val's boat) but then decided to open the envelope. It turned out to be the second letter I had sent to the broker who was a friend of my mate Justin in Port Vila. In it I stated that my budget was $200,000. You will recall that he had replied that I would either have to come down in size to a forty-footer or forget about the idea altogether. Attached to my letter was a complimentary slip from the broker who must have been a friend of Val's. "This might be the best offer you will get," it stated simply.

The Bugger ... he'd known all along!

'Val, I have just found a letter in the navigation station that I sent to a broker last year.' I'd had to climb three quarters of the way up the mast to get reception on my mobile phone.

'Oh that one,' he replied casually, as I was swayed by the wind.

'I'm a little confused here. Why didn't you tell me about it?

'Are you a religious man?' he questioned.

'Not really,' I replied, hoping that he wasn't going to try to engage me in some sort of philosophical debate while I hung on for dear life forty feet above the deck.

'Neither am I, but I have come to learn that God or the Gods or whatever, work in strange ways. I was afraid it might scare you off.'

'On the contrary, if you had shown me this at the very beginning we wouldn't be having this conversation.' By some innate knowing I realized that this was the sign that I had been looking for all along. Religious or not we were both singing off the same hymn sheet. 'You have yourself a deal!' I affirmed.

11

'Until one is committed!'

Sailing around the world means a lot of different things to a lot of different people and depends on whether you are the one standing on the pier or the one sitting in the boat.

'Are you not afraid of hurricanes or pirates or sharks?' was the most common question we had to deflect from people who, in all fairness, didn't know any better than we did before the idea had taken possession of our souls. As part of a confidence building exercise, I had done the research to convince Darling and anyone around her who might have an alternative, but potentially fatal point of view, that we were just as safe on land as at sea. There were many facts and figures that I could quote, but the following two are pretty compelling.

3,500 people die in motor vehicle accidents around the world on a daily basis. That's the population of a small town, wiped out, every day, by a seemingly benign function of life. New Zealand, at 400 deaths annually, has one of the highest fatality rates per capita in the world. This fact was brought into stark contrast two weeks after we purchased Edvina, when the eleven-year-old daughter of one of our friends ended up in an intensive care unit for two weeks following a near-fatal car accident just a couple of kilometers from home. We were safer sailing around the world with our two children, than driving in our four-wheel-drive Nissan Patrol.

The second fact is, that of the type of cruising that we were planning to do, almost 80% would be spent either moored, anchored or otherwise attached to a safe harbor in or on the way to an exotic destination. The remaining twenty percent spent at sea would take place as we travelled in between hurricane seasons, 96% of which would involve good or at least safe weather. The remaining 4%, approximately seven days of an entire cruising year, might involve bad weather, but only one day of this could potentially sink us. In the case of minority rules, we had decided not to let the potential of one bad day ruin a perfectly good adventure.

In addition to the facts and figures I thought it just as important to listen to the sage advice of those who had literally *climbed the mountain before us*.

The first is a statement by W.N. Murray, the leader of the Scottish expedition to conquer Mount Everest back in the fifties.

Commitment

Until one is committed, there is hesitancy, the chance to draw back, always ineffectiveness. Concerning all acts of initiative (and creation), there is one elementary truth, the ignorance of which kills countless ideas and splendid plans: that the moment one definitely commits oneself, then providence moves too. All sorts of things occur to help one that would otherwise never have occurred. A whole stream of events issues from the decision, raising in one's favour all manner of unforeseen incidents and meetings and material assistance, which no man could have dreamt would have come his way. I have learned a deep respect for one of Goethe's couplets: "Whatever you can do, or dream you can -- begin it. Boldness has genius, power, and magic in it. Do it now!"

Every cruiser we met in Vanuatu gave us the same piece of advice ... Do it now!

Another came from the novel 'The Power of One' by Bryce Courtenay ... "I had to teach myself to never consider the consequences of losing a fight. Too much cross-referencing of the consequences of failure robs one of the single minded concentration to win."

Probably the most important one of all was this one attributed to John F. Kennedy, former President of the United States. "The stories of past courage can offer hope, they can provide inspiration. But they cannot supply courage itself. For this, each man must look into his own soul."

Following the bucket list wasn't just about fulfilling a promise or visiting exotic places. It was an adventure of the soul. It was to boldly go where we had been programmed to think we could never before go. To invite Godzilla into our back garden to play with our kids and trust that no matter what happened ... we could handle it. It was as much about the child within *us* walking our talk and daring to be the player in the arena of life, perhaps even bloodied, rather than a spectator yelling from the stands. Sailing around the world was to be our big fat hairy audacious Everest.

Were we scared? Hell yeah! But it wasn't hurricanes or pirates or dragons on the horizon that had us by the short and curlies. It was giving up the idea of safety that comes with leading a so-called 'normal' life. It was swopping the imagined certainty of our freehold house, busy practice, permanent job, a regular income, money in the bank, big cars, social status and a hospital down the road for the uncertainty of everything we didn't know about life that was determined by who knows what?

When I look back now, the scariest period was not the journey, but selling off our hard-earned investments one by one to 'divest' in a boat that could very easily lead to not only financial, but our physical demise as well. The scariest day, and I'm talking diarrhea, dry retching and migraines, was when we handed over the check to Val in payment for Edvina, because we knew there and then, that the line had truly been crossed and there would be no turning back.

The biggest boat I had ever owned was a twelve foot dinghy. The biggest boat I had ever sailed was twenty-one feet which I managed to run aground. It had been twenty years since I had actually sailed a boat and that was over the incredible distance of twenty-six miles. Short of the few charter trips we had done to convince Darling that 'this was the life' I had never taken a boat offshore. Our first leg was to be a thousand miles of blue water sailing.

While we had next to no sea time, our two years of picking the minds of crews in Vanuatu who had trod the boards before us made for an enormous resource of knowledge essential to making Edvina ready for the journey.

The 'To Do' list was enormous and we faced working ninety hours a week for the ten week window we had to make her shipshape. The learning curve during this time wasn't just steep, it was vertical and folded back on itself on occasion. I had always thought that once you started living the dream, the highs and lows of life would go away. What struck me most was how the emotional rollercoaster still prevailed. The 'holy shit what have we just gotten ourselves into' was still there on waking, every day, especially in the early days. However, as we gradually overcame our doubts, a door opened up to a new reality that we could never have imagined. We started to get a glimpse of a new set of real possibilities that had been hidden by our fears. Once we got out of bed and got started on the 'To Do List,' each item crossed off was like a deposit in the 'confidence account' that made the next day that little easier, until one day … this way of living became our new *normal*.

Besides getting Edvina ready for sea, the biggest challenge we faced was finding a suitable crew. While we might have been winging it, we had grown smart enough to know that we couldn't begin the trip without at least one experienced person to help us out. With only four weeks to our departure, we were cutting it close in finding the right person, but Captain Keith had warned us that the "wrong person" would spell disaster from the beginning. This was personified by a long line of dismal, dead beat, gone in the head (two of them) stoned (one of them) mostly ancient applicants who never even made the short list.

And then the words of W.N. Murray rang through.

'Gidday, I'm calling from Sydney. I'm inquiring to see if the position for crew is still available?' Somehow our advertisement for a crew that we had placed in various yacht clubs and marinas around Auckland had found its way to Australia!

'Mate, you're a long way from home to be applying for the position,' was my first response. 'Do you have any experience?'

·'I have just spent the last fifteen days sailing from Auckland to Sydney. I arrived here yesterday, but I'm keen to go again!' he declared with enthusiasm.

'Well, this is the way it is. If you decide to come all the way from Sydney and we don't like the cut of your jib, we won't take you.' I explained our interview process and how many other applicants had failed to meet our requirements and how we would not be responsible for a wasted trip. He rang off saying that he'd think about it.

Two days later, just as we were sitting down for dinner after another long day of preparation, there was a knock on the side of the boat.

'Ahoy, anyone on board?' a voice shouted.

I climbed the companionway ladder to the cockpit to answer the call. Standing on the marina at the stern was a stranger.

'Gidday, I'm Kent, I called you from Sydney.' I was flabbergasted *and* impressed, but did my best to hide it as I ticked off the box called *enthusiasm* that was number one on our checklist.

At twenty-four, Kent ticked all of the boxes in terms of attitude (arrived with a bottle of red wine) sense of humor (didn't mind when one of the kids accidentally spilled a glass over him) physique (built like an Olympian) laughter (lots) tattoos (one on each bicep to accentuate his warrior intellect) a qualified carpenter (great for helping with the maintenance) offshore experience (just enough), but most of all, the kids liked him ... and so did we.

He joined us the next day in the preparation dance of two steps forward and one step backwards until we finally began to know Edvina as a living, breathing being who let us know in return how she was feeling by coughing, spluttering, creaking and farting until we had, one by one, cleared out the cobwebs and sorted out all of her gnarly bits. With two weeks to departure she finally began to purr.

I'd love to tell you that when the day of reckoning arrived we were ready. The truth is ... you are never ready. You prepare as best you can, tick all the boxes, cross off your lists and double check that everything is in place, but the day comes when you *have* to throw off your attachment to the living, breathing land of certainty that you are deeply rooted to and head out into the unknown. Ready or not, we were committed and felt confident enough that if the worst came to the worst, it would be nothing short of an act of the Gods.

We were hoping for success. Failure we had decided we could handle. Our motivation to press on though was the fear of ending up back on the middle ground that we had worked so hard for so long to break out of in the first place. All we needed was for our luck to hold.

12

"Fortitudine Vincimus!"

It is the pioneering spirit, that inborn desire that we all possess to break out and *live the dream*, that helps us rise up and be the best version of ourselves. Once embraced it becomes a force to be reckoned with that pushes through a great deal of the negativity, self doubt, fear, enculturation, desperation and all of the other stuff that has a tendency to stand in your way. Not that all of this shit isn't necessary. We need to be tested, to harden our resolve and reaffirm our course again and again so that when the going gets really tough, we have the fortitude to push on through. Nothing could be truer than when it comes to the physical and psychologically debilitating nature of seasickness.

'Be warned. It's less about sailing and more about punching north to get out of New Zealand waters,' Captain Keith stated ominously when I'd asked him to confirm the rumour I heard from other seasoned skippers. 'Regardless of what the weather man tells you, you will most likely be sailing uphill, against the wind.'

Finally, it had all come together. After years of dreaming, months of preparation and weeks of delay waiting for the best weather window, we departed Opua on the fourth of May 2000 on a big high, both meteorological and psychological. On the companion-way ladder I had stuck a magnetic plaque from "Alice in Wonderland" written by Lewis Carroll ...

"There's no use in trying,' said Alice. 'One can't believe impossible things!'

'I daresay you haven't had much practice,' said the Queen. 'When I was your age, I always did it for half an hour a day. Why, sometimes, I've believed as many as six impossible things before breakfast.'

We, and that included Kent, had spent so long dreaming and working towards the impossible. Now suddenly, we were living it. It was surreal, to have dreamed the dream and made it real. To be the guy in the boat with his back to the mainland rather than the guy on the pier yearning for the sail on the far horizon.

Besides the total vulnerability of travelling the unknown road, the hardest part about beginning the adventure was leaving our family and friends behind. Our sad and tearful farewell though, was tempered by the enormous support and encouragement that we had received, including a threat of disownment if we dared to back out at the last moment.

The skies were blue, the day was warm (as much as a winter's day could be) and our spirits were high, if not floating. With full sails set and a fishing line trawling off the stern, fair winds carried us out of the Bay of Islands at a gentle six knots. By midnight, the only remaining sign of shore was the lighthouse of Cape Reinga, the furthest tip north of New Zealand. I don't remember much after that.

According to our log, we shortened sail on two occasions during the next twelve hours, including taking down the mizzen altogether. The next step would be emergency storm sails. By the following morning, the expensive weather report I had paid for turned out to be about as useful as the seasick tablets we had taken the previous day. Except for Kent, we were all sick as dogs. Forewarned, we were all armed with at least one sick bucket, bottles of water and a pre-selected place on Edvina to brace ourselves as she began the hard work of punching north as predicted by Captain Keith.

How strong was the wind? I don't know other than it blew the gauge off the top of the mast. How high were the waves? It's hard to tell when you are hugging the cockpit floor like a teenager after a drunken binge, but they sometimes engulfed the entire length of Edvina and stopped all twenty tons of her dead in her tracks. Each time however she found her feet and charged the next monster with the resolve of a battleship intent on breaking through 'No Man's Land.' Time and again she gave as good as she got without complaint, which unfortunately, was more than could be said for her crew. By the middle of the second day they were completely miserable and the kids were showing signs of dehydration. Darling and I were not far behind them.

At one am the following morning a terrible clanging on the side of Edvina alerted us to the fact that the anchor and fifty foot of chain had broken loose from the bow. The drag alone knocked two knots off the essential speed necessary to make headway. Fearful of the threat that we might founder in a trough or the chain wrapping around the propeller, Kent and I fought our way to the bow. There, my choice in crew was proven as he applied himself, on three occasions completely submerged, to the heroic task of recovering the anchor and chain and lashing it safely back in position. Our immediate relief at success was short lived by Darling's frantic shouting when we made it back to the cockpit.

'Fire!' she shouted. 'Fire!' The most terrible warning you would never want to hear on a boat. 'There's a fire somewhere down below!'

'Get the kids on deck,' I ordered as I charged down the companionway to find that the saloon was already beginning to fill with an acrid rubbery smell. Kent sprang into action behind me and disappeared down the aft hatch to where Poppit and Jack were sleeping. With no sign of flames I immediately suspected that the smoke was coming from the engine room, which was a shock because we were not using the engine. I grabbed an extinguisher and saying a 'Hail Mary,' I made my way down past the galley and carefully opened an access door, only to be forced back by thick billowing smoke. To my great relief though, other than a screeching, whirring sound, there was still no sign of flame.

It took a minute or so for the smoke to clear. When it did, I could see the last strangled remnants of an engine belt that connected a pulley on the propeller shaft to a pulley on an alternator mounted on top of the gear box. A brilliant idea that generated electricity for the entire boat, but the pulleys had become misaligned and the friction had caused the belt to become red hot. I was in two minds as to whether I should use the fire extinguisher (because of the mess it would make) when the belt disintegrated and immediately stopped smoking. *Pheeeeeewwwww!*

'Three days,' Captain Keith had advised when I asked how long it takes to get over the sickness. I began to wonder if he had lied about that part as we entered our fourth day at sea. Our only connection to the outside world was a twice daily radio schedule that we maintained with Russell Radio by high frequency single side band radio. We reported our position (Hell), exchanged weather conditions (atrocious), and the state of the crew (barely alive), in return for the crackly reassurance from three other yachts fighting the same battle in our one million square mile vicinity that none of them were close to surrender.

"Fortitudine Vincimus!' *By endurance we shall conquer,* I kept telling my crew. Up to that moment I had fortified myself with the legendary Ernest Shackleton's favourite quote from the story of "Endurance" … the account of the incredible hardship he and his men had suffered when they were stranded in Antarctica after their ship was crushed by ice. His epic account of the human ability to endure the most harrowing of circumstances trapped on ice for more than a year, made our own hardship by comparison pale into insignificance.

As Captain I had decided early on that the best way to rule our little ship was by consensus. That included letting the kids know what lay ahead and allowing them at the very least to voice their opinion, including their fears. Knowing there would be hard times, we wanted them to be educated and up for the challenge. Home schooling as a consequence wasn't just about one and one equalling two. It was more about un-schooling the kids so that they had the sense to think outside the box of prejudice, superstition and F.E.A.R. (false evidence appearing real) However, by the fourth day, just as a part of me began to wonder how much longer 'we' could endure, the youngest of our crew finally brought it to a head.

'Your son wants to see you,' Darling reported from below decks. Dismissive of my rank, I had been summoned by the cabin boy! As I made my way to the aft cabin I could see that in spite of the fact that everything had been battened down, reefed down, strapped down *and* secured … the inside of Edvina was like the inside of a tumble drier. There were sick buckets everywhere with the remnants of bile and long emptied stomachs, the stench of which permeated the entire boat on a long tail of stale air.

'I want you to get me off this *fuckin'* boat now!' Jack demanded when I entered the aft cabin. I was shocked by his profanity. If the tables had been turned and I had spoken to my own father in that tone of voice … he would have obliged immediately!

'I can't,' I replied, searching for some logical explanation that he could hold onto. 'We are three hundred and fifty miles from the nearest land.'

'You can get a life boat can't you?' he implored.

'I wish I could,' I tried to sympathize, 'but the lifeboat only has a range of three hundred miles.'

104

'What about a helicopter? They have a range of over six hundred miles!' he shot back.

'I can't, son. As bad as it is, we are not in an emergency situation,' I tried to reassure him. 'I'd end up having to pay for the helicopter which would cost a fortune and I haven't got any money left because I have spent it all on the boat,' I lied. No money, no rescue, my simple logic defined that we were stuck with the situation.

'You have a fuckin' Gold Card, haven't you?' as if it was the answer to everything.

With that, my hardened heart softened. It had occurred to me to tell him about Ernest Shackleton and his men and the fact that they didn't have a Gold Card. That today's mighty oak is just yesterday's nut that held its ground. That at times like this the best attitude is a 'fuck you' one that I had learned in the school of hard knocks … but there is only so much you can expect from a six year old.

'You have been a trooper mate and I'm really, really, really proud of you.' I sat on the bunk and took him in my arms to comfort him. 'Hold your nerve son. Give it another twelve hours, okay? If it doesn't settle down by then we will head for the closest land.'

'Promise?' he appealed in a miserable whisper.

'Pinky,' I said and held out my finger.

He grabbed it with both hands and nearly twisted the bloody thing off! Little did the cheeky bugger know that twelve hours would bring us just shy of the halfway mark. Regardless of the conditions, from there on in, it would be just as easy to press on as turn back. I hoped, from the advice I had been given, that either the storm would abate, or we would recover from our seasickness.

Later that night, as I sat crouched, cold and shivering under the weather dodger in the cockpit, I knew that I too was coming close to the end of my tether. That the hardened resolve that had served me for so long was beginning to turn to mush. I began to question my judgment, doubt my determination, slate myself for driving my family so hard. Edvina had already proven herself beyond any measure of doubt and I knew that she could go on forever. The same though could not be said of Kent, our rock, who through no fault of his own, was beginning to fray around the edges. The only one *not* to get sick, he had carried the greatest burden of coping for us all, which was more than he had signed up for. Without Kent we would never have made it this far. It occurred to me, as another monster wave came crashing over us, that if anything happened to him, we might not make it back either.

At four in the morning, when I was at my very lowest, I decided that as soon as Kent came on watch, we would turn around and run with the storm back to Aotearoa.

'Don't give up mate!'

Half asleep with nausea and exhaustion, I was suddenly startled by a voice that didn't belong on the boat.

'Lewis!' I jerked upright on seeing him sitting on the opposite side of the cockpit, barefoot, in a pair of jeans and a faded denim shirt that had the top three buttons opened. I was alarmed by his presence, that he wasn't clipped on by a safety harness and that he should have been soaking wet ... but he wasn't. He sat for a moment with his head above the dodger and into the wind, seeming to relish the spray as it blasted his face and flattened his hair. He crouched down then, and leaned his elbows on his knees, laughing at the thrill of it all. The air around us then began to grow still. I was suddenly aware of being bathed in a reassuring comfort, as if a warm blanket had been wrapped around my entire body. Then Lewis smiled.

'You think this is hard?' his voice was gentle, no more than a whisper. *'This is living, really living,'* he smiled. *'You have the bull by the horns now mate!'* He leaned back against the cockpit edge and drew a full breath of cold sea air into his lungs. *'Adversity is the anvil upon which our dreams are forged ... you have to learn to savor it!'* He drew another deep breath. *'I know you think that you are in hell right now, but believe me ... this is nothing!'*

'I'm all in, Lew. I don't think I can hang on much longer.' I found myself replying, punch drunk, as much by watching my children suffer as by the conditions that prevailed.

'You should try chemotherapy sometime. Now that will really make your blood boil!' he shook his head as if reading my mind. *'Most fears are born of fatigue and loneliness. You are all just tired and worn out. Kent included!'* He moved purposefully then to the back of the cockpit and braced himself behind the binnacle upon which the steering wheel and compass were mounted. *'A decent meal and a good night's sleep and you will be good as gold,'* he shouted above the wind, satisfied that we were on the correct heading. *'Hang in there mate. By this time tomorrow it will all be over!'*

I rubbed my eyes to make sure that I wasn't seeing things. When they cleared, he had disappeared.

Sometime later I heard the sound of static squeaking, as if someone was turning the dial on an old radio to find a favorite program. Suddenly, a fix was made and 'boom, boom,' ... we were surrounded by the blaring sound of a German military band as Edvina charged each wave. A minute later the tuner changed again and Mick Jagger complained about 'getting no satisfaction!' Then the Ink Spots came on and crooned in harmony about being 'dumped by some floozy!' Lewis was gone, but his warmth remained and while it was still hard to judge the conditions in the pitch dark, I for certain, felt better in myself.

When Kent came on deck two hours later, I decided not to mention the experience, or the decision I had made not to turn around. No more waves had washed over the boat during the latter part of my watch so my last instruction was *that it was business as usual* before climbing below to follow Lewis's advice and get some sleep.

Later that morning I awoke with a new-found energy. When I went on deck, the wind had eased, the decks were dry and we were making almost eight knots on a full set of sails that Kent had shaken out just an hour before. A few minutes later Jack appeared on deck in a full set of waterproofs and sat beside his stoic sister who had endured the entire drama with little complaint.

'How are you doing, Big Man?'

'Six hours to go!' He was determined to hold me to my promise. Fifteen minutes later, Kent finished his watch and made his way below to the galley. A short time later, the most deliciously warm savory aroma you can ever imagine began to waft through the hatch above the stove.

'What are you cooking down there? Jack shouted. It had been four days since he had shown any interest in food.

'Toasted cheese and marmite sandwiches … do you want one?' Kent ducked his head tentatively out the companionway in the hope of a favorable answer. The doubled barreled question created a dilemma for Jack. Say 'no' and he would get to invoke the promise (false) I had made of turning back, or say yes and give up his hunger for the certainty of continuing the journey. I knew by the way he glanced at me, and his sister, that given the choice, he would have held out for the deadline which was only two hours away. But his body let him down once again and, urged on by the rumbling that echoed in all of our stomachs, he agreed to "trying a taste." Kent and I exchanged glances knowing then that we had this thing beaten.

Two entire sliced bread pans, a half a kilo of cheese, a jar of pickle, two pots of tea and a "sing song" later we had all defeated the monster that had savaged our bodies for four days straight. The lowest part of our trip turned into the highest. A make or break experience that could have sunk us, just when we were getting started … but it didn't. By late afternoon the wind had died to almost nothing. The following morning the sea was like a mill pond and our stomachs were busting from a 'half way party' that included everything from homemade egg McMuffins to Hokey Pokey ice cream while the stereo blasted out "I believe in miracles" by Hot Chocolate. To work off the excess, we dived overboard into water, which according to our chart, was five thousand two hundred feet deep, before turning on the engine and motoring the last four hundred miles of the journey to Port Vila. Our senses were so honed that we could smell the traditional food of the islands cooking in a ground oven, almost fifty miles before sighting land. We finally picked up the quarantine buoy at four in the morning, eight days after leaving New Zealand.

To celebrate the occasion, I had purchased a special bottle of merlot and it was while searching for a corkscrew that I rediscovered some mail in the navigation table. It had been delivered at the very last moment, just when we were departing Opua and then forgotten when conditions prevailed. Among the envelopes was a letter from the New Zealand Coast Guard stating that I had "failed" my final examination in Ocean Navigation!

13

'You have to go through the hard bits

to get to the good bits!'

Lewis was right. On this voyage we were to discover time and time again, the inseparable connection between our physical, emotional and spiritual wellbeing. That the circumstances we found ourselves in were much more likely to be determined by our morale and resilience, rather than the situation itself. To honor this, and restore our confidence for the next big leg of the journey between Vanuatu and Australia (1,400 miles) we planned a two week gentle cruise around the outer islands. It was a great idea that started out with snorkelling with dugongs, diving on ship wrecks and visiting isolated villages to meet the natives. However, by the time we had returned to Port Vila, it ended with blood poisoning (me) cerebral malaria (Jake) an emergency dive to rescue Kent who had passed out at a depth of forty metres due to a non-symptomatic ear infection, and a new 'To Do List' that required an extra week of maintenance to restore Edvina to seaworthy condition … again. As a consequence, the kids were far more dubious about their next offshore adventure.

'If it gets too tough we will turn back,' I reassured them as we departed Port Vila and ventured out into the deep blue Pacific. Sure enough it blew up rough within hours of leaving. We could have pushed on through (it was nothing like New Zealand) but turning back was more about restoring faith and keeping a promise than anything else. It turned out to be a promise well kept. We departed again a few days later in what can only be described as glorious conditions.

The perfection lasted for three days during which our previous experiences of Hell were contrasted by the rare, but very worthwhile glimpses of Heaven … reading on deck by moonlight at two in the morning as you sail off the wind at eight knots while all hands sleep peacefully in their bunks below. Shooting stars the size of comets, a sunrise and a moonset on opposite horizons at the same time, both so big, you cannot work out which is East and which is West, while you listen to Neil Young singing "Old Man" on the stereo. To top it off we stopped in Noumea, the capital of New Caledonia, for a few days' R&R to catch up with some cruising friends.

Our spirits emboldened, our courage restored, we charged across the remaining thousand mile gap to Australia. There had been times early on when we'd felt like chucking it in, but every time the fun or adventure went out of it we always came to the realisation that we were pushing too hard, going too fast or stretching too far. More reasonable expectations, tempered by a short rest in an exotic anchorage to recharge our internal batteries, always did the trick and returned us to our center. For every challenge overcome there was a reward of some sort that spurred us on to step back up to the plate and try again.

'What's the biggest thing you have learned so far from our trip?' I questioned Jack. It was a fatherly attempt at sharing parental wisdom as we departed the Whitsundays islands following another ten days of perfect cruising, snorkelling, diving, fishing, bbqs on the beach and lazy days in the sun.

'You have to go through the hard bits to get to the good bits,' he shared.

The boy has gotten the lesson. Step by step we climbed our Everest, inspired to greater heights of achievement.

As we sailed north inside the Barrier Reef towards Darwin, (another 1,400 miles) the days got warmer, our pale skins got darker and our smiley faces began to glow with the confidence gained from sailing record distances in conditions that a couple of months before would have defeated us. We met other cruisers heading in the same direction with kids on board and shared similar war stories that helped us all to develop new strategies for thriving. As such, our learning curve began to flatten out so that the scales of enjoyment tipped merrily in our favour.

'I never thought we'd make it this far!' Kent confided after we had crested the tip of Cape York and committed to the final leg to Darwin. By this stage we had travelled over three thousand nautical miles. Darling and I were happy to acknowledge the same sense of disbelief, but it was contrasted by a new found confidence that had been forged on the *anvil of adversity* that Lewis had described.

Darwin for us was the new point of no return. Beyond, lay a different language, different people, different values, different laws and really deep creeks if you lost your paddle! Our malaria scare in Vanuatu instilled a greater sense of vigilance so that we made extra measures in preparation for travelling through the tropics. Stowaways, we had learned, were the biggest threat. Mice, rats, reptiles, snakes, spiders, bugs. Anything that could carry pestilence and disease that was common to the warmer climates but, like malaria, not always detectable because of their long incubation period.

Were we scared?

Not really!

We had served our apprenticeship, and while still learning, we felt competent, especially in the company of other boats who were just as eager to continue ... once our 'To Do Lists' were finished. Cruising, we were fast learning, was as much about 'boat maintenance in exotic places' as it was about adventure. Our first venture offshore had required three months of hard work for one week of sailing. Now we were down to a week of hard work for the same distance travelled. Broken parts along the way included our G.P.S. chart plotter, depth sounder, toilet, radar, generator, refrigeration, electronics, roller furling sails, outboard motor, toilet (every boat has a f*&$#n toilet story), shaft alternator (again) V.H.F radio, battery charger, three broken toes, two fractured ribs, battered spirits and a busted budget swollen beyond recognition with invoices for just about any conceivable thing that could be broken on a boat.

Was it worth it? Absolutely! We were boldly going where we had never gone before and the experience being gained was priceless. Along the way, I managed to find time to pull out 'The Christening' and add more depth and colour to the landscape of the story. It still had a long way to go before I could send it off to a publisher, but it occurred to me that Kate and Paddy's journey in many ways mirrored our own and that we were all on a major voyage of self discovery.

In contrast, Scotty and Angel and their kids were now stuck in U.K. and miserable, in a non-profitable partnership that had failed to compensate them for the freedom they had traded in return. It was a good reminder to keep on going, and so we did, jumping off the top of the known world into Indonesia.

14

'It will make you or break you!'

Kupang, Roti island, then west through the Flores, Rinca, Lombok and Bali. From there, north through the notorious South China sea to the jungles of Borneo. One minute you are reading a yachting magazine in the comfort of your home on a stormy night in New Zealand about the Kumai river in Kalimantan and the Orangutan sanctuary. The next, you are anchored beneath a flame tree five thousand miles from home and chasing monkeys off your deck who will steal anything that is not tied down.

From there west again through two storms, one that shredded our genoa (the front sail) and we finally arrived in Singapore. After three months of sailing through what was now the Wild East (because it was behind us) there was a collective and palpable sigh of relief from everyone on board as we pulled into Raffles marina and tied up to a real jetty in the most organised and civilised city on the planet.

Rashard was delighted with our progress. We had crossed the imaginary halfway line (Equator) and now, confident of our ability to make it to Oman, he began processing the paperwork to eventually receive us.

When we finally departed Singapore for Phuket in Thailand, we did so without our faithful and trusty Kent who, by mutual assent, had found another boat in greater need of his services than ours. On then further north to Malaysia and the Malacca Straits where generations of pirates with real guns still hijack real ships and steal their booty. Thankfully, while tense and exciting, we had a safe and uneventful journey. Two days after we got through the worst area, an oil tanker was hijacked and they got away with twenty thousand barrels of diesel. A week later another ship was boarded and they took $120,000 in payroll that the purser had just taken on board for the crew. We didn't really have much to worry about. Edvina was carrying 290 litres of diesel and about $60 in four different currencies. Slim pickings for a hungry pirate. If chocolate had been on their list of priorities it might have been a different story. Darling had reserves stashed that would have sunk a smaller boat. The gauntlet run, we settled into a gentle routine visiting the famous island of Penang and then on to Thailand for Christmas. Five months and 6,740 nautical miles from good old Aotearoa.

"It will make you or break you!' was the most consistent piece of advice we had been given on the nature of families sailing together. Proof of that was the number of abandoned boats left for sale at brokerages by families that had not only parted way with their boat, but each other as well. Proof however, was also in the families that we met along the way who, through mindful determination, had created the opposite result. 'All for one, and one for all!' became our call to action and it stood us in good stead on many occasions. It wasn't so much the good times, but rather the experiences and challenges that we'd had to face and overcome together that were the making of us. We were closer, stronger, happier, more in love and held a greater respect for each other than ever before. Sufficiently blooded, we now shared that unique bond forged in adversity that is similarly common with combatants who have fought alongside each other and survived against tremendous odds. By endurance we had conquered the fear within, as much as the threat from without. It is impossible to put a price on the confidence gained.

When you break out to discover new lands, you also encounter new people as well, all making the same journey. Ordinary people from all walks of life ... a school teacher, a banker, a builder, a urologist, a retired couple spending their kids' inheritance. An eccentric artist sailing by herself. All had chosen to grab the same proverbial bull by the horns and do something 'extraordinary.' Those who shared our journey, the league of extraordinary gentlefolk, watched out and encouraged each other, so that the extraordinary became the ordinary and the life that our children had initially been reluctant to embrace, now started to seem normal.

So much so, that there came a time on our journey when the strongest winds had been met, the highest waves overcome and the worst conditions all paled in significance to the nightmares that we and our friends had first imagined for us. Where all pain had been embraced, all hardship forgotten, all loss subsumed, so that everything that came after was weighed, measured and found wanting! Where our daughter Poppit stood on the aft deck *defiant* at an oncoming wave that towered above us and shouted "is that all you've got?" Where our little son Jack was heard whispering to his sister "A.F.T." (another f*&$%#n temple) supposedly out of earshot when the novelty of sightseeing and adventure had been overshadowed by a greater desire to return to Edvina and simply play with his friends.

Besides boat maintenance in exotic places, we were to discover that for every high there was a low, for every happy a sad, and for every seeming good there could be a bad. It was as much a journey *within* that had the unforeseen dark side of homesickness, loneliness, isolation, boredom and danger that comes with the territory, not to mention food poisoning which struck us all down with a vengeance the week we arrived in Phuket! When you travel on the Wild Side of life with the ones that you love, you cannot expect it all to be plain sailing.

At the beginning of our voyage, we didn't know if we were going to make it to Vanuatu, let alone Thailand. Now suddenly, our next stop was Sri Lanka to accept a special invitation.

From the very first day we left New Zealand we had placed a well-known tea company on our multi-mailer list. The idea was that if we ever got that far, it might be a good home-schooling experience for the kids to try and visit the factory. What amazed us was that for every mailer we sent, we always received a reply with words of encouragement and an invitation from a guy named Merrill in the marketing department.

'When you get to Sri Lanka, please make sure you come and visit us. We would love to hear more about your adventure!

After a fantastic and uneventful trip of seven days (thank the Gods) we berthed in Galle Harbour in the Southern tip of the country. I decided to do some research before heading north to Colombo to meet our new best friend Merrill. It was then that I discovered that he was the owner of the company.

That's when it got interesting!

15

'Be reasonable - do it my way!'

On the appointed day at the appointed time, Merrill almost failed to show … almost.

'My sincere apologies. Only for you have come so far I would have cancelled.' He arrived three quarters of an hour late to our hotel. His driver held his left elbow to steady him as he sat down shakily in the chair opposite us in the lounge. 'I had an accident two nights ago just after we made our arrangements. Slipped and banged my head and wrenched my spine in the shower. I have a splitting headache and my balance is shot,' he explained in a soft voice, wincing with every word. 'I'm booked to fly to London to see a neurologist at the end of the week, a damned nuisance!' he stated eloquently, but then he apologised to Darling for his language.

I looked at Darling, who acknowledged my thoughts.

'We just so happen to be neurologists of the Chiropractic kind.'

'What is a Chiropractor?' Merrill grimaced again as he changed position in his chair.

'Your new best friend,' I smiled. Fifteen minutes later I was examining him on the bed in our room. Sure enough he had a significant whiplash and a nasty hematoma on his left hip with a subluxation of his left sacro-iliac joint.

'Can you give me anything for the pain?' he appealed.

'Of course.' I adjusted him gently.

'What the blazes?!'

'I get that a lot.'

I turned him over and I adjusted him again. Five minutes later he was walking the length of the hotel corridor without his driver's assistance. Within half an hour his headache had reduced dramatically and his blurred vision had cleared.

'My God, but you are a miracle worker!'

'Not really. It's more a case of being in the right place at the right time. Injuries like this often take weeks before you feel relief and months before they stabilize.'

Merrill's problem now created an ethical dilemma. I knew from experience that he would need at least three days of intensive treatment followed by a break of a week for nature to run her course and then three more days of adjusting to stabilize his spine. We had only plans and the budget to stay in Colombo for two days.

'Keeping you in Sri Lanka will save me a ton of hassle. I am more than happy to make arrangements to accommodate you.'

Three days later, he insisted on giving us his brand new Seven series BMW and a driver to take us on a scenic tour inland that ended on the 'Somerset' plantation in the mountains of Nuwara Eliya. It was an amazing experience for the kids to participate in picking the tea, knowing that a few days later, it would be packed at the height of its freshness in Colombo. Even better, our driver, through local connections, organized a private jungle trek on the elephant that starred in the Indiana Jones movie *The Temple of Doom*.

As we travelled throughout the land, we were reminded time and again of just how lucky we were. In contrast to our unbound freedom, we had been witness on our voyage to the rape and pillage that had been Colonialism. The scars that we had first seen in the slums of Vanuatu had scratched their way along the entire length of our journey. The hit and run without reproach, the inevitable decay and detritus that had been left behind, was especially prominent in Sri Lanka. It was to shape our plans to eventually 'colonize' the Middle East with Chiropractors.

On our return to Colombo we were met by a much better Merrill. He was making such a great recovery that at seventy years of age, he was seriously thinking of taking up tennis again after a twenty year break! While Chiropractic had effected an amazing transformation in his health and vitality, it paled in significance to the inspiration that Merrill had on our thinking.

Merrill Joseph Fernando was born on the 7th May 1930 into a middle-class family of modest means with five children and strong ethics in work, Christian values and fair play. In 1948, Sri Lanka gained independence from the British. As a consequence, the long-held monopoly on tea tasting, which was reserved for British nationals, slowly abated. By 1952, Merrill was among the very first Sri Lankans to travel to London, the Mecca of the tea world, to train in the art and science of tea tasting. Little did they know that they were training a man cub to be a lion!

He learned his trade well, but he also observed the dysfunctional aspects of a business upon which his country was heavily reliant. Ceylon Tea that was being handpicked and produced according to a traditional and artistic process was being treated as a raw material and shipped at nominal value to Europe where value addition, branding and packaging took place. That meant that his country received a tiny percentage of the ultimate profits, while the middle men, - mainly large corporations - benefitted disproportionately.

On return to Sri Lanka and still in his twenties, he was among the first of his countrymen to own his own tea estate and to export tea in bulk to the USSR. *Melton* was his pride and joy which he transformed into one of the top producing estates in the country. However, *Melton* was nationalized (stolen) by the Sri Lankan Government under the guise of land reform in the late seventies. It broke his heart. This so-called nationalization would eventually bring the tea industry in Sri Lanka to its knees.

'Believe it or not, I seriously considered emigrating to Ireland,' he surprised me during one of his treatments. 'I used to blend and supply tea to Barry's.'

'No way!' It was my turn to surprise him. Barry's had been the brand that had ultimately brought Darling and me together all those years before in America!

'Luckily, I had very good friends and clients overseas who supported and encouraged me, so I remained in Sri Lanka and started my own tea production company.'

By doing so, he literally created a storm in a tea cup. Overcoming strong resistance and dissuasion from the status quo, he imported the first tea bagging machine into Sri Lanka. Listening to him tell his story was like David and Goliath at its very best. A tale of values overcoming the sometimes amoral machinations of much bigger and more powerful players. Despite threats to his own future, he did not fear to challenge the more powerful competition for the greater good of all. Furthermore, he refused to compromise his values or cut overheads by blending his tea with inferior brands to save money. Years later, he would rename the company Dilmah after his two sons Dilhan and Malik.

I loved his story. In many ways it was similar to the beginning of Chiropractic and how our original founders had fought for years to challenge the status quo and keep the profession pure and unsullied by not mixing it with any other form of inferior healing art.

Ultimately, Merrill's passion and drive accrued to the benefit of the Sri Lankan stake holders, including the workers in the tea plantations whose living standards needed to be improved.

'The Middle East has oil. Sri Lanka has tea, but it comes with a responsibility,' Merrill stated solemnly. 'We must not only be loyal to our consumers, but also our workers by offering a product that is authentic, of good quality and embodies integrity and social justice.' In this respect, his thinking was far ahead of its time. Half a century ago issues such as fair trade and social responsibility of business were virtually unknown.

During a personally guided tour of his three story tea packaging center in Colombo, I noticed a framed poster on "Success" by Ralph Waldo Emerson that hung behind his office desk. It read:

To laugh often and much, to win the respect of intelligent people and the affection of children, to earn the appreciation of honest critics and endure the betrayal of false friends, to appreciate beauty, to find the best in others, to leave the world a bit better, whether by a healthy child, a garden patch or a redeemed social condition, to know that even one life has breathed easier because you have lived ... this is to have succeeded.

I smiled and nodded my head in agreement, feeling lucky that we could not relate to the part about betrayal by false friends.

Then, as if to underscore his determination, he pointed to a sign on the front of his desk.

"Be reasonable - do it my way!"

We all laughed.

Dilmah, we were to discover, is the only vertically integrated tea company with its own tea gardens, state of the art printing & packaging facilities, tea packing, and investments in every segment of the industry that can deliver tea from the plantation to consumer in less than eight weeks. Compared to the years that some teas remain in bulk storage I could see why Dilmah tastes so good.

We learned a lot from Merrill and came to understand that at the end of the day, you have to have a vision that goes beyond just making money. Here was a man with the world at his feet who could have been long retired and living out his twilight years in a style he richly deserved. Instead, he had shunned the privileged life and still worked sixty hours a week for the vision of a greater future for his company and his country. In a land that had been torn by civil war, he sought to make his country a better place by means of hard work rather than looking for a handout from some international organisation or taking to the gun. Merrill's life and the bizarre connection that we had made through Barry's tea, became an inspiration and a framework for a future of 'fair exchange' in Oman.

Our goal in introducing Chiropractic to the Sultanate was to create something that would far outlast us. It was inevitable that at some stage we would have to move on. In doing so, we would endeavour to leave Oman a better place by establishing a Chiropractic Center that represented the standard by which all other clinics would be measured in the Middle East.

By now we'd had almost a year to think about what we wanted to achieve. Like many new graduates, our early experience in practice had been very much like the early part of our voyage ... too much pressure and too much stress with a learning curve that folded back on itself once too often. Oman was an opportunity to reinvent ourselves.

16

All that I would have missed!

From Sri-Lanka we travelled south to the Maldive islands for a two week holiday before the final jump across the Indian Ocean to Oman. At fourteen hundred miles, it was to be the longest section, metaphorically, mechanically and in mileage! The winds that started us off with the promise of a twelve day passage died on the second day. Our gearbox died on the third! Had it been the start of our journey from N.Z. we would have been up the creek without a 'you know what' as the currents pushed us further away from land. However, by now I was so mechanically minded that I almost welcomed the challenge of stripping the damn thing down and after six hours of 'obstetrics and gynaecology' we were back on course again.

My biggest concern though was Darling. On land she had seemed fine, but was now sicker than ever with vomiting and nausea and a malaise that confined her to our bunk for most of the voyage. Despite our almost paranoiac vigilance, I'd found a dead cockroach in a routine check of the bilges before leaving Thailand and so began to harbour the terrible fear that she may have contracted some sort of tropical disease from a stowaway. Was it Malaria? Dengue fever? Leishmaniasis or Chagas disease? These terrors are prevalent and unique to the tropical and subtropical regions we had just passed through. Insects such as mosquitoes and flies are by far the most common carriers. Vaccines are not common and many of the diseases do not have a cure. We had a medical reference book on board which had helped us to diagnose and treat Jack's malaria, but none of the descriptions enclosed matched Darling's condition. Would the doctors in Oman be able to recognise it?

Then, as if in answer to our prayers, two days from Muscat, the most amazing thing happened. The winds suddenly returned and blew in our favour like never before and Darling made a miraculous recovery. With all hands on deck, Edvina rose to the occasion and with full sails set she surfed the final three hundred miles in a 'goose wing' fashion. Edvina by now was our Siren, our Mistress, our home away from home and our 'high maintenance bitch' (they all are). It's hard to imagine an inanimate object of hardened steel having a soul, but we had grown to love and cherish her as one of our family.

As we rounded Ras al Hadd, the most eastern tip of Oman that juts out into the Arabian sea, we were joined by a pod of whales migrating in the same direction. In the enormous distance that we had travelled, we had longed for, but never come across any whales. Now here we were in convoy with the giants of the ocean. We took it as a sign of good fortune, an omen from the Gods as to what lay ahead. By midnight, we were anchored in a perfectly sheltered bay a couple of miles from Muscat. We would wait there until morning to clear customs.

Christopher Columbus once said that "in order to discover new lands, you must be prepared to lose sight of shore for a long time."

He was wrong!

In order to discover new lands you must be prepared to lose sight of shore for a very, very, very, long f*&%#n time!

We had made it and celebrated with a veritable feast of treats that we had saved for the occasion.

A couple of hours later, after Darling and the kids had finally succumbed to sleep, I relaxed on deck and sipped a celebratory rum under a diamond-studded sky and reminisced about the trip that we had just completed. It seemed like only yesterday that we had, in our blinding ignorance (hindsight is a great thing) made the commitment to find a boat. Now here we were, over ten thousand miles later, hardened mariners who were just about to start another adventure as landlubbers. In spite of the hardships and challenges that we had faced, my heart was filled with a deep appreciation and gratitude to Lewis for his inspiration and support, especially at the beginning, where his surreal and unexpected appearance comforted and inspired me to push on through the worst moment of the storm.

I thought also about my own journey and how my life had really just begun under that granite bridge all those years before. That in order to escape from that dark place, I'd had to give up the landscape of what I knew for a very, very, very long time until I found a better state of mind. How the dragons in my head had been no more real than the dragons on the horizon. How the inner journey had involved just as many storms and challenges as the outer journey, but just as many blessings as well.

It occurred to me then, what if I had managed to pull the plug and passed on into the abyss? God, what if? All that I would have missed!

As Darling and the kids lay sleeping below, I sat there thinking that all was good with our world. That there was nothing that we could not do, no ocean that we could not cross, nor mountain that was too high to climb. Whatever it may have cost to make the journey, it is impossible to put a price on the degree of confidence and self-belief that we had gained from the experience.

Musing about what would happen next, my peace was broken from a desperate rumbling of floor boards in the saloon below followed by heavy footsteps up the companion way ladder. Suddenly, Darling burst into the cockpit, scrambled across the deck and just managed to lean her head over the side before throwing up her dinner.

In answer to my wondering, she bowed her head and shook it slowly in defeat.

'I think I need to go to a hospital.'

Book Three

1

'A Stowaway'

'C'mon!' I honked the horn for the second time. I'm not normally impatient in traffic, but *this* was an emergency.

'Take it easy. I'll be okay,' Darling mumbled, putting on a brave face as she leaned on a pillow against the door sill of Rashard's Jeep for support. It was a piece of shit and I hadn't driven for over a year which made manoeuvring through tight traffic that much more frustrating. Muscat Private Hospital was on the far side of town and we were fighting peak hour traffic.

Anybody who has worked in the Middle East will tell you that the bureaucracy is horrendous. Despite the fact that Rashard's brother was head of ports in Oman, I watched Darling's life fade before me as Customs clearance took three times longer than any port we had cleared on our voyage. I couldn't tell them she was sick. That we might all be infected. I'd heard too many stories about the harsh treatment some yachties had received after failing the strict and often draconian clearance procedures that some countries still adhered to. The last thing we needed was to be banished to some isolated quarantine area by an overzealous customs officer who held sway over our lives.

Rashard's return from his first pilgrimage to Mecca the previous day only added to the agony as everybody in the know wanted to "praise Allah" and kiss his hand.

'Bastard!' I shouted when an Indian in a commercial van jumped lanes and robbed me of a green light that would have sped up our journey. I don't know who was blowing off more steam, me or the radiator, when we finally reached the hospital, but I became almost apoplectic over the paperwork that was required to get registered!!

Finally, finally we were ushered into a private room to meet the doctor.

'How confidential is this conversation?' was my first question after we had made introductions.

'We treat all conversations with the strictest of confidence,' but as if to reassure, she closed the door to our consultation room behind me. I wasn't being paranoid. I was in damage control and wanted to make sure that I could handle the fallout if Darling was as bad as I suspected. Edvina and the kids were happily parked at the marina in Muscat. If the worst came to the worst, I wanted to be the one to tell them the news and not some overly officious customs agent who couldn't speak English.

In the process of giving a case history I described the tropics we had passed through and listed off the diseases that I knew were endemic to those areas. When a push came to a shove and her questioning became more emphatic around potential exposures, I finally owned up to the stowaway cockroach that I had found in the bilges. The doctor was empathetic and genuinely concerned and wrote copious notes at a furious rate as I listed off the maladies I suspected. As she questioned Darling about her specific symptoms, I informed her of our medical background and peppered her with a number of suggestions to try and speed up the diagnosis process.

Then, suddenly, she stopped.

'I think I know what it is!' she declared.

'What?' I was beside myself. It was possible that Darling's very life hung in the balance of the answer.

'I can't be sure until I do a number of tests to confirm. Come!' she smiled, and without any further explanation she took Darling by the hand and led her to an adjacent room. Fifteen agonizing minutes later they returned.

'I can confirm your diagnosis. You are right!' she stated with a voice that had been hardened over the years by delivering bad news.

Darling refused to give me any eye contact. 'You do have a stowaway.'

My shoulders dropped.

'But it's not on the boat,' she clarified.

'What do you mean?' Where else could the damn thing be, I thought, wondering why Darling kept looking at the floor.

'It's in her stomach.'

'In her stomach? Oh God, what is it?' My heart sank at the thought of some of the massive tapeworms and insidious parasites that we had studied in microbiology in University.

'In Latin the condition is called *Gravida* or *Ingravesco*, but I much prefer the French term of *Lourd de sens*,' she replied, and waited to see if the penny dropped.

'English, what do they call it in English?!' I wanted to shake her! I hadn't read anything in the diagnosis or first aid book that sounded like those conditions.

'Your wife is pregnant.'

'She's what?'

'I'm going to have a baby!' Darling repeated.

'You are whaaaat?' I was still confused, but then I saw the blue stick that confirmed the diagnosis in her hand.

F*&%#k!!!!!!!

2

What to do?

I don't know which was greater, the sense of relief that Darling was okay or the feeling of idiocy on my part as we made our way back to Edvina and the kids. Of course she was pregnant, the signs were now obvious, but it was so left field of any of the plans that we'd had, real or imaginary, that I had never considered it an option. Nine years was a long time between babies!

'You knew, didn't you?!' It was exasperation more than an accusation. 'Why didn't you tell me?'

'I wasn't sure. It's different. I didn't have any sickness with Poppit and Jack. Are you mad?' Darling asked.

'As a maggot!' I replied, shaking my head, but half smiling to acknowledge the fact that I had been party to the passion that had created our dilemma. Talk about out of the frying pan and into the fire. I was too distracted to be of any real assurance. The last thing we needed was a baby.

The initial relief of arriving safely in Oman was easily overwhelmed as our brains tried to work out the logistics of which was the better option. The first was to get back on the boat and haul ass for home. In this case it would be a four month grueling "uphill" sail through the Red Sea and the Mediterranean to family in Ireland (NZ was too far and against the winds). The second option was to stick around and take our chances. According to the doctor, the baby was due the second week in November which gave us only seven months to get organized. A piece of cake if you live in Auckland and are only ten minutes' drive from the North Shore hospital. We were now in the Middle East which was the middle of nowhere when it came to having babies.

Living on the edge for the last year had been precarious, but there had been luck involved ... lots of which we had worked hard to get. The success of the trip in many ways had depended on it. But adding a baby created a much more complex equation. Whether we established ourselves in Muscat or headed for home, the real question was ... 'would our luck hold?'

The doctor had reassured us that the sickness would pass in a matter of weeks. If we were going to head for home then we would have to wait till Darling felt better. While this was good news for Darling, it piled the pressure on by shortening the time slot we had for making it back to Ireland.

'What to do?'

If nothing else, probably the most significant lesson we had learned on our journey was to be patient and prepared and have faith that we had the ability to overcome whatever challenge we faced. We had done it so many times it had become second nature. It was all just a matter of pacing ourselves.

'Let's just take a break and recover before we make any decisions,' I broke the silence as we drove into the marina. While the trip from the Maldives had been a success, it had taken a lot out of us and I for one, didn't feel like going straight back to sea again. 'We can use the time to make a more detailed reconnaissance. Who knows, things might look better by the end of the week.'

Darling looked visibly relieved.

And they did. Better than we could have imagined. The Gods seemed to conspire so that without really trying, other than driving around sightseeing, we found a villa in a central location in the Business and Consular district that was perfect for a practice. When we told Rashard and his wife Salwa of our dilemma, they were so anxious for us to stay that they proposed an agreement that would make us not only equal investment partners, but give us full control of the clinic. It was a very generous gesture on their part which minimized our sense of vulnerability and left us feeling more in control of our destiny.

Within days of landing, Darling started to feel better. The kids were happy, the schools checked out and the expatriate community was more than encouraging about us not only having a baby, but the massive potential that a new clinic would achieve once established.

The big surprise though was Scotty and Angel who had been living vicariously through our voyage while stuck in a rut in the U.K.. Despite their hard work, the partnership they had engaged in had not been a success and they were looking for something more adventurous. Their discontent resonated with our own sense of the isolation. Being an adventurer can at times be a very lonely business. However, a throwaway comment on our part about our need for another doctor to help with the demand once the clinic got going, eventuated in a series of lengthy discussions around them joining us for the long haul in Oman.

Suddenly the big hole in our social fabric was starting to look like it was going to be filled by not only one of the best Chiropractors in New Zealand, but our best friends *and* the Godparents to our children. While nothing formal had been agreed, it was the potential promise of the perfect "trifecta" that was to begin to tip the balance in favor of us staying in Muscat and making a go of it.

Being a proponent of Murphy's Law, there were a thousand other things to be considered, but as we started to find our land legs, the enormous sense of confidence that we had gained from sailing half way around the world started to smooth the bumps and fill in the blanks of what lay ahead.

'Well, what do you think?' I asked Darling tentatively as we relaxed in the cockpit of Edvina with a traditional sundowner a week after we had landed. I for one, was beginning to chomp at the bit over the potential if we stayed. It would be hard work and there were still a lot of unknowns to be dealt with, but I felt that the risks would be outweighed by the financial rewards and the unique lifestyle that Oman had to offer. On a completely separate note, I had in mind also an idea for a second draft of 'The Christening' which I wanted to work on. If we went back to sea then it would be delayed for who knows how long and my Muse was starting to give me shit over it!

'So long as I can have a home birth and Angel and Scotty can join us, then I would be happy to stay.' It was a statement as much as an answer, a caveat over my enthusiasm that balanced out the unknowns and gave her something to anchor to. Poppit and Jake had been born at home with great success. If she could have Angel by her side, then all would be right with our world.

'Fine!' They were both *big asks*, the success of which would be largely out of my control. However, she had been crazy enough to get on the boat for me in the first place, so despite any reservations I might have had, (quite a few!) I was just as crazy about her to at least try and fulfill the promise. Insanity would turn out to be the operative word.

3

'Insanity'

Decision made, the following morning we awoke energized and hit the ground running. There is nothing like a new baby on the way to motivate you. We had no insurance, health or otherwise, so we needed to not only have the clinic open by the time the clock stopped ticking, but also be in a positive cash flow so that we could afford any unforeseen 'baby' expenses.

It was then that the real bureaucracy began!

To ensure that all of the rules and regulations have been adhered to, no new enterprise is deemed legal until it receives the official stamp from the proper department.

Rule number one:

"Don't even think of opening your clinic, business, factory, or pizza parlor before you fulfill all of your obligations, lest you have a strong desire to be heavily fined and immediately shut down!"

On this new adventure we were soon to discover that there are a ton of entities who all charge a *reasonable* fee (bastards) for clipping your ticket. They include the Department of Health (sub office), the Department of Labor (sub office), the Department of Town Planning, the Department of Labor (health clearances) the Business Registry office, the Ministry of Health (Head office) the Ministry of Labor (Head office) Police Clearance (Residents) Customs Clearance (again!) the Department of Health (labor clearance) Police Clearance (Interpol) The department of this, the department of that, the Department of every f&%$#@g thing under the sun and on and on and on... Each document had to be stamped by the Sub Deputy, the Deputy and the Head of Department, not to mention the Minister and often his Personal Secretary.

Had it all been in the same building it might not have been so bad, but they had to have an office, sub office and Head office, not to mention Ministry, strategically positioned on opposing sides of Muscat. I remember on one occasion driving for eight hours in a single day back and forwards across the city just to get the signature of one official.

The conversation went like this ...

'He's not here right now.'

'He's praying.'

'He is sleeping.' Nowhere was open between eleven am and three pm. Too hot to work.

'His wife is having a baby'

'No, no, no, you have to have this signed by the Ministry first and then bring it to us to sign!'

'No, no, no, he has no idea what he is talking about. Bring it to Khalid. He knows what to do. Get him to sign it and then bring it to the Ministry and then back to us.'

'Khalid is praying!'

'Khalid's cousin's sister just had a baby. Come back tomorrow.'

'Khalid has been transferred, you need to see Hasan! Come back tomorrow.'

'Hasan who?'

On and on and f*&^%$g on! And this was *with* a PRO (Public Relations Officer)

A PRO was essential to handle all matters Arabic pertaining to all of the Ministries and their sub departments. A good PRO could speak English, smooth the way, make your life bearable and with a bit of luck, help you to have your business open in a relatively short period of time. A bad one could make your life a misery and take over a year. This one was an eejit! He was an uncle of Rashard's who was unemployed (figures) and owed him a favor so Rashard appointed him to assist us because he was busy with his other businesses.

'Six weeks?!' our lawyer laughed, when I vented my frustration over the mountain of paperwork that stood between us and our plans to be open. 'You would have to be a member of the Royal family to achieve that!' he declared. 'If you had wanted to be open by the beginning of August then you should have started in January!'

We were hemorrhaging money big time. The cost of the set up and our living expenses were almost twice what we had budgeted (Murphy's Law). The villa was leased, painted, furnished, signposted, phone and power connected, business cards and headed paper delivered and ready to go three weeks after we had landed. By the fourth week we had our advertising campaign worked out and the newspapers scheduled to go. The special treatment tables had been paid for (ouch) and were on their way from America. With a bit of luck they would arrive by the end of the fifth week. All we needed was the sign-off. I was damned if I was going to let bureaucracy get in our way.

If paperwork was the mountain that had to be climbed, then I got in behind and pushed, pulled and tugged Rashard's uncle every hour of every waking day to get the job done ... and it worked. With three days to go to our deadline, everything in the now two-inch-thick application folder was signed and sealed. It just had to be delivered to the Minister of Health's personal office for his final sign off.

It was then that said PRO lost the entire file *and* suddenly became un-contactable!

'F%$#*&%#@&%$^#K!!!'

By now, we had already invested our entire cruising budget, a thirty percent contingency *and* were leaning on our credit cards to the point of meltdown. The heat was back on, outside as well as inside the practice. Almost overnight, temperatures had risen beyond forty degrees, which was making living on the boat untenable.

Rashard, we were beginning to find out, was about as useful as tits on a bull and away overseas on other business for at least two weeks. In all of the challenges we had faced since leaving New Zealand, this was the furthest we had found ourselves up a creek!

Going into emergency mode, we bought some cheap mattresses and a fridge, grabbed the bbq off Edvina and moved into one of the bare airconditioned rooms upstairs in the clinic. This in itself was illegal and totally contravened the rules of the application process for a clinic license, but we were desperate. The thousands of dollars of emergency food that Darling had stored on board Edvina now came into its own (told you so!) and we lived off anything that could be canned, bottled or rehydrated in a pot of boiling water. Insanity! Anywhere else in the world we would have already been open for business. Then, just as we were about to arrange an emergency loan from family overseas … the most amazing thing happened.

Two weeks after the file was lost, I was at the airport clearing customs for our new adjusting tables. Thankfully, I didn't need a f*&%$n PRO! During the process, I approached a man to get directions and he just so happened to be the Senior Pilot for His Majesty's private airline *Royal Flight*. Upon hearing my Irish accent, we got to talking and it turned out that he had been trained by my childhood best friend's father who was the senior pilot of *Aer Lingus* the Irish national airline! If that wasn't crazy enough, guess who had a serious back problem? His boss's nephew *His Royal Highness* (H.R.H.) Said Hytham bin Tariq Al Said, the expected successor to the throne!

'Would it be possible to make an appointment for you to look after him?' the pilot inquired.

'I can't!' I explained our dilemma using the least amount of expletives that I could subdue.

'That shouldn't be a problem,' the pilot smiled. 'Royalty and rules don't always mix!' He pulled out his mobile, made a call and a half an hour later I scheduled my first official appointment at the clinic!

That afternoon H.R.H. arrived with an entourage that included an orthopedic specialist, a neurosurgeon, his personal G.P., *his* nurse, (all Indian) his secretary, the pilot, a driver, two heavily armed body guards and at least three other people whose purpose eluded me. Introductions were made. As it turned out, during our license application process, I had already met two of the *big guns* in the group, so we were ready to rock and roll.

M.R.I. scans were presented, x-rays discussed and lots of opinions thrown around. The medical diagnosis was a herniated disc that would need a surgical repair. However, the room fell into a curious silence once I started my examination.

Was I nervous? Hell yes! I knew there and then that the success or failure of our yet-to-be-opened practice might boil down to this single consultation. The last thing you want to do with a member of the Royal Family is look a fool in front of his personal doctors! In the heel of the hunt though, I needn't have worried. They were fascinated by the Chiropractic tests that I used to analyze his spine and my unique interpretation, as I talked them through his x-rays. The enthusiastic discussion that ensued shook off the last of my nerves and my hands quickly worked to isolate a right Sacro Iliac subluxation that had not shown up in any of their investigations. When I pointed this out, heads wobbled, tut tuts were made and a general sigh of relief was exuded when I announced that His Highness would no longer need to have back surgery.

'Is that it?' the orthopedic surgeon looked quizzical when H.R.H. climbed off the treatment table after I had spent no more than two minutes adjusting him.

'No, it will take a series of visits over the next few weeks to stabilize his spine.' I pointed to some degeneration on the x-rays to clarify my explanation.

'Yes, yes, but that, I mean, you hardly touched him!' He looked around the room to see if any of his colleagues were of the same opinion. More heads wobbled.

'That's it. His body will do the rest. All he needs is a helping hand.' It occurred to me to make a joke about me *not* being J.C. (Jesus Christ) but in a Muslim country I doubted that anyone would get it.

His problem now solved, H.R.H. returned the next day for treatment, by himself, with an offer to help us overcome our own predicament. While the rules would have to be adhered to, he assured me that if we went ahead and opened, that no-one would bother us while the paperwork was being processed. He even went so far as to recommend a reliable PRO.

Talk about cutting it fine. Six weeks to the day after we landed we opened for business.

4

'She's a hard road!'

'You can't do this!' were the first words Rashard uttered on his return from overseas. He had dropped by unannounced to see how the license application was going. To his horror he found a waiting room full of people and our new receptionist Linda, whom we had employed without telling him.

'You don't know the ministry like I do!' he ranted as he pulled me into an empty adjusting room to avoid embarrassment. 'They will shut you down and ban us from ever trading in the future if we don't comply with the license requirements before opening!'

'Take it easy Rashard, they won't shut us down.' I reassured, but he was too intent on toeing the line to give me a chance to explain.

'They will, they will!' he wrung his hands, half breathless with worry. 'If they find out, we are doomed!'

'They already have,' I smiled.

'Who has?'

'The Ministry.' After all we had been through with his useless PRO, I actually found myself savoring his discomfort.

'The Ministry! Oh my God, what did they say?'

'That they would be grateful if I would make an exception and look after His Royal Highness.'

'His Majesty!!' Rashard screeched.

'No, no, his nephew, Saeed Hytham Bin Tariq.' I explained what had happened. It took a few minutes to sink in, but he soon calmed down when he began to realize that not only were we actually open for business, but had attained the Royal seal of approval. It might not have been his Majesty that we had under our care, but it was the next best thing which carried massive kudos that could be slipped into any conversation. Suddenly all was well with his world.

Magnanimous in our initial success, we decided to overlook the fact that his incompetence had almost sunk us. Saving face is more important than owning up or taking responsibility. Our luck had held and the day had been saved, so in the end, that was all that mattered. Regardless of what had happened with his uncle we decided to give Rashard the benefit of the doubt and let it go. Besides we were practically broke and needed to put all of our energy and focus into creating a cash flow.

To do so we pushed the boat out with the media and short of running down the street buck naked, there was very little I wouldn't do to attract attention to the practice. Fortunately the Arabs are wheelers and dealers by nature, and like most humans, (who love something for nothing) couldn't resist our FREE ASSESSMENT promotion. As a consequence, we were quickly inundated with a flood of enquiries. However, most weeks were saved by last minute appointments and upfront discount cash deals that could be immediately deposited in the bank to save our asses ... again and again and again! The early months were spent living hand to mouth as every bill that was paid was replaced by two more that threatened to put us on the rocks. It was a crazy, scary, daunting task, but living on the edge can also be very exciting. We'd had a year on the boat to form a vision for the practice.

Now open, our policy was simple. All men and women have a spine ... so that makes all men *and* women equal. There was to be no palaver or special treatment for the privileged classes, religious zealots or husbands with righteous attitudes. It ruffled a few feathers, but the really big shots like H.R.H. were more than happy to be treated as normal human beings in a country where being a member of the Royal family is often a burden.

Our second patient was an Indian road sweeper I found limping outside the practice from obvious back pain.

'I have no money!' he declared when I said that I could help him.

'God is good!' It is an Arabic saying that wipes the slate clean of any obligation he might have felt before I could persuade him into the clinic. So long as I had time early on, I was happy to look after anyone who crossed the threshold, regardless of their ability to pay the fee. However there would come a time when that would no longer be the case. Having spent time with Merrill Fernando in Sri Lanka we were very clear with our mission. The practice would need to be up-market to make a profit. With a population of two million people there was no way Darling and I could look after everyone. We made a decision therefore, to look after the movers and shakers of society who could not only afford our care, but influence the very future of Chiropractic in the country.

To set the standard we had sofas instead of chairs, chandeliers instead of lights, marble floors and thick rugs, coffee tables and an antique beverage stand that included coffee, tea (Dilmah) fresh dates and lollies and copies of the newspaper in English and Arabic. Our longterm vision was to eventually replace ourselves with local Omani who would become Chiropractors. In doing so, we had plans for a free clinic that would be set up as part of their training.

My respect for the Royal Family was reinforced a week later when I saw Hytham and Sanje (the road sweeper) sitting drinking coffee and engaged in conversation in the waiting room, neither knowing nor caring where the other was from.

"She's a hard road!" is what I wrote in my diary at the time. Twelve hours a day, six days out of seven, physically shattered and brain dead at the end of each week. Our cruising life was well and truly over. It was hard work all around, especially for the kids who had to put up with a grumpy bastard of a father who couldn't afford to relax for a second as he navigated the survival of the practice through an ocean of consecutive dilemmas. More than once I blew off steam by getting smashed on what little rum that we had on Edvina, wondering what madness had made us decide to take on this challenge.

The amount of head injuries and busted bodies that showed up in the practice in the first few weeks inspired us to contact the national radio station and kick start a road safety awareness campaign. In a country that had no ambulance service, "click, clack, front and back," became the call to action to reduce the insane number of people being killed or maimed for the want of simply wearing a seatbelt. Combined with our tag line "spine in line makes you feel fine" and a "free assessment", the campaign was successful also in helping to promote our new practice ... which made us even busier!

Darling was well, but equally exhausted as she balanced female patients with pregnancy, motherhood, nest building and massaging the ego of a husband who had gone from being "Captain of his Ship" to playing second fiddle to an idiot (Rashard). It was quickly becoming obvious that he had no idea what he was doing. Half of her wish was fulfilled by the knowledge that our midwife in Ireland had readily agreed to come to Oman and deliver the 'stowaway.' Scotty and Angel though didn't know whether they were coming or going. Scotty's business partner had suddenly departed for greener pastures which left him in control of their destiny. After years of disappointment, it was the first real opportunity he'd had to make a go of it in the U.K. but they were torn. Stay living in a place they hated … just for the money, or walk away from it all after years of struggle and start afresh from scratch again. Whatever their decision, we knew within weeks of opening that we would need a second doctor and decided to cover our bases by advertising internationally.

Finally … finally, after what seemed like forever, it started to come together. We had dotted the *I's* and crossed the *T's*, lined up the ducks and paid our pound of flesh. We were by no means out of the woods, but the light at the end of the tunnel was no longer an oncoming train. Most of all, Poppit and Jack had adapted well and were happy living on land again. They had made great friends at school, joined the tennis and swimming clubs and spent most weekends either hosting or attending sleepovers.

On top of this I had managed, somewhere along the way, to do a redraft of Kate and Paddy's story in the first three chapters of 'The Christening'. I did not know whose life was having more ups and downs, but all going well, I expected to finish the manuscript within six months.

'Cheers!' Darling and I toasted in a rare moment of relaxation. We had snuck off to the Intercontinental Hotel for a drink and some food without the kids to celebrate our busiest week. Eight weeks after we had opened for business, we managed to stem the financial hemorrhage. It was early days yet, but we had finally begun the ascent from the nightmare world of overdraft towards the land of *positive cashflow* where a man can dream of better places.

'The future is looking so bright we gotta wear shades!' Darling chimed as we chinked glasses. It was our favorite affirmation. The one we used the most when pushing through the hard times. Had we gotten back on the boat we would still be "punching north" somewhere near the top of the Red Sea. Instead, we were sitting in the comfort of a five star hotel watching the sun set on a turquoise blue horizon.

Halfway through the second glass, our peace was disturbed by my mobile phone. Saleh, our new PRO, had done such an amazing job in cleaning up the mess that the last one had made that I felt obliged to take the call.

'He f&%$#@n what?!' I shook my head in disbelief, when he told me the news.

5

'What to do?

D-Day for baby was the first week in November. With three months to go, our time line was critical in making sure that without any family, we had all of the support we needed in place for the big event. This included Saleh, our recently acquired "irreplaceable" PRO that Rashard had just fired.

'Why?' I shouted down the phone when I finally got hold of his dumb ass. It was the last straw. I was beside myself with frustration

'He was ripping us off!'

'He did the job I asked him to do which is more than you can say about the first one!' I countered.

'He charged five times the price. The man is a thief. I refuse to pay him that much money!'

'You are not paying him, we are and you didn't pay the last one either!' I reminded him.

By some small twist of fate I had bumped into his uncle in a coffee shop a couple of weeks before. The encounter was more than awkward, until a friend at his table, who spoke halting English, apologized profusely on his behalf for the loss of the original file. He explained that he wasn't a real PRO, but rather an out of work clerk who had no idea what he was doing. On top of this, Rashard had refused to pay him until after the license had been approved.

Overburdened with expenses connected to the process and otherwise unemployed, he had simply run out of money!

For the first time, I truly understood his situation and felt terrible about the pressure that I had put him under.

'I need a Pee-Rrrr-Ohh Rashard. I can't run the practice without one!' I stated through gritted teeth.

The previous day I had handed him a blank check and asked him to countersign and pay Saleh for his services. A simple request. Instead he had insulted him, called him a thief to his face and paid him one third of what he had requested. (I would have happily paid him double). The problem now was that my signature on the check made me party to the subsequent loss of face that had ensued. Saleh stated that while "there were no hard feelings," he could no longer represent me as long as I was in partnership with Rashard. When I asked him to recommend someone else, he politely declined.

'We will find another one!' Rashard stated stubbornly, but before he had a chance to justify, I slammed down the phone.

He'd had it coming, but in many ways so did we. Up to then we had been too busy to notice, or perhaps willingly ignored it, but it was time to have a second look between the lines and take stock of life in the Middle East.

With the benefit of hindsight, to understand the Arab psyche you have to look to the desert. It is by nature, a ruthless and unforgiving environment where survival and longevity is less about being the fittest, but more about being clever enough to get someone else to do the work! Historically, the cheapest form of labor had been slavery (which filled the gap quite nicely for thousands of years thank you) but with the embracing of western values, the task has fallen to those who willingly work for the lowest price. Haggling being a national sport, the measure of a man is often the number of people he can get to work for him for the least amount of money. The players in this game are mostly educated Asian expats who, surplus to requirements in their own country, are brought in to fill the middle ground. It works for the most part, but slavery mentality being the modus operandi, any chance the locals get they will try it on.

A good example of this on the home front was Violi, a wonderful Filipina lady and qualified school teacher who we had employed to help with managing the kids and the house. She worked nine to five from Monday to Friday, had weekends off and we paid her extra to babysit. Compared to New Zealand, her wages were well below minimum rate, but compared to the Philippines she was earning more than her brother who was a qualified GP. In contrast to this arrangement, our next door neighbor employed two house staff for the same amount as we paid Violi, had them work twelve hours a day, six days a week, gave no extra for babysitting for which there was at least three nights a week and kept a lock on the fridge so that they would not steal food.

When it came to the practice the FREE ASSESSMENT meant FREE ASSESMENT. It didn't mean free treatment, nor did it mean that we were negotiable on our fees. By nature, the Arabs who came to us in the early days tried their hardest to bargain us down.

'What is your best price?'

'The fee that I just quoted.'

'No, no ... in Oman we do not fix the price. I can go to the doctor down the road for less than half of what you are charging me! What is your best price?'

'If the doctor down the road was any good you wouldn't be here!'

'That is not the point (even though they had just made it). He is a medical doctor, you are just a physio and they earn less!'

'If you want a physio then go to a physio. If you want Chiropractic then you will have to pay our fee.' This was especially nerve wracking in the early days when any amount of money would have helped our cashflow crisis, but to give in would have ultimately defeated us.

'My friend Ibrahm says that Chiro-what-is-it and physio ... it is all the same. I don't see why I have to pay any extra!'

'Your friend is wrong!'

'Are you saying my friend is stupid?'

'No (yes) but your friend does not know anything about the true value of Chiropractic.'

'Your advertisement said that the treatment is free!'

'No, it says that the assessment is free.'

'If I go to the hospital treatment it is free!'

'Well then go to the hospital!'

'I did.'

'What happened?'

'It did not work. I want to come to see you, but you have to change your fee,' and on and on and f*&$#n on!

Fortunately our travels through the markets of Indonesia and Malaysia had prepared us for this mentality, so were able to knock it on the head within the first few weeks of opening. The posturing and haggling was not only time consuming, but draining and demeaning of our specialty. Fed up with the scratched record of 'best price' we restructured the fees and devised a method of "special discount" (20%) for advanced payment regardless of the number of visits a patient had over a set time period. Once explained, they were delighted with the choice. In truth though, it still worked out the same as our original fixed price, but they couldn't resist a bargain!

All of this we could get used to, but Rashard's early charm combined with our willing naiveté had led us to trust that he too believed in a world of fair exchange. His actions though told a different story. Among other things ... we didn't like the subservient attitude he demanded from his "house maid" or the way he expected the staff at his wrought-iron factory to kiss his hand just because he had been to Mecca (this one was really wearing thin). He rarely showed any appreciation for how hard we worked or any sense of understanding when things went wrong. Most of all, he was beyond reproach when he was responsible. All added up, and with a baby just over the horizon, this made us feel very vulnerable.

Once formed, a business partnership with an Omani is an exclusive relationship that cannot be dissolved or swopped for a better partner. It's either all or nothing and if it is not to be, then the Expat has to leave Oman for two years before they can return and engage with a new partner. Technically we were broke (the only thing keeping us afloat was our cash flow) so if the partnership ended, it would leave us up the wazoo.

'What to do?' ... as the Indians love to say. More importantly though, how to do it? There would have to be a face off which was likely to lead to the inevitable shouting match (on my part anyway!) We had a clause in our contract that was designed to resolve any conflict through arbitration, but our limited experience of Arab life left us unprepared us for a situation like this. The biggest problem was the whole concept of 'loss of face' or 'saving face.' In Arabic the expression '*Hifz Ma'a Wajh*' translates literally to 'save (*Hifz*) face (*Wajh*) water (*Ma'a*)' where an individual is trying to maintain dignity and prestige, particularly in times of confrontation. For a westerner it was no big deal, a temporary embarrassment, but for an Arab, to lose face is as bad if not worse than the loss of a limb.

Short of a knock-down drag-out fight, I didn't have a clue what to do, nor did I want to be running to a lawyer every time we had a problem. While there were a lot of things that our new business partner reflected about the culture that we didn't like, he had, in truth, provided us with a very unique opportunity.

A full week passed before I finally resolved to bite my tongue and was just about to give him a call, when a surprise e-mail arrived unexpectedly.

Dear Gary,

I'm writing to apologize for dismissing Saleh without consultation. As sole director of the practice you have every right to be angry and I regret this decision. I have been under pressure with my other business of late and have been finding it very hard to keep pace with how quickly the practice has been developing. I'm used to being in charge and making the decisions, but realize now that this is an area entirely outside my experience. It's a whole new game for me, some of which I find intimidating. I hope that you won't let this incidence come between us and that we can continue to work towards the future success of the clinic.
You have my full commitment
Rashard.

Pheew! To our great relief, Rashard had come up trumps and saved the day. The line in the sand had now been drawn (excuse the pun) which was a relief, and everybody knew where they stood. With a few short months to D-Day our ultimate goal was to establish a stable and secure foundation for the clinic and our future in Oman. We now had all of the pieces in place and that included the trust from a partner who would back us 100% and not pull the rug from under us when it mattered the most.

The last part of the jigsaw to complete was to find another Chiropractor to join our team. This was going to be the trickiest part, but with Rashard's full support we now felt confident that we had the stability to attract the right person. Inundated with inquiries from all over the world, we finally made a shortlist of three potential candidates before whittling down to a Canadian D.C. who had been practicing in Zimbabwe for the last twenty years. With impeccable credentials and a list of experience as long as your arm, he was motivated to escape from the social implosion that was Zimbabwe and knew a great opportunity when he saw one.

But then the best news of all came through and Darling's prayers were answered!

6

'Anything is better than this shithole'

To our great surprise, Scotty and Angel had had a change of heart. One disaster too many had made them decide that they were sick of the UK and they wanted to relocate and join us. For Darling this was the icing on the cake. It would not be until two months after D-Day, but her wish list was now complete and she was happy to wait. We weren't just getting one of the best Doctors of Chiropractic in New Zealand. We were getting our best friends and instant family to boot.

'Talk about the Gods rowing in behind you!' Darling said when she heard the news.

For me I was no longer so sure. The experience of vetting potential associates had made me appreciate more the degree of *absolute* commitment the practice demanded in making it a success. Thinking that Oman might be any easier than the UK, was the wrong way to go about it. We had already made a heavy investment financially and emotionally, but there was still a lot of grunt work to be done.

'You gotta come down and see this place. It's a lot different than we first thought!' I advised over the phone.

'Can't do it … it's too hard to get anyone to cover for me,' Scotty replied. 'Anyway, anything is better than this shit hole!'

148

'Seriously,' I said, pressing the point on our second *and* third conversation within the same week. I wasn't happy about them making the big move without doing the same sort of reconnaissance that we had done. In their heart of hearts a lot of expatriates hated the Middle East and were only there for the money. It would be a disaster if they discovered that Oman might be no better than the U.K. but Scotty was adamant about committing sight unseen.

If you take a liberal amount of good will, mix with a pinch of stupidity, season with naivety and allow to simmer for several months in a state of high emotion … you pretty much get an idea of what we agreed to in the end, but I'm getting ahead of myself *again*!

7

'I'm Listening!'

'Wake up!' It was just after midnight. 'C'mon, wake up. You have to sort this out!' Long time no hear, it was "Tony" calling me from slumber. 'You can't do this ... you know you can't ... you already have enough on your plate!' he echoed, bang, bang, bang over the agreement that we had made with our best friends.

'I want half,' was Scotty's answer when we had sat down to iron out the nitty gritty of ownership, division of labor and overall responsibility. It was an enormous ask, magnified by the fact that he offered nothing in return.

'Don't do it!' my inner voice (Mr. Hopkins) had whispered when we shook hands over the arrangement. Now he was shouting at me as I walked around the house under the pale moonlight to try and clear my head.

What had swayed us to agree to giving them half? The emotion of the moment; the desire to please, a belief that somehow, all would be better with our worlds. Scotty had originally taken an underperforming practice in Auckland and achieved legendary status by tripling it in less than a year. If he wove his magic and only doubled our new clinic, then his contribution would be worth every metaphorical penny that they *wouldn't* be investing. This wasn't part of the discussions nor was it mentioned in our agreement. It was just taken for granted.

However, having had a few weeks to cool off, I was no longer persuaded by this twisted logic. Since returning to Muscat, I'd sent Scotty several long e-mails outlining our vision for the clinic based on our travels experiences and time with Merrill Fernando. This included our mission statement, commitment to service and the long term objective of sponsoring local Omani to train as Chiropractors and ultimately replace ourselves. The correspondence included facts and figures, projections and contingencies and asked a ton of questions to try to flesh out any unexpected and perhaps unrealistic ideas on both sides.

In return I received nothing, other than excuses about a crashed computer and not enough time to read.

'It's not fair,' Tony harped on. 'You have put your entire lives on the line. They are putting nothing up front *and* planning on maintaining two associates in their practices in the UK as a fallback position!'

This did not come anywhere close to what I felt was required to make it a success. I walked the floors for another hour before I made the call.

'Can't do it mate!' were my first words when Scotty finally answered the phone. It was a difficult conversation, bordered by disappointment and the guilt of reneging on our agreement.

'We have had too many ups and downs for me to give you any guarantees for the future. Now with a baby on the way...'

The silence that followed echoed my uncertainty. If we had learned one thing from cruising, it was about the importance of enjoying the journey. The minute you had to cross a line at a given time the joy factor was lost and it became a race against time that invited all sorts of dramas and disasters.

Scotty's response was surprisingly short, but full of understanding and I felt a tremendous sense of relief wash over me when I put down the phone. Sometimes you don't realize how much pressure you are under until it has been lifted. I slept soundly that night for the first time in weeks. The reprieve lasted a little less than twenty four hours when Scotty called me back.

'We understand where you are coming from, so this is what we can do. We can't afford to make the same financial investment as you guys (seventy thousand dollars) but we can come up with ten thousand. How does that sound?' It was their buy in ... their bit of skin. It paled in comparison to what we had already invested, but they were putting their money where their mouth was and this was sufficient to grab my attention.

'I'm listening!'

'Beyond that we promise, like you guys, that we are in it for the long haul. There will be no fallback position. We will take it as it comes and be fully responsible for our decision. We need the practices here in the UK to support our initial transition, but if they take a dive, then we will abandon them!'

Above all else ... these were the words that I wanted to hear. Commitment, commitment, commitment. The idea of a written contract had crossed my mind, but they had been our best friends for twenty years, god parents to our children and named as executors of our will. If we couldn't trust them, then who could we trust?

8

'One Mississippi, two Mississippi ...'

'Wake up!' It was five thirty am. 'Come on wake up!' a voice called me from the worst night's sleep I'd had in a long time. This time though it wasn't the *Voice*. It was Darling who had been walking the floors on and off all night in a disturbed and highly agitated state. 'The baby is coming!' she finally announced.

'Are you sure?' It was still three weeks till D-Day and our midwife was nowhere in sight. I'd been hoping instead that it was just Brackston Hicks contractions, but when her waters broke we knew that it was game on.

F#*$k!

'I'll organize the kids, you pack a bag!' I ordered. Within twenty minutes we were on our way at high speed to the Muscat Private Hospital. Despite the fact that we were already registered, there were more paperwork and forms to be filled out than you could shake a stick at ... each one about the length of a contraction. The obstetrician was called, a stranger, unfamiliar with our case, and we were ushered into a room that reeked of foreboding. Darling was hooked up and plugged into all sorts of machines and monitors. It was nothing like the home births we were used to.

'I feel like pushing!' Darling announced about fifteen minutes after our arrival. It was the exact same time that the Obstetrician noted a blip on the baby's heart rate monitor.

'The baby is in distress. We have to get it out now!' she announced.

Then all hell broke loose.

Without consultation or warning, the obstetrician and a nurse literally grabbed Darling and manhandled her onto a hospital gurney. Somewhere in the background an alarm sounded and before I knew it I was running full tilt as they pushed Darling at a headlong dash through the hospital corridors. As we rounded each corner more doctors and nurses joined the fray. In a strange way it was reassuring, but my heart sank on the last bend when I found that it led to a dead end with two large doors marked *Operating Theatre.*

'No!' Darling cried out as we burst through the theatre doors. This wasn't the way it was supposed to happen. We were used to softly lit rooms with luxurious sofas, warm baths and hot compresses, gentle music and heaps of time, to dilate and communicate, cogitate (not complicate) on honey and fresh fruit for energy, and time, lots of it, to hold hands and reassure and cajole and encourage and breath in unison to the rhythms of nature and the beat of a new life that would arrive in its own good time.

'Get him out of here!' a voice screamed. Before I knew it, I found myself being manhandled to a 'holding' area back down the corridor in a room beside the nursing station. A security guard was placed on the door to prevent me from leaving.

Two things occurred to me simultaneously. The first ... that I was big enough to charge the bastard and escape back to Darling. Two ... it takes a good obstetrician four minutes to deliver a baby by emergency c-section.

'Hold!' the *Voice* commanded as I worked out how many steps it would take to reach the guard. 'Hold!' *Tony* repeated, this time in warning, as the guard (gorilla) sensed my intention and braced himself, knowing better than me how to hold the line. In that moment of hesitation, it finally occurred to me that the last thing the surgeon needed was a mad fucking Irishman breaking down the door. Frustrated, I turned away from the guard to hide my tears of shame for not having fought harder to stay with my Darling in the first place.

'He is a good Doctor!' said the guard, an Arab, about twenty years older than me, speaking gently when he could see that I was no longer a threat. 'He has delivered many babies. Your wife will be fine,' he

154

reassured. But I wasn't. Like Darling, I was shit scared, out of my depth and alone.

'One Mississippi, two Mississippi, three Mississippi four, I started counting (I had left my watch at home in the mad rush). When I reached four minutes I persuaded myself that it was all over, but started counting from zero again because it gave me something to focus on and helped to calm me. I did it over and over, again and again as a second alarm went off and an excited voice on a loud speaker called out for another doctor to attend the theatre. 'One Mississippi, two Mississippi, three Mississippi, four.' I watched more staff run past with oxygen bottles and equipment, until a half an hour had passed. Somewhere in the melee a nurse rushed past the window with a Chinese baby swaddled in a blue towel and I reassured myself that any minute now they would bring me news of my own baby. 'One Mississippi, two Mississippi, three Mississippi, four …

'It's taking a long time,' the guard finally said in commiseration when an hour had passed. The counting was no longer working and he could see that I had stopped pacing the floor and was eyeing the door with renewed determination. 'If you wait here I will go and ask what is happening … okay? Please, wait, or you will get us both into a lot of trouble!' he appealed.

I nodded, but only half intended keeping my promise. I'd give him five minutes. 'One Mississippi, two Mississippi, three Mississippi, four. At least fifteen minutes passed before he reappeared at the door.

'The doctor will be here soon,' he confirmed. There was a burden to his voice and a detached look to his eyes that avoided contact when I appealed to him for more information.

Ninety minutes after Darling was rushed into theatre, the surgeon finally appeared at the door. He looked haggard and drawn, as if he had been through a war. There was blood on his gown and tragedy written all over him.

'I'm sorry for the delay,' were the first words he said as he steered me towards a chair. The last thing I wanted to do was to sit down. 'There were complications during the delivery … your wife had an allergic reaction … to the anesthetic. … I'm sorry,' he repeated … 'please accept my condolences.'

155

9

'All for one and one for all?'

Take a long carving knife with a curved blade in your right hand. Hold your victim firmly by the shoulder with your left and using all of the strength that you can muster, drive the tip of the knife up under his sternum. Now twist it, so that it breaks free from the bones that are stopping it, and, putting your shoulder and entire body weight under it, drive it deeper, through the heart, so that there is nothing left but the hilt showing.

My legs buckled and collapsed from under me. That's why I needed the chair.

'Put your head between your knees and take some deep breaths,' the surgeon instructed in a precise, practiced tone, as he knelt down in front of me and held my shoulders to stop me falling off the chair. 'That's it … breathe.' And with his mouth beside my ear, he drew deeply along with me. 'Get me a bucket, he is going to throw up!' he shouted at the security guard.

I wasn't, but then, as if on cue, a wave of nausea washed over me and I felt the bitter taste of bile rise from my stomach and burn the back of my nostrils. 'Hurry!' the surgeon shouted, but the security guard was too shaken to take any notice. Luckily a nurse had followed the doctor in support and a bucket appeared between my legs as the first wave of vomit exploded from my mouth.

With that my eyes watered, light turned to darkness, sound became muffled and my mind warped as a tide of emotion swelled in my chest threatening to drown me. I could hear a voice through the fog, but I don't know what the surgeon was saying.

Somewhere in the distance I heard the cries of a new born baby, a distinct tone of the first breaths taken, but I recognized them from twelve years before. The haze suddenly cleared and there I was, holding our first born daughter, whom I had just caught as she entered the world. We were surrounded by laughter and relief and the sound of gentle music and the congratulations of the two midwives we'd had in support. The room overflowed with joy and I was in awe of this thing called new life, but more in awe of my Darling who, in a sea of pain, had remained dignified and regal as she delivered our first child without a whisper of hesitation or fear. This was a glimpse only, of the power that she possessed. Four years later she brought this power to full force in another home delivery, a ten pound son, when a lesser mortal would have surrendered to surgical intervention. Now she was gone. My Darling, my wife, my love, my life … all else paled in significance. The *Voice* had not lied. I had loved her before I had met her … truly, madly, deeply, beyond realistic or mortal explanation. 'One Mississippi, two Mississippi, three Mississippi, four …

In that moment of realization, I suffered the long pointed needles of a thousand regrets, of the thousand lost opportunities to tell her how much she had meant to me. I should have been more devoted, I should have been more caring, but life had swayed me with untold distractions and a million excuses and silly justifications of what it was to be a man.

We had been happy. Truly. Beyond the petty arguments that infiltrate and try to defeat happiness, but it was only now that I fully knew it.

We had been in love. Truly. A love that had borne us two wonderful children, but it was only now that I understood the gift that she had given to me.

We'd had our ups and downs, but finally, through adventure and adversity, raging storms and blazing sunsets, we had become comrades in arms, sailing around the world, believing that somehow we could make it a better place. Now my best mate was lost to the depths of despair.

Sweet Jesus, what use were these thoughts now that I could not tell her. What use was this love when the person I wanted to share it with the most was gone? I was suddenly envious of the blind man who had never known a sunset. Of the deaf man who had never heard the sweetness of music in his ears. Like the prisoner held in solitary confinement, I had time to kill, time to burn, time to waste and eventually justify, but what use was any of it when I didn't have the time to say goodbye. To tell her the thousand ways I had loved her smile and the way that she had called me Dorkus.

It was only now that I finally understood.

'Ah, I see you have heard the terrible news.' It was the pediatrician who brought me back to my senses. Somewhere along the way he had swopped places with the surgeon who had been called to another emergency (poor bastard) 'You need to talk to your children. They are worried about you.'

'My children!' I had forgotten they had been left behind when we made the mad dash to the operating theatre. 'Where are they? I have to go and see them. Tell them what has happened. Oh God what do I tell them?'

'Don't worry. I have just been with them. They have told me about your boat and all of the great adventures that you have had. Amazing!

'Where are they?'

'They are with your wife!'

'With my wife?'

'In recovery, it's down the hall.'

'Recovery? But the surgeon? He gave me his condolences!' My mind was like mush, still mixed with confusion, my mouth a sea of self pity and bile. 'Condolences, *condolences*,' I searched for a more hopeful explanation, but then suddenly, I realized with equal amounts of devastation. 'The baby must have died!'

'No,' he paused. 'It's much worse than that,' the Pediatrician stated sadly.

'What could be worse?' I couldn't imagine.

'It has Down Syndrome!'

'What?'

'It has Down Syndrome!'

He didn't say the baby, or your new daughter or *third born blong Yu*. He said "It!" then waited for gravity to set in.

It was the single happiest moment of my life and the single most terrible combined. Alive! My Darling, my wife, my love, my life. She was alive! But the joy was overshadowed by the specter of having a child with Down Syndrome. Nobody wants an "It" in their lives.

He handed me a consent form to sign for the baby's care.

'Boy or girl?'

'It's a girl.'

'Where is she?'

'It is in I.C.U.' (that "It" thing again) He waved at the nurse and the security guard to dismiss them. Then he pulled me to one side of the room out of earshot. 'You don't have to live with this *thing*,' he advised.

I was shocked, disbelieving the words that I had just heard. The "It" had now become a "*Thing*."

'In my country (Poland) there is a place that you can send it. Not an institution,' he shook his head to assuage any guilt that might be connected. 'It's more like a hotel. You are a doctor. You have plenty of money. We can take care of the details and you can get on with your life.'

'One Mississippi, two Mississippi, three Mississippi, four.' This wasn't happening to me. Mine was a world of live and let live. A world where you don't go around being scared of imagined monsters or ghosts or the specter of a child who has the power of Trisomy Twenty One. I was a doctor, a healer, a giver of life. I belonged to a world that did not offer such *tantalizing* choices.

Had the pediatrician been a stranger, then I might have understood, but he was my friend. We had a professional relationship. He had referred me several children and their parents in the short time since we had opened our new clinic. We'd had long discussions on treatment protocols and expected outcomes and the similarities and complimentary natures of our professions. I in return, had referred a number of children to him in a similar light. To take the greatest of care, to do the right thing, but now I could no longer trust him.

Torn between going to see Darling and the desire to see our new child, I instinctively chose the latter. If Darling was in recovery with Poppit and Jack, then she was going to be okay. But what about our new daughter they now called "It." Only two hours new to this world, I had to be sure that they were looking after her. I went to leave the room, but the pediatrician tugged me back again, persisting.

'If you walk out that door then there is nothing we can do!' I felt like a lunatic being dragged back from the edge of a precipice.

'One Mississippi, two Mississippi, three Mississippi, four.'

The part of me that he appealed to that *might* be open to making such a choice was barred by the promise that I had made to my children when we set off from New Zealand on Edvina.

'All for one - and one for all.'

That no matter what happened, they would always be safe. Maybe I was a lunatic, but my little girl's life was likely in peril and as a new member to our crew, I'd be damned as a father if I was to abandon her.

'Not on my ship and not on my watch!' I stared him down, calling his bluff. The hell he was threatening me with would be no worse than any hell we had already been through.

'You will be on your own!' he called after me when I walked through the door.

10

'Dead man walking'

On the way to the ICU I was met by the director of the hospital who had sought me out especially.

'I'm sorry for your tragedy,' he began and took my hand and held it in both of his to comfort me. 'I have already spoken to the Board and they have asked me to extend their condolences and advise you that we will be happy to make a substantial discount in your final bill.'

Another bastard. I wasn't looking for empathy or sympathy or people to hold my hand and feel sorry for me. His condolence was an insult, further exacerbated by his offer to discount the fee for our daughter's delivery, as if her arrival could not be justified as worth the full amount.

If bad news spreads like wild fire, then the air was thick with the sympathetic smiles of those who had gotten wind of our so-called tragedy. Short of someone calling out "dead man walking" the pediatrician had been right. I was completely on my own.

When I reached the I.C.U. he had somehow overtaken me by way of a back corridor and was busy giving orders.

'At least ten days,' he replied when I asked how long it would take to get my daughter out from under the lights.

'Ten days?' It defied all logic.

161

'She has swallowed muconium (fetal feces) in utero. I have aspirated her airways, but you can never be sure. With her low muscle tone and underdeveloped lungs we are concerned about her being overpowered by infection.' He pointed to the numerous electrodes to which she was hooked up to monitor her every breath. Temperature high, blood pressure high, heart rate all over the place, oxygen saturation rate 80%. Through calculated words, chosen for their power rather than their caring, he magnified her condition tenfold so that it rendered her totally dependent on him for her life. If she was to make it, it would be because of him and no one else. 'The next three days are critical!' he stated, grim faced, as if somehow, the measured signature of his machines underlined the truth.

I was alarmed by his statement that she might not make it. Alarmed by the incubator and bright lights, the beeping machines and the smell of disinfectant. How could an environment of such sterility and detachment hope to give her any chance at life.

'Has she been fed yet?'

'She is on an IV drip,' he replied pointing to a clear plastic bag of fluid that hung from a stand and a tube that snaked down under the sheet into her body.

'No, I mean breastfed.'

'No, it is too dangerous. She is three weeks premature and we are concerned about her swallowing the wrong way and getting more foreign matter into lungs. Anyway, she is too weak to do it!'

What ensued then was a heated discussion about the merits of at least trying to breastfeed, in particular the benefits of colostrum for her immune system. (Not to mention the importance of bonding) As the doctor in charge, he wasn't having a bar of it. The rules had changed. I had crossed the line. We were no longer friends or professionals with shared opinions. That I was the father of this child carried even less merit. This was his turf and I had no right to question his authority!

Left with no doubt as to where I stood, he finally excused himself in a huff. Because of her condition, there was a mountain of paperwork to be filled out. I remained with a Filipina nurse who was appointed sole charge.

'She is very pretty!' she half whispered in defiance of toeing the line that the pediatrician had set. It was heartfelt, genuine, but coming from someone who had no authority, it was a pebble in the ocean, the ripples of which were overpowered by the waves of prejudice that prevailed.

Intimidated, I found myself having to ask permission to hold my new daughter. Equally so, the nurse hesitated, looking to the door through which the pediatrician had departed.

'Just for a minute, okay?' she whispered. Her concern left me in no doubt of the risk that she was taking, but even still, she reached into the incubator. 'She is very floppy. It is part of the condition,' the nurse explained as she carefully handed me my new daughter's limp body. Fortunately the wires and tubes that connected her to the monitors were long enough to stretch out of the incubator.

First-time fathers all have two left hands when it comes time to holding their new baby. I already had two children under my belt and had cared for hundreds in practice. In spite of my experience, I had been made to feel that she was a ticking bomb waiting to go off at the slightest of mistakes. 'One Mississippi, two Mississippi, three Mississippi, four.' I was shocked by her size (small), her fragility (utterly defenseless), her vulnerability (the whole world against her) and her almond shaped eyes. Then it struck me. It wasn't a Chinese baby that I had seen being taken from the delivery theatre hours before. It was my own daughter! F&^%$#@&^%$#!!!! I should have been angry. I should have thrown a wobbly and kicked some ass and complained to the highest level that my daughter was not given to me the second she left the delivery room! I should have, but our eyes met for the first time and suddenly … there was light and love and warmth and humanity. I knew then that nothing else mattered, but that I should sing to her to welcome and comfort her for the short time that she might be with us.

'Hush, little baby, don't say a word, Dadda's gonna buy you a mockingbird.

And if that mockingbird don't sing, Dadda's gonna buy you a diamond ring.

And eef dat dimond ring turns brass, your Dadda he is going to buy you a looking glass!' the nurse (to my surprise) joined in, stroking my little girl's head.

'And if that looking glass gets broke,' (we both chorused) 'Mama's gonna buy you a billy goat!'

163

And on and on, smiling and making a racket till we ran out of words and I found myself making up my own verses ...

'Hush little baby don't you cry, Daddy's going to sing you a lullaby ...'

'Hush little baby please don't die. Please don't die, please don't die!' I found myself repeating over and over in tears.

'Who said that she will die? She is not going to die!' The nurse stood back in shock.

'The pediatrician,' I blubbered. 'He said that with the infection she might not survive!'

'What infection?' she demanded

Having no other proof, I pointed to the monitors. And then I had to make a second take. To my great surprise, all of the readings had normalized. Even her temperature had dropped!

'He said that she might not survive!'

'He is a bully!' she stated. 'Yes!' she repeated when she saw my disbelief. 'We all call him "Dr. Short Ass" behind his back. He is such a little man!' Her face twisted as if she had swallowed something bitter. 'This girl ... she will *not* die ... she *is* strong. Look, see how she wants to feed!' It was true. Every time I stroked her face, her lips pursed open and closed like a goldfish trying to latch onto my finger.

It's hard to be brave when the whole world seems against you, hard to make a stand when there is no-one to hold your hand. Had I Darling to help me hold sway against the sea of prejudice that I faced I might have felt stronger, but my best mate lay wounded and inconsolable. But now, I swear, the Gods had sent me this Angel in the disguise of a four-foot nothing seemingly meek and subservient Filipina nurse to stand beside and give me her back!

'Really, she will be okay!' she smiled in gentle reassurance. 'What does a machine know about the beat of a baby's heart?' She brushed aside the monitors with a swipe of her hand. 'You must listen to dis now!' she tapped her own heart. 'You must be strong for your baby!' she punched her fist in the air.

However fucked up I might have been at the time, (really fucked up) my instincts as a father were finally starting to fire on all cylinders. That's when I got angry! Angry at myself, for not having fought harder to stay with Darling. Angry, that my power as a father had been diminished and rendered impotent by the stamp of the pediatrician's so-called authority. Why had I not been shown her before now? Why had he left her to bake under bright lights instead of having someone hold her and comfort her, *that she might die at any moment and never know that she had been loved.* Angry at the whole world for their attitude towards this helpless child. Was I was being made to stand aside and allow someone who really didn't give a fuck to care for her? I don't think so!

Was I scared? Yes, beyond shitless, I could barely breathe, for I too had been indoctrinated and shackled with the same prejudice since I was born. No parent wants a child with Down Syndrome, but as I held my daughter and sang to her for the first time, just like I had with Poppit and Jack, I began to experience a new kind of love within me that I had never imagined existed in this life. A new source of strength that I never knew I contained. I began to realize that Down Syndrome was not the problem. The problem was the waves of ignorance and ironclad prejudice that had been breaking over and threatening to drown me from the moment I knew of her condition. If I was angry before, then this new source of strength made me angrier than I have ever been at any other time in my life!

'Fuck you!' I thought, of anyone who might try to steal this new love that I felt for my new daughter. 'Fuck you!' for trying to take away what little courage I had. Fuck *me* for thinking the same thing just an hour before. Fuck you Mr. Pediatrician, that with all of your years of experience, you had not the wisdom to see the goodness that I held in my arms. Whatever the outcome, whatever the consequences, whatever the down side, I decided there and then that she had a better chance being cared for by me than a wolf in sheep's clothing.

Then I went to get reinforcements.

11

'There is going to be a war!'

It took me half an hour to round up the kids, *shell shocked*, and find Darling, *devastated*, her body plundered of her power and the birth that she had meticulously planned and so looked forward to. She was further distraught that she had been moved from the recovery unit to the far side of the hospital away from her baby that she had yet to see. There was no time for comfort or consolation. No time for explanations or the holding of hands and shedding of mutual tears. As far as I was concerned, so long as one of our children was separated from us, then we had a "man overboard situation!" There would be time enough later on for a family cuddle.

'I want you to feed the baby!' I wasn't asking. I was telling. I knew what condition she was in, but hoped the urgency in my voice would be sufficient to overcome her weakness and spur her into action.

'I don't know which way is up right now, but I'll do whatever you think is best!' She lay on her side in the fetal position, clutching her stomach to try to relieve the pain. There was no way that she was going to be able to walk across the hospital to the I.C.U. I wasn't too sure (yet) how far I could bend the rules, but felt that hijacking the incubator to bring Darling her new baby was outside the realm of possibility. Then I had an idea.

'Poppit, get the doors!' She was confused at first, but when she saw me kick the release brakes on the bed, she cottoned on and ran to open the double doors that were designed to allow a bed to be moved between rooms. 'Jack, Mum's bag, grab it!' I pointed to her overnighter that was hanging from a chair. 'Hook it on the head of the bed and guide it after me, okay!' A look of disbelief passed between them. The sort that borders on the raw excitement (and terror) of breaking the rules! Just as quickly, as if throwing off the invisible shackles of authority that had been holding us all powerless, they sprang into action.

The bed moved easily. We stopped at the doorway momentarily, three heads looking out into the corridor. When the coast was clear, we heaved Darling out and took an immediate left and then left again without scraping any walls. Ahead of us lay a one hundred meter dash along an empty hall way, at the end of which stood the elevators. The I.C.U. was two floors below.

'Okay, everybody be chilly!' I slowed my pace to a gentle walk. It was as much to calm the beat of my own racing heart as the kids whose chests I knew must be thumping. 'We are out for a Sunday walk. No need to draw attention. We make the lift and we are home free, okay?' I asked for confirmation.

'Holy shit, I can't believe we are doing this!' Jack's voice echoed off the walls. You'd swear we had just robbed the crown jewels! My conscious effort to contain our adrenalin and appear normal made every step feel as if we were wading through a river of glue. It was all going well though, until suddenly, a doctor and a male nurse appeared out of a side door half way between us and the lift. My heart missed a beat when they turned in our direction, but they were so deep in animated conversation, that they walked towards us unnoticed.

'Gidday!' I nodded with all of the confidence I could muster as we passed each other, but they hardly acknowledged.

'Pheew!' Jake whispered out of the side of his mouth. We had just passed the halfway mark.

'Excuse me. Hello!' two voices called out in unison. When I turned to look behind, the nurse and doctor had been stopped by another nurse from Darling's ward. She was pointing in our direction. 'Where do you think you are going?' The doctor started walking back towards us.

'No, you are okay, we are grand, we are just out for a bit of a walk!' I replied, waving with the back of my hand to dismiss their concerns, but our pace had noticeably quickened. 'Poppit, get the lift!' I whispered, but she was already ahead of me.

'Hey, come back here!' the doctor called. The glue had now become unstuck and Jack and I were pushing Darling at full flight down the remainder of the hallway.

'I said stop!'

But Poppit already had the doors open. We made one hell of a racket as we crashed to a halt inside the lift. Jack flipped him the bird as the doors jammed shut. The expression on the doctor's face was priceless! We all laughed with relief and disbelief at what we were doing.

'All for one!' I called out as we watched the dial tick off the floors. We had broken the mold. Shattered the illusion. Taken our power back.

'And one for all!' the kids chorused. When the lift doors opened again two floors below, I knew that they were ready to fight their way into I.C.U. Whatever it took to save their sister.

I had expected the same doctor to leap the stairs and confront us, but when the doors opened he was nowhere to be found. When we reached the ward it was empty save for the Angel that guarded our baby.

'Oh my God, what are you doing?' the Filipina nurse was wide-eyed at the sight of us pushing Darling through the doorway.

'We are going to feed the baby!' I could tell by her uneasy submission that she might still be on our side.

'I will have to go and tell him, it is my duty you understand?' She shrugged her shoulders apologetically.

'It's okay. Tell him that I went crazy and threw you out if you have to!' I joked as we maneuvered Darling's bed up beside the incubator. The last thing I wanted was for her to lose her job.

'I will go the long way. It will take me at least ten minutes to find him. It should be enough hopefully to get you started!' She fussed over Darling and packed pillows gently behind her so that she could sit upright.

'There is going to be a war!' she hummed when she walked out the door. You could tell by her tone that she was looking forward to it.

12

'Be quiet!'

The monitors were all over the place when I reached into the incubator. The first time had been easy with the nurse to help, but this time, even my kids held their breath as I removed the ticking time bomb from her case.

'See the monitors!' I pointed, as I handed Darling our new daughter, but they were all too distracted to understand the significance. Charged on adrenalin, I wanted her to get started straight away. To try to latch her on and give her a good feed, but there was too much cooing and cuddling and crying and the singing of "twinkle, twinkle little star," as Darling and Poppit and Jack welcomed their new sister to our family.

'You have to feed her!' I encouraged, trying not to sound agitated. Any minute now the storm troopers would arrive, but Darling, her power beginning to restore from gazing into the depths of her new baby's dark almond eyes, silenced me by placing the tip of her finger on my lips.

'When we are ready!' she stated calmly.

F$%K!!!!!!

In the distance, I could now hear doors opening and closing, the sound of footsteps and voices arguing as they fast approached. Then it occurred to me ... what if he had the security guard in tow? In a fit of desperation I looked around the room for something to defend myself, but all I could find was a clip board with some papers attached. I looked for a suitable chair to jam against the door to block entry to the I.C.U. but all too soon they were upon us.

'What do you think you are doing? This is my ward!' the pediatrician virtually screamed, as he burst through the door followed by a battery of nurses. There were no security guards in sight.

And then the Gods smiled upon me.

I met the little fucker face to face, halfway across the room.

'I am withdrawing my consent for you to look after this child!' I said holding the clip board up to his face. He had to arch backwards to stop his nose from banging into it.

'You cannot do this!'

'Yes I can. As the father of the child I have absolute authority in this matter. You will desist immediately!' I stated. On the clip board, I had discovered the "Consent to Care" form that he had made me sign. I tore it up in front of him. He was incredulous!

What followed then was a heated battle of wits over infection and brain damage, blood sugars and oxygenation levels and all of the medical terminology he could throw to disarm and defeat me. Among his claims for the medical and moral high ground, he declared to have a superior education, years of international experience, the backing of the hospital board and the support of the three nurses *and* a fully qualified midwife who stood beside him.

What gave me hope was the denial from said midwife with the perceptible shake of her head. Either way I didn't give a fuck. I had two balled-up fists looking for an excuse to have the last word, but before I got a chance to use them there was a shout from behind.

'Be quiet!'

It was Darling.

Suddenly the room was silenced. When we turned to look, the matter was once and for all settled as to who was really in charge.

'The baby is feeding!' She gave a withering look (10 *mega ton)* that was locked and loaded and aimed directly at the pediatrician. The hairs on the back of my neck stood on end as I watched him visibly shudder. She pointed then to the monitors. Once again, all of the readings had normalized!

'That's my girl' I thought ... 'game, set and match to the mother!'

Defeated, the pediatrician turned and stormed out of the room. The battle may have been won, but I knew that the next few seconds would truly decide our fate. If the rest of his team turned and joined him, then I was probably munted. Already way out of my depth, I knew that there was no way I could handle this on my own. But they didn't! Rudderless, they just looked at each other until the midwife shrugged her shoulders and defaulted to what they do best.

'Would ye mind if we have a wee look at the baby?' She had the broadest of Scottish accents. It was thick like honey, warm and hot chocolatey so that it melted my battle hardened heart and sweetened the bitterness that had just left the room. A nod from the Filipina nurse, that I could trust them to do the right thing, was all I needed to give up a little ground.

'Of course.' Any other hospital in the world would have had me sitting on my arse at the front entrance by now. (I doubt if any hospital in the world has a training manual that deals specifically with a father taking over their I.C.U.) I wasn't proud of this fact. It should have been a 'joint venture' between parent and professional, but the pediatrician had turned it into a pissing competition. Fortunately for us it was the weekend and their lack of staff made a counter assault nigh impossible.

'What is her name?' the midwife enquired as she and the nurses fussed around mother and child.

'Molly,' Darling smiled. (Luke had it been a boy)

'Mollee!' the Filipina nurse had trouble wrapping her tongue around it.

'Like Molly Brown, on the Titanic.'

'Unsinkable!' Jack and Poppit chimed.

That afternoon, I was summoned to a meeting in the hospital Director's office along with the obstetrician and the pediatrician. After the morning's debacle it was a request that I welcomed. I am not normally aggressive by nature, but instinct had gotten the better of me and having cooled off a little, I was anxious to restore some sort of normality to the situation.

The pediatrician however, wasn't having a bar of it. He was sullen and disinterested in any form of reconciliation other than his authority being completely restored. To my surprise the Director put a stop to his whingeing just as quickly as he had started.

Somewhere along the way it had been discovered that the obstetrician, who readily admitted to having panicked, had also failed to gain consent to perform an emergency c-section on Darling. She was sincere, apologetic, and to my further surprise admitted to being equally devastated by what had happened. Considering the circumstances, it could have been swept aside as a minor technicality, but in a court of law 'no consent' left the hospital with its pants down and ass exposed to the whooping of a lifetime.

I wasn't interested in litigation, nor anyone being brought to heel. Responsibility lay on both sides and I reassured the obstetrician, now in tears, that the only story Darling and I were interested in was one with a happy ending. At the same time though, I knew by the look on the Director's face that I had the moral high ground. That they were vulnerable to me changing my mind. So I proposed a deal.

'The midwife and nurses will look after Darling and Molly. You have my consent to oversee her care until discharge,' I said to the pediatrician. It was as much about *saving face* as anything. 'If her condition escalates (as he still professed to fear) then you have my permission to be the primary care provider, so long as we are engaged by *informed consent* every step of the way.'

The obstetrician and hospital were now off the hook. With the benefit of hindsight, I chose also, to accept the Director's generous offer of discount on our fee and as a gesture of good faith, I settled our account in cash there and then. The Director practically fell over himself to shake my hand and accepted the proposal unreservedly on behalf of the hospital. Under his watchful eye, the pediatrician had no choice but to reluctantly accept the agreement.

Deal done, I returned to Darling thinking that the remainder of our stay would be at the very least tolerable. What I hadn't banked on was the pediatrician's total lack of benevolence. The little prick turned out to be gargantuan in proportions and had every intention of interfering with anyone who tried to help when I wasn't around.

What he hadn't banked on though, was that the cavalry was just over the horizon!

13

'I must insist!'

'Angel ... help ... to come!' It was Scotty on his mobile phone
from the U.K. The connection was crap. I had to get him to repeat,
several times, but lost the signal in the end. Somewhere along the way,
I had managed to call family and friends overseas to tell them the
news.

'F%$k!'

'Hard luck mate!'

'God's a bastard!'

'You don't deserve it!'

Silence ... devastation ... tears ... pity ... followed by several
offers, heroes all, prepared to dash at a moment's notice into the fray.
But I declined. While battle weary, we had managed somehow to hold
the line. Now that I had a truce with the hospital the real pressure was
off. On top of this, several expat families whom we barely knew,
gladly extended their help without being asked. I felt that we had
enough support to get us through. Besides, it wasn't like we were just
down the road. For all intents and purposes we were on the far side of
the world.

'It's too big an ask!' I stated that evening when Scotty managed to
make a better connection.

'You are not asking. *I'm telling you!*' The line crackled with emotion. 'I have already dropped her to the airport. She will be there in the morning!'

Given the choice, I would still have said no. Had I fired off a flare or sent out a "Mayday" it might be different, but there is something about sailing around the world that makes you fiercely independent. We had weathered the storm and with the help of our newfound friends, I felt we could manage the situation. However, she was on her way, so I had to concede that for Darling's sake, it would be good.

Angel's arrival the following morning was a reminder of the truly special bond that we all shared and harked back to the days when I had subbed for Scotty in prenatal classes. Circumstances were different, the distance she had travelled was greater, but the spirit remained the same.

"All for one and one for all," I briefed her on what had happened on the drive to the hospital. There, an emotional reunion released a flood of tears (even the nurses cried) that washed away some of the terror that Darling had been through the day before.

A daughter of a New Zealand Army Medical Officer with three home births to her credit, Angel had no intention of taking prisoners when it came to looking after her best friend. Her name defied a toughness, the wrong side of which you did not want to get on. It didn't take her long to work out who was on our side and who wasn't.

We should all have been allowed to settle with a good night's sleep the previous night, but he had insisted on waking us every hour, on the hour, to "check up on baby." Because I had wound down, I had unwittingly put up with the disturbances as an overzealous attempt on his part to make amends. As a consequence, we were all shattered from sleep deprivation.

Fortunately, Angel could see through his machinations. 'The baby is fine!' she stated when he entered the birthing unit to perform another hourly check, just after we had arrived.

He ignored her.

'I think they could all just use a break now,' her suggestion still polite, but he continued with his routine.

'No, I must insist. We have an agreement,' he nodded in my direction, his hands clasped in prayer around his stethoscope, head slightly bent, obsequious to the point of being the faithful servant. *Nothing was too much trouble.*

'And I must insist that you fuck off and don't come back here until you are summoned!' she glared. The nurse in attendance had to turn and face the wall with a hand covered mouth to suppress her shocked laughter.

'Don't make me repeat myself!' Angel admonished and pointed to the door. He hesitated, looked to me for support, but when it wasn't forthcoming he realized he had no choice, but to depart the scene. 'When we want you we will send for you!' she called after him as he retreated. The likelihood would be never.

There is nothing more reassuring than having the backing of your best friends. Nothing more consoling than the shoulder of someone who helps to bear the weight of your pain. Within an hour, I too was sent packing to my own bed, secure in the knowledge that Darling was now safe from disturbance.

However, there are some things your best friends can't help you with. Some things you have to deal with on your own. When I arrived home, too wired for sleep, I faced a barrage of e-mails and phone messages of well-meaning condolences that echoed the war that was taking place between my heart and my head.

While the battle against the outer world of hospital Dictators and public opinion had largely been won … the inner battle was still raging. From her very first breath, my loyalties were torn between the part of us all that fights for the sacredness of life and all that is supposedly good, and the equally conflicting desire to euthanize that which is seemingly bad. In so doing, be freed to return to a perfect world. Just because you don't say it, doesn't mean you don't think it. Just because you deny it, doesn't mean that you are not sorely tempted. I recalled seeing programs on TV where the new born, unfit for "life as we know it" was nurtured to death without food or water. God forgive me, but my head was wrecked from these tantalizing choices that kept flashing through my own mind.

Can you imagine then, three days later, leaving the hospital? As I walked down the marble stepped entranceway I knew that if I dropped Molly on her head and she died, that no-one would mind. That no-one would give a damn. There would be no investigation. No inquiry. We would just get further condolences and 'hard luck mates' … 'but at least you can get on with your life.'

The hardest part though was having to tell Poppit and Jack who knew that something was wrong, but had yet to be confirmed. Fortified by Dutch courage, I sat them down on our first night home with the intent of breaking the news in some light that would give us all hope for the future, but I couldn't.

175

I'd had three days of continued sniping from the pediatrician. Three days of mental retardation, lifelong dependence, social isolation and future financial strain. Instead of talking, I started to cry. What should have been tears of joy were instead tears of shame and tears of pity, for the overwhelming challenges that life would place against her. How could something that I could practically hold in the palm of my hand be so monstrous?

'She's special Dad! Isn't she?' Poppit announced, looking to her brother who nodded in agreement.

'What did you say?' I was taken aback by her choice of words.

'She's special!' she repeated looking to me for reassurance that they had made the right guesstimation. It was the first time someone of significance in our life had used a word that described their new sister as anything other than a retard. My heart soared for the joy of it. My tears dried in an instant.

You might see now, that my obsession with having her breastfeed against medical advice, ran deeper than some naive desire to be a *new age* Dad. The truth is that I had needed a win. Some singular, solid, irrefutable proof that I could use to counter all of the evidence and prejudice that was being weighed against her. If she could breastfeed and *survive* then she might be capable of overcoming greater challenges later on. Who knows, one day she might go to school or maybe learn to drive a car. It was a stretch, I know, a clutching at straws, hoping against hope, but in that single moment of victory, my baby girl, like her brother and sister before her, hath climbeth the mountain (excuse the pun) and latched on for all that she was worth! And for that moment, and the one where her brother and sister chose to love her unconditionally, I was prepared to suffer the slings and arrows of all who were demented, and fight the good fight for her.

Little did I know that a war was beginning to brew that would test us all to the very core.

14

Busier than ever

Angel returned to the UK more determined than ever that they join us as soon as possible in the New Year. It had been a whirlwind trip, but her visit had also served somewhat to offset my concerns about our future working arrangements. On the one hand it was good news. In a world of isolation, their eventual return would mean instant family, best mates, business security, and eventual time off.

On the other, well, the timing was lousy. We had already been stressed to the max with the practice before Molly arrived. Coping now with the challenge of a special needs child created a whole new level of tension. Our isolation was further magnified by the fact that in an oil rich country, where his majesty could afford to have his own personal airline with two Jumbo jets at his disposal, there were no services whatsoever for children with Down Syndrome.

We should have been chilling out and spending time together as a family. We should have been processing our emotions and giving time and nature the opportunity to restore our lives and adjust to a new normal. Instead, I was now busy building the practice to dizzier heights to accommodate Scotty and family. During this time, Darling, still in recovery mode, was approached for advice by an Arabic family who also had a daughter with Down Syndrome. And then another. And then another, all thinking that being a doctor of some sort, she would know best how to raise a child with special needs. Other than a confidence born of adversity, we didn't have a clue, but it did not stop word from spreading that we were specialists in the field.

Busier than ever, our lives seemed to be measured by exhaustion, sleepless nights and the number of crises that we could fit in, in any single month. In our fridge there was a bottle of expensive French champagne. On my writing desk lay a Cuban cigar. Both untouched. Somewhere along the way the fun had gone out of life and instead of celebrating the arrival of our new child, we all marked time and lived for the day when Scotty and Angel arrived in late January and we could take a break.

With Darling out of the practice, Linda now became the glue that held it all together. Without any formal training, she rose to the occasion and became my trusted confidante who helped to keep me pointed in the right direction. At home, Violi fluffed about like a mother hen who cooked and cleaned and tucked everybody in and saw to it that we didn't starve.

Ten weeks, it felt like a life sentence, yet it was barely enough time to complete their visa applications (Inshallah!). On top of this I had to organize a separate visa for Darling's mum, who was anxious to visit for the Christmas holidays. Six separate applications, forty-two pages, each to be stamped by God only knew how many separate departments.

'Our PRO will organize everything!' Rashard declared but the unsuspecting bugger could not speak English, so it was left to me to fire his ass and complete the process myself.

By now, I was determined to beat the system and all of the players involved so that I would no longer be at their mercy. However, administration being my greatest weakness, I soon faltered and spiraled into a dark hole of bitterness and resentment as I found that all of my time, energy, joy, money (thousands) and sense of humor was being sucked dry by the bureaucratic process. With three weeks to Christmas I had already been kicked back twice on minor technicalities. I now faced the onerous task of telling Darling that, short of a miracle, there was no way I was going to have a visa for her mother to visit.

And then ... the Gods sent us their right hand man!

15

Abdullah

It was a Saturday, holy day in the Middle East. The one day when the entire country comes to rest. Me? I had been working since six that morning, processing F%$#%*g applications and howling like a wounded dog every time a call to prayer sounded from the local mosque down the road. My resentful, bitter and exhausted demeanor had reached a new low. The previous day an entire department at the Ministry of Labor had laughed out loud at my request that 'in light of my family situation,' they give my application special consideration and expedite the process. BA%$#&%DS!!

Frustrated and starving, I was just about to go home for lunch when a Baisa bus pulled into the driveway and discharged a lone Omani passenger. He was disheveled and dirty, but you could tell by his classic hunched posture that he was in a lot of pain as he limped towards the entranceway. Well … so was I. My mental anguish knew no bounds. After yesterday's berating at the Ministry, my sympathy for the local population was by now at rock bottom. I knew that if he arrived in a Baisa bus that I was unlikely to get paid for my care. Having already performed over thirty free spinal assessments that week, I was damned if I was going to answer his knock on the door!

The problem was his persistence. When no answer came he shuffled around to the window that looked into the waiting room and

179

knocked again. Then to the window on the other side that looked into the treatment room at the front of the building. All of this I coldly observed as I hid in the shadows of reception where he could not see me. Twice he did this, shuffling over and back, over and back, each step a torture in itself until finally, he came back to lean against the front door and knock in a slow repetitive pleading. His desperation greater than my resentment, he finally wore me down with his childlike whimpering. You have to be in a lot of pain to cry unobserved.

"A Salam Alaikum," I greeted on opening the front door.

'Docta! Plees. De pain. Eet is terrible. Plees help me?' he begged, massaging his neck. 'I piss my pants!' he pointed to a urine stain that had dried on the front of his dish dash. 'If you don't fix me then I have to go to de Eendia (India) for de surgery. Already my docta, he has made de plan.' There was no apology for disturbing me on my day off, nor was there any promise of compensation. While this was more a measure of the pain that consumed him, my feigned sympathy was motivated by only one thought. How quickly I could get rid of the bugger?

'Come,' I yielded, making a mental note that I would need a bucket of disinfectant to wipe down the treatment table. I led him slowly through the waiting area to the closest adjusting room. He was short in stature with a square head that sat on a thick neck connected to broad shoulders. His flat featureless face was covered in a five-day shadow that threatened to overpower his moustache. But it was his eyes that grabbed my attention. Despite his anguish, they were alert and darting. Like the forked tongue of a snake that tests the air, they absorbed every square inch of the room as he shuffled his way across the marble floor. My senses piqued as we passed the reception area. I found myself wondering if I had left anything of value in view that might be worth coming back later to steal.

'You will have to trust me!' I sat him down and began my assessment. Normally I would take a detailed case history and provide an explanation with each step of the examination, but his English and his anguish (and his body odor) were so bad that I decided to get it over with as quickly as possible.

It soon became apparent that his neck, while in severe spasm, was not the root cause of his problem. Further examination revealed a problem in his upper thoracic spine that was connected to significant dysfunction in his pelvis caused by a short leg syndrome. F*&^%$k! Getting rid of him wasn't going to be as straightforward as I had hoped.

180

'Okay, lie on your side … no, this one!' I tapped my right shoulder when I could see that he was confused. It took a good minute to work through the pain as we maneuvered him onto his side. 'Try to relax,' I gently modified his position. A loud crack echoed from his pelvis before I had a chance to adjust him.

'Wallah Docta, you break me!' he cried out. Just as quickly though, he relaxed. The terrible spasm that had wracked him for five days had virtually disappeared.

'Are you okay?' I was equally surprised.

'Okay, okay!' he nodded, panting in short breaths, his eyes whirling around in his head as he performed a systems check on every part of his body. When no pain was found, he exhaled a deep sigh of relief. 'Wallah Docta, you fix me!'

'No, there is work to be done, but it sounds like we might be off to a good start!' I smiled despite myself. There is nothing more satisfying than knowing that you have saved someone from the knife.

'No Docta, you fix me … reely, I have no pain!' he gestured with his hands as he sat up, but as quickly the pain began to return and he had to lie down again. Three gentle adjustments followed and then he was back on his feet, straighter and in reliably less discomfort.

'You will have to come back,' I stated, to temper his joy at immediate relief. 'Hopefully it will save you from having to go to India.'

'Inshallah!' he nodded.

'You make de visa, Docta?' His eyes scanned the reception area on our way to the front door. The entire reception, including the computer table and filing desk, was covered in stacks of neatly assembled pages that made up the application process for Scotty and family. Having run out of room, the table in my private office was entirely covered with similar (now defunct) application papers for my mother-in-law.

'I'm trying!' I said, bitter at the reminder, but surprised by his astute observation.

'You need help?' He stopped, keen to show his appreciation by being of some assistance. It was a genuine offer that served somewhat to console the fact that I wasn't being paid, but I dismissed him with a vague explanation that all was under control. I'd had enough disasters already without the likes of him throwing another spanner in the works.

That afternoon he returned upright and clean shaven. His hair was oiled back and he wore a brand new dish dash and highly polished sandals. His transport this time was a Toyota Echo, (the smallest of the Toyota range) driven by a friend who remained in the car.

'Wallah Docta, I am so happy!' he grasped my hand with both of his. 'You save me go to de Eendia. Ten weeks de surgeon tell me. Ten weeks you save me!' he was giddy like a child as we began his second treatment.

I was in a better mood for his improvement and less disheveled state and adjusted him within a matter of minutes. 'Ah, you finish de visa!' he stated in a celebratory tone as we passed reception. The area was now cleared of all paperwork.

'No, not yet.' I pointed to six chairs in the waiting room to which I had transferred the applications. I'd put in another three hours of work that afternoon only to discover that I had taken another step backwards by missing a vital signature required from some obscure department or other.

'Plees Docta, it not a problem. I help you wid dis!' he pleaded. My desperation and his transformation was such that I was sorely tempted, but I still demurred based on my stubborn notion that I would somehow beat the system.

When he arrived for treatment the following morning at nine o'clock I was already in a sweat. Both waiting rooms were full and the phone was going crazy with bookings from a radio show that we had done the previous week. On top of this, the Ministry of Health had just called to announce that they would be there at twelve o' clock precisely (Inshallah) to do an inspection as part of my application for Scotty. To keep up with the pace, Linda directed patients through three separate treatment rooms, one of which was my private office at the back of the villa. There, I found Abdullah and another man shuffling through and rearranging the visa applications!

'Dis is my driva, Hilal,' he nodded out the window to a brand new Toyota Rav in the car park.

'What do you think you are doing?!' I was mortified as I watched him change the sequence of the application to God knows what. Had it not been for a waiting room full of patients I would have marched them both out of the clinic and told them where to shove it.

'Please Docta, you take away my pain. Let me help you!' he pleaded.

'He can help you!' his driver chimed in. 'You must trust him!'

'Yes!' Abdullah resounded. 'I trust you … no? To help me … yes! Now you must trust me!'

I was stunned that he would use my own words against me, but then suddenly, I had a brainwave. I picked up the defunct visa application for my mother in law and handed it to him.

'Wat's dis?'

'It's for my wife's mother. I want her to come for Christmas. Can you make the visa?' I knew from my recent experience that he couldn't, but figured it would shut him up and allow me to get on with my business.

'Ah Docta, Christmas, it only three weeks away!'

'I know!' I smiled triumphantly. It was nice to be sticking it to one of the locals in the way that they had been sticking it to me.

'Dis is it. Dis all you want?' he nodded to the mound of paperwork that I had snatched off his driver.

'If you get this for me, then I will give you this job to do.' To save face, I expected them to walk out the door and never be seen again.

Abdullah shrugged his shoulders. He turned to his driver and they proceeded to "tut tut" as they tore page after page from the sheaf until there was only one left with a photo of my mother in law stapled to it. He removed the photo, placed in his pocket and then balled up the application and threw it in the bin.

'You want make me look like stupid, eh?' he nodded to his driver and they left the room.

'Up yours too!' I thought, glad to be rid of the both of them.

Later that evening I sipped a large consolation rum on the back doorstep of our home as Darling and I swopped notes on our day. Hers good. Mine crap and about to get worse with the announcement that her mother's visa was dead in the waste bucket in the practice. I was just waiting for the rum to kick in before I ruined her Christmas.

'Dad, there is someone at the front door!' Poppit called from the kitchen. 'He says that his name is Abdullah.'

"*A Salam Alaikum,* Docta, sorry to disturb you,' he apologized sensing my surprise. I had not given him our address. 'Madam!' he bowed tipping his official headdress when Darling stepped from behind, curious to see who was calling. Parked in our driveway was a brand new Lexus with his friend Hilal standing beside the driver's door.

'He my driva,' Abdullah explained to Darling. 'I bring you de visa for your mother!' Ignoring me completely, he leaned forward and handed a piece of A4 paper to Darling. It had official writing and a photocopy of her mother's picture in the top right corner.

'But?!?!?!!!!!'

'You didn't tell me we have a new PRO!' Darling was delighted that her mother's visit was now confirmed in time for Christmas.

'But?!?!?!!!!!'

'I am not PRO,' Abdullah replied.

'But?!?!?!!!!!'

'But I have PRO company,' Abdullah smiled.

'F&*$#%$#K!!!!'

16

'The Ego hath landed'

Embarrassed for having thought of him so badly, it was the glass of rum I still held in my hand that saved my butt.

'Do you like rum Abdullah?' I rattled the ice in my glass, knowing that he could probably smell it from where he was standing.

'Docta, I am Muslim!'

'I know, but it's twenty-year-old Mount Gay, with chilled Schweppes Tonic and a splash of freshly squeezed orange juice,' I teased. It was thirty degrees in the shade.

'You must come in Abdullah, please. I will make you some coffee instead to celebrate the visa,' Darling intervened.

'No, no Madam, it not necessary. I just make de visa for you to say thank you for your husband,' but his eyes did not leave my glass.

'Yes, yes, you and your friend are our guest. Come in out of the heat and meet our children!' Before he could object any further she took him by the hand and led him into the guest lounge of our house.

To overcome my discomfiture, I mixed three large rums while Darling made coffee, three more after we had finished the coffee and three more which finished the bottle. It was enough to loosen our tongues and with that we told each other our stories.

Abdullah Saif Saleem Al Kiyumi hailed from the small village of Wadi Al Kabir, a genuine oasis, two hours into the desert. He owned a Toyota Echo, a Toyota Rav, a top of the range Lexus, a top of the range Mercedes saloon, a Mercedes Convertible and a Range Rover. How could he afford this? Well, he also owned a PRO company that employed anything from five to fifteen PRO's. Why? Because he had the agency for producing GAP fashion wear for the US market and needed more than one PRO to look after his eleven hundred employees!

So what was he doing in the Baisa bus? Well, he also had six children and a "good wife" who threw him out of their house on occasion when he came home drunk and called her Milanna, the name of his Russian girlfriend! He had no formal education and could barely write his name, but he was a *Master Connector*. A fixer and procurer of all things legal and otherwise that endeared him to every level of society from Prince to pauper, Government Minister to vagabond and many of the nefarious swindlers you meet in disguise in between. Just the sort of guy you want on your side when you want to get things done!

'Please Docta, let me make de visas for you. It like you crack my neck. For me it is easy,' he tossed his hands in the air like a magician. He was also a master charmer. By the end of the night, there was something endearing about this lovable rogue that finally made me trust him.

Two weeks and a shitload of money later (I could have bought a new car!) Scotty and family were signed off and legal to enter! Every signature came with an official receipt. Every visa came with a subtotal of itemized costs on his company headed paper that was written off as a genuine business expense. Had Abdullah thrown in a fee for his personal assistance, I probably would have had to sell one of our children, but he didn't. Instead, he called me "brother," introduced us to his family and appointed himself as our personal PRO who, from that day forward, was never more than an hour away.

Christmas came and went, but was mostly a non-event. We were all just too exhausted and emotionally washed out to make the effort. As a last resort Darling's mother threw the turkey and ham into the freezer and dragged our sorry asses down to a local hotel to make the best she could of it for the kids. It was a valiant effort made all the more meaningful by having Supermamma (Nana) to share it with, but within a week her presence was just a memory.

186

Finally, following several weeks of further delays, Scotty and family touched down to a great fanfare of laughter and tears as we made fools of ourselves and each other in the arrivals terminal. Finally, we could drop our guard and think that we were no longer vulnerable. Finally I could allow myself the luxury of a day off, to get back to play, to reconnect with the aliveness and the vitality of imagination that our adventure used to afford us. To return, hopefully, to a space where a man could dream of the future instead of always fighting a rear guard action. As we walked to the car with Scotty on one side and Abdullah on the other, I began to think that the days of being worried, anxious, insecure and vulnerable were over.

However, it was a sideward glance from Scotty, a drawing back of the curtain that hides the window of truth to the machinations of the mind that hinted differently.

There and then I should have called a halt, nipped it in the bud, and stamped on its carcass. I should have admitted our mistake and taken the blame (that would come later). Wined and dined and thanked them for visiting, then just as quickly, sent them home. But I didn't. I was too set on future plans. Too determined to make the impossible come true, but that split second had been long enough for me to realize that the *Ego hath landed!*

17

'Chick Ching'

'You need another drink!' Darling motioned to the air hostess who was busy serving beverages.

'Yeah Dad, take a chill pill!' Poppit and Jack laughed as they scrolled through the video screens on the seats in front of them. 'We are supposed to be on our holidays!'

They were right, but, but I was finding it impossible to wind down with all of the alarm bells that were going off in my head. The three weeks before our departure to South Africa should have been fun while Scotty made the transition into practice. Instead, they had quickly turned sour as the mood of relief swung to one of unexpected resentment.

'Everybody is just trying too hard!' Darling had appeased at the end of the first week when we found ourselves having to remind each other that it was *they*, uncalled, who had come to support us in our hour of need. That Angel had made a difference in the few days that she had been with us. We had been looking forward to their company and rolled out the red carpet on their arrival, but there is a big difference between being grateful and being made to feel beholden.

'You are just tired,' Darling empathized at the end of the second week. By now the subtle cues had become so amplified that I had begun to lose sleep. I was aware that I was worn out. That Scotty was fully charged and *probably* just trying to make his mark, but my best friend just wasn't acting like the guy that we had remembered. There was a hardness to him that comes from too much time spent at the coal face. A bitterness from too many disappointments. In particular, I did not like how he referred to the adjusting rooms as a "rotary milking shed" and kept making the sound of money "chick ching" every time we started a new patient.

Outside the practice we had problems with some of his attitudes towards the Asian and Indian population. On one occasion I had to phone a graphic designer friend to apologize for Scotty's condescending behavior.

The more slack I cut, the more I felt that I too was being condescended to. It was like this thick Paddy was good enough for digging trenches and laying foundations, but when it came to the business of "building" a practice, I was expected to stand aside and watch him weave his magic.

The third week almost ended it completely when we found out that the $10,000 that we understood to be part of our agreement would not be forthcoming. We had been relying on the money to replace a significant part of our hard-earned reserves that had been burnt up (again) in processing their visas. These included some very costly extras that Scotty "had to have" for practice.

'You are being over-reactive!' Scotty brushed my concerns aside when I tried to take him to task on the matter. 'In a couple of months we will be making so much money that you will look back and laugh as well. Seriously man, you need to take a holiday!' He was in breach of our contract and offered no promise of compensation in the future. I was fobbed off instead with a horse's ass excuse, literally, about the money being "tied up" in some lame nag that his ex-business partner was trying to sell in the U.K.

Too late to cancel, we boarded the plane with a reassurance from our trusted PA Linda that she would contact us if there were any problems. All that I could do, as I nodded off to the effects of my second wine, was hope that Scotty was true to his word and that I did not have to fly home early.

We were greeted at Cape Town airport by our good friends from Iowa who had returned to South Africa to live. Knowing the year that we had been through, they showed us a glorious time that allowed us all to recharge our batteries and reconnect as a family. Surrounded by the remnants of Colonialism and apartheid, it was also a great perspective for the kids to see how lucky we were to be living the life that we had chosen in Oman *and* the life that had chosen us!

Slowly but surely we were also discovering that the arrival of a child with Down Syndrome was not the end of our adventure, but rather the beginning of a new one. That we had been blessed rather than cursed, given a gift rather than a burden. That the silver lining contained within our 'perceived' misfortune shone with the twinkling of a star that was really a diamond in disguise and our lives were far richer for the experience.

An example of this was the Early Intervention Group that Darling had started by default only a few weeks after Molly was born. Within a few short months it had grown to fifteen families, all Omani, who considered Darling 'the expert' and looked to her for leadership. She was no more expert than the woman on the moon, but what qualified her more perhaps were her outspoken views against any excuse that demeaned the life of a child with Down Syndrome or any child with different abilities for that matter. In a Police state dominated by religion and testosterone, she could have easily been silenced, but hers was recognized as a voice for the 'greater good' and embraced by the community and the media alike.

In this short time, doors began to open into a world seldom shared with expatriates. We experienced an outpouring of gratitude on a weekly basis that was more 'soul-filling' than any profit we might ever hope to make in our practice. We were no longer strangers in a foreign land, but felt rather like a missing piece of a jigsaw that had been found and embraced by all of the other pieces to make them whole. Having a child with Down Syndrome in their lives may have led to being lost, misguided, confused or just plain out of their depth, but not one family in the group felt in any way cursed or a had a sense of the tragic about them. We were, all of us, amazed by the children that we had been gifted. Like any so called "normal child" they farted and pooped, cried and slept, and for the most part stole the heart of anyone who held them for more than ten seconds! Regardless of the added work, the Group was something we all looked forward to, in particular the fathers, who doted on their sons and daughters and celebrated the reaching of every developmental milestone as if it were Olympian in proportions.

Darling as a consequence may have been tired, but she was inspired. It wasn't long into our break that she showed the best signs of recovery when she began to wake most days with at least one idea that would better serve the Group.

For my part, I measured it by the fact that my '*Muse*,' had started whispering to me again and gifted me several new scenes for 'The Christening' that I could use in the next redraft. By the end of the second week I began to admit that I had probably been overly sensitive from too much time spent in the trenches. This notion was reinforced by an upbeat e-mail from Linda announcing that all was okay. That Scotty, as hoped, was weaving his magic and patient numbers were on the increase!

I was very proud of the fact that despite all of our trials and tribulation, the practice had turned profitable before his arrival. The additional growth now meant that whatever future financial challenges we faced, we would likely surmount them.

The hard work had been done. What mattered most was that we were all together on this adventure. All we had to do was bide our time, let the practice grow and have fun and enjoy the journey.

However, it was the most bizarre of coincidences, and I mean *the most bizarre* of coincidences ... on the last night of our holiday, that connected us to the final character in our story.

Book Four

1

'H%o#y S&%t!

We were sitting in a restaurant with our friends having a good old time, reminiscing about our great holiday and how far we had all come since graduating. We were halfway through telling them about our plans for Oman when I locked eyes with a guy making his way across the dining room towards us.

'Am I right in saying that you are a Chiropractor?' He stopped at the head of our table.

'We all are!' we announced in unison, wondering at how he knew.

'I'm Anthony,' He had a Canadian accent and pointed at Christo's shirt. 'It was the Chiropractic logo on your tee-shirt that caught my eye.' The logo in question was no bigger than a twenty cent piece. 'I've been practicing in Zimbabwe for the last twenty years.'

If we were impressed at how he had spotted the logo from the far side of the room, then we were even more impressed at his purpose for being in Cape Town.

'I've just finished running an ultra-marathon.' (90 kms!) That sort of introduction is enough to kick off any conversation and with it, we shared our stories. His was one of a whirlwind three day visit to compete in the race before returning the next day to Harare. It was only by chance and a last minute change of plans that he had come to our restaurant.

'Did you say Oman?' he quizzed when we had told him of our adventure to date. 'I've been corresponding with a Chiropractor in Muscat who has just opened the first Chiropractic center there!'

'H%#y S&%t!

Of all the Chiropractors in the entire universe, we marveled at the fact that it was Anthony whom we had short listed to work with us before Scotty and Angel had decided to join us instead.

Our conversation was cut short when he was summoned back for the main course with the rest of his group, but I promised to keep in touch. Sooner or later, we were going to need another doctor.

2

I was fit to burst

It's remarkable the difference a few weeks of rest can make to your attitude and enthusiasm. Our energy now restored, we landed in Muscat ready to give it one hundred and ten percent alongside of our best friends. Before our return, we had been further buoyed by another e-mail that announcing that "business was now up by twenty percent" Go Scotty!! This was a tremendous relief and sufficient to put the tensions of the first few weeks down to both sides being overanxious. He had pulled it off and I was excited again about pushing the envelope to the next level.

It was a different game now. We had dragged ourselves over the physical, mental, emotional and financial hump that every business has to scale in order to get started. We had defeated resistance and built up the necessary momentum essential to reach the rarified airs where opportunity awaits. It was exciting and far less daunting now that I had Scotty as my wingman.

We were welcomed to a spotless house, delicious meal (good old Violi!) and several bunches of fresh flowers from Angel as a homecoming present. On the coffee table in the lounge were several brochures for 4 wheel drives, itemized, dissected and highlighted. A big red grunty Dodge Durango sat on top as the obvious favorite and Scotty talked animatedly about the 'crazy' test drive they had already been taken on. The size of the dunes, the depth of the valleys, horsepower that would pull the hind end off of an elephant. It was just a matter of organizing the finance. I promised to look into that the week coming.

We made a point of staying away from the practice for the weekend. To bask in the afterglow of our holiday and Scotty's mutual success, we took Edvina down the coast, caught some tuna and celebrated over a barbeque and a Sangria-poached sunset.

My renewed goodwill however began to be tested on our first day back in practice. Scotty was now six weeks on the ground. When he took me through the appointment book on the Monday morning I found that the patient visits had actually grown by twenty-four percent. However, because our unique monthly fee structure covered an unlimited number of visits, the income remained the same.

I was in too good a mood after our holiday to be particularly concerned. I had expected the numbers to drop while I was away. The fact that we were still in profit was an achievement in itself. What I hadn't expected was for Scotty to lay claim to a greater share of the profit as a consequence of his "increased service." Nor had I expected him to become belligerent when I pointed out the fact that he hadn't actually contributed to the bottom line.

'If we were charging a fee per visit we'd be making a killing now!' His mood was accusatory, as if he was being short-changed. Suddenly there was blame in the room and I found myself having to back off, lest he try to lay it at my feet.

To prevent an argument over "who said what" I printed off four 'sent files' from our Hotmail account that specifically spelt out the philosophy of the practice, our working agreement and profit sharing from day one. They amounted to almost twenty printed pages, some of it rambling, all inviting an opinion, but none of which he had responded to, other than to proffer an excuse that his computer was on the glitch. It had annoyed me at the time. They had taken a lot of effort to construct. In particular, two whole pages were devoted to the reasoning behind how our unique fee structure had evolved. I was even more annoyed because their purpose had been in anticipation of circumventing this kind of situation.

He was visibly taken aback, as if it was the first time he had seen the e-mails. More so because they negated his argument.

'I want to introduce a fee per visit with my patients. It's the way I have always worked. How else can you expect us to make any money?!'

'The fee is not based per visit, but rather on a per case basis.' I pointed to the relevant pages. 'It's a win-win!' I tried to counter his pessimism. 'The more people we introduce to care, the more we are rewarded. As the word spreads the practice grows!' I was unwilling to yield to the word "*My*" or change our fee. Both were divisive and a recipe for contention. There is a big difference between *inspiring* your patients to lift their game and spend a bit more on a monthly fee for the sake of their health, and charging like a rhino for the sake of your own wallet.

He wasn't impressed.

Neither was I, but I was determined to keep us on an even keel.

'Come on Scotty! We are in this for the long haul. You are living with us expenses free. Your share of the profit is easily covering your costs and you are making money in the U.K. Give it a few months and the practice growth will take care of it!' We had been on the ground long enough for me to be confident of where we were going. Having overcome the bureaucracy, the Omani people had turned out to be the most gracious, gregarious and considerate of all the people we had treated around the world. They made for wonderful patients who were proactive and appreciative of our specialty and happy to refer their family and friends for treatment. On top of this, and after considerable negotiation, L&G, (responsible for developing oil resources in Oman) had just come on board and given us full scholarships to train two doctors in the New Zealand College of Chiropractic.

'You can take care of that!' was Scotty's answer to my enthusiasm. He was even more ambivalent to the Early Intervention Group who he saw as a drain on our resources.

Scotty and Angel had been spending up large since the day they had arrived, staying in flash hotels on the weekends and buying all sorts of mementos and souvenirs from the souk (market) like clay pots, traditional Omani rugs and antiques.

On the seventh week he approached me again about the Durango. 'I've been shopping around and found the one that I want!' (Fully loaded) 'It's a steal!' he bragged about the price that he had negotiated a price for a brand new vehicle. All we had to do was get the practice to finance it!

The alarm bells were now clanging off of their rockers. As the owner of the business, Rashard would have to sign for the Durango. Based on Scotty's lackluster performance I couldn't justify it. When I suggested that I could get them a fully loaded Isuzu Trooper (similar to our own vehicle) for half the price, a single glance between Scotty and Angel let me know that "it would just not be big enough!"

By the end of the eight week Angel let slip that the cash flow that they had been relying upon from their clinics in the U.K. had just about dried up. Their associate doctors had not only dropped the ball, but were chewing up the cash reserves that they had left to cover costs. As a result, other than the income he was making from our center, they had no money. None, nada , not a sausage! To further thwart him, our steady growth curve had leveled off during this time!

I knew the Gods well enough that they were just messing with our heads. That it had been the nature of the beast all along to go through fits and starts and then settle before jumping to the next level. For Scotty though, the financial constraint was like being shackled into a strait jacket. His blame became international and knew no bounds. His associates "lacked the drive, the oomph, the killer instinct They didn't have the spine!" There was a subtle innuendo loaded between the lines that also pointed my direction.

Twice over the ninth week he tried to get me to change our fee structure. I refused. It was an act of desperation whose short term gain would have resulted in long term negative consequences for the practice. We were a health center, not a bank and I wasn't going to let him overextend us to prop up his practice in the UK which by now had become a major distraction in our lives.

By the tenth week, when he finally realized that I wasn't going to yield on the fee, he surprised me by resorting to a different strategy

'What if I pay you half of the set up costs?

'Come again?' We were sitting opposite each other in the waiting room. He'd just made us coffee. It was the first time in days that he had been in a good mood.

'If I give you half of the set up costs, then we could split the income.' He spelt it out slowly, like he was doing me some kind of favor. A very conservative estimate would knock him back thirty seven thousand dollars. That didn't include the original ten that he had already defaulted on.

'But you said that you didn't have any money.'

'I know, but what if I came up with it?' he gestured with his hands, like pulling a rabbit from a hat.

'But ... you ... haven't ... got ... any ... money!' I spelt back slowly, letting him know that I wasn't buying it. Up to that moment we had given him the benefit of the doubt, made allowances for his behavior and put it down to stress, but now I was pissed. We had put everything we had on the line to make the practice a success. I had burned the midnight oil and sent long e-mails outlining our vision and identifying the challenges and pitfalls. Time and again I had encouraged him to visit, but he'd declined. Not only had we overcome our own challenges, but when we should have been enjoying our success, we had chosen to dig deeper, beyond the depths of self-preservation, to make it a place for two families to share the adventure. I had worked thousands of unpaid hours to get the clinic started, (900 free spinal exams in six months) endured sleepless nights, endless fights with bureaucracy, living on the edge financially and never missed a day, even when Molly was born. His offer in short was an insult. Not only had he totally underestimated the level of commitment necessary to make a life in Oman, but that they had totally overestimated their role in our relationship. We weren't the ones who needed rescuing.

'Didn't you read the e-mails I printed off two weeks ago?' I had to go and retrieve them from my desk. 'Look at this!' I shuffled through the pages until I found the one that explained ownership of the clinic. 'It's Rashard's. All of it. No expatriates are allowed to own property or any form of business in this country! I can't sell you what I don't own!' This single fact put paid to any ideas he might have for buying his way out of trouble.

'What about all of the money you guys put into it? Doesn't that make you a fifty percent shareholder?' He was indignant.

'No! It opens the door to opportunity. Same as the Key Money,' I reminded, turning over the pages once more till I found the one that dealt with the matter. "All going well, what we make in the future will justify the expenditure," I quoted word for word, then handed him the page, 'it's the fourth line from the bottom,' I pointed to the sentence.

My attitude would have been different if they had *bought in* and made the commitment from the very beginning. We could have used their contribution as a contingency to help them, but we were now overextended (again) and I wasn't prepared to go any further out on a limb. It was true that a large wad of cash would solve part of the problem, but the reality of his offer meant that we would only be buying into their problems.

By this stage I was pissed off, brassed off, F#$@*d off and exasperated. There is a very fine line between bravado and idiocy and I for one was tired of walking it. For too long we had already trodden the financial tightrope to get the practice established on a solid footing.

We were not about to be dragged out on the wire again. At least not under these circumstances.

The only thing that was holding it all together by this stage was our history. We were best friends, 'cousie bros' and godparents to each other's children. There was no denying that they were in the shit, but the reality was that we were all in this together. As bad as it was, it would be a disaster if we were to let it fall apart. They would have to uproot their kids *again* and relocate back to the U.K. (a major ordeal at the best of times) Not to mention that all of the hard work, sacrifice and expense that we had gone to would end up being for nothing.

Darling and I were still motivated in making the partnership a success, but a decision had to be made. A decision that harked back to our agreement the previous year and pre-empted this dilemma. Drop the U.K. and commit all resources and all efforts one hundred percent to Oman as we had done, or … drop Oman. Scotty's answer then had been clear and implicit that they would "drop the UK" but caught in the grim headlights of reality, he was now torn and indecisive.

A decision delayed is a decision made and while we waited for their container of household effects to arrive, I prodded and probed, encouraged and cajoled him on a daily basis for some sort of clue. The longer he deferred, the greater the tension. As we held our collective breaths, our home life reached the point where Poppit and Jack had nicknamed him the "Angry Man" behind his back after he'd read them the riot act over some minor misdemeanor committed while playing with their children.

Finally, the inevitable happened and it all came to a head in the practice after another frustrating day of distraction, when I found out that their container had never been sent in the first place.

'Why?' I was fit to burst. 'You were supposed to have sent it while you were on holiday in New Zealand!'

'Because I'm not doing this shit, that's why!' He turned in the confines of the reception and, facing off, he pointed his index finger at my chest. 'I'm … (poke) … not … (poke) …working … (poke) … for … (big poke) … nothing!' (shove) he spat. I could smell the bitterness in his breath.

My first reaction was to use my forehead to knock some sense into his head. To let him know how tired I was of his shit, but I have never read any management books that advocated violence as a solution to a dispute. Anyway, he stormed out of reception and headed for the main door.

'What about the Durango?' When I put the idea of financing it through the practice on hold, he decided that he would take matters into his own hands. Within a week he had whipped every dealership in Muscat into a frenzy for his business, but one by one they fell by the wayside when he could not provide a guarantor. Still he persisted.

'What happens if you decide to go back to the U.K.?

'I'll park it at the airport on the way out!'

That was the last straw.

3

'Don't let an argument ruin a great friendship.'

Darling phoned ten minutes later to find out what was going on. In the background I could hear Scotty and Angel locked in a heated argument. There was no way I could go home. I needed to cool off, to sort out what to do next. I never imagined that it would come to this.

Seeking solace, I went down to walk by the sea, but ended up kicking my own ass from one end of the beach to the other in frustration.

'I shoulda made him reply in writing to every e-mail I'd sent!'

'I shoulda made him visit in advance!'

'I shoulda made him sign a contract under legal supervision before they had stepped foot in the country!'

'I shoulda insisted he front up with the key money before their arrival!'

'I shoulda knocked his ego on the head the very first day, before it had a chance to ruin everything'.

'I shoulda listened to the voice that had warned me from the very beginning' ... "don't, don't, don't!"

'I shoulda, I shoulda, I shoulda!'

'F$#K! ... F$#K! ... 'F$#K ...!!!!!'

From the very start we had been upfront and worn our hearts on our sleeve and done everything we could do to prepare them for Oman. In hindsight, I now think that he had never committed, but taken us for a ride instead with no real intention of paying for the ticket. That he wore his heart in a holster, but had ended up shooting himself in the foot.

I could have saved the day and made it easy for them. I could have rowed the boat out and gone another six more months without drawing any profit in order to subsidize their folly, but I couldn't.

By the third lap of the beach I arrived at the conclusion that they had come to the Middle East for all of the wrong reasons. That in their hearts they were mercenaries, not missionaries and were more interested in "taking" profit than making it.

By the fourth lap I was battered and bruised from shoulda'ng all over myself. All that remained was sadness. He was supposed to be my best friend. My bruvver from another muvver, but this wasn't how best friends treated each other. We were all at fault. We had all gotten it wrong (horribly) but instead of manning up and admitting the role he had played, he was acting like a bollix.

Signature or no signature, parking the Durango at the airport would have serious repercussions for the practice and in particular Rashard. Word would be spread, our names would appear on a "black list" connected to bad debtors and it would make finance for future developments very difficult, if not impossible. Not to mention the adverse effect it would have on my partnership with Rashard. What saddened me the most was that parking the Durango at the airport wasn't just irresponsible, it was premeditated. Scotty had clearly been on the ground long enough to know how deep the shit he'd be getting us into.

As I write this now I feel like a f*&%$#g Ejit. "Vigilance … vigilance!" I can hear Captain Keith implore. It was my own fault for being suckered in the first place.

"Don't let an argument ruin a great friendship," kept ringing in my head. I knew from this moment that there was no way forward. That our adventure together was over and possibly our friendship along with it. I was tired of the battle of egos. Tired of the pissing contest that had become a distraction from the mission of the practice. I was fed up with his unwillingness to cooperate and his constant undermining of my hard earned experience. The only real effort he had made in the last three weeks or so was to make me look like an idiot in front of our patients and staff. The irony was that he was right! Only an idiot would have put up with a complete lack of fair exchange that he had demonstrated from the very beginning.

The question now was how to put an end to it without a major fall out taking place?

It wasn't just me and Scotty. Darling and Angel and the kids were involved. How could we handle it without it leading to permanent acrimony?

I didn't have the answer, but after another two laps of the beach I finally came to the conclusion that we had two choices at our disposal. End it well, or end it badly. Given the choice, I knew the one Darling and I would make, but the reality was that it was now out of our hands.

If Scotty chose to end it well, then I decided that I would continue to swallow my pride for the few short weeks it would take them to transition back to the U.K. (and hope that time would heal and we could reconcile our differences in the future). If he chose the latter, I would end it there and then. Give him a rocket for all the stress that they had caused us and demand that they leave our home and stay somewhere else until they left Oman. If he wanted to turn it into a poking match then that was okay. He could go ahead and make my day. I was well and truly ready for him!

With this in mind, I headed for home, safety catches off, locked and loaded, my heart pumping a thousand beats per minute. Based on Scotty's recent behavior I held little hope that he would find in our favor. Either way I was determined to end it.

4

'It's important to tell the truth!'

By the time I reached home I had changed to a less confrontational strategy and come up with a speech to support it. There would be no *blame*. Frustration maybe, with a few expletives aimed at how their associates had let them down. I would talk about the unfairness of it all after such hard work and high hopes. That it was an untimely and sad ending, but that a decision had to be made. We all needed to move on, that sort of thing. The *best* would be wished for *everyone*. Anything I could find to deflect responsibility and focus our bile elsewhere.

At the same time though I would keep my fists in my pocket or behind my back, whichever made me the least vulnerable. I'd already worked out (from a Jack Higgins novel) how I would sort him out if the need arose. On a scale of one to ten, I was four parts scared, four parts ready to "take him down" and the rest was close to tears. The sooner I got it over with the better.

My heart sank though when I found the house empty save for Violi working in the kitchen.

'She has gone to the beach. She is very sad!' Violi lamented when I called out Darling's name. 'Scotty and Angel, they have a beeg fight. Now dey are going to go back to de U.K!' Her tone was a little less

206

disappointed, she had already hinted a couple of times that she too had had enough.

'Really?

'Really! Dey have gone to the travel agent now to make de ticket. I tink they will leave very soon!'

Just like that. It was over. The decision it seemed had been made, but more importantly, they had made it for themselves.

There was an end in sight now that didn't require the spewing of guts or the breaking of each other's hearts.

Darling returned, subdued and disappointed. I didn't tell her about the poking incident or the Durango. I boiled the kettle instead and made some Dilmah which we shared on the front porch.

Scotty and Angel arrived shortly after and announced their decision.

'It's for the better,' Scotty saved me from making my speech by laying the blame squarely on the shoulders of his associates. Two weeks (fourteen days ... three hundred and thirty six hours ... one million, two hundred and nine thousand, six hundred seconds) and they would be gone.

End it well or end it badly, the whole thing sucked. I didn't know if I could be nice for that long.

The upside of them continuing to live with us was that everyone was obliged to get on well. We shared meals, went to the beach with the kids, watched DVD's and pretended to make each day count as the clock ticked down to the inevitable.

The downside was having to ignore the elephant that stomped around our house with blame written all over its backside. With the benefit of hindsight, it would have been better to have a shoot-out, bring it to the ground and kill the bastard. The problem was that in ending it well, I had come off a war footing and dedicated myself to good behavior and being as supportive as I could while they made their shitty transition.

Every day I felt sorry for them. Every day, as I watched the kids fawn over Molly and thought about *what could have been,* the pangs of regret would get so strong, that in spite of the Durango I'd start thinking about throwing together some sort of rescue package. The Gods though would intervene with the truth.

'Ah, Docta Scotty, why you leaving?' Abdullah questioned, disappointed when he heard the news. There was a ton of paperwork connected to their departure that had to be processed.

'Because the practice is not big enough to support two families!' It was in total contradiction to what we had already agreed - that they were returning to the U.K. because of their associates.

Darling and I were sworn to this "fact." If it all turned nasty and their associates took them to court, they had to make it look like the associates had failed to live up to the terms of their contract. It was ironic that he was accusing them of the selfsame crime of which he was guilty.

'I thought we agreed that you were going back because of your associates?' I questioned, taking him to task after Abdullah departed.

'It's important to tell the truth!' Scotty replied smugly.

I'd had enough shoulda's to contend with at that stage without having to add another one that covered smacking him! The second time he told his lie I just gritted my teeth. One million, one hundred and twenty three thousand, two hundred seconds and they would be gone!

I'm not going to say that it got easier after that, but the bigger the elephant got, the more I disowned any sense of impending loss that might be connected to their departure. When the moment finally arrived we were glad of it. We spent the day skirting each other and pretending to be busy, I with the practice, Scotty with suitcases and the one hundred kilos of souvenirs that they had bought in their ten short week stay that had felt like forever. I arranged transport so there would be no prolonged or agonizing farewells at the airport.

The final moment arrived where Scotty and I had to face off and say our farewells. We had done this many times over the years when we had separated for far sides of the world. Passionate, raw, unabashed, man love. The same again when reunited. This time it was different.

This would probably be the last time and we both knew it. If ever there was a moment a person might want to show how they felt in their heart, this was the moment. "End it well, end it well," I kept telling myself as we embraced, rough, tough, unyielding. More like a clinch, it was the sort of hug that could just as easily have ended in a wrestling match, but it didn't. We held on for all we were worth, heart to heart, cheek to cheek, till the tears we shared felt like they might wash away the madness that had prevailed.

In that moment I felt forgiveness. A window opened, my hope rekindled and I experienced the possibility of a new beginning sometime in the future. Then he kissed me, on the cheek, bristle on bristle like oft times before, but it was different.

I'm not a religious person, but it felt like I'd been kissed by the devil!

5

Doctor "Z"

Sail around the world, write a book that helps people, make a movie. I had forgotten. We had been so caught up in the drama that was Scotty and Angel, that I had hardly put pen to paper. Immediately after their departure I felt this incredible compulsion to cleanse myself. To shower, shave, shower and shave again, especially the part of my cheek that he had kissed, as if to stop some debilitating or *deadly* virus from taking root.

'Is it just me or do you feel like you can breathe again?' I asked Darling the following morning when we woke up. It was the first time in weeks that I was actually excited about going to the practice.

'It's a beautiful day!' Violi greeted us with glee as she arrived to help with the kids. In a country where the sun always shines, it was no more beautiful than any of the other day, but her smile said it all as she hummed and went about the business of stripping down the guest bedrooms and putting our house to rights again.

'Thaaaank God!' Jack stated that night. It was the first time we had dinner on our own as a family in ten weeks.

'For what?' I already knew, but we thought it important that the kids be allowed to acknowledge the fact that we had no more wild life tramping around our living room.

'The Angry Man is gone … duh!'

It was a moment of light relief, kind of, but it was also a sad ending to "what could have been."

A week later the feeling persisted. I couldn't get the idea of the "Angry Man" out of my mind. It just wasn't like him. There had been a motor bike accident outside our home one night, not long after they had arrived in Muscat. An inexperienced rider lost control and smashed through a barrier fence. It was like a bomb going off, loud and nasty, with bits and pieces of bike flying everywhere and the man left badly wounded among the destruction. Neighbors came to assist, his family ran for help, but it was Scotty who lay on the oil stained dirt beside this stranger. He held him tightly in his arms, rocked him back and forth and soothed his wailing until he eventually convinced him that he wasn't going to die. For those brief and heroic forty five minutes my best mate shone just as I had remembered him, but just as quickly the darkness returned when the victim was carted off to the hospital.

'Wallah Docta, it is the rules I tell you. He can't come back for two years from now!' Abdullah reassured me in the second week as if he had been reading my mind. 'By that time he will make his life someplace else!' Abdullah was confident. It took a long weekend away on Edvina to sooth our imaginations. By the end of third week I had two new chapters written for 'The Christening' and settled back somewhat into a normal routine.

Then the practice went ballistic! It was like the Gods had been holding back, waiting until all of the right pieces were in place before making their move. One minute I am joking with my PA Linda about trying to be a writer. The next, I am gasping for breath, running from adjusting room to adjusting room. Our spinal care workshop doubled overnight and then tripled until it was standing room only as we averaged forty people in the class! Patients waited sometimes an hour and a half to be seen until I had to add extra hours, then extra days to cope to with the demand.

From our first day in Oman, our oft precarious existence had been about as secure as Edvina anchored to jelly. Now, like a stretched breath that could only be expelled after driving through a long tunnel, it was a huge relief to be able to relax and breathe again. We were now confident of a long term future in Muscat.

While I was run off my feet, Darling had found her niche and was head down and bum up with the Group. Some of the families were making round trips of hundreds of miles. Others stayed in Muscat for weeks at a time to work with the therapists that Darling had organized to help in the development of their children.

To be surrounded by so much love and appreciation in one room was a glorious experience. It had an unexpected healing effect that helped the individual families discover the blessings of having a child with Down Syndrome. It also mirrored our own lives and reassured us that on this journey we too were not alone.

Unfortunately, as our dreams and plans finally came together, Scotty and Angel's were falling apart. Their associates had refused to take their dismissal lying down and a punching match had ensued over who was responsible for the shambles. Angel was in touch with Darling on a weekly basis to give a running commentary. In the one corner was Scotty, huffin' and puffin', knuckles bared, hoping for a swift knockout. In the other were his two opponents, a husband and wife team with a profoundly handicapped child whose high needs required the stability of a settled life which they were not about to give up without a fight. From a distance of almost three thousand miles we were incredibly relieved that we had not had to resort to this method in the parting of our ways.

After all that had happened, it was inevitable in our isolation, that we would share our version of "the truth" with our families. However, in a profession as small as ours, there were two things that we had not counted on. The first was the three degrees of separation that connects all Chiropractors. The second was the measure of ill feeling among other doctors about their past dealings with Scotty.

My brother told Chiropractor "X" (who we didn't know) he told "Y" (didn't know him either). Before you know it, sides were taken and the Chinese whispers reached all the way to Doctor "Z." Unfortunately the "Z" in question was one of those who'd had a run in with Scotty in the past. Unfortunately, because *he* knew Scotty's associates! Seizing his opportunity, he passed on his version of "the truth" which they gladly used against Scotty. It was all hearsay, but caught once again in the machinations of the Gods and the sticky web of his own deceit, Scotty needed to blame someone. So the finger was pointed back at me for "breaking my word". If I'd stuck to his version of "the truth" then he would have had less of a fight on his hands. But where do you draw the line? What if the drama had escalated to court and Scotty demanded that I swear on the bible? That's when I decide that Scotty was right ... "it's important to tell the truth!"

Either way it did not matter. Scotty prevailed in the end and retook possession of his practice. The dust settled ... eventually, but not without adding to the bitter taste that they had already left behind. It would be two years before we faced off and spoke of the matter. Two years of what "shoulda" been the best in our lives, but the Gods, being more determined than we were, had other plans!

6

'Told you so!'

'Molly's not right.' Darling had made the remark several times
before, but I had ignored it in favor of her being overly protective. You
spend so much time making, pretending, forcing and believing that
"she'll be right mate" that you fail to see something is wrong right
under your nose. She had been sick, but she had recovered, just like
every other kid. She was sleeping fine, no cold or flu, no runny nose or
gastric reflux, no temper tantrums or pooey nappies, but *just not right*.
The kind that no matter how hard you try, deny, pretend or ignore, it
casts a shadow over everything. Intuitive and immeasurable, the idea
began to keep us awake at night, wondering if the doctors and
specialist pediatrician who was taking care of her had missed
something.

As luck would have it, a friend of a friend knew a nurse who
knew a family from South Africa who had a teenager with Down
Syndrome. To help in her development they had taken her as a baby all
the way to Wales in the U.K. to an early intervention program. We
contacted the family who spoke of their great success and highly
recommended it. The program included a full physical and mental
assessment that would insure we were ticking the boxes and doing
everything possible for Molly's healthy development.

'It will be perfect for the Group!' It was all Darling talked about these days. However, when she made contact, she found to her bitter disappointment that there was a six month waiting list.

Two days later they called us back. There had been a cancellation. Would we be interested in attending? They gave us the weekend to make the decision.

For me, I wasn't so sure. Dubai was a one day return trip. We could go there for a second opinion to make sure that nothing was being missed. Beyond that, our efforts in raising a daughter with Down Syndrome might have been compared to a "living experiment," but I felt that we were doing a good job. Certainly better than anyone else in Oman.

'It's the far side of the world!' I resisted.

'It's not. It's a six hour plane journey and a two hour road trip. We can do it in our sleep!'

'It's f*$#&n expensive!' I countered. We would have to close the practice for a week.

'Isn't your daughter worth it?'

The distance and the expense were the least of my worries (kind of!) My biggest frustration was that life was becoming one damn thing after another. I was supposed to be keeping a promise to my mate. As it was, we had sailed only half way around the world and I had only a half-written novel (on five floppy discs that were likely to disintegrate before I got the story finished) All I needed were a few drama-free months to knock the bastard out, but every time we started to make progress, another distraction reared its ugly head.

'It's just a week!' Darling admonished.

'I know, I know, but everything is just a week!' It occurred to me to send Poppit along, but she was too young to be burdened with the responsibility. 'Can't we do it by internet?' This comment resulted in a scathing look that took me a week to recover from!

If the Gods had waited for Scotty and Angel to leave before lending a hand with the practice, then my Muse had muscled in and taken center stage reminding me (from the other shoulder) that I had yet to complete 'The Christening'. Most writers claim they require at least ten redrafts before they are happy with their story. 'At this rate it's going to take me another twenty years to finish the F$#%@^&*k book!'

'Who comes first, your stupid book, or your daughter?' It was the first time Darling had ever given me shit over my writing.

Of course our daughter came first. Knowing Lewis, I'm sure he would have understood if I had given up on my promise altogether. We'd had a big year and it was inevitable that Murphy had more in store for us, but ... and this was a BIG but, I had the story living and breathing inside of me now. Somewhere along the way, I had developed a paternal attachment to Kate and her beau. I know this sounds crazy, (duh!) but I was now as worried about them as I was for my own children.

It was like I had written the first draft with dark glasses that had a tendency to fog. The second draft was coming through now a whole lot clearer, but was cause for consternation. 'The Christening' had started as a simple story. Girl (Kate) meets boy (?). They fall in love. I didn't know his name, so to keep the story going I'd used simple Irish logic and called him Paddy!

Kate was orphaned as a child and raised as a social outcast in an institution for the delinquent and homeless. On her eighteenth birthday she was required to leave. She was penniless, but with a lot of luck, had managed to make a life for herself working for an elderly Dutch couple in their small cheese factory in the south-west of Ireland. She has a sharp mind, is quick of wit and it doesn't take her long to become an indispensable part of the business. Her greatest asset though is her beautiful voice which she uses to great effect at the local weekend market in charming the customers to buy more cheeses. It is there that she meets Paddy. He has his own stall selling children's wooden toys.

Paddy comes from the wrong side of the tracks. His family is moneyed and titled with a background in farming. He is a great sportsman and captain of the local hurling team. His father, nicknamed "Lordy" by the local, is a bully who is determined to lead his son's life in whatever direction he sees fit, regardless of the tensions it causes between them. In the first draft Paddy flies his own biplane and takes Kate on romantic joyrides to the family's private island and a surprise weekend trip to Dublin.

The second draft is a cause for severe anxiety. Suddenly it's a war story and he's flying Spitfires! What the hell does he think he's doing? What about her? Pregnant (he doesn't know because she doesn't know), with her own battles to be fought against a world of prejudice and bad people who do bad things to the weak and vulnerable.

As a father of three children, I felt responsible for her welfare and his safety (the F&*%@n eejit) Wouldn't you be worried if one of your own had gone off to war to fly Spitfires where the life expectancy was only ten days! This was serious shit. If he got killed (not if, when) then what would happen to her and the baby? She could hardly go it alone.

And yet I was gripped. Couldn't let it go. I have always wanted to fly a Spitfire! To feel the G forces in a tight turn, a steep dive or a barrel roll with Jerry on my tail. The rush of adrenaline. Deadly fire. Evasive maneuvers. Jerry outsmarted and now in *my* gun sights. The punch of my cannons, daga, daga, daga, daga ... boom! A victory roll over the base on my arrival home. All shot up, but safe with another swastika painted on the side of my cockpit.

But this was just me day-dreaming. He was in it for real, with real bullets and real blood. What if something terrible happened?

I was troubled mostly for two reasons. The first was that I didn't know how it ended. My muse (bitch) had left me hanging. I had a beginning and a middle and some of the bits in between. I had most of the characters, but not all of them and certainly no clue as to who were the good guys and who were the bad guys or what Kate was truly up against. I didn't trust the Gods or my muse for that matter. Too many Irish stories end in tragedy and I don't like unhappy endings.

My biggest problem though, was that I didn't believe what the muse was telling me. Paddy has now chalked up a string of kills that put him among the hallowed ranks of one of the highest scoring fighter aces in the R.A.F. with a bunch of decorations to prove his bravery. It was too big, too fantastic. Who would believe me when I had nothing to prove it? I'd left school at fourteen, never studied history and there was no access to history books in Middle East. As a kid growing up I'd had pictures on my wall of all the heroes like Johnny Johnson (highest scoring RAF) Douglas Bader, (Reach for the Sky) Sailor Malan, George Beurling, Stanford Tuck, Alan Deere. They were either Brits, Kiwis, Aussies, Canadian or South Africans. I'd heard somewhere that a few Irish had trained as pilots, but to the best of my knowledge none of them had amounted to anything.

I was confined to land, but my head was now stuck in the clouds. How could I explain this to Darling who had no interest other than her new found mission to save the world?

'Think of it as an adventure, like the road trips we used to go on!' She massaged my ego (twisted both arms). Before you know it, the bookings were made, the practice sorted, the kids farmed out to friends and we were sitting in the reception area of the Early Intervention Center in Wales and it was fantastic (told you so!).

Not only did it reaffirm the work that we were doing with Molly, but that there was so much more that could be done for her and all of the Group back in Muscat.

On the first two days of our stay Molly was assessed by a physiotherapist, an occupational therapist, a nutritionist, an ophthalmologist and a general practitioner. Several lay parents who had become early intervention specialists by way of raising their own children to living independent lives also gave a hand.

By lunch time of the third day our heads were spinning with the latest research and excitement for all that we could now do to help our baby girl. Every minute of every hour of each day spent was worth its weight in gold so that the burden of expense that had weighed heavily on me diminished and finally faded beyond question to the value that we were being gifted in return. Had I known from the start how many light years it was going to put us ahead of ourselves, I'd have gladly paid double for the opportunity!

That afternoon we had time to chill while the early intervention team devised a program for Molly which they would share the next day. Feeling confined, we chose to venture into a nearby ancient village square where we heard there was a farmers market that was worth strolling around. Anything to help our brains unwind! It had the usual stalls that included clothes, foods, preserves, coffee, second hand tools, children's clothing and a book stand that boasted a Collector's Edition category ...whatever that was.

It suddenly occurred to me, as I gravitated towards the book stand (Darling was busy checking out the children's clothes) that it had been a week since I'd heard from the Muse. A whole week! Before leaving Muscat, she had driven me crazy, but up to that moment, she had remained silent (probably something to do with Darling!). I chose to use the time to study front covers and back covers, font sizes and introductions, spines and bindings until a very pleasant hour had passed unnoticed.

'Come on, the movie is starting in five minutes!' Darling startled me and tugged my elbow in the direction of the theatre that we had chosen to see *About a Boy* with Hugh Grant.

'Hang on!' I pulled back, a book in hand. A word in the title on the spine had caught my eye, but upon turning it over, it was the picture on the front cover that blew my mind.

"*Fighter Ace*" was the name of the book.

It was a historical biography with a close-up black and white photo of a pilot sitting in the cockpit of a fighter plane staring right at me.

The aircraft was a Spitfire.

There was a large shamrock painted on the cowling in front of the cockpit.

The name of the pilot?

Wait for it!

"Paddy."

The book was about Brendan Fergus "Paddy" Finucane, the second highest scoring fighter ace in the RAF during the Second World War!

Why was he called "Paddy?"

Because he was Irish!

'F*#K and double f*#k!'

'Told you so!' my Muse whispered.

7

'A broken heart'

I don't remember any of the movie. What I do remember is borrowing the usher's torch and annoying the crap out of Darling as I scanned through the biography and quoted every fact and figure that I could find.

'Twenty one years of age. He's the same age as Kate!'

'Shush, I'm trying to watch the movie!'

'Tangerine!'

'Tanger what?"

'Tangerine, by Jimmy Dorsey. It's their favorite song, remember, at the big party he throws with his brother at the Manor? It says here that he used to play it on the gramophone before every mission as a talisman!'

'Shush (curiosity). What's a talisman?'

'It was a ritual. A kind of a good luck thing they did before each mission. Some pilots used to stick photos of their girlfriend on the cockpit instrument console!'

'Pass the popcorn!'

'Aw man, this is great!'

'Pass the (beep) popcorn!!'

'Could you please be quiet!' (disgruntled Pommy voice in the dark coming somewhere from my right.)

'Says here his father fought against the Brits during the First World War. He hated them!'

'We are surrounded by Brits, you idiot!' Darling squeezed my hand. 'Shush!' (Hugh Grant is kissing Rachel Weisz.)

I couldn't believe what I was reading. Everything the Muse had told me was true. It was no longer fictional or beyond fantastic. There were photos and citations, news clippings and excerpts from his flying log to support the facts. Then suddenly.

'Shit!'

'What?'

'He gets badly wounded!' I was half way through the book. For Kate's sake, this was the last thing I wanted to hear.

'Can I have my light back!' It was the usher. (Pommy bastard had complained). I had to surrender the torch before I had a chance to discover Paddy's fate. I was determined to finish reading the book straight after the movie, but the weather had different ideas and lashed us all the way back to our B&B. It didn't matter. By the serendipitous hand of fate, I had the facts and the figures, the dates and the times and the photos to prove my story. In twenty-four hours we would have Molly's Early Intervention Program locked and loaded and be ready to hit the ground running when we returned to Muscat.

'I feel like the King of the World!' We pulled into the driveway of our B&B. Suddenly, way out of left field, it had all come together. Life couldn't be better!

Then we found a note stuck to our bedroom door that was one of those grim reminders that the Gods never give you anything without taking something in exchange.

'Please ring the Early Intervention center asap!'

I lost the toss (so much for being King of the World!) and did so while Darling changed out of her sodden clothes.

'Ah yes … Molly,' the Director answered hesitantly. 'I know that we are not supposed to meet till tomorrow, but we have some news that we think important to discuss. Can you come down now?' He did not offer any further explanation.

Twenty minutes later he greeted us along with the G.P. who had done Molly's physical assessment and a stranger with the ominous title of "Cardiologist."

'I found something disturbing in Molly's heart that is not noted in any of the medical records that you have brought with you from

221

Oman.' The G.P. looked at the stranger, uneasy at being the bearer of bad news.

'Molly has a V.S.D.' The stranger cut straight to the chase. 'A ventricular septal defect is a hole between the right and left ventricles of the heart. Commonly known as a murmur, what happens is ....'

'We know what it is.' I stopped him short.

'I knew there was something wrong!' Darling held Molly closer to her chest.

'What else?' We knew from our own training that there was a raft of potential complications connected to the condition.

'We can't be sure until certain tests are done,' the G.P. piped up.

'The point is,' the cardiologist placed his hand gently on Darling's arm to comfort her. 'Surgery is normally performed on this type of defect within days of birth. Weeks at the latest. Left too long it can cause irreversible damage!' Irreversible was 'dead by seven years of age'.

'What's too long?' I put my arms around Darling who was already in tears.

'Six months, at a stretch.' The Cardiologist was grim faced.

Molly was already eight months old.

8

'Ho, Ho Ho!'

Take a sleepless night and multiply it by ten, add a heavy dose of jet lag and a six day week of catching up with a backlog of patients while running around Muscat like a blue-arsed fly trying to find answers from doctors and pediatricians who gave us nothing but excuses as to why they had missed the hole in our daughter's heart … and you might have a fraction of an inkling of what was going on in our own hearts.

So much for hitting the ground running! Our life was now one big grandfather's clock, tick, tock, tick, tock, every second irreversible and precious, every beat of our little baby's heart one step closer to failure.

'Why don't you have the surgery done here at the Royal?' suggested an Irish acquaintance I bumped into by chance at the marina. In anticipation of having to travel to Ireland for several months for the surgery I was busy making plans to have Edvina hauled ashore for safekeeping.

'I know, I know!' he empathized when I told him our tale of woe about the incompetency that we had already been through. 'The heart department is different though. It's run by an Iraqi doctor who trained at the Mater Hospital in Dublin They are famous for pioneering heart surgery and have one of the lowest mortality rates in the world!'

Not exactly the words of encouragement that I was looking for, but it was enough to make me think twice about how we might avoid the logistical nightmare of closing the practice and moving to live in Dublin.

As it turned out, it was also a time to face off against certain prejudices that you deny harboring within the depths of your own heart.

It's one thing to trust a Filipina lady to care for your children in your own home, for your gardener to be from Bangladesh, your builder from Syria and your banker a Palestinian. When I needed work done on Edvina, my go-to guy was a Sri Lankan, my car was serviced by a Jordanian and when I wanted the "second opinion" of an incompetent pediatrician, there were several nationalities and two private hospitals that I could readily choose from. However, when it came to handing my little girl over to a stranger to have her sternum split with a glorified skilsaw and her heart stopped so that they could use scissors and scalpels to do a repair job ... before hooking her up to a set of jumper cables ... the last thing I wanted (may God forgive me), was an Iraqi or an Indian or anyone else other than a white man to do the job. I wanted one of my own, rotund and jovial, dressed in red, with silken white gloves and a fluffy beard to go "ho, ho, ho" and promise me that all of my Christmases were going to come in one and that my baby girl, (may God protect her) was going to be okay.

Our first visit to the "Royal" was overwhelming. The sights, the sounds, the sea of humanity. The language barrier, which was a stumbling block at the best of times, was enough to make us drive straight to the airport and jump on a plane back to Ireland. Unlike the small private hospitals that we had grown used to, the Royal was a sprawling edifice of open spaces and long corridors, marble tiled from floor to ceiling with locks on every ward to prevent relatives from setting up camp (literally) in the ward with the affected member of their family. Foreign in every sense of the word, the pervasive smell was a tug between desert musk, disinfectant, and frankincense.

As we joined the queues to be processed, the unwelcome novelty of being the obvious foreigner in line for assessment attracted a steady stream of uninvited attention. Women covered from head to toe in their traditional dress would come up and touch Molly's white face and run their hands through Darling's long wavy hair and wonder at my willingness to allow her the freedom to 'display' herself. In saying this, there was no hostility, only nervous banter and friendly apologies.

Others approached in broken English for us to explain the meaning of a referral letter written in English, the way you would ask a stranger for directions in a foreign country.

Ill at ease, we slowly began to realize that everybody was in the same boat and just as lost and frightened as we were. That we all had to give up our lives and those of our loved ones to complete strangers. I envied them for their ignorance and their absolute faith and the fact that they were surrounded by family and friends. As the days passed quickly I was grateful for their community and silent reassurance. For the way that they would come up to me and rub my shoulder with one hand and look me in the eye and smile while gently touching their heart with their other hand and then their mouth and finally their forehead, before bowing and clasping their hands in silent prayer. 'God is good,' they would repeat, 'God is good,' over and over, probably the only three words they knew in the English language. It is at times like this that there are no atheists in the trenches. It was enough for us to anchor our souls to in the upcoming storm.

Our first meeting with the specialists was a f*^#&n nightmare. Unaware that we were fully conversant with the ghastly language of surgical procedures, they only stopped when I pointed to how Darling had turned pale.

'We will have to sedate her to keep her still for an echocardiogram.' One of the doctors handed a script to the attending nurse to prepare Molly.

'Will it hurt?' It was the first of many times that Darling would ask the question.

'No, of course not. It is just a sedative. She will be fine!' He ushered us out of the room so that he could attend to someone else.

An hour later, Molly sufficiently drowsy, we were crammed into a small consultation room. The Cardiologist and two assistants pointed at images, mumbled under their breaths and scribbled notes because they now knew that we knew what they were saying.

'How big is the hole?' I was fascinated that I could see her heart beating on the screen.

'Big enough to drive a bus through!' He shook his head in dismay at how something so big (fourteen millimeters) could have been missed by so many people.

'Can it be fixed?'

'We must operate as soon as possible!' I could tell from the deep furrow in his brow and the worry in every gesture that he made across the screen that the dice were loaded heavily against us.

'We will need twenty units.' His colleague addressed me.

'Sorry?' My mind was beginning to twist.

'Your daughter has a rare blood group. In Oman, it is the responsibility of the family to organize the blood for the surgery. You don't have to have it by Tuesday of course. We have a small bank of blood for our surgeries. So long as you promise to make the contribution in the next month it will be sufficient.'

'What has Tuesday got to do with it?

'We will be doing the surgery on that day.' Unbeknownst, the head of surgery had applied and received special dispensation from the hospital board to have the procedure performed in Oman. Only later would I find out how massive the exception was that they had made in our favor.

'But we haven't decided whether or not ...' I did not want to blurt out in front of him that we were still considering Ireland an option.

'You must understand the seriousness of this situation!' The Cardiologist almost shouted. 'Her heart is already a third larger than it should be!' He pointed to the screen. 'It should have been done long before now!' He shook his head, as if they shouldn't have to be responsible for cleaning up someone else's mess. 'Please, (give up all resistance) sign here!' he pointed to a *Consent for Surgery* form and gave me a card with a barcode printed on it for access to the ward where Molly was already booked. 'We will do the best that we can. We always do!' It was as much a rebuke to my unwillingness to surrender my prejudice.

We had four sleepless nights to organize our shit for the worst day of our lives. It felt like being strapped to the front of a runaway locomotive as it headed straight for a concrete wall.

9

'Okay, okay, stop!'

'I'm fine, I'm fine!' I lied, brushing off helping hands as I struggled to stand on jelly-like legs after donating my unit of blood. There were seven of us in the room. Darling, Rashard, his wife Salwa, my P.A. Linda and a couple more friends who had immediately put their hands in the air when I put out our appeal for help. 'Breathe in, breathe out, breathe in, breathe out, put one foot in front of the other and keep moving!' I had to keep telling myself, to stop from completely falling to pieces in front of everyone. Darling, in survival mode, seemed to be coping better, but I'd finally hit the wall. My mind had turned to mush at the sight of the blood and the persistent images seared in my brain from all of the sleepless nights thinking about what they were going to have to do in order to save our baby girl.

'It is at times like this that we must be strong for our children!' Rashard gripped me vice-like by the arm, pulled me back from fainting and braced me so that I would not fall. I was indebted to him, for the pain it caused brought me quickly back to my senses. Difficult to deal with at the best of times, he made up for all of his shortcomings in that single afternoon by having half of his extended family also donate their blood. By the end of the day the twenty units were surpassed and almost doubled! It was an enormous relief. A metaphorical transfusion of confidence which, combined with the knowledge that my mother was flying in to support us the next day, allowed us to sleep for twelve hours straight.

I have always found that the best defense against fear is *decisive action*. Full on, dawn till dusk, fall into bed 'too tired to be anything but glad the day is over' sort of action that creates momentum and moves you from the inertia that threatens to drown you. We were determined therefore, on the run up to the surgery, to fill our days with any excuse for activity, escape, adventure, fun, special treats or last minute distractions. Anything that would take our minds off the inevitable.

It was a success, mostly, that gave us several hours of reprieve at a time, to live in a normal world as a happy family doing happy things. Nevertheless, the moment we stopped to rest, or take a family photo, the words "high risk" and "mortality rate" always settled on our shoulders.

You'd be inclined to think that after the challenge of sailing around the world in Edvina, punching through storms, narrowly missing twisters, Molly's nightmare arrival, (Darling's close shave with departure) and establishing the practice would pretty much have prepared us for anything. The hard reality of life though, is that in spite of our professional training and all of our worldly experience, nothing prepares you for a hurricane. There is no such class as Hurricane 101 or Tsunami for Beginners. Apocalypse Now, means now! Not ready? Steady? Brace yourself, here comes the Apocalypse!

The persistent question was how much to tell Poppit and Jack. Should we "scare them to prepare them" or just allow them to enjoy these last few days of calm with their Sis in ignorant bliss.

How do you explain to a ten-month-old child what is about to happen to them? The surgeon had advised us that all going well, the procedure would take about five hours. Other than ourselves, my mother was the only one who knew that it could just as easily go the other way. That her granddaughter, whom we all adored, might not be coming home.

When we finally checked into the hospital on the eve of the surgery we were looking forward to a quiet night to settle Molly (and our nerves). Instead, we were faced with an unexpected welcome from the registrar.

'We have to insert a surgical line into her groin for the anesthetic tomorrow. It's a straightforward procedure, a little nick. Nothing to worry about.' He could see the look on Darling's face. 'It will be over in a matter of minutes!' he assured. He was so offhand and disarmingly professional that we believed his every word.

On his third attempt to insert the needle (with me holding Molly in a full Nelson), Darling folded from the intensity of Molly's high pitched, heart rending squeals and left the room in tears.

'I have done it a hundred times before!' The registrar shook his head, exasperated at his inability to find a vein in Molly's groin.

'It's always the way!' I tried to put him at ease. My baby daughter's groin was starting to look like a pin cushion. 'The easy looking ones turn out to be the hardest!' I added, knowing that he was probably just as flustered by our unwillingness to be parted from Molly until the absolute last minute before surgery.

'Okay, okay, stop!' I instructed and brushed his hand aside gently when his fourth attempt was faring no better.

'But we have to get this line in for the surgery!'

'I know, I know, but not this way. She is too distressed. Let's just take a little break and everyone can calm down and then we will try again, okay!?

'Yes, of course!' he nodded, visibly relieved by my suggestion. 'Here, take one of these,' and reaching behind him, he tore two tissues from a dispenser on the wall and wiped his brow while handing me the other for my eyes. A few minutes of long slow deep breaths passed until Molly calmed down. Then, I had an idea.

'Can you sing?'

'I beg your pardon?

'Sing!'

'Hush, little baby, don't say a word,' I held Molly close and sang into her ear, 'Dadda's gonna buy you a mockingbird!' Having been adopted as her lullaby since her birth, the song had the immediate effect of calming her.

'And if that mockingbird don't sing,' I rocked, 'Dadda's gonna buy you a diamond ring!'

She smiled.

'Brilliant!' The doctor joined in.

'And if that diamond ring turns brass, your Dadda's going to buy you a looking glass,' I nodded to the Doctor to "get on with it," and stroking my little girl's head, I held her tight so that she could not wriggle.

'And if that looking glass gets broke,' we both chorused with Molly screaming in harmony after the needle was inserted, 'Mama's gonna buy you a Billy goat!'

'It's done!' the doctor shouted seconds later, his hands held high in the air in triumph. 'It is done!' he repeated again softly, taking Molly's hand and gently stroking it, apologizing to us both, equally glad the ordeal was over.

10

'I'm sorry!'

Instead of running from the hard reality of life there are times when you have to play the hero and charge headlong into it. To "face the f#&@*r." Eyeball it, nose to nose, then shove, punch, kick, scream, cry, scrape, chop, shit, spit, shoot (being heroic is often messy). Whatever it takes to climb on top and beat the bastard into submission. I'd heard this from a Vietnam vet who then told me that being the hero is never what it's cracked up to be. He added further, that there are times when surrender is in fact the best part of valor. That there is honor sometimes, in the laying down of arms, where men on both sides can go home and live out the rest of their lives with their families.

On the morning of the surgery, I woke up angry at the choice I was being forced to make. At having to give up my power. My every instinct was to come out fighting. To shove, punch, kick, scream, cry, scrape, chop, shit, spit, shoot, whatever it took to protect our baby girl … and yet I knew that this was not the solution. For all that my healing hands had done to help others, I was angry now at having to hold them by my side, incapable of helping my own child.

On the way to the hospital (Darling had stayed overnight) I drove down to the sea and prayed to all of the Gods that ever existed that when the time came, I would have the courage to "Kia kaha" (stand strong) and not fight but rather surrender, in the hope that my daughter would come home to our family.

Every fiber of my body was on edge when I arrived at the hospital. Like entering an inhospitable no man's land I could sense death looming around every corner. After a sleepless night of foreboding, I found Darling equally agitated. The only way we could keep our emotions in check was to pace from ward to ward with Molly asleep on Darling's shoulder.

To make it easier, we had willingly accepted the surgeon's suggestion that Molly be sedated, so that at that final moment, we would remember her as asleep, dreaming, unawares. Unfortunately the Gods had other plans (f*&$#rs) which caused a two hour delay in the surgical roster. By the time we were summoned on intercom from the far side of the hospital, we were deeply upset that Molly was fully awake, aware and as equally disturbed as her mother.

'We are ready,' the team leader of a group of nurses greeted us a little too happily when we finally arrived at the entrance to a long corridor that ended at the operating theatre. Two sat behind a counter filling out paperwork, two stood beside a gurney that was to be used to wheel Molly (supposedly asleep) to theatre. I could hear the footsteps of at least two more (reinforcements) walking along the corridor towards us. Seven in all, I could easily deal to them, but I had made a commitment to keep my clenched fists firmly by my side.

'I will take her now,' the lead nurse said gently. Instead, Darling handed Molly to me.

'I can't do it,' she whispered, eyes streaming, shamefaced by her lack of strength.

'Please, the team is waiting!' I too stood frozen, my arms wrapped around my little girl, heart to heart, cheek to cheek, my head shaking gently from side to side.

'I'm sorry,' I whispered into her little ear. 'I'm sorry!' I kept repeating as my tears ran down her cheek, but still I could not release her.

There was consternation among the nurses, how to handle such a display. That I might bring the wrath of the surgical team down upon them for such a delay.

One of the nurses that appeared from the corridor was junior to the team leader, but the eldest of all the staff, and, sizing the situation up, she immediately approached me without introduction. She took my hand and squeezed it, stroked Molly's head and then reached across to Darling to comfort her.

232

'I too have a daughter,' she smiled and continued to make a fuss over Molly. Within seconds Molly was smiling with her little hand gripped around the nurse's pinky finger. 'Would you like me to take care of her?' It was a suggestion only, nothing personal if I refused. Her head nodding in understanding at the heartbreak her role would play in the event of an unhappy outcome.

'Please bring her back!' I begged through whispered tears. I dropped my arms in surrender, and finally let her go, knowing that it was the only way that I could save her.

I could tell you that I surrendered to a higher force. That the nurse who walked away with my baby girl was an angel. That her touch came with an unspoken trust and that suddenly, I *believed* everything was going to be okay.

I didn't.

Quite the opposite.

What I had needed was something more powerful to which I could anchor my soul. Something so profound, that if it all turned to crap and the Gods I'd prayed to on the beach abandoned me, that I would still have enough faith and courage left over to carry on.

That something was a story.

Above all else, my greatest belief is that it is stories that save us. Stories of love, stories of adventure and stories of great deeds that have been done. For contained within every story of hardship, difficulty, danger, misfortune and hard times, is the "silver lining of adversity" that lifts us when we are down, strengthens us when we are weak, acts as a balm to sooth our pain and offers hope when all else seems lost. Time and time again in the past, it is stories that have saved me.

From the poster under the bridge all of those years ago that promised me a better life in Australia ... to the gay guy in the bar in Sydney whose story about losing his arm made me feel better about losing my mind ... to the rhino charging me down on the African plains who made me realize that I wasn't so stupid after all ... to my good mate Lewis on his death bed whose own story inspired me to stop talking shit and turn my bucket list upside down and truly live my dream ... to Merrill Fernando's story of Dilmah tea ... to Shackleton's story of *Endurance* on the Antarctic ice cap which made our own hardship pale in significance as we "punched North" to get out of New Zealand.

I didn't give the nurse our baby girl because I trusted her, but rather because she reminded me of a story of loss that might make my own more bearable, a story of pain so great, that it might extinguish my own, a story of God that it might just restore my faith, a story of courage that it might strengthen my weakness and if all was lost, a story of love that would lift and inspire me to go on.

She reminded me of the story of Maggie.

11

'I too have a daughter!'

What's on your mind?' I ventured, his hesitancy begging me to dig deeper with my questioning. We'd covered the usual areas of spinal health … pillow, posture, nutrition, ergonomics, cause and effect, prognosis (good) long term maintenance (essential).

'It's my daughter, Maggie.' He pointed to the list of the seven areas of life that I had on the wall in my adjusting room (spiritual, mental, physical, family, social, career and finance). His finger came to rest on *family*. 'She has been through a hard time. Still broken up. I have been thinking, maybe … that you might be able to help her?'

The following day I met a blue eyed blonde with a crooked face covered in heavy foundation that failed to hide the scars of tragedy that still twisted the very core of her being. Forewarned, I tried to keep the consult light, but she was so fragile, so devoid of personality or joy, that it was impossible to "crack her" with a joke or a laugh. When she answered 'car accident,' as the cause of her disfigurement, I knew not to dig too deep. My examination of her contorted spine and badly broken pelvis told of the terrible heartbreak that she had experienced. Or so I thought at the time.

Within a few weeks she began to make progress, but then just as quickly, she disappeared. Six months later, she showed up again (by herself).

'I wasn't ready.' She confirmed my previous assumption. 'I was stuck, but I'm doing better now.' That her father was not with her was a good sign of recovery. If she was prepared to come on her own, then I was confident that she would stick with her program.

I never take the credit when a person makes a good recovery. It's a team sport that takes two to play, where both sides rely on the body's innate ability to restore itself, but "amazing" would be the best way to describe her progress. I can still remember, a few months later, her first real day without physical pain. How she smiled (still pretty!) like a spring flower blooming. She had a hope in her voice that dared to be happy. A spring to her step that made up for a limp that was now only perceptible to the trained eye.

Then one day, she showed up with her father in tow and behind him, a big dark cloud.

'I'm pregnant!' she announced. 'It wasn't planned. I have a new man, he's nice,' she faltered, somehow ashamed. As if she had broken some vow that she'd made to protect herself.

'None of my children were planned!' I joked, trying to bring levity to her situation.

'I'm terrified!' she whispered, looking past me to the middle distance, where the living are separated from the dead.

'How many weeks are you?'

'Not many.' It was as if she was trying to discount the life within her. She looked to her father to explain, then she left the room.

He hesitated, worried that he might delay me, or that I did not care, that the quiver on his lip might make him seem a lesser man, or that the pain of telling me was too much to bear.

'You need to know her story. Why she is so scared. She is talking about having an abortion!'

'I understand.' I didn't, but invited him to sit down on a chair beside a table that had a box of tissues and a jug of cold water.

He began to share his story in snapshots and short sentences:

'I am senior project manager for Al Hambra (Civic) I was on a job. We were about to do a continuous pour of concrete on a flyover in the central business district. Our biggest job to date. Massive. Risky. Most of the company's resources tied up. If we got it right, then my sponsor could write his own checks after that.' He didn't mention what would happen if he got it wrong, but it was easy to guess that the future of the business and his own was also on the line. *'We had been planning it for months. We were very confident. I had just started the pour. There was no turning back. Then I got the call. It was her*

236

partner. They'd had an accident. I could hear my daughter in the background screaming!'

His hand shook as he took a sip of water.

'You know that there are no ambulance services in this country?'

'I didn't.' The thought had never occurred to me.

'It was carnage. Two trucks, my daughter's car. So there are three things you should always carry in your car.' He reached for a tissue, his eyes starting to well up. *'A fire extinguisher, a first aid kit and an angle grinder! I told my 2 IC what had happened and then I walked off the job, literally. Grabbed two of the workers closest to me and got in my pickup and drove away. It was rush hour. The traffic was backed up, so I drove along the margins. Up one way roads, across traffic islands, broke all of the lights. My boss ringing me. His boss ringing him. Eventually my sponsor on the line "Why wasn't I on the job? Everything was on the line!" I told them all to get fucked, that my daughter was more important than their little bridge. It took twenty five minutes to get there.*

'Destroyed. Crushed from both sides, petrol leak, a fire had started. The engine bay was already engulfed. Her boyfriend useless. Been drinking. Sitting on the road with his head in his hands. Shaking. Crying. The police standing around. Everyone had their backs to the car. Ignoring the flames. I couldn't find her, searched everywhere. Thought that she might have been thrown clear. Then I heard groaning coming from the car. She was trapped. One arm between the seat and the door. One leg caught in the floor well. Blood everywhere, her face mangled, her hair matted, her lips torn so that she could only mumble.

'She was pregnant. In labor. Two weeks early. On their way to the hospital. It was a roundabout. He'd gone around the wrong way. I could see the baby. On the floor in a pool of blood. Dead. My first grandchild!'

He paused to clear his throat and blow his nose.

'I tried, but I couldn't reach. Nobody was doing anything to rescue her. There was the smell of burning flesh ... my own daughter's! One of my men grabbed the extinguisher from the pickup and fought the fire.

'Once we got started, people seemed to be moved to help. Two expats showed up out of nowhere. We dragged the car backwards to stop the fire moving into the front passenger area. I grabbed the angle grinder from the back of the truck. A police officer gave me a first aid kit. Someone held a towel between her legs to try to stem the blood. Sparks flying from the grinder. Two more extinguishers. Fear of

explosion. A crow bar. Somebody showed up with a crow bar!' He shook his head. *'Six of us rocking the car to try to tear panels off. My baby grand-daughter dead in pool of blood on the floor, did I mention that? Placenta beside her. It took a half an hour. More fire extinguishers. My men. I didn't even know their names at the time. Heroic. Finally, we were able to lift her free. Blood dripping all of the way to my car. Laid her on the back seat. Somebody, an Indian I think, handed me the baby completely wrapped in the cloth of his blood-stained turban!'* He held out his hands in a similar gesture.

He paused, drank from the glass of water I gave him, wiped his eyes, apologized, took a deep breath and kept talking.

'The hospital was pre-warned by the police car that escorted us. We were doing a hundred miles an hour at one stage (if anything had gone wrong!) Emergency ward. They stemmed the flow of blood. Drips, fluids, but couldn't stop the internal bleeding. No idea where, without performing surgery. She has a very rare blood group. All of their small bank used up. They contacted Dubai. Too far to deliver. Nothing more they could do. Moved us to a private room, Sedated. Slowly dying. I was holding her hand (her mother in the U.K.) My tears running down her cheeks. Praying to God. Begging, fucking begging I was!' He trembled, water spilling from his glass as he tried to get a grip on himself. *'The doctor had said that it was just a matter of hours.*

'An hour or so passed. I don't know. There was a commotion outside the ward. My sponsor' (bitterness in his voice) *'made one of his grand entrances. His two eldest sons were with him.*

'I was angry. Angry at God, angry at the world, angry at the hospital that they could not save her. Angry that of all the people, I did not want to share these last precious moments of my daughter's life with this fucker! He knew it by the way I looked at him.

"I too have a daughter!" *he admonished, that I should think such terrible thoughts. "I too have a daughter!" He whispered, placing his hand on my shoulder. He stood by the bed and took my daughter's hand and patted it. Then he closed his eyes and recited a very long prayer in Arabic. Beside him, his own physician and his personal assistant spoke in hushed tones to the attending doctor in the room. When he finished, he touched his hand to his heart, then his mouth, then finally his forehead before he placed it momentarily on my daughter's forehead.*

238

"Do whatever it takes!" He turned to his physician and his assistant aware of the nature of the conversation that had taken place. They quickly rushed from the room.

"I have asked my God for help. Now, we must ask your God as well." He took my daughter's hand again.

"Our father,
Who art in heaven,
Hallowed be thy name
Thy kingdom come
Thy will be done."

'I swear to you. The power of that man. I loved him and hated him in equal amounts. Everybody in the room was praying, even the doctors!

'A half hour passed, then horns started beeping, people shouting. I was on the window side of the bed. There was a commotion outside, down in the car park. I saw a group of porters run out of the hospital and set up two long trestle tables side by side with boxes and bags and all sorts of equipment. There must have been ten nurses with them. Two of the company buses that transport our workers from their quarters to the building sites arrived. Packed like sardines. At least one hundred in each bus. The men were quickly unloaded and made to line up single file in front of the nurses. Syringes were drawn, blood was taken and each man was numbered with a black marker on his wrist and told to stand in the shade while his sample was sent to the lab.

Fifteen minutes later a nurse came running out. "Number three. Number three!" A man raised his hand. Five minutes later "number three" was sitting on a chair outside our room. By some divine miracle a match had been made and they were drawing blood as quickly as they could from his arm.

"Fifteen minutes," the physician announced.

"Inshallah!" My sponsor leaned over my daughter to get closer to her ear. "You will not go now. You will stay!" It was a command, a pleading, a prayer, from a father to a daughter. As if by holding her hand he was keeping her alive!

'Five, ten, then fifteen minutes passed. Suddenly, there was shouting from outside of the room.

"No, no!" we heard "number three" cry out.

"But you have to!" someone shouted angrily. Then a scuffle broke out.

239

"You cannot take it!" the high-pitched voice shouted back, defiant. *There was silence for a few moments. Then the physician came into the room.*

"Your Excellency, he won't give us the blood!"

"What?!"

'*I have never seen the man so enraged! He stormed out of the room. I followed for fear of what they might do to the poor man.*

"Number three" was cowering in a corner, holding his bag of blood so that it could not be snatched from him.

"You cannot take it!" he cried. *"You cannot take it!"*

'*My sponsor clicked his fingers. Had it been up to his sons, they would have set upon the man and killed him for his blood if they'd had to. But he didn't. His personal assistant stepped forward and handed him a small leather bag. From it he drew a hand full of Rial notes. Thousands. An entire year's income for the man and his extended family back in India.* *"Number three's"* eyes suddenly turned wild.

"I don't want your money!" he chided, insulted by so profane a gesture.

"Then what is it that you want?!" Unused to being denied, my sponsor raged, ready if need be to take the blood from the man himself.

"I want to give it, myself!"

'*We were all stunned, every one of us. I swear, had they chosen to take the blood, there would have been no witnesses in the room to testify against them!*

"But of course. Please. I am deeply sorry!" Our sponsor, truly apologetic. Humbled by this man's profound gesture. *"Please!"* He motioned to the room. *"We must be quick!"*

"Number three" entered, the bag of blood held tight to his chest. He was a small man, shy, timid, about my own age. He walked straight up to me.

"I too have a daughter!" He extended both hands to give me his blood. *"I'm sorry that I cannot give you more!"*

"God is good!" my sponsor replied.

'*Within an hour they had found two more units (600 men). A military helicopter arrived with three more (it's not what you know!) enough to do surgery. By the end of the day she had been stabilized in intensive care. She had survived ... imagine!*'

'God is good!' I found myself saying.

'Then her partner skipped the country the next day, on the pretext of avoiding arrest over the accident, and never came back! How do you heal those kinds of wounds?'

There was a long pause. A shaking of heads. 'Bastard!' It was the only word of consolation that I could offer. I didn't know anything then about how to fix a broken heart, but it occurred to me that we could do something about collecting blood.

'We'll do an appeal.'

'A what?' It brought him back to the present day.

'A blood collection!' It was the only thing I could think of that might make a difference. 'I will put up some signs around the practice. If we start now, you might be able to collect and store enough blood in time for the delivery. She can probably donate her own blood!'

'You can do that?'

'I think so!?' (I didn't know.) I was clutching at straws, trying to offer hope. I had organized an appeal years before in America for an African-American kitchen-hand whose Momma had needed surgery. It saved them a fortune from not having to pay for the blood. 'If we can, (it was a BIG IF) then it might be enough to give her the confidence to follow through.'

I had him stand at the reception and proof the signs for Linda.

However, by lunchtime I was already having serious regrets about offering too much hope where there might be none.

12

Speedy Gonzales

'I have that blood!'

'I beg your pardon?'

She was a new patient. The very first person I saw that same day after lunch. I was taking her case history to decide how I could help her. Asking her about accidents and falls and previous illnesses to build a picture about her health.

'Your sign on the wall!' She nodded to an A4 page stuck on the wall behind me. 'I have that blood type. So does my best friend who flies in tomorrow for a two week visit. We belong to a kind of club in the UK who donate for emergencies!'

'No way!'

'Yes way!' She smiled. 'We can probably organize four units between us in the next two weeks. But she will have to join the club!'

I organized a meeting with Maggie the very next day. They used two large boxes of Kleenex to persuade her to hang on. By the end of their holiday they had her mind made up. Four weeks before Molly's surgery, after a trouble-free pregnancy and delivery, Maggie brought Michelle, her new baby girl (on the way home from the hospital) to have her spine checked!

Maggie's journey to hell and back made all that we were going through pale in significance. The encouraging part was that in spite of her horrendous experience, she had recovered from the depths of despair to bring a new life into the world. It was a consolation of sorts, a balm for our own heavy hearts. Something that we could anchor ourselves to if our own little girl did not make it.

*****

'They are finished!' a nurse approached, bringing us back to reality. She wasn't the one to whom I had entrusted Molly's care.

So caught up had I been in remembering Maggie's story that I had lost track of the time. When I looked at the clock on the wall of the cafeteria where we were waiting, I estimated that three and a half hours had passed since Molly's surgery had started.

'How is she?' Darling begged. She could also see that we were an hour and a half short of the estimated time that the surgeon had advised.

'It is best that the doctor speaks to you.' Avoiding any further questions or eye contact, she led us, numbed, from the cafeteria back to the room where we had said our goodbyes to Molly.

'Please, wait here.' She gestured to a small sofa across from the desk in reception. 'I will go and get the surgeon.' Tired of sitting, we stood hand in hand and watched her walk down the long corridor where we could see a group of theatre staff outside of the operating room. The nurse interrupted and quickly silenced their post-surgical chatter by pointing in our direction. A man in green garb and a hair net leaned down to hear what she had to say. He glanced at us briefly, shook his head at the nurse, spoke to the staff who quickly dispersed, nodded his head and then shook it again as he looked at us once more.

He then proceeded to wash his hands methodically in a sink for a period that seemed like forever, as if in doing so he could delay the unavoidable.

I was just about to break through the invisible barrier that separated us and dash down the hallway to stare fate in the face and end the agony, but the doctor and nurse finally turned and began walking towards us.

'One Mississippi,
Two Mississippi,
Three Mississippi,
Four ...'

As they closed the distance, he avoided all eye contact, seemingly more preoccupied with a blood stain (my daughter's) on the left sleeve of his gown.

'She was such a trooper,' were the first words that I overheard him say to the nurse. They hadn't quite reached us, but the echo off the walls was enough to warn me of the grim reality of the news they would deliver together. 'You must be strong!' he instructed the nurse.

'You are the father?' he questioned on reaching me. 'I am Dr John. Dr Taha was called away to Dubai this morning for an emergency meeting so I had to do the operation. Has anyone explained to you what has happened?'

'No,' I shook my head, both of us now too choked up to speak. My arms strained under the weight of supporting Darling.

'I am so sorry. They should have told you before now. Perhaps you would like to sit down?'

'No.'

'She was very strong. Fought so hard, right to the end.' He looked at the nurse for support. She nodded in agreement. 'There were complications. There always are. I have been doing this now for twenty years and it is never straightforward.'

Somewhere along the way, in exchange for giving up my power, I had made a pact with myself that if my daughter did not survive … I would kill the surgeon. That I would take his neck in my hands and crush his larynx. Slowly. So that as he felt his own life slip away, he could look into my eyes and see the unholy rage that all fathers have felt at the loss of their child.

Now that the time had come, this *imagined* rage had abandoned me. It was replaced instead by a terrible sense of pity for the man. For having fought so valiantly to try and save my daughter's life, his only reward now was to deliver such tragic news.

'I expect that you are both exhausted!' Darling had chosen to share her burden with the sofa. 'But listen to me now. You must be strong. For your daughter's sake,' He bent down and took her by the hand. 'I know that you will want to go home and share the news with your family, but before you leave, I want to come and say goodbye to Molly. To try and feed her.'

It took a lifetime to register. Then another to sink in. Almost the same length of time again before I dared to ask.

'She made it?'

'What do you mean?' The surgeon was perplexed.

'They told us five hours. It's just three and a half since you started. We thought …?!'

'His nickname is "Speedy Gonzales".' The nurse smiled.

'But you said. In the corridor!' I pointed to the nurse.

'Said what?'

'About being strong, you said!'

'He was talking to me about my new promotion. How the person I am replacing has worked so hard!' She laughed.

'The operation was a complete success from start to finish. Her heart had already shrunk back to its normal size before we closed, so everything will be okay for the future. If it had not been for one or two minor hiccups I would have finished it in under three hours!' he bragged.

I don't know how many times we kissed and hugged them.

'Please, I am married!' Darling made no attempt to stop. 'This is my favorite part!' he confided.

The knowledge of success fortified us with the confidence needed to make the first tentative steps into the I.C.U. To ignore the tubes that drained from Molly's chest and all of the wiring that connected her body to the various monitors that hummed and beeped into the night.

Three very long days later, we thanked the staff for the umpteenth time and made our final departure to bring Molly home.

Safe for the moment, it would be *Speedy Gonzales* who would save all of our lives in the not too distant future!

13

'The eye of the storm'

I had a dream on the night that Molly came home from hospital. I was on Edvina, alone, kinda. We'd just made it through the worst type of storm that you can ever imagine. The seas were now calm, above us blue skies, the air was tropical and balmy with a wall of cloud receding in the distance. I had taken my wet-weather gear off, grabbed a bottle of rum and two glasses and made my way to the bow (the sharp end). There, I found Lewis sitting at the foot of the mast. For some reason I wasn't surprised. This wasn't the first storm we had been through together. I sensed though that this time he had enjoyed it less, for he was saturated, exhausted and edgy.

'What a doozey!' I poured two large shots from the bottle then surveyed the rigging for damage. The sails were frayed, but repairable. Warps (ropes) were strewn around the deck, a couple of our fenders had been lost overboard, but the dinghy, which had taken a hiding, remained intact where I had double strapped it behind the mast.

'*Slainte*!' (good health) I toasted.

'Gather your energy!' he warned, unexpectedly.

'It's over, isn't it?'

'Vigilance!' he pointed his glass to the wall of weather that I only noticed for the first time. It surrounded us on the horizon of every quarter. He dropped his head back and swallowed his rum in one large

246

gulp. 'You think that you have made it?' The rum burned the back of his throat, but he held out his glass for another shot.

'This is just the eye!'

The Eye of the storm ... a region of mostly calm weather at the center of a strong tropical cyclone or hurricane.

14

'To be sure, to be sure'

'Wallah, Docta, you need to get some help!' Abdullah complained goodnaturedly after waiting almost an hour to see me for an adjustment. Normally I would skip him ahead of the queue. However, when you have H.R.H. sitting in the waiting room with his wife and three children, two government ministers, the Mayor of Muscat *and* his mother, you have to be careful not to upset the wrong people! Just shy of three months out of surgery, Molly's recovery was nothing short of miraculous. Save for a fading red scar that ran the length of her small chest, she was thriving. The operation had been a complete success.

The problem with commitment is once you start, there is no turning back or slowing the momentum down to a more manageable pace. The practice as a consequence was getting out of hand. We were on a growth trajectory that I could no longer manage by myself. For the first time in years I had a waiting list that sometimes stretched to weeks (no matter who you knew) and patient waiting times that were starting to become embarrassing.

'You are a little rushed off of your feet Doc!' The third comment from an expatriate that day was enough to make me start openly admitting it.

'Actually I have been looking for an associate for some time and have narrowed it down to a Canadian doctor in Zimbabwe!' It was true

... kinda. At the same time I was trying to "make hay while the sun shone." Having no health insurance, the surgery had cost us an arm, a leg and half a hind quarter. The upshot was the need to rebuild our depleted finances ... again!

'Not Dr. Anthony?'

'Yes actually! How did you know?' I was blown away. Of all the doctors in all of the towns in the whole wide world, he had guessed the very Chiropractor I'd been talking to.

'He was my Chiropractor when I lived in Zim!'

'No!'

'Yeah, in Harare. All of the expats used to go to him.'

'What was he like, as a doctor?' I was still in disbelief. I didn't mention the fact that I had met the guy briefly in South Africa.

'He was great. Had a huge practice. I know several people here in Muscat who used to go and see him. He's a good man!' my patient nodded.

By the end of the week, I'd found five more of our patients had lived in Zimbabwe and that they had all attended Anthony. It was the most bizarre thing. To have met the guy in Capetown and now have all of these clients who recommended his care. I wasn't too sure what the Gods were up to, but after the debacle with Scotty I took it as a sign, as if they were trying to make it up to us!

As long as I was a sole practitioner we were vulnerable and tied to the clinic. Sooner or later I would burn out and the practice would become a burden. Another doctor therefore was essential. It would mean more preparation, more expenses and more delays to finishing 'The Christening' (the story of my life), but I felt it was worth it for our future security and the sustainability of the business.

With Abdullah at the helm, the fickle winds of bureaucracy were easily navigated. Police clearances were sought, letters of good standing from the Zimbabwe Chiropractic association received, (Anthony had been a former president!) and contracts sent and discussed at length by e-mail and phone. "To be sure, to be sure" we invited him for a visit to make sure he liked the place and that we liked the "cut of his jib" before making the final commitment.

He was nervous, intense, and determined to be liked. The fact that he carried a well-worn leather-bound bible most places was a tad overkill, especially in a Muslim country, but I took it as a sign of conviction. Better to have a Christian on board than a Crusader.

When he finally "checked out" and ticked all of the boxes, there was only one last question that needed to be asked before signing him up.

'Is there anything about you or your life that is not in any of your clearances, that might be detrimental to the practice?'

'No.' His smile was emphatic. We felt reassured that we had been vigilant and done enough due diligence to safeguard our future.

Next to going cruising, it was the beginning of the most exciting phase of our lives. It was like everything that we had ever worked for and sacrificed and all of the challenges that we had been through were to prime us for this single purpose.

I realised that we had not been fully prepared at the beginning. That the rollercoaster ride of getting started had been essential to strengthening our resolve and weeding out those who were less than 100% dedicated to our mission. I had this innate sense that we had passed the test and were now suitably qualified to get on with the task of building the practice.

The Early Intervention Center in Wales had been a tremendous source of inspiration. By similar design, Darling was now getting the chance to live her dream of building a specialist health center for children with different abilities. She was busy making plans to do a fund raiser to bring specialists to Oman to up-skill the local therapists on the latest research and approach to supporting early childhood development.

With Zimbabwe going through an economic implosion under Mugabe's rule, Anthony was delighted to be offered the opportunity to get out and start a new life. Nine months after Scotty's departure, he arrived and immediately set to work. Having scored a remuneration package and a bonus incentive that made his income in Harare look like small change, he was more than happy to dedicate his energies to help grow the practice.

Rashard was in the same boat. His investment had paid off and he was now receiving a generous return with an expected increase in his dividend as Anthony came on line. Half of my time with Rashard was still spent with my eyes raised to the heavens, but most of it could be done with a handshake over coffee or even better, over the phone. An unexpected benefit to him and his family was the recovery of his nephew Quasai from epilepsy (petit mal) under our care.

Finally, it all came together. It had taken almost two long years to lay the foundation, but we felt that we had found that ideal balance.

That our life was as much about giving as it was receiving. That we were making the world a better place (certainly for children with special needs in Oman).

With Anthony on board for the long haul and my trusted P.A. Linda to assist him, I was able to cut back my hours, pull out Paddy's biography and begin a serious phase of writing.

As I sat down at the practice computer to fulfil my promise to Lewis, I found myself humming the hit song from *Tales of the South Pacific* by Rogers and Hammerstein.

"Happy talk, keep talkin' happy talk,
Talk about things you'd like to do.
You got to have a dream,
If you don't have a dream,
How you gonna have a dream come true?"

I was finally back on track .
Living the dream.
Fulfilling my promise to my mate.

Book Five

1

A knowing as powerful as a whisper

Paddy was hurt. Badly. A piece of shrapnel from an exploding canon shell passed within three inches of his manhood and nicked the femoral artery of his right leg. Not badly, but enough, that in the g-force of sustained battle he lost almost a liter of blood in under three minutes. Sufficient to fill most of his bucket seat and make the control pedals slippery as it drained down his leg onto the cockpit floor. At first he took no notice. He had so much adrenalin surging through his body, it really did not hurt that much. That and the fact that he was too busy fighting off the twenty-three Messerschmitts that had bounced his squadron from the sun while they shot up the shipyards of Le Havre on the northern coast of France. It didn't take long before the blood loss commanded his attention and upon realization he dived for the deck and pushed the emergency boost all the way to the stops to get him home. Despite a tourniquet which he had improvised from the straps of his head gear, it was touch and go whether he could remain conscious for long enough to make it home. He did, eventually, only to pass out at the end of the runway after a belly landing caused by a damaged hydraulic line that controlled the undercarriage. Ten more minutes and I would have been writing a condolence letter to Kate from his wing commander!

Brendan's biography made for incredible reading. Gruesome in places, it described the perils of daily combat that all of his men faced, sometimes for months on end without reprieve. The attrition rate was such that promotion was rapid and by the time I was half way through his story, he had been appointed a Squadron Leader, where a few months before he had only been a wingman!

Putting his biography down, I switched on the computer to begin the weekend with an evening of writing in the quiet of the practice reception. Wouldn't you know it, headlights flashed through the window. It was Abdullah in his Mercedes 500 SEL. He'd been to our house, found I wasn't there and come straight to the practice to see me. He had gotten into the habit of dropping in unexpectedly from time to time, to shoot the shit over a rum or two which I really enjoyed. However I was anxious to get a good night of writing done, so decided to cut him off at the pass by meeting him at the front door with a rain check for the following weekend.

'Ah Docta, I have just come from meeting with Mr. Anthony,' he surprised me when I answered the door. 'This man, he is planning to make big problem for you!'

'What do you mean?' He'd caught me off guard. Before I knew it, he settled into one of the sofas in the waiting room and I knew the night was shot.

'He wants me to make visa. To be his sponsor instead of you and your crazy Rashard!'

'But he can't. It's against the law!

'I know Docta, that's what I'm telling him, but he insists. He say he will pay me plenty of money!' Abdullah laughed.

'Can you do it?'

'Docta, you are my friend. Why you say such a thing?'

'I know, but can you do it?' His loyalty was undoubted, but I was intrigued by the idea. I had heard that it could be done. If anyone could make the switch then I figured (probably like Anthony) that Abdullah could do it. It had crossed my mind every time my *crazy* Rashard had pissed me off.

'Docta, only his Majesty can make the visa!' he reassured. 'This mister Anthony, he doesn't want to do de work for you. He want his own cleenic. Say he can make more money that way!'

Something about the guy had been bugging me for the last few weeks. I couldn't put my finger on it, but he'd gone off the boil and was less receptive to my leadership. Blinkers on to get the book finished, I had made excuses by putting his lack of commitment down to the stresses of moving and adapting to a new environment. Technically more qualified, I sometimes sensed a resentment from him for having to work for someone ten years his junior after being the boss of his own busy practice in Harare. After the debacle with Scotty I had expected to have some problems with any associate we engaged, but because of the strict rules on sole sponsorship, it had never occurred to me that he would try to double-cross us.

'What else?' No rum had been mentioned. I had never seen my friend look so serious.

'This man Docta, he has de *black heart*. From first day I tell you I do not like him, but you do not listen!' He tut tutted and shook his head. He had said it more than once, but I had brushed the idea aside. I had patient testimonies, clinic references, association approval, police clearances and a serendipitous meeting organized by the Gods in a faraway country to counter his poor judgment.

'What you want I should do Docta?'

'I don't know.' I was still reeling from the news. Abdullah's comprehension of the English language was questionable at times. A month before, after I'd made an inquiry, he had processed a visa for me that I had not wanted. ($500 down the drain!). There might be a simple explanation that he had misunderstood Anthony's intention. At the same time though there was also a chance that Anthony was being opportunistic and using us as a foothold to get into the Middle East.

It is not unusual for a doctor to join an established practice under the guise of being an associate only to set up a year later down the road in competition and steal a large percentage of the patient base. To prevent this from happening we had advised him from the very beginning of the law that protected sponsors from being used like this. I considered Anthony too smart *and* too vulnerable to do something so stupid. Discovery would lead to instant dismissal and oblige him to return to Zimbabwe which was just not an option. Had Abdullah chosen not to come to me I would never have suspected a thing.

'Don't tell him we have had this meeting and don't make the visa. I will have to think about what to do.' It was likely still a misunderstanding.

'Wallah Docta, you my friend I tell you. That's why I come. Even if I could, I would never make visa for this man!' With that he stood up to leave. 'I go now, see my wife. Too much trouble for me this woman!'

'Have you been stupid again?' I smiled.

'Agh, my Russian girlfriend she is the stupid. She text me … my wife she read … beeeg fight! I am Muslim. I can have four wives, but I don't want. I only play with my girlfriend for the fun. I never leave my wife, you understand, I love her, but she is crazy sometimes!' he said tapping his head.

'They are all crazy!' I joked as I walked him to his car, glad that he wasn't going to burn up a night of writing after all. Glad again that he was my friend.

As I returned to my writing desk it occurred to me that whatever had happened, I was going to have to sit Anthony down and set him straight. That I may have given him too much leeway to begin with and as such, he was trespassing boundaries without knowing it (maybe). One was Abdullah. He had proved himself to be an exceptional friend, whose services were not to be used (or abused) under any circumstances without my consent. I had come to rely heavily upon him for support in running a tight ship and I didn't want anything or anyone rocking our boat.

Decision made, I sat down at the computer equally determined to do justice to the combat scene that I had just read about in Paddy's biography. To get in the mood, I picked up his book and flicked through the pages to engage my senses in order to breathe life into the lines that were forming in my head. Ready then to roll, I tapped the keyboard to wake up the screen. Immediately, I noticed that something was wrong with one of the icons on the screen when it finally flickered into view.

Wrong in the sense that it did not belong there. Wrong in that the title "Divorce Proceedings" had nothing to do with the practice. Internet was not fully accessible in Muscat at the time so I had given Anthony permission to use the practice computer to correspond with his contacts overseas. No harm in that, but something else was wrong, and forewarned by Abdullah, I knew an alarm bell when I saw one.

While the file had nothing to do with practice business, I felt compelled to click on the link and read the proceedings. The ethical dilemma I faced in doing so (it was none of my business), was overruled by a *knowing* as powerful as a whisper, that in spite of our due diligence, Anthony was in fact up to no good.

2

A thunderbolt in bold

Unused to the legal jargon connected to a divorce, it took me a minute or so to unscramble the first page. It looked like some form of discussion document. Anthony was arguing his position on each point of the "causes of divorce" as laid out in paragraph after paragraph by his wife. The hairs on the back of my neck stood on end when I latched onto the magnitude of the contents.

Two things of significance came to mind. The first, that Anthony's wording was in stark contrast and conflict with the explanation that he had given us for his divorce (irreconcilable differences) Two, that we had a serious problem on our hands. There were four pages in total. By the end of page three my first impressions of him had changed from a lonely middle aged guy struggling to build a new life, to that of being a nasty bastard who most likely deserved what he got. Just when it could not get any worse, a thunderbolt in bold text leapt from the last page and struck me right between the eyes …

That under no circumstances was Anthony to be allowed in the company of his young son without qualified adult supervision

as laid down by the rules, following an investigation by the Canadian Department of Family Welfare.

My heart sank. I had to read it again. And again. This wasn't happening. This was a guy who carried a bible almost everywhere he went. Insisted on saying grace when we ate together and frowned when I used profanity ... the condescending bastard! The week before, he had proudly announced that he had just been appointed Youth Leader at the Christian Church for expatriates. It didn't register at the time, but his obvious disappointment at our declining his offer to be a voluntary Doctor at the Early Intervention Center suddenly made sense.

Whatever hope I may have had that this wasn't true, it was slowly torn asunder upon reading and rereading the document. Regardless of the allegations of child molestation, I had little doubt, from *his* written responses to his wife's claims, that her motivations for divorce were genuine.

'Why me?' We had worked hard, weathered the storms, taken the hits and rolled with the punches to get to this point. I had truly thought that we had arrived. That nothing else could go wrong. That we were doing some good in the world and that the universe was finally supporting us in "living the dream." What the hell had the Gods been thinking?!

To be sure I wasn't seeing things, or in case the file might get deleted, I printed off a hard copy and read and reread it until I had some semblance of a plan of how to deal with the matter. I couldn't imagine what Rashard (panic britches) was going to say, but Darling for one was going to hit the roof! To be sure to be sure, I printed off two more copies for safe keeping, then looked up the phone directory for a law firm from whom I could seek advice. A thousand different scenarios ran through my head, all bad. All amounting to one thing. Unless he could persuade us otherwise, we were back to square one in trying to find an associate.

'Divorce can be a very nasty business! It is not unusual that a wife will make such statements to strengthen her case ... really!' the lawyer stated the following morning at my surprise. 'You must speak to the man, give him the benefit of the doubt and get his side of the story.' He handed me back the document.

That afternoon, I was too distracted to write. I decided instead to do a 100 hour oil change on Edvina's engine as a way of organizing my thoughts which were in rapid oscillation between denial (I will wake up and it will have been all a bad dream), frustration (this is not

259

my idea of living the dream), resentment (for having my dream spoilt) and hoping against hope that his wife was in fact a liar.

Later that evening, Rashard must have shook *his* head a hundred times as he read through the divorce document.'

'Fuck!'

'I know!'

'What did the lawyer say?

'That I should listen to his side of the story.'

'I think it is a good advice.'

'What about the meeting with Abdullah?'

'It does not surprise me. Sooner or later most people try to change sponsors. That's why his Majesty made the law.'

'Do you want to be there?'

'No, I trust you will make the right decision. If we have to, we will sit him down later and remind him who he works for!'

He'd surprised me … again. Regardless of saving face, I had been embarrassed because I was responsible for getting us into this mess. I had expected him to have a conniption. To go off the rails and dance around like it was the end of the world. Instead he gave me his full support. It was another test of our sometimes shaky working relationship, but when the chips were down, like Molly's surgery, he rowed in behind. It was good to have him on board.

After a sleepless night, I decided not to beat around the bush when I started our weekly practice meeting the next morning.

'I found this on the computer desktop last night. I'm hoping that you can explain it.' I handed him the document.

Wide-eyed surprise would be the best way to describe his first reaction. There was no shaking of heads nor turning of pages. He knew exactly what the document contained.

'It's a copy of my divorce papers!' He might as well have been hit by a bombshell. I could tell by the catch in his voice and the defensive body language that he was rattled.

'It's none of my business I know, but as the director of this clinic I'm concerned about some of the accusations that your wife has made. In particular, the bold text on page four. It is inconsistent with the explanation you gave us during the application process.'

Unseeing, he reluctantly leafed through the pages, while his brain raced ahead to try and form some sort of reasonable explanation. In spite of the air conditioning, a slight patina of perspiration broke out on his forehead. He tried to wipe it off without me noticing.

'It's not what it seems!' He casually flicked the papers onto a small table beside him, dismissing their contents. 'It looks terrible … I know … but none of it is true! She is trying to screw me for an unfair settlement. Look, I was really pissed off when I wrote that. I never sent it in the end. In fact I thought that I had deleted it!'

'Go on,' I gestured without saying a word.

'She has made these allegations to try and strengthen her case. That's all. It's a Canadian Government department ruling, but they have no jurisdiction in Zimbabwe nor Muscat for that matter. She knows this. That's why she states it all happened there. There has never been a court case. No charges have been laid. I have never been given the opportunity to defend myself!'

'Why didn't you tell us at the start? If this gets out, it will look really bad for the practice.'

'You are right, I should have, but after all of the problems you said you had with the last guy, I was afraid that it might get in the way. I'm sorry, really!'

He couldn't apologize enough.

'I know how this must look. It's just that guys my age don't get many opportunities to start over again and I was afraid I was going to be stuck in Zimbabwe forever. Have you spoken to Darling about this? I can imagine the impression it must have made.'

I didn't bother to repeat the expletives she had uttered when she had read the document.

'It looks terrible, I know, but I have lost contact with my daughters and my son because of her. She wants me to support them all, but this stops me from going home to Canada to practice. She has completely cut me off by getting this government department involved.'

I don't know which was working faster, his brain, his mouth or his hands, but he was persuasive, genuine, even sincere as his body language changed from being defensive at the beginning to being open and apologetic and then finally pissed off.

'You know what Martin Luther King said the week that he was killed? "There is nothing worse than being right against a government that thinks you are wrong!"' He pointed to the bold text that prevented him being around his son unsupervised. 'Imagine how you would feel, if Darling did that to you and your kids!'

'Look Anthony, I'm sorry for your troubles.' I was, genuinely. I had gone into the meeting fully prepared to dismiss him on the spot. Now I wasn't so sure. Perhaps the lawyer had been right, I thought. His argument was persuasive enough that I began to feel like we had been overreacting. 'There is no judgment here. No hard feelings. It is just that you have placed us in a very difficult position. Had we known about this, we wouldn't have taken you on!'

'I understand, but am I not doing a good job? Surely the end justifies the means?'

I was stumped by his question. The answer clinically was yes, but there was more to it than that. I wanted a team player and regardless of the allegations, his recent meeting with Abdullah had proved otherwise.

'There's more to it than that. It's a matter of security. I'm responsible for the practice and my sponsor's interests.'

'But I have told you the truth!' he pleaded.

'I know, I know,' I tried to sound sympathetic. 'But you have put us in a *very* difficult position!' I shook his hand to end the meeting, 'but I'm going to have to run this by Rashard.'

About what, I wasn't sure. The end justifying the means? The Mission of the practice? Take him on face value and carry on regardless? They all had a certain ring that could be used as an excuse to serve our mutual purposes. So long as he toed the line we could all get on with our lives. I wished Darling had been there to hear his side of the story.

3

'But he hasn't done anything wrong!'

'Look, I'm trying to be pragmatic here. He has already cost us a fortune. If we let him go, we are back to square one. I need another doctor to support me in practice!' I tried to explain to Darling as we discussed my meeting with Anthony that evening. She was busy writing a report to be used for fund raising for the group.

'What do you mean?' If she was all for getting rid of him after I had told her about his meeting with Abdullah, then the divorce papers were like a red rag to a bull.

'Well, better the devil you know, than the devil you don't. Rashard is confident that we can make him toe the line!'

'Over my dead body!' she countered.

'I knew you'd say that!' The last thing I wanted to do was spend another year running around like a blue-arsed fly (and getting no writing done) until we found yet *another* associate.

'The way I see it, we have two choices.' She closed the lid of her laptop. 'The first is to get rid of him.'

'What's the second?' I didn't hold much hope for the second being anything better.

'You sell our souls and that of our children to the Devil and you keep him on.'

Ouch!

I knew that keeping him on staff was to tread the fine line between what was right and wrong. How I could do so without condoning Anthony's behavior was the sixty five thousand dollar moral and ethical question.

The following morning I received an unexpected call from Rashard.

'I have just had a very interesting visit from Anthony!'

'What the hell is he doing calling you?' I was furious that Anthony had disturbed him at his place of work.

'He explained about your meeting last night. He was very distressed, but felt that as the sponsor of the clinic he had the right to give me his side of the story. He's concerned that you might make the wrong decision.'

'And?'

'We spent over an hour together.'

'I'm sorry Rashard, I can't believe he bothered you at work. I made it very clear to him at the beginning that I am in charge.'

'It's okay. These are exceptional circumstances. He was very convincing. I'm inclined to think that we should keep him.' He had an upbeat tone, as if he had solved our little problem. 'What do you think?'

'I have decided to let him go!' I countered. The word pragmatic had suddenly disappeared from my vocabulary. The choice was motivated by the same part of my brain that had declined Anthony's offer to work as a doctor at the Early Intervention Center. Rashard was off limits as far as Anthony was concerned. If he was prepared to go behind my back and undermine my authority, then as far as I was concerned he had "crossed the line" of culpability.

'But he hasn't done anything wrong!'

'What about the meeting with Abdullah?' I was now convinced that Darling was right. This guy was going to be more trouble than he was worth.

'I questioned him about that. He says that it was all a misunderstanding. I have made it very clear who is boss!'

'And who is that?' I demanded. The last thing he had expected was a show down.

'I think you are overreacting.' He avoided the question. I could sense him tense at the end of the line.

'I'm not happy about this. You and I have an agreement. It's my responsibility to protect the interests of the practice.' I didn't want to have to pull rank or shout him down. But it was important to establish who was in charge. 'You said that you trusted me to make the right decision. I believe the right decision is to get rid of the guy.'

'What about my dividend?' He finally blurted the truth.

'What about the thousands of dollars I have already blown in processing his visas and work permits?' I shot back. 'Regardless of the money, the last thing I want to do is to lose another doctor, but you have to think about the long term picture. If he is not telling the truth, then where will we stand? We brought him into the country. We are his employer. *We* are responsible!' I stressed. 'Did you know that he has just been elected the youth leader at the local church for Christ's sake!'

'He didn't mention it,' he tried to sound offhand.

'I'll bet he didn't. If he is prepared to molest his six year old son, then you can only imagine the field day he will have over there. What's that going to do to the practice?'

There was silence at the end of the line.

'How strong is your case against him?' Rashard finally asked.

'What do you mean?'

'We have passed the three month trial period set down by the Labor Department. He is now considered a permanent employee.'

'So?'

'So, unless you have a watertight case, getting rid of him is going to be a nightmare.'

To be honest, I had no idea what the laws were at the time, but I was surprised by his concerns.

'I have an agreement with Anthony, that if for any reason the associateship does not work out, then we will support him in moving to Dubai or any of the other Arab states of his choosing. Clinically he is sound, so I could give him a good reference which should negate any necessity for a knock-down drag-out fight in the courts.'

'What if someone calls you to back up the reference and wants to know why he was dismissed?'

'I'll just say that we over-estimated the market and that Muscat is not big enough to support two Chiropractors,' I lied, thinking that Scotty's twisted version of the truth had some use after all.

'You had better be right!' He surprised me by hanging up the phone. It wasn't the first time that he had done it. I was more surprised though by the tone of his voice. One second upbeat, the next stressed, it now contained something that bordered on fear. I wondered what else had transpired in their meeting.

I called my lawyer to discuss the matter. He was very much in favor of my idea to support Anthony into a clinic somewhere else, but named the case for dismissal as one of *non-disclosure* in the event that Anthony decided to take us to court.

'He wouldn't do something that stupid would he?' I'd put myself in Anthony's shoes thinking that the last thing I would want was this kind of information being made public about me.

'It depends on whether he is innocent or guilty. Right now all you have are allegations. They could just as easily be false, which could make the matter very complicated for you. If he takes you to court, then the onus will be on *you* my friend to prove the case. No matter how much you trust the hairs on the back of your neck or the feeling in your gut, neither will be accepted as evidence. You will have to come up with a better argument!'

I hadn't thought of that one either.

'That is why you should sit down with the guy and try to resolve it in a friendly way and keep it outside the court.'

While I was pissed at his non-disclosure and the fact that he had gone behind my back, I was still confident that we could resolve this matter in an amicable way. Regardless of the law, the short term discomfort and expense of getting rid of Anthony was far outweighed by the gut feeling of knowing that we were better off without him.

However, something about that gut feeling had me thinking that he may not be equally forthcoming as I called him to a meeting over our decision.

4

A live one on our hands!

The scene was already set when I arrived at the practice. Anthony had made coffee and brought fresh dates from the market. Presuming the best, his handshake was friendly and bore confidence in the way he poured the coffee from a height into two cups that had already been sugared. As we made our way into my office, he had a lightness to his step and a cheer in his voice that told me he had not been in contact with Rashard since their last meeting. The news therefore was like a sledgehammer.

'But they are only allegations!' he cried in disbelief at my decision to let him go after we had sat down. 'Nothing has been proven. I'm the innocent victim here!'

'I'm sorry, I have seen a lawyer and this is what I have been advised to do. I said at the beginning that there was no judgment on this and I mean it.'

'Let me speak to your lawyer, I'm sure I can convince him otherwise!'

'Anthony, I know this is very bad news.' (It would have been a conflict of interest for my lawyer to advise us both.)

'But … you have to listen to me, to give me some chance to defend myself!'

'It's not about defending yourself, nor is it about judgment. Personally, I don't care either way.' My tone of voice must have surprised him. 'Seriously, it's a big world out there. We agreed at the beginning that if it didn't work out, for whatever reason, that we would do our best to help you relocate. It doesn't have to be the Middle East. Look at Arthur C. Clarke, one of the most famous authors in the world. He lives in Sri Lanka for this very reason. Thailand and Vietnam are far more accepting of this type of lifestyle. You could establish a practice over there for buttons and no one would ever bother you. Seriously Anthony, I'm live and let live, but this country has the death penalty!'

I couldn't believe what I was saying. It was like I was condoning his behavior.

'But nobody has to know about this. I mean it's just you and Darling and Rashard. Surely it could be kept a secret?' He was desperate.

'I'm not the one who let this slip. Luckily it was in the practice, but next time it could be in the public domain. What about my lawyer, or Abdullah? It just takes the wrong person who thinks that they are doing their civic duty and we will all be screwed.'

'You told Abdullah?'

'I had to discuss this with somebody other than a lawyer. Abdullah has thousands of employees. I figured he would have the experience to deal with it.'

'What did he say?'

'Same as the lawyer, but worse. Anthony, I have a wife and kids to think about. I am duty bound to protect the interests of my sponsor. Rashard and I have both invested heavily in the practice. You haven't. If anything were to happen, God only knows what it would do to our reputation.'

'But when I spoke to Rashard he was supportive about me staying! Has he not talked to you about it?' It was the first he'd mentioned of their meeting.

'I know, but Rashard is not the law, nor does he operate above it. The death penalty is the death penalty. Do you know what Arabic justice is? They take you out into the desert and make you dig your own hole and then they shoot you in the back of the head. Abdullah tells me that the desert is full of bodies!' Overly dramatic I know, but I was letting him know that his meeting with Abdullah had been a waste of time.

'But they are only allegations. Nothing has been proven. There is nothing registered in the courts. Even if there was, Zimbabwe is such a mess that you would never be able to find it!' He wasn't just arguing his case now. He was arguing for his life.

'Anthony ... again ... I'm sorry. The decision has been made. You can't stay with the practice. As I said we will do our best to help you. I will give you a great reference. We have a spare treatment table and some other equipment you can take to get you started somewhere else.'

A long period of awkward silence followed. A long period of him staring into the middle distance, shuffling in his chair, searching for an answer I would buy. Beginning a sentence, but just as quickly ending it in case he put his foot in it. Long pauses and fatal sighs as his desperation to maintain a "front" slowly died between the two of us.

'What if I was to come to you and Darling?' he finally suggested.

'What do you mean?'

'When I get the urge, I could come to you and you could counsel me and we could work through it together.'

I couldn't believe what he was saying. He hadn't said "if" he'd said "when!" We were no longer dealing with the allegations. We suddenly had a *live one on our hands!* I berated myself that I had not made the effort to record our meeting.

'Anthony, I really wish that you hadn't told me this! (NOT) First of all, I'm not qualified. Based on what you have just told me it would make me complicit to everything that has happened in the past and an accessory to anything that might happen in the future, if my counseling did not work. If this was to become public knowledge for any reason it would be seen as irresponsible on my part that I knew about your history and continued to employ you. You have made a mistake. A big one. We all do from time to time.'

The part of me that was trying to sound sympathetic and supportive was now in a wrestling match with the part of me that wanted to drag him from his seat and knock his head off for what he had done to his son. His admission however had been strategic. There were no witnesses. A last ditch effort to win me over. I kicked myself again several times for not recording the meeting. Either way, I still had to get rid of the bugger!

'Please don't fight this decision. We will work with you so that you can find somewhere just as good to make a new start.'

Another long pause.

'What do I tell my patients?' His shoulders sagged. I didn't see it as a victory, but rather his submission to the idea that moving on peacefully was the better option.

'This dismissal is effective immediately. I will take over your patients tomorrow. It's best that you take your stuff with you today.' I considered it best that he stay away from the practice.

'What about Linda?'

'I will just tell her that you had a serious family issue. She will understand. Let me know what you intend doing and where you want to go.' I stood up and offered him my hand in appreciation for doing the right thing. The meeting had lasted well over an hour. 'We will do our best to row in behind you.'

There are a lot of things they don't teach you in Chiropractic College that you learn from years of practice. One is reading a person's mind through their posture. Call it body language, call it intuition, but you can tell when a person is happy or sad, in a good space or needing greater support, committed to their care, or pissed off because you haven't played Jesus Christ. As Anthony walked away with his belongings under his arm, the thinly veiled air of condescension that had tolerated my authority was now pulled off to reveal the fury of a bad loser. For someone who didn't like profanity, he had 'fuck you' written all over him!

5

'Arabic, Arabic, *Arabic*!'

A week passed quietly without any word. I called Rashard twice
to see if he had heard from him, but he was just as much in the dark.
There had seldom been a day in the three months that Anthony had
worked for us that we didn't have some sort of contact. The relief at no
longer having him in the practice was quickly overshadowed by the
knowledge that the longer it took for him to make contact, the more
likely it was that he was up to no good.

This was confirmed ten days after his termination when I received
a summons to the Disputes Tribunal at the Labor Court to answer for
1st Chiropractic in the case of "Unfair Dismissal" brought by one
"aggrieved" Anthony Christink. At least this is what my lawyer
explained. Save for my name, the entire document was written in
Arabic. I tried to contact Anthony directly over the next three days to
have a "face off" and sort it out as we had originally agreed, but he
wouldn't return my calls.

'You don't need a lawyer for this. Just someone who speaks
Arabic,' my lawyer stated. 'There will be an arbitrator who will listen
to the case and work to help both sides settle it. They don't have the
power to rule for either side, but will use their legal training and
experience to see if an agreement can be reached without it having to
go to court. Don't worry about this. This is his way of getting a better

271

settlement, that is all. If you present the divorce papers along with the proposal you told me about to help him move on, then you should not have any problems.'

'Are you sure?' I had zero experience in these matters.

'Believe me, whatever happens, Dr Anthony will not want this to go to court. It would take years to settle and cost him more than he could ever hope to claim.'

As reluctant as I felt, it sounded straightforward.

'Wallah Docta, I will do it!' Abdullah volunteered when Rashard said that he was tied up with an international audit at the Air Traffic training center on the scheduled date. 'I have been one hundred time before. It easy, I tell you, I know what to do!'

The hassle of attending the hearing was compounded by the inconvenience for Linda of having to reschedule all of the patients at the practice which was now top heavy without two doctors to serve it. I would have to work extra hours after the court hearing to try to catch up on my ever expanding workload.

When we arrived at the court as scheduled, we found that the time was arbitrary and dependent on the case load that day (huge). The building was compact, the waiting room overcrowded, the air fetid from poor ventilation and years of bitter disgruntlement. The whole environment felt more than intimidating, but with a glowing reference for Anthony in my briefcase and a relocation package that would help him set up almost anywhere within a matter of weeks, I felt hopeful that one or two sessions would end it as advised by my lawyer.

Anthony and his interpreter were nowhere to be seen. When our names were finally called, they appeared from behind an opaque glass screen. Without introduction, we were led into a room so small that the walls were marked by the stain of shuffling bodies. I'd say the place had not been decorated in over twenty years. I was pleased to find that the judge sitting behind a huge desk on my left was female.

As an act of good faith I intended to shake hands with all concerned, but instead, my confidence was shaken when Anthony introduced his interpreter as his "lawyer". In spite of the judge's obvious ability to speak fluent English, she immediately set the tone by insisting that all of the proceedings take place in Arabic.

We were totally unprepared. I had no Arabic. Abdullah's ability to interpret into English was limited. It was the equivalent of tying our hands behind our back and throwing us in with the sharks (excuse the pun). Not knowing any better, the meeting thereafter quickly descended into a farce.

'Arabic, Arabic, Arabic, Arabic?' the judge addressed me directly. I hadn't a clue what she was saying.

'She want to know why you are here?' explained Abdullah.

'Because I have been subpoenaed!' I shrugged, wondering why I was being asked to go first. I had assumed that it would be up to Anthony's lawyer to make his case.

'What this word "supenade?"' Abdullah replied, confused.

'A letter from the court, Dr Anthony,' I handed Abdullah the subpoena.

'Arabic, Arabic, Arabic, Arabic,' Abdullah explained and handed the letter to the judge.

'Arabic, Arabic, Arabic,' she showed the subpoena to Anthony's lawyer who acknowledged by handing her his business card.

'Arabic, Arabic, Arabic, Arabic?' the judge addressed me again.

'She want know why you have fired Mr. Anthony?' Abdullah explained.

'I found this on my computer two weeks ago. It is the divorce papers for Mr. Anthony and his wife. It states …' I wasn't sure how to word the next few sentences. To protect the reputation of the practice, I had kept the knowledge of Anthony's deepest darkest secret under wraps. Only Darling, Abdullah and Rashard knew about it. Had we been sitting around a table in the privacy of a lawyer's office it would have been easier to talk about Anthony molesting his son, but in front of a judge? I was surprised that Anthony would want it known either.

'*Arabic, Arabic, Arabic, Arabic!!!!!*' Before I knew it, Anthony's lawyer leaned forward and snatched the divorce document out of my hand.

'*Arabic, Arabic, Arabic, Arabic!!!!!*' Abdullah shouted and tried unsuccessfully to retrieve the document, but the lawyer prevented him by holding it behind his head.

'*Arabic, Arabic, Arabic, Arabic!!!!!*' Abdullah appealed to the Judge.

'*Arabic, Arabic, Arabic, Arabic!!!!!*' The lawyer shouted back.

'Arabic, Arabic, Arabic, Arabic,' the judge explained in a calming tone, waving my friend to sit down. 'Please!' she finally appealed. Abdullah was fit to be tied.

'He say you cannot present this in the court because it not in Arabic!' Abdullah nodded at Anthony's lawyer. 'He say the rules say it must be in Arabic translation!' The judge acknowledged with the nod of her head.

'Arabic, Arabic, Arabic, Arabic,' Abdullah spoke again to the judge, but pointed at Anthony.

'Arabic, Arabic, Arabic, Arabic!!!!!' Anthony's lawyer objected. *'Arabic, Arabic, Arabic, Arabic!!!!!'* He ranted, crushing the divorce document with his hands and throwing it on the floor at Abdullah's feet.

'Arabic, Arabic, Arabic, Arabic!!!!!' Abdullah spat, picking it up, opening it out and flattening it on his lap. *'Arabic, Arabic, Arabic, Arabic!!!!!'* He repeated and again pointed at Anthony. We were about two seconds away from a fist fight.

'We all speak English here!' I shouted, losing my cool above their ranting. 'I haven't come to argue a case - I have come to offer terms for dismissal!'

'Please!' Anthony's lawyer interrupted and turned to the judge and begged in Arabic that we speak *Arabic*, before I had a chance to finish.

'I am sorry.' She was genuinely apologetic. 'But I am bound by the law. If the defendant insists, then we must proceed in Arabic!'

'Arabic, Arabic, Arabic, Arabic!!!!!' Abdullah cried out in frustration.

'Arabic, Arabic, Arabic, Arabic!!!!!' Anthony's lawyer shot back totally unfazed. 'Arabic, Arabic, Arabic, Arabic,' he then spoke to the judge.

There was a long pause, followed by a sigh of frustration from Abdullah and then further silence.

'Does somebody want to tell me what is going on here?' I finally broke the tension.

'The defendant's lawyer states that your representative is not qualified to argue this matter,' she kindly explained. She held her hand in the air to prevent Anthony's lawyer from making any further objection to her communicating in English. Something in the way she spoke told me that while bound by the law, she was embarrassed for the unnecessary way in which Abdullah had been humiliated and made to lose face in front her. 'I think in this case it would be best to adjourn until you can find a lawyer to help you,' she advised.

We had been duped. The idea that an honest agreement could have been arrived at between civilized men had faded to something more sinister and malevolent. *Will the real Anthony please step into the spotlight!*

If Anthony or his lawyer thought that having me ruled out of the proceedings and making a fool of my friend was a clever move, then they were wrong. Far from being a fool, Abdullah's genius was his innate ability to break the most complex of problems down to simplest of steps. To help in solving *my* problem he had announced on our way to court that morning that he had been able to locate a sponsor in Dubai who was willing to take Anthony on without too many questions. Had he been truly clever, Anthony would have been now sitting on a golden opportunity. Instead he had shown his hand and I knew if he wasn't careful how he handled Abdullah, he would end up using it to dig his own grave.

'It was an ambush!' I had a meeting with my lawyer later that afternoon to seek further advice.' He could tell that I was pissed off.

'It does not surprise me. I told you. He will use the court as a means of negotiation to get a better settlement, that is all! I will give you Medani, my best Advocate. He is like a lion in court. The next time you go in there it will be a different game!'

I had my doubts.

When Medani read through my evidence for dismissal that Anthony's lawyer had refused to allow me to present to the judge, he wasn't so sure either. He was a small man, of Sudanese descent, with a serious face that was too tired to smile from all of the injustices that he had witnessed in his own country.

'Regardless of the allegations, it is his language that concerns me!' he echoed my sentiments, by pointing to Anthony's responses to his wife's accusations. 'I think that we will need to be careful with this one!' was his final piece of advice.

6

'Round two …!'

He wanted a lawyer to argue my case. I got one. He wanted the divorce document translated into Arabic. I did it. I even agreed to closing the practice (again) so as to fit in with a date that would work best for *his* lawyer. You'd think after that, that he might play ball.

'Arabic, Arabic, Arabic, Arabic,' Anthony's lawyer spoke to Medani as soon as the formalities had been dispensed with.

'He objects to you presenting this document as evidence. Legally, you are supposed to provide it before the proceedings so that he has the opportunity to prepare a rebuttal,' Medani explained.

'You were given this the last time we were here and you threw it back at us!' I gestured my frustration at their unwillingness to engage in negotiations.

'It is true, but it had not been translated,' Medani kept a level tone. 'For the record,' Medani spoke in English, 'and the benefit of my client's understanding, I am now presenting you with this as evidence for cause of dismissal.'

'Arabic, Arabic, Arabic, Arabic?' Anthony's lawyer responded.

'Do you have anything else you wish to present?' Medani interpreted.

'No.'

'Arabic, Arabic, Arabic, Arabic.' Anthony's lawyer spoke to Medani and then to the judge who nodded.

'They request time to consider this document. The judge has approved so we must finish for today,' Medani looked me straight in the eye and nodded that I too should concede to the request.

'Arabic, Arabic, Arabic, Arabic?'

'They are asking that we meet again in two days' time.

In spite of the fact that it was my busiest day in practice and would cost us a fortune to cancel, I nodded in agreement, just to get the whole mess sorted.

Medani though had different ideas as he leafed through a small pocket diary that I could see was blank on every page. 'Arabic, Arabic, Arabic, Arabic!'

'Two weeks?' It was the first word Anthony had spoken in all of the proceedings.

'Arabic, Arabic, Arabic, Arabic!' his lawyer argued that his client had no work and therefore no income. The judge in turn appealed to Medani, but he refused to concede. Having accepted their request for time to consider the document, he had a right to name his date.

'I know this man,' Medani acknowledged Anthony's lawyer out of earshot, as soon as we cleared the court. 'We went to law school together many years ago in Darfur. He is a brilliant lawyer. *Very* clever. He could end this today if he wanted, but it is obvious to me that this is not the first time Mr. Anthony has been in court. I'm sure that he is the one directing the proceedings!'

The two week wait was hard on my nerves. It helped that I was flat tack with the practice and helping Darling with the Intervention Group and writing e-mails to my lawyer, and doing my best to not be a grumpy father, but lack of sleep was taking its toll.

Captain Keith had always advised us to keep a wary eye on the horizon for that unexpected storm that was impossible to predict, but you knew was coming. I was beginning to get that sense about Anthony from Medani; that beneath the surface lay something ominous that you would never want to take your eyes off.

Rashard as usual was nowhere to be seen. He was named as sponsor in the case and therefore liable, but I was responsible for dealing with the matter. Ultimately we expected to win, but it surprised me that the "worry wart" was not on the phone every day. At the same time though I was grateful for his confidence. It was a relief to not have him winding me up any more than I already was.

It was less about fear and more about frustration. I was confident that we had the moral, legal and financial high ground to fight the case, but it was a massive distraction that put the brakes on the practice and my finishing 'The Christening.' We had put two years of hard work into building up momentum. Instead of "rowing in behind" as promised, he put on the anchors. Mostly though, it was my inability to speak Arabic that riled me. As captain of the ship and master of my own soul, I felt vulnerable from having a stranger do my bidding in such critical circumstances.

'Round three …!'

'Arabic, Arabic, Arabic, Arabic,' Anthony's lawyer waved the divorce document in his hand and then pointed it at me.

'He says that it is a piece of paper that contains the name of the defendant, nothing more,' Medani explained. 'There is no proof that it is genuine and like the wrongful allegations it contains, that it has been constructed by you to defame his client!'

'You can't be serious!' Effectively Anthony's lawyer was calling me a liar. Funny how liar and lawyer are pronounced almost the same.

'Can you prove that this is genuine?' Medani asked.

'I printed it off the computer that Dr Anthony was using at our clinic to correspond with his wife!' It couldn't be any more genuine than that. Could it?

'*Arabic, Arabic, Arabic, Arabic!*' Anthony's lawyer argued, not needing any explanation.

'He says that the only thing it proves, is that you got it from a computer that *you* own. Therefore it could be just as likely that you have made it up!'

'What?' I couldn't believe what I was hearing. Out of the corner of my eye I caught Anthony turning his face away to hide one of the many sniggers I had grown used to him making when he knew that he had again tripped us up.

'*Arabic, Arabic, Arabic, Arabic!*' his lawyer argued on and on and on and on.

'He says it is just a document. Anyone could have written this. Unless you can prove otherwise, then you have no business presenting this in court.' Medani delivered the news straight-faced and solemn. Another day wasted, and he requested two more weeks to consider the matter before the next hearing.

'Did you know he could do this?' I was fuming as we left the court.

'It was one of many things that he could have done,' Medani mused as we drove back to his office.

'So what do we do?'

'If you have some other way that you can discredit him, then his lawyer may persuade him to think twice about dragging this out, rather than risk losing the advantage they have gained.'

'What advantage?' I was surprised that he would make such a statement.

'You must not only demonstrate "just cause." More importantly, you must be able to prove it. So far you have failed to prove anything. If you continue to fail to do so in the next few sessions, then you will have provided them with just cause for unfair dismissal.'

'What ...?'

'Did it ever occur to you that he might have planted the document on your computer with the intention of you finding it and acting as you have done?'

'No way!' It was crazy. I wasn't buying it, but then again, being the one who was no good at playing games, I may have played right into his hands.

'You said so yourself. You cannot prove the divorce papers are genuine, therefore...' He let it hang.

'What do you think? I mean about the papers. You believe they are genuine don't you?'

'What I think does not matter. If you cannot prove their authenticity, then I have nothing to argue your case with, which means you may have a more serious problem than you think.'

'But ...'

'The reference you showed me for Dr Anthony. Is it the truth?' Medani changed the subject.

'For the most part. I have embellished it somewhat to make him look good. I had a few complaints when he started, but nothing serious. You get that when doctors change patients.'

'See if anyone will make a formal complaint. In writing. They must be prepared to back it up if the court demands it. Even if you only get one, then you will have a better chance of bringing him to heel.'

By the end of the week I had three letters of complaint, all from women, all genuine, including one on headed paper from a member of the royal family describing Anthony in no uncertain terms as a "creep."

The grievances included inappropriate touching, suggestive behavior and a penchant for flirtatious and *procreative* language.

I should have been happy, but I wasn't. According to Medani, this was valuable ammunition that could potentially have Anthony fired on the spot. However, it was also more of a reflection of how big an idiot I had been. To be frank, I was shocked and ashamed at how I'd missed the signs that were now evident once I began to take notice. I'd allowed myself instead to be blinded by my "vision" and my "mission" for the practice and the Early Intervention Center. To fulfilling my promise to Lewis, instead of keeping an eye on the horizon for that inevitable storm in whose clutches we now found ourselves gripped.

'Round Four ...!'

'Arabic, Arabic, Arabic, Arabic ...!'
'He is objecting to you presenting these letters of complaint (already translated). He says that they are not the reason for dismissal. For all he knows they have been solicited and fabricated in favor of the clinic,' Medani interpreted.

'These are genuine. The three patients who wrote them will be happy to attend this hearing and testify to their authenticity,' I stated, happy to have something more tangible to argue the case. He could object all he wanted, but Medani had negotiated with the judge in the last meeting that in order to save time, either side could present evidence at the time of the hearing.

'Arabic, Arabic, Arabic, Arabic ...!' Anthony's lawyer argued brushing aside the letters of complaint that Medani placed on the judge's table.

'Arabic, Arabic, Arabic, Arabic...!' Medani disagreed.

'He says that you have yet to prove the original case for dismissal. That failure to do so is unjust and defames his client's good reputation.'

'What!' Had we presented the letters to the Chiropractic board of New Zealand or the U.K. Anthony would have been up shit creek without a paddle. Regardless of the allegations about his son, dismissal would have been upheld, an investigation ensued and heavy penalties imposed including possible loss of his license to practice upon testimony of the complainants. If I had been Anthony and had to choose between a glowing reference or three letters of complaint for inappropriate and unprofessional behavior, I knew which choice I'd be making.

My big problem though is that I wasn't Anthony and this wasn't the U.K. or New Zealand. That there was no Chiropractic Board. Therefore, unless I could prove that he had molested his son then I was the one who was going to be up the creek.

'Arabic, Arabic, Arabic, Arabic,' Anthony's lawyer reached into a file in his brief case and handed the judge and Medani two manila folders with several sheets of paper contained within. 'Arabic, Arabic, Arabic, Arabic,' he repeated, pointing to different paragraphs that had been highlighted on each page. *'Arabic, Arabic, Arabic, Arabic!!!'* he accused pointing at me, then the pages, then to Anthony who sat and shook his head with the expression of someone who had been deeply offended.

'He says that none of the complaints are true and that he can prove it. Furthermore, that it is you who are in breach of contract. That you promised him, before he came to Oman, that the company would cover him for medical and dental care and emergencies, and that he would receive the annual trip home that all expatriate employees are entitled to as per the labor laws of Oman.'

Medani gave me one of those "you didn't tell me this!" looks.

'Arabic, Arabic, Arabic, Arabic!' Anthony's lawyer interjected.

'Also, he says that you have underpaid him by 50 rials per week since he started working for you.'

'What …!' After making me look like an idiot he was now making me look like a liar in front of my lawyer who had nothing to deflect or deny his argument. I was aghast. Even more so when I read through the contracts and discussion papers. The text had been changed! The figures modified! By how much, I could not be sure, until I compared them to the original documents. The problem was that they looked like the original documents that I had sent.

'Arabic, Arabic, Arabic, Arabic?' Medani questioned.

'Arabic, Arabic, Arabic, Arabic!!!!' Anthony's lawyer was offended that we should doubt *his* evidence and pointed to the top of each page.

'He says that they are original documents as marked by the Hotmail and Zimtel (Zimbabwe telecom) headings. He says that he can forward them to us from his computer to verify them.'

We were stumped. I realized there and then that Anthony had no intention of backing down. That he had been on the offensive from the very beginning. Not only had the letters of complaint failed to knock him off his perch, but suddenly Anthony's allegations of *my* breach of contract were now making me look like the bad guy. The labor laws in

Oman rule harshly against employers who take advantage of their employees. The judge, whom I had thought would be sympathetic to our case, was now looking at me with a different set of eyes.

'Arabic, Arabic, Arabic, Arabic,' Medani immediately requested another break to "consider his client's position."

7

The last straw

'Come on. How did it go?' Darling cajoled when I finally got home that evening from the lawyer's office. It was obvious that she had been having a good day, but I was raging at Medani's boss. The last thing I wanted to do was talk.

'He promised me a lion, but I end up with a f&*$#n pussy!' Darling laughed as she set the table for dinner.

'You think? You should see the documents he has presented in court accusing us of breach of contract.' Whatever happy day she was having, it suddenly hit the kitchen floor.

'What did Medani do?'

'He should have read Anthony the riot act for lying in court and threatened him with perjury, but no, what does he do?' I ranted. 'He just sits there and lets it all happen without putting up any sort of fight!'

Not only was I was frustrated, I was beginning to grow suspicious about what was really going on between the lawyers. Every minute I spent with Medani, either in person, or on the phone, cost us. Every e-mail I sent or received was invoiced "for consideration" which was a minimum one hour billing. Whatever Anthony's courtroom strategy was, I was starting to get the feeling that the lawyers for both sides were playing us for all we were worth.

'What really pisses me off is that I know the truth about Anthony and no-one, not even the judge, has bothered to ask me how I know.'

'Come on, ask me how I know ... ask me, ask me you dumb bastards!

'How?' Darling played the part to soothe me.

Because he told me, that's how! He sat across from me in our clinic and told me!

But then again, technically (I had grown to hate that word) he didn't. He had said, and I quote ... "if I get the urge."

"If I get the urge to what?" I could hear Anthony's lawyer question as I searched for my bottle of rum. 'What the hell does that actually mean?'

'You will give yourself a heart attack if you keep going on like that,' Darling admonished and pulled the bottle from the freezer where I had forgotten I had hidden it. 'What is Medani going to do about the contract?'

'He spent the whole afternoon "sighting" the documents!' I poured myself a triple shot over ice.

'What, doesn't he believe you?'

'It's not about belief. Any idiot can see that the contracts had been altered. He says that he wants time to discuss them with his colleagues and consider strategy and the possible outcomes for defense purposes. It's all money!' I said holding my hand up and rubbing my fingers like Fagan.

They were playing on my inexperience ... *"If you can't prove the document is genuine then he can have you for unfair dismissal and possible defamation"*... and magnifying my fears ... *"You will have to make a big pay out or release from contract, or both. He could end up setting up down the road!"*

While ours was not a battle for survival (at least not yet) it was definitely starting to hurt. Patient numbers were down, expenses were up. He had me physically exhausted and stressed out.

However, by allowing Anthony to dictate courtroom strategy, his lawyer wasn't doing him any favors either. The more he dragged out the case, the more bridges he burned. It should have been win, win for both sides, but the only winners so far had been the lawyers.

'What do you think is making him so belligerent? Darling asked. It was a question I had been considering a lot lately. It had been almost three months since his dismissal. Had he run with the deal we had originally been prepared to offer, he would have been set up in Dubai or somewhere comfortable by now. The fact that he had just presented altered documents in court was beginning to make me think that the guy was actually nuts!

As crazy as it was with Anthony, the experience made me thankful for Scotty and Angel. While our partnership had ended badly, it hadn't ended in court and for that I was eternally grateful. It would have been a nightmare. Thankfully, Darling was now back in weekly contact with Angel who had her own tale of woe about *their* latest associate who had been caught having sex in a car park with an underage girl!

Scotty and I had yet to talk. Put it down to bruised egos. It was a guy thing and it was stupid, but I found it hard to let go, when dealing with shit that was a constant reminder of past experiences. Sooner or later though one of us would give in. I would get drunk or he would get nostalgic, then one of the girls would twist an arm, a phone call would follow with several awkward moments then riotous laughter, like nothing had ever happened. We had been through too much for it not to happen. Just not yet, but it was good to be in contact through the girls.

The following morning I regretted the rums and vowed to stop drinking until the case had ended.

'You have a call,' Linda announced between patients. As I picked up the phone I was grateful for having such a great P.A. on my side. Responsible for the day to day running of the practice, she was the only other person I had confided in besides Rashard and Abdullah about what was going on with Anthony.

I had been expecting an update from Medani, so was surprised when H.R.H. came on the line.

'I have just finished a meeting with Dr Anthony.'

'You what?' I was incredulous. What the hell was Anthony thinking?

'He tells me that you have dismissed him?'

My immediate reaction was to tell him that it was none of his business, but it always pays to choose your words carefully when dealing with a member of the Royal family.

'With all due respect, it is a private matter. I'm sorry that Dr Anthony has dragged you into this.'

'It is no problem. He has shown me the papers for divorce from his wife and explained the nature of the allegations. It is not my business to get involved (oh yeah?) but my biggest concern is my friend Mulallah.'

H.R.H. had referred his friend, a minister of state, to me several months before with severe neck pain, but he had failed to make a complete recovery. When I asked Anthony for a second opinion, he scored gold by using a completely different adjustment and had assumed Mulallah's care until the day he had been dismissed. I had since become proficient in the necessary adjustment, but Anthony had ingratiated himself so much to the old man that he refused to see me after that.

'He is in pain again.' Unfortunately Mulallah had a habit imbibing too much Johnny Walker Gold and passing out on his sofa, or his chair, or the back seat of his car or wherever he happened to get pissed that day (most days). 'I was wondering would it be possible to make some arrangement?' H.R.H. inquired. He was referring to the practice. We had a special treatment table which Anthony needed to perform the necessary adjustment.

I understood his concerns. He was obliged by friendship and culture to make the call. Very often it was a way of solving a problem, opening a door, making an introduction or sometimes bringing peace to a long-standing problem, but Royal intervention or not, there was no way I was having the little bollix back in the practice.

'Did Anthony show you the letter of complaint from your sister in law?' I asked him.

'No, he did not mention it!'

Not all Royalty are obliged to act like Royalty. Some just want to be normal and act accordingly. Had Anthony known this, he wouldn't have gone feeling up H.R.H.'s sister-in-law in the first place!

'I think if you speak to your sister-in-law it will be easier for you to explain to Mulallah why he should come directly to me for treatment in the future. Dr Anthony is not going to be around for much longer!'

It was the last straw. I realized that it wasn't Anthony, but me who was nuts. That I was the one who had been playing pussy. I had given up my power and held out for the idea that good sense, self-preservation and finally, the lawyers would prevail through fair play. It was one thing for Anthony to try to negotiate for a better settlement in order to move on. I could understand that, but this time he had gone too far. In doing so however, he had also done me a favor. His going public to one of the highest ranking members of society negated the so called "charge of defamation" and meant I no longer had my hands tied behind my back. It was time to get down and dirty and bury him in the hole he had been digging for himself from the very start.

8

'Dr Feelgood!'

The decision to go on the offensive was liberating and opened up a whole world of options that had been prevented by legal process or doing the right thing. It wasn't just me against Anthony anymore. Steeled by inspiration from the Early Intervention Center, it was now Darling and I *fighting the good fight* to protect all children, but in particular those more vulnerable and less able to protect themselves.

The gloves were off, the Marquess of Queensberry Rules dumped in favor of bare-knuckle fighting. Anthony had muffed his chances of a friendly resolution by hitting below the belt for the first six rounds. Under Abdullah's coaching ("we are going to fuck him") we were going to line him up and deliver a knockout punch.

Our first move was to defer the next court date. When the judge, who was by now just as fed up as we were, asked for "just cause" Medani answered "back pain" which was reasonable. Except when you are married to a Chiropractor! (Two can play at being belligerent!) While Medani ran distraction, Abdullah and I got busy pulling pins and chucking hand grenades.

The first of three targets was the Department of Health. With letters of complaint in hand the aim was to discredit Anthony and have his license revoked, thus putting the onus back on him to prove his innocence. Target two (Immigration) and three (Police) would be hit with the collateral damage of involvement by allowing him into the country, thus drawing them into a shit fight and blaming each other. This all according to Abdullah our strategist!

'Please Docta, let me do all the talking!' he politely ordered as we drove down the highway to lay siege to our first objective. 'I know how to handle *these* people.' We were no longer bound by the rules of court (English is the second language of the Omani) but once again, for the sake of culture and being taken more seriously, it was better for him to handle the dealings in Arabic. Sure enough he was true to his word!

'Arabic, Arabic, Arabic, Arabic!' Abdullah gesticulated, postured, ranted, tapped the finger of blame squarely on the table and generally bullshitted the Head of the Health Department for Muscat about Anthony's unconscionable deception and reprehensible behavior.

'Arabic, Arabic, Arabic, Arabic?' The head of Health Department for Muscat replied. 'If what you say is true, then we will investigate,' he kindly replied in halting English. 'If you can provide complaints from wherever he comes from overseas it would be better. You can show that he was hired under false pretenses. If you have this, then you can blame the Police and Immigration for letting him in and they will have to deal with the matter!'

'Just as I tell you,' Abdullah stated as we left the office of the Head of the Health Department. 'Now we go and get the Police!'

As we drove across Muscat to Police headquarters I thought about the Zimbabwean Chiropractic Association. To be honest, I had never contacted them to check up on Anthony's *actual* references. Instead, I had taken them on face value, the recommendations of his patients in Oman and placed my faith in the serendipitous maneuverings of the Gods. Contacting the association now was another angle. A way to outflank and corner the bastard. I was starting to feel lucky when we reached Police Headquarters.

'Arabic, Arabic, Arabic, Arabic!' Abdullah gesticulated, postured, ranted, tapped the finger of blame squarely on the table and generally bullshitted the head of the Head of Police for Muscat about Anthony's unconscionable deception and reprehensible behavior.

'Arabic, Arabic, Arabic, Arabic?' The Head of Police for Muscat replied.

'If what you say is true, then we will investigate,' he kindly replied, again in English. 'If you can provide complaints from overseas, then you can show that he was hired under false pretenses. If you have this, then you can blame the Department of Health and

Department of Immigration for letting him in and they will deal with the matter!'

Abdullah nudged me under the table. Our luck was building momentum as we left Police Headquarters for the department of Immigration.

'*Arabic, Arabic, Arabic, Arabic!*' Abdullah, now well rehearsed, gesticulated, postured, ranted, tapped the finger of blame squarely on the table and generally bullshitted the Head of Immigration about Anthony's unconscionable deception and reprehensible behavior.

'Arabic, Arabic, Arabic, Arabic?' The Head of Immigration replied.

'If what you say is true, then we will investigate!' he kindly explained, in beautiful English 'If you can provide complaints from overseas, then you can show that he was hired under false pretenses. If you have this, then you can blame the Police and Department of Health for letting him in and they will deal with the matter!'

Abdullah nodded his head in thanks. By the time we were finished, Anthony would be begging for mercy!

My next stop was to contact the Zimbabwe Chiropractic association and get said information. The task initially proved impossible when none of the contact numbers that Anthony had supplied on his references would connect to the persons mentioned. (Smells like a rat eh!) Desperation being the mother of invention I had the bright idea to contact one of his former patients now living in Muscat. To go through an old address book and see if they could help me to find the other Chiropractors in Harare.

'Dr. Feelgood was his nickname! There was a collective sigh of relief among us when he left!' I had managed to track down the President of the association in Harare by phone. He was more than happy to share his own experience after I explained the purpose for my call. 'He first came to Zim to associate for a Dr Telon, another Canadian. Worked with him for a year or so, then opened up down the road and took all of his patients with him!' It sounded like a familiar story.

The news of Anthony molesting his own son held little surprise, but helped fill in the gaps as to why his family had returned to Canada and his wife was now divorcing him.

'Have you ever had any complaints against him?

'How do you think he got the nickname?'

'Why wasn't he taken to task?'

'He was one of the first Presidents of the Chiropractic Association here, so it made it very difficult. As you know by now he is very litigious and threatens to sue anyone who might dare to complain against him.'

'How does he get away with it?'

'It is a different culture down here now with Mugabi in charge. Nobody gives a shit anymore compared to years ago. It is much easier to change Chiropractors than it is to take legal action.'

'Do you have any of the complaints in writing?'

'I'm sure there will be something on file. I will talk to my colleagues and see if we can dig them up. Does he still carry that damn bible everywhere?'

'Yes!'

'The bugger would have prayer sessions and healings in his clinic, for Christ's sake! Nothing to do with Chiropractic, but it really appealed to the religious types over here.'

'I need the evidence in writing. Do you think you can help?'

'I feel sorry for you man. The guy is a sociopath. It will take a week or two, but I will see what we can do.'

I was kicking myself as I rang off. How I could have avoided all of these problems if I had made the effort to call him in the first place. My only consolation was that they were on side to help and it was just a matter of time before we received the ammunition we needed to knock Anthony off his perch.

Our confidence was boosted the following week when, true to Abdullah's prediction, the police hauled Anthony in for questioning and gave him a grilling that lasted most of an afternoon.

To add to his grief I had heard that to save money, he had hunkered down in a spare room of a large villa belonging to one of our patients who had two young children. A brief e-mail followed by a short phone conversation soon flushed him out and, adding insult to injury, Anthony was forced to seek digs in one of the more shady and lower socio economic parts of town. A massive blow for someone who was used to living in relative luxury with house staff to look after him.

As we waited for our new allies in Zimbabwe to send the ordnance for the final offensive, we decided to sail down the coast to our favorite anchorage for a long weekend. It was there, cocooned in the safety of our dear friend Edvina, that we drank hot chocolates with the kids by starlight, played Monopoly until two in the morning and decided that in spite of our challenges that our life wasn't just good …

it was great! That facing off against Anthony paled in significance to meeting a hurricane at sea, or the Twin Towers, or the tsunami that had wiped out thousands of innocent souls on a beach that we had once anchored off. We celebrated that we had the best practice (and practice manager) in the Middle East, that we had made a bunch of new friends and found our niche where we were able to give back as much as we received. The kids were well, Molly was a gift, and that in a world full of broken hearts and broken dreams, Darling and I were still together.

The following week, fully restored, Abdullah and I drove back to receive the expected good news from the Heads of Department.

9

'The man is ruthless!'

'Wallah Docta, this not good,' my comrade in arms stood up and began pacing the reception room, worried. We had been sitting for more than half an hour waiting for the Head of the Police to give us an audience.

'I'm sure he is a busy man,' I volunteered, but was equally concerned. Abdullah never had to wait for anyone.

'When he want something from me, I get it straight away, yes!' he nodded to the secretary sitting uneasily behind his desk which blocked access to his boss's office. 'You call him again,' Abdullah pointed to the phone. 'Now!' he gesticulated when the secretary made no effort to fulfill his wishes. He still refused to pick up the phone.

'Wallah, I do it myself!' Abdullah ignored the protests of the secretary. He pushed his way past, gave a cursory knock, then disappeared, shutting the door behind him to prevent the minion from following. Raised tempers quickly ensued. A file was slammed on a table, then more voices, less volatile, so that the secretary had to lean his head towards the door to hear what was being said. Silence followed, then conversation (civilized), the door swung open and the head of Police walked out and stood right in front of me. (SHEEIIT!)

'We have our doubts, but we do not have any proof because you have not provided any,' he pointed back to Abdullah who remained

293

dejected in his office. 'We have spoken to Mr. Anthony who of course denies everything, but there is nothing that we can do. He has no charges against him that we can find and he has a clean record since coming to Muscat!' he shrugged and handed me a copy of a police clearance from Zimbabwe.

'Did you call the police who wrote this?'

'Of course!' he tried to lie, then backtracked. 'They have been impossible to contact! Get the evidence you promised and go to the Department of Health and tell them you don't want him. If it is good enough, then they can contact me, but you must understand, we are bound by the law. We can't go arresting a person because someone suspects them. We must have proof!' He led us out of reception with our tails between our legs.

'Why he not call?' Abdullah demanded as we retreated back to the practice instead of our planned visit to the Department of Health. He was referring to the President of the Zimbabwe association who had yet to come back to me. The lack of contact, like the long wait at the Police office, had an ominous ring to it.

'I don't know.' I was beginning to worry. It had been over two weeks since we had last spoken. Long enough to find a few files and send them. In spite of this, we had gone into the Police headquarters confident that the grilling they had given Anthony was all it would take. Instead, it looked like we had jumped the gun. Worse still, he had survived the ordeal, and the Police, whom we were now offside with, had effectively found in his favor.

'We need the letters before we can go the Health,' Abdullah reminded me when he dropped me off at the clinic. I knew well enough to head straight to the phone and started dialing.

'He is busy with patients,' his secretary answered. At first she had been surprised by the distance, but hushed tones in the background quickly made her change her tune. 'Can you call tomorrow?' Then the next day, and the next until I tracked down his home phone and caught him by surprise.

'I'm sorry man, it's crazy here. Mugabe is really fucking things up. The phones don't work, e-mail is down, you can't get bread anywhere and petrol is like liquid gold...'

Excuse after excuse after excuse, until I had to stop him and ask straight out if he was going to help us.

'You don't know how hard it is here!' More excuses. 'Nobody has any money. Sooner or later Anthony will get a job and have cashflow.

294

Then he will be able to hire the best lawyer in town for peanuts and sue us all from overseas.'

'Are you or are you not going to provide me with anything to defend myself?' I finally demanded.

'We just can't take the risk. There are only five of us,' he pleaded, as if surrounded by a posse. Anthony could come back and sue us,' he stated again. 'Is there any chance of work up there?'

I couldn't believe what I was hearing. He was refusing to help, but then asking me for work.

'Things are desperate here, inflation is crippling, it's impossible to make a living. You know a loaf of bread costs a small fortune!' he begged as if starving. 'Even I feel for those black bastards on the street!' It was one more reason why Anthony should have behaved himself. 'The man is ruthless!' He finally rang off when I could see no point in furthering the conversation.

Our visit to the department of Health the next day was far less encouraging. After making a scene two weeks before, Abdullah now had to go back and take a sip of his own medicine.

'I have his statement,' the head of the department held a piece of paper in plain view. 'He has been to visit,' he explained further when he could see the surprise on our faces. 'You did ask me to investigate, no?'

'Yes.' I already knew his answer.

'Clinically he is good … yes?' he addressed me.

'Yes.'

'All the complaints come from women, yes?'

'Yes.'

'You have no complaints from men, no?'

'No.'

'No problem then.' He dismissed my concerns with a wave of his hand.

'But this one is from Her Highness!' I reached across his table and picked up the original letter of complaint thinking that it might carry some weight.

'Of all the people in Oman, she can afford to go anywhere in the world!'· he stated as he lit up his second cigarette of the meeting. 'Women, they are always complaining,' he smiled to Abdullah who for once was obliged to agree with him. 'I asked you for complaints from overseas. Real ones. I'm trying to help no?!'

He was, but he wasn't. I could tell that he had already given up.

'You want my advice, yes?'

'Yes,' but not really. The guy didn't give a shit about our problems.

'If you want to avoid these kinds of complaints then get a lady doctor!' He smiled, as if he had just made a joke, then picked up his phone and asked his secretary to escort us from his office.

'Arabic, Arabic, Arabic, Arabic!' We saw no point in going to Immigration after the Department of Health. This was confirmed by Abdullah's expression as he spoke to his contact by speaker phone on the way back to the practice.

'He has been there as well,' he confirmed. It didn't matter what we did … Anthony was always one step ahead of us.

'What the hell is wrong with these people?' I was stunned. We had been expecting a tidal wave of support, but the little bollix had an answer for everything. It was like he was mocking us with his ability to frustrate our every move.

I was further shocked when Rashard, who had spent most of the time out of contact, showed up at the practice unexpectedly that afternoon with the suggestion that we "re-instate" Anthony and get on with business.

'You are not serious!' The thought was revolting, but he was my sponsor and I was obliged to at least listen to him. 'He has put us through hell in the last three months and now you want me to re-instate him?'

'He will behave himself now,' he reassured me.

'Really? What makes you think that?'

'He is broke. I'm sure of it!' Rashard was confident.

'How do you know?'

'He called me last night. He says that he will drop the charges of unfair dismissal if we give him back his job.'

'And what did you say?' I couldn't believe we were having this conversation.

'I said that I would speak to you. There will be conditions of course.' (He was almost chuckling) 'He will have to sign a new contract. We have him where we want him now!' Rashard sounded victorious.

'He's a child molester!' I struggled to contain myself.

'They are only allegations. Nothing has been proven.'

'He's a fuckin' child molester. He told me himself, there in that room!' I pointed to where we had sat. 'You have no idea what we are dealing with here, because you haven't bothered to come to the court. There is no way in hell that he can come back to this practice. *No way!*' Now I was shouting.

'But he has no charges against him!' Rashard argued, his own temper flaring. 'We have the capacity. We should be using him!'

'Not for all of the money in China. Not morally, not ethically, not even over my dead body!' I wasn't having a bar of it. I stopped short of telling him that he should be ashamed of himself. That a *good* Muslim would know *in his heart* what the right thing was to do, but somehow I managed to stop myself from causing him to lose face. 'I'm sorry, (NOT) but I am non-negotiable on this. There is to be no more contact. No more intercessions. He deals with me and only in court. That's where he started this shit so that's where it will end.' I tried to sound more confident than I felt.

Rashard huffed and he puffed and said that he was only trying to help. That I was right and blah blah blah. Two minutes later he took off for some important meeting he had to attend.

After three months of firing blanks and riding the rollercoaster around in circles we were back to square one. He still had us for "unfair dismissal".

'We are going to look like idiots going back into court next week!' I was updating Darling that night on the day's events.

'I can't believe the bloody Police did not suspend him until he provided real proof!' If hell hath no fury like a woman scorned, then Darling was on fire as she grilled me over and over on every move made, every Government department contacted, every option exhausted and every legal loophole exercised in order to *"get rid of the bastard!"*

By the end of her tirade I wasn't too sure whose side I was on. I was about to go looking for consolation in a glass of rum when she came up with a crazy idea.

'There's one person we have not spoken to.'

'Who's that?' There was a twinkle in her eye that stopped me short of reaching into the freezer.

'His wife!' she announced and picked up the portable phone from the kitchen counter.

'Yeah, right! There are thirty eight million people living in Canada and you are just going to pick up the phone and call her!' I'd had sufficient frustration for the day for my hand to find its way back to the freezer.

297

'Can I have international directory please.' She clicked to loudspeaker.

'I'm looking for (name withheld). It might be Ontario. I don't have an address, but am hoping you can help me. It's a family emergency!'

There was a pause, a click, the audible sound of fingers on a computer key board, another pause … 'Please hold for the number!'

10

'He's a walking nightmare!'

Thirty-eight million to one, give or take. Those were the odds as Darling dialed the numbers dictated by the operator. Statistically, we had a better chance of winning the lottery. Even if we did get through, I did not hold much hope based on our experience with the Chiropractors in Zimbabwe. The rum was halfway up the glass by the time I added the ice, when, eight thousand four hundred and fifty-four miles away a Canadian voice answered the call.

'Hello.'

'I'm calling from Muscat, the Capital of the Sultanate of Oman, in the Middle East. I'd like to speak to (name withheld),' Darling introduced herself.

'Speaking!' followed by (holy shit) silence.

'I understand that you and Anthony are going through a divorce.'

'That's correct.'

'I'm wondering if you would be prepared to talk about the circumstances surrounding the matter?'

'Who did you say you were?'

Darling explained.

'And you are calling from … Oman?'

Darling confirmed.

'Sure, I'd be happy to talk to you,' she agreed in an educated voice. Her initial wariness soon forgotten, she was quick to get down to the nitty-gritty of her soon-to-be ex-husband. 'Highly intelligent, two-faced, devious, dangerous, manipulative, opportunistic, perverse, vindictive, litigious, a liar and a bully. He has divided our family, persuaded our daughters to blame their younger brother for having to relocate back to Canada (where he missed them!) Because I never gave him his day in court in Zimbabwe, he denies any wrong doing because no charges had been laid!'

Darling introduced me over the speaker phone and then I related the problems we were having with him in the court.

'He will do everything he can to frustrate the case. He will add fuel to the fire, and snow you under with legal jargon and any challenge that he can think of that has nothing to do with the case.'

'Sounds just like him,' I agreed.

'He's a walking nightmare,' she continued. 'It's like he thrives on this stuff. Just when you think you have him beat, he bounces back. It's been two years now and my lawyer is going nuts trying to pin him down to a settlement.'

'It's like he is reading our minds,' I confirmed.

'More like your e-mails.'

'I thought that sort of thing only happened in the movies,' I laughed. The rum had kicked in.

'They tried to hack through the computer firewall at the insurance company I work for. I nearly lost my job.'

'What do you mean "they"?' I was not laughing anymore.

'I can't say for sure, but Anthony never works alone. He has this tremendous ability to recruit people just like him. I was interrogated by security at my company for several hours. I had to account for every name they came up with. There were a whole lot of names I did not recognize. It was all very confusing until they started talking about Oman. I mentioned Anthony was there and they finally put two and two together. That's why I recognized you when you called. Your names were mentioned as well.'

'How did they find out all of this stuff?' I was fascinated.

'They hacked into his e-mail.'

'Nooo!'

'Yes!' it was her turn to laugh. 'I work for the biggest insurance firm in Canada. We have over a thousand employees using internet every day. The company spends something like ten million dollars on security every year.'

'Do you think that we could talk to them about Anthony?' I was suddenly hopeful. 'They might be able to give us something we could use in court against him.'

'No, I'm afraid not. They are like the CIA. You don't know that they exist until there is a problem.' She was quick though to respond to our silent disappointment. 'Perhaps there is some way in which I could help?' she offered, sounding hopeful.

'We are in deep shit.' Deeper than I wanted to admit. 'I know that he has no charges against him, but is there anything you might be able to send us that would demonstrate "beyond reasonable doubt" that the court order preventing Anthony from being around your son unsupervised holds substance?'

The momentary silence that followed our request was measured by how much she thought that she could trust us versus the loss she would make if Anthony found out that she had helped.

'I will need an e-mail address. A new one,' she instructed. 'Open it from a computer that Anthony has never used. Make it sound like a rest home or some hospital and send me the address by fax at my work. He can't hack a fax.'

Darling scribbled the number on a piece of scrap paper faster than my heart could beat.

'We have a court date a week from now. Everything has to be translated into Arabic before we can present it. I don't mean to pressure you, but!'

'For obvious security reasons, I keep everything at work. I'm on the way there now (eleven hour time difference) Check your inbox first thing tomorrow morning. I should have it to you by then. Will that be time enough?'

'Are you serious?'

'Someone has to make him accountable for his actions. God knows I have tried. If you have better luck, then perhaps you could give me something in return to support my claim for divorce?' We readily agreed.

Deal done, we followed her instructions, then settled down so for the longest night of our lives. Sleep was out of the question so we watched two movies back to back (Titanic and Pearl Harbor) took several walks around the block in the early hours of the morning and from five am, checked the inbox every half hour or so ... empty, empty, empty! I was dead to the world on the sofa when Darling woke me at seven thirty am.

'It's here!'

When I looked at the inbox, there were seven separate e-mails including two from Dr Telon, the Chiropractor that Anthony had ripped off when he first went to Zimbabwe.

'Where are you going?' Darling questioned when I suddenly stood up without opening any of the files.

'Shower, coffee, breakfast. Then I will read them.' I headed up the stairs to our bedroom.

'But!' We had agreed that we would open the e-mails together.

'I know. We have waited this long, we can wait another half hour!'

'But!'

I wanted time to think. To get my head into a better space. The last three months had been a rollercoaster of emotion whose final destination always ended in disappointment. There was no guarantee that the information was going to be of any use to us. Furthermore, on my early morning walk, after speaking to Anthony's wife, I had realized, but couldn't put my finger on it, that there was something far more sinister going on. He was fighting too hard. Taking too many risks. Burning too many bridges. The same question kept nagging me over and over. Why had he not just moved on peacefully? What was he holding out for that made him so tenacious?

11

George@marina.net.omantel.

The first e-mail was an apology. How she should have made an effort to find and warn us about Anthony after he had tried to break into her internet account at work. That there had always been something "odd" about her husband, but that she had never suspected for a moment that she had spent almost eighteen years married to a child molester. There was "before" and "after" the discovery. How before, she now regretted, their life had been a sham. How after, it had been nothing but a nightmare. She hoped that the information that followed would in some way compensate for all of the trouble she could have prevented.

The second was a scan of a document of testimony by their son (the victim) outlining in graphic detail the specific nature of the offences, dates and times as best he could remember, methods (revolting) and threats of punishment (chilling) if he attempted to tell anyone. The horror, dictated in a court setting, ran two full pages, was notarized by her lawyer; hard copies of which she had already sent to us by courier post.

The third, which took almost ten minutes to download, were the court notes of the hearing held in Ontario to investigate the offences. Anthony had been given three months' notice for the date of the hearing, but had failed to respond or attend. While it had no powers to prosecute an offence made on foreign territory, the findings were scathing and, as dictated in the divorce document, prevented Anthony from being in company with his son without adult supervision on Canadian territory.

The fourth, as a suggestion, was an introduction to Dr Telon. While Anthony had done the nasty on him years before, she, as a member of the same church mission, had gone to great pains to maintain a friendship.

The fifth was an introductory letter from Dr Telon outlining his experiences in Zimbabwe and dealings with Anthony. The sixth was a character reference (NOT) for Anthony that Dr Telon said I was welcome to use at my discretion. Neither of these would be of any use in court, but it was good to know that we had finally met a Chiropractor who would give us his back!

'You cannot argue against this,' Medani announced after he had studied the documents in their entirety later that morning. His lips were pursed, he shook his head, 'just a child!' he mumbled, as he drew a bright yellow pen across the page to highlight the worst parts. 'I can say now with confidence, come the next meeting, that *this* will end it!' He held the testimony of Anthony's son in his right hand.

The next people we showed the evidence to were Poppit, and Jack who was only two years older than Anthony's son at the time of the offences.

'Always trust your instincts when it comes to people,' I pointed out and explained the paragraphs that Medani had highlighted. A lengthy explanation ensued about the analogy of "having the wool pulled over your eyes" but in the end I was rewarded for my troubles with the label of *Daddy Dorkus* as they reminded me of *their* outspoken dislike of him from the very beginning.

"Trust your instincts, trust your instincts, nag, nag!" In spite of Medani's reassurances, that *sinister* feeling followed me to the practice the next morning and distracted me all day as I saw patients back to back. It was three days to what would hopefully be the final court session,.

'Naseem is here,' Linda reminded me. I was an hour behind schedule when I finished with the last patient that evening.

Every technophobe has a go-to guy and Naseem had been my savior on several occasions when I had just plain screwed up. In this case, my laptop had shat itself the previous week and would not eject a floppy disc that I had been using to back up 'The Christening'.

I found him in reception after Linda had signed out and gone home. His wife had given birth to their first child back in Mumbai around the same time as Molly was born, so we had lots to talk about as he put my laptop through its final tests before handing it over. When he connected the phone line to make sure I had internet connection … the *nag, nag, nag, nag* suddenly became incessant.

'How would I know if someone had hacked into my e-mails?' I think that I was as surprised by my asking the question as Naseem. 'I mean, how hard is it to break into someone else's e-mail address?' I shared a brief outline of the problems we were having with Anthony. About the divorce papers I had found on our computer, the falsified documents he had presented in court and the comments his wife had made in relation to "they" reading our e-mails.

Naseem looked around to make sure that we were alone before providing the answer which was as much ethical as it was technical.

'I have some friends I studied with in University in India. For them, it is no problem,' he wobbled his head in affirmation. 'All they need is the e-mail address and maybe a few hundred dollars.'

'Seriously?' It sounded too easy.

'Really,' he spoke quietly, still afraid that he might be overheard. 'If you want, I can organize. It will only take a week or so.!'

I was intrigued by the idea, but just as quickly dropped it. Putting the ethics to one side, I couldn't see how it would serve us. In a week it would all be over. I walked back to my office to get some cash to pay for my computer. While doing so the phone rang and I got caught up in a long-winded conversation with a regular patient about the possibility of bringing his elderly mother in for care. I was halfway through our chat when Naseem appeared at the door of my office and forced me to end the call with the incessant waving of his hand.

'Come quickly Doctor, you will want to see this!'

I hung up.

As I followed Naseem back to reception I was shocked to see that the practice computer was turned on and that he had logged onto my e-mail address.

'You have a big problem!' He sat me down, confused, in front of my inbox. At least I had thought it was mine, but there was something I did not recognize about the addresses.

'It is Doctor Anthony's inbox,' Naseem clarified.

'No way … how did you … I thought…?'

305

'He has saved his password to your computer,' Naseem smiled. 'When you type in his address, the computer automatically logs onto his account.'

'F#*k!'

'Yes,' Naseem laughed, but shocked me further by logging off from Anthony's account in front of me.

'What are you doing?' I couldn't believe it. We were so close to having some sort of clue what he was up to.

'It is okay, look!' He punched the keys in rapid fire and signed on again. Sure enough, the Gods, who seemed to have set us up and then abandoned us, were back on our side as Anthony's e-mail inbox reappeared.

'You must read!' Naseem encouraged at my hesitation. 'A man who molests a child has no morals or ethics. You must read and find a way to beat him.'

My hesitation had nothing to do with morals or ethics or indecision. I was thunderstruck instead by the name that kept repeating itself every third line or so down the inbox.

Our decision to come to Oman was based largely on having a marina facility big enough to safely moor Edvina. That confirmed, other than Rashard, our point of contact was George, the marina manager. *George@marina.net.omantel.*

George tracked and reported our voyage in the marina newsletter. He advised us of weather patterns across the Indian Ocean when we departed on our final leg from the Maldives and he was the very first person to welcome us ashore in Muscat. On the ground, he became our trusted adviser for everything; the best mechanic and maintenance persons for Edvina, schools for the kids, the best place to live and practice, the best place to purchase practice furniture and office supplies *and* just as important, a babysitter that we could trust (his stepdaughter). *George@marina.net.omantel*

George was on our Birthday list, received an invite to Molly's "welcome to the world party" *and* was a special guest at our family Christmas Eve celebrations. The best thing about George though, was that he had recommended the best P.A. I have ever had the good fortune to work with.

'Tell your mum to get down here now!' Poppit answered the line when I called home, wondering why I was running so late.

'You need to be here!' I didn't explain any further when Darling came on the line concerned at my tone. 'Quickly!'

I scrolled to the bottom of the inbox, clicked the previous page, and then the next, until I found the first time the address George@marina.net.omantel appeared. It was just one week after Anthony had joined us. He had met George at our home as part of a social gathering we had organized to welcome Anthony to Oman. To begin with, the correspondence between Anthony and George averaged about once a week as Anthony sought advice on everything from the best place to live, how to exchange money, where to buy a car etc, etc.

However, when Anthony was dismissed, it ramped up to as much as three times a day until the present day. The tone too had changed, from one of friendly banter and the occasional on-line joke, to interpretation of the labor laws, legal largesse and constant referral to "strategy." Our good friend George, manager of the marina, was giving legal advice to Anthony on how to go about suing us for *unfair dismissal*. Our trusted friend George, caretaker of Edvina, was the one who had referred Anthony to his *personal* lawyer the Rottweiler. George, manager of the marina … married to Linda … my P.A.

12

'This ... is ... very ... serious!'

The word *sinister* has many different meanings: disturbing, ominous, creepy, baleful, threatening, menacing. By the time Darling arrived, I was halfway through printing off most of the correspondence between Anthony and George. My brief explanation was followed by incomprehensible silence as the magnitude of the discovery settled upon us. We would never have believed, only that we were seeing it unfold before our very eyes. Evil I decided was the best interpretation.

'George?' Darling kept repeating, 'Linda?' Thankfully, Linda had gone home before the discovery had been made.

Concerned that Anthony might log on at any time and find out that we were trawling through his inbox, we stopped reading the individual e-mails and started printing everything off from the time he had arrived in Oman. That finished (almost midnight) we decided to do the same to his sent items. I printed, Darling collated. When we had filled one ring binder, we started another. We ran out of ink halfway through, but thankfully we had a spare cartridge. It was just after three a.m. when we finished, the third binder almost full.

'What are we going to do?' Darling voiced my own confusion as we drove home. I shook my head not knowing how to answer. My mind was numbed from a twenty-hour day and the implications of what we had just discovered. I didn't want to think. I wanted to sleep instead and awake to find it was all a bad dream. I was dreading the contents of the binders.

Darling made some strong coffee in anticipation of us reading through the hard copies after I dropped Violi home. When I returned though, I found her fast asleep with Molly still latched on in our bed. The desire to put my head down beside them, even for a few hours, was far outweighed though by a familiar name that kept appearing on the sheaf of e-mails that we had just printed. *Medani ... Medani ... Medani.* Forty-five minutes and three cups of coffee later I had confirmed what Anthony's wife had warned. That Anthony had been reading and downloading all of the correspondence between myself and Medani. It made sense now, how he had always managed to keep one step ahead of us. What sent me into orbit (along with the coffee) was the fact that he had somehow hacked into Medani's e-mail account as well!

I have never taken a day off practice due to sickness in my entire career, but at six that morning I made an exception and called my "trusted" P.A. to cancel my day due to a migraine, which was half true. I had gone twenty-four hours without sleep and the coffee was no longer working. I realized that not only was I in no shape to practice, but needed the time to A) sleep and B) visit Medani and spill the beans.

She replied that she understood how the last few months had been stressful and what with a baby at home with special needs, she often wondered how I coped at all. (condescending bitch). Rest assured, she would reorganize the day, the remainder of which she thanked me for having off. She wished me well for the following day as we would be closed so that I could go face Anthony in court.

Medani had made an exception and given me his personal mobile phone number. I called him at seven am, related the nature of the "development" and organized an emergency meeting first thing after lunch. At seven-o-five I was asleep before my head hit the pillow!

'This ... is ... very ... serious!' Medani said as he leafed through the binders. I had marked his name and any correspondence to or from him in red highlighter. 'I have already spoken to my boss this morning. I will have to go and show him.' Medani left me sitting in his office alone. Almost an hour later he returned and summoned me to a large conference room where his boss, *his* business partner and the four other lawyers who worked in the firm sat grim-faced around a circular hardwood table. The briefest of introductions was followed by a stony silence as they avoided eye contact and stared instead at the three binders stacked neatly in the middle.

'The law has been broken here.' Medani's boss finally spoke and pointed to the folders.

No shit Sherlock! I could hear my son Jack say. 'What do we do about it?'

'None of this could be presented as evidence to support your case in court. *You* would be immediately sued for a serious breach of privacy!'

'But *he* left his password on *my* computer. There has to be some sort of legal precedent!'

'Please!' he raised his hand to stop me. 'If you want to pursue this matter any further it will cost you a minimum of fifty thousand U.S. dollars, half of which you will have to deposit today, the remainder in installments over the next three months.

'Fifty thousand?' We had already racked up over ten grand by this stage.

'At least, and I warn you that it comes with no guarantee of success. If, by some miracle he sticks around long enough for you to win a case against him … you won't even get your expenses.'

'But he has hacked into your e-mail addresses! Surely it is in your own interests to do something about it?'

'Only if you guarantee to pay us. If you don't, then, based on the massive volume of work it will take, it is more in our interests to drop the case.'

I was shocked. My gut feeling, from the energy in the room, was that a decision had already been made … the bastards were angling to dump us.

'We took this on as a simple case of unfair dismissal. Had you informed us that he was capable of breaking into our e-mail, we would never have accepted the case.'

'I didn't know myself!'

'We would expect this answer.' He looked at me steely eyed. He might as well have called me a liar.

'I am supposed to meet with him in court tomorrow. How am I supposed to handle it without legal representation?'

'I am sorry, but if you cannot afford to pay our fee, then my advice would be to settle with the man. It will cost you far less. Medani will inform Dr Anthony's lawyer today that we have withdrawn.'

'You can't do this. It's ridiculous!' I stood, reaching for the moral high ground from which to make my appeal.

'The decision has been made.'

Except for Medani, his colleagues nodded in agreement and that pretty much summed up three months of legal advice. I was sure that there was some sort of precedent that prevented them from doing so, but assumed also, that they could find another argument to support their decision. Either way, I would need a lawyer to prove it.

The consolation offer from Medani's boss to "not bill me for any outstanding hours" as he led me to the front door with the three binders tucked under my arm was of little consolation. I had paid my last fee installment two days before.

I don't remember driving back to the practice other than some idiot cut me off at a roundabout. It was my fault, (I was trying to contact Medani on my mobile, but he would not return my calls) but I thought seriously about ramming the bastard!

One minute you are King of the World, running in front of the wind with all your sails set, nothing is impossible. The next you are an Infidel, a castaway in a foreign land where the word 'impossible' is a polite way of describing how f&%#*d you really are.

So far, all I knew was that Anthony had hacked into our e-mails. How? I had yet to work it out. It was a highly specialized skill of which I was pretty sure he had no clue. As for Linda and George? I was still in a state of shock, but from what I knew, or thought I knew, neither of them possessed the expertise. Remembering what Anthony's wife had said about his ability to engage allies, I figured a fourth party had to be involved. I had run out of time highlighting Medani's name on the e-mails before going to his office, so had no idea of what was happening in the six hundred or so pages we had printed from Anthony's inbox. The only thing I knew for sure was that I had less than twenty hours to work out what the hell was going on before our next court date. I had tried to contact Abdullah to cancel the meeting, but he was out of range in Dubai. The idea of engaging another lawyer at such short notice, without knowing what we were really up against, was out of the question.

When I reached the practice I was surprised to find Darling already there, sitting in front of the computer with almost a half of ream of printed paper stacked beside her.

'Anthony's wife called. They have been trying to hack into her account again, but the security guys have cut them off.'

'So have our lawyers!'

'What?' she followed with a series of expletives, as I attempted to explain. 'The f*$#&in sharks!' she ranted when I mentioned the fifty K.

'What's with the printing?' I was past being angry, but I could see that she was back on Anthony's e-mail again.

'Anthony's wife said that the security guys at her work have been much more open this time, with names and dates etc. They said Anthony has been "profiling us" from the very beginning.'

'What do you mean?'

'They have been reading our e-mails from the first time we made contact with him, remember, just after we got back from South Africa. He has been building a picture. Making sure that it was safe for him to move, then looking for a weakness to exploit once he got here.'

'You keep saying "they". Who are "they"?' My head was spinning faster by the minute.

'His name is Saul. He works for Zimtel, which is the equivalent of Zimbabwe Telecom,' Darling reached for a smaller stack of pages that she had separated from the main pile and pointed to Saul@zimtel.co.zim at the top of the first page. 'I'm trying to separate the pages. Everything with Saul's address over here and everything else, which looks like ordinary correspondence to friends and family, over here.' She took another page from the printer and placed it in the larger stack. 'I have one more month left to catch up to when Anthony arrived here in Muscat. Then we can sit down and study it properly.'

13

'This visit is completely off the record!'

'This is starting to look like something out of a Grisham novel!' My head was spinning with all of the twists and turns.

'I'll take *before* he got here. You are more familiar with the court stuff, so you take *after* he arrived.' Darling handed me a couple of highlighters and then headed off to the female waiting room where she began to spread her pages on the floor. I stayed in the male waiting room, which was twice the size, and began to follow her lead. It was a study technique we had developed years before at Chiropractic College for Final Exams. Spread out the pages on the floor, scan, and then highlight in the color green, the information that we thought was relevant to the test. Use pink to underline what was likely to show up. Go over the green with the pink (makes brown) to focus on what was vital, then summarize it down to no more than seven flash cards. We were looking at over six hundred pages of copied e-mails to sift through by ten am the next morning.

Two hours later she reappeared with eleven sheets of paper and laid them on the only empty space she could find on the floor. 'There isn't a lot to go on, but this is where it starts.' She pointed to the first sheet. 'Anthony is asking him for our password. She pointed to the second page. 'There it is! The third e-mail thanks him and acknowledges that "he is in." '

Being a faster (and impatient) reader, I had finished before she had explained page five. He described us as young, friendly, helpful and highly motivated. After his return from visiting us (page six) he portrayed Muscat and our new clinic as the perfect set up. However, he changed his tone from depicting us as ideal to one of idealistic and naïve and therefore considered our situation one which would serve his short term transition, while he made better contacts for long term *independence*.

'Two-faced bastard *Bible basher* eh! It shows you how arrogant he is, that in spite of the warning we gave him about the sponsorship rule, he still thought he could get around it!'

'I don't like how he describes the children, especially Jack,' Darling stated through pursed lips. The word 'beautiful' on page seven, was colored in dark brown and circled heavily in pink.

With fewer pages to throw away than Darling, I had a much bigger job on my hands and was less than a third of the way through my stack of paper.

For the first couple of weeks or so, Anthony wrote heartily to everyone to brag about all that was good in his new life, including us whom he described as his "*Business Partners*."

His wife though was the exception. To her he maintained a front of desperation (Zimbabwe in meltdown) desolation (being separated from his kids), poverty (unable to provide financial support) and blame (it was all her fault). There was no mention of him working in Oman. Her pleading in turn for a resolution and divorce was met with the tactics we had become familiar with in court including, denial, diversion, delay, counter suit and everything else that she had warned he would throw at us. His total lack of good will was best reflected in the arranged phone consultations they had, where he would only make himself available at two or three in the morning, her time.

Besides his wife, the contents of his sent box was what you would expect from someone who had just shifted to a strange new world to work with even stranger people (us) They included a combination of emotions that tic-tocked between novelty, hope, elation, wonder, bragging, depression, homesickness, frustration (at how slow it is to get anything done) loneliness, new contacts, renewed confidence and finally momentum. This was echoed in a note to his father in Canada in the sixth week where he described Abdullah as "the fixer" and hoped to be changing sponsors soon.

The eight week was a turning point. He finally realized that there was no way of getting around the 'rules' and that he was tied to his sponsor. However, in another e-mail later that week, again to his father, he was encouraged by his "friend" George who had suggested that the Gulf State of Qatar had no Chiropractors and was therefore "wide open!" (highlighted in pink)

This coincided with his waning interest and motivation working with us. Totally unaware of what was going on behind our back, we put it down to a "settling phase." To help remedy this we had done two things. The first was to invite him over for a morale-boosting dinner with George and Linda! It had been a fun night (I had thought) where we drank too much, shared a lot of stories and everybody hugged and kissed as they departed into the early hours of the morning. The second was to arrange for Rashard to have a friendly chat with him and remind him of the unique opportunity he had been given to come to Oman.

The language used in the e-mails that followed our evening together was disparaging in his description of "our veiled attempt to make him work harder" and that he had not come to Oman to be somebody else's "lackey". I was surprised though, to find that his time had been "better spent" with Rashard, who "understood" his frustration and had advised him that "patience would bring better things!" (highlighted in pink ... what's with the underlining?)

The plot thickened after that, with Anthony and George making plans to travel to Qatar, and Anthony in turn relaying these plans to his father, who, it was starting to become obvious, played a significant role in any decisions that he made.

The trouble with interpreting the e-mails was that a lot of the dots were missing. Anthony referred to meetings that he'd had and satisfactory outcomes, but venues were not mentioned and he did not name the other parties that were involved. The more engrossed he became in these plans, the more dissatisfied he was working with us, so that I could have graphed the pattern of decline in his performance to coincide with his increase in confidence at his soon to be expected departure. (Highlighted in green.)

The day that I confronted him over his divorce papers was matched by a threefold increase in e-mails and two long and very expensive phone calls to his father. No longer smug, or self-confident, Anthony was like a panicked kid caught red handed with the cookie jar, terrified of the punishment he might receive.

His father's words in return were calming and reassuring, as if speaking to a child. He called him "son" and that no matter what, they were in this together.

Anthony replied to his father as "Dad" and kept telling him how much he appreciated his "unconditional support." It didn't take long to read between the lines and see who had been molesting whom. That Anthony was very much "his father's son!" (highlighted in pink and green)

If his father's words calmed him, then his confidence rebounded in a reply letter after his meeting with Rashard. I don't know what was said, but he was now back to his old arrogant self again and reassured his father that his sponsor would sort me out (interesting assumption … highlighted in green and pink and circled in red.)

Then I'd fired the bastard!

I was so immersed in highlighting pages and making notes that it was eight pm before I knew it. Darling had long gone home to feed the kids. What brought my attention to the time was a white taxi pulling into the car park outside the clinic. I was determined not to be disturbed, but then I saw Medani climb out of the car.

'I had planned on giving you this tomorrow, to celebrate the end of court!' he handed me a gift after I (reluctantly) answered the front door. 'It is from my father, to say thank you for your care. He can walk much better now and has returned to Darfur.'

An awkward silence followed. I was still upset by the way his firm had dumped me and that he would not return my calls. However, he had made an effort to make contact, and acknowledged the free care that I had provided to his father, so I decided to yield to good manners.

'I have just made some coffee.' (It was going to be a long night.) 'Would you care to join me?' The disemboweled binders laid out on the waiting room floor required him to side step several times to reach the coffee stand.

'I am ashamed about all of this,' he pointed to the pages after we sat down. 'They should not have dropped you like that. We are talking about children … little children … they should be doing something!'

I was surprised by his admission, but grateful for his candor. It was as if I was meeting the real Medani for the first time.

'You must understand that this visit is completely off the record. If my boss knew that I was speaking to you in this way,' he paused to sip his coffee or perhaps check his thoughts. 'It is why I left Darfur. I had my *own* firm,' he stated with a vacant stare, looking into the past. 'It was a real legal firm, not like the one I work for now. *Very* successful. I employed thirty lawyers and just as many secretaries and assistants, but I had a big mouth. I wasn't afraid to speak out, so the Government threatened to kill me.'

I couldn't believe what I was hearing.

'I had to leave, on principle. I hoped to find somewhere that I could speak my mind, but,' he shrugged his shoulders. 'I am almost sixty now. I cannot afford to be brave any longer. I have to keep my big mouth shut and think of my family. It would be impossible for me to get another job!' His shame was palpable. His frank confession was sufficient to erase any previous resentment I may have felt for his not having made a stand on my behalf.

'I appreciate you coming by to tell me this,' I leaned forward, and with the simple gesture of tipping coffee cups, all was forgiven. 'So what do I do now?'

'The evidence that his wife has sent to you, it is genuine, but … a man of these resources!' he pointed at the pages on the floor. 'There is no telling what he is up to. Also, I have spoken to my colleagues. They have me convinced now that so long as he has no charges against him in Zimbabwe, technically, he will still be legal to work in this country. This means his case for unfair dismissal can be upheld.'

Why was I not surprised?

'No matter what happens tomorrow, you must drive this into court!' He gave me a stern look as he put down his coffee. 'A real court and not this nonsense that he has been wasting your time with! I have seen cases like this dragged out in the proper court for three to four years. The cost alone is prohibitive. Even if he was to win, in the end he will lose!'

'Surely he would have been better to move on?' I hoped Medani had an answer to the question that had been bugging me from the very start. 'I could have opened three practices with the amount of energy he has put into fighting this stupid battle.'

'I have thought this too … unless …' Medani's expression was grave.

'Unless what?'

'Do you trust your sponsor?'

'What?'

'Sponsors are not to be trusted. The only thing that they are loyal to is the money.'

'But he is suing my sponsor as well!'

'So long as you are involved, but without you, they could come to some arrangement. The case could then be dropped as part of a new deal.'

'But Rashard would never!' Then suddenly I wavered. His recent visit and suggestion that I re-instate Anthony took on a new and more *sinister* meaning. 'I have a legally binding contract!'

'So do I.' Medani finished the last of his coffee and stood up to leave. 'And I am a lawyer!' he stated wearily. 'No matter what happens, you must go in there tomorrow, present your evidence, and drive it into court!'

'Then what?'

'It will buy you lots of time. After that, who knows? I might have a different boss by next month and you can come and hire me to fight for you in court,' he stated without a hint of humor. After all he had told me, I could see now why he never smiled.

'Masalamah Doctor!' He extended his hand.

'God be with you too!' I took a firm grip and we shook. It was to be the last time I would ever see him.

14

The "Still" in number 1

Rashard, Rashard, Rashard. Sick with the thought that our business partner was caught up in this mess, I scanned every e-mail from Anthony's inbox, immediately after Medani departed. Three hundred and seventy pages later, I switched to his sent items and repeated the process over again. My guts churned and my hands were sweaty as my heart thrashed at ten beats per, every page, twice over, so that my head was spinning an hour and a half later when I finished.

Nothing. Not in his inbox, not in his sent box. There were forty-five pages printed from his deleted box, but none of them contained the word Rashard. I sat back in the sofa, relieved ... but not convinced. If Medani, as a lawyer, did not feel safe with his contract, then I had no right to feel that I was any better off.

'Come on Lewis, talk to me!' It had been two months since I had dreamt of meeting my mate in the "eye of the storm" where he had warned me of impending trouble. Two months and not a word! Anthony, George, Linda, Saul ... I could handle them all, but Rashard! I stood in the center of the room and took a bird's eye view of every page on the floor *knowing* that I was missing something.

What did I know?

1.   That Anthony had been molesting his own son from a very early age.

2.   That it was very likely that Anthony had been molested by his own father.

3.   That he had a contact named Saul who could hack into and read our Hotmail and change the text of documents and use it in court.

4.   That Anthony had been involved with Linda and George who had been giving him legal advice from the very start. (highlighted in pink with a question mark about George's sexual preferences)

5.   This was no longer a case of unfair dismissal.

6.   I had found no evidence (yet) but I had a nasty feeling that my sponsor was involved.

7.   Why?

It wasn't enough. I still had more questions than answers which left me with no choice but to go back to the start and read and highlight every page to try and piece the whole thing together. To help in the process I stuck *Post It* stickers on the edge of relevant pages and started to collate them back into a folder in a linear flow from day one. By midnight I had a single binder with less than thirty pages. (Still two hundred on the floor to study) By two am the binder had swollen to sixty pages. There were just fifty left to read. It was like trying to find a needle in a haystack … or not. The last thing I wanted to find was that my sponsor was involved!

On his good days, Anthony was confident, business-like and short, to the point of ruthlessness. On his bad days (a lot) he wrote prolifically, to anyone and everyone in his address book, wandering through every emotion from arrogance to loneliness, elation to despair, an overinflated view of his self-worth balanced by desolation and rootlessness. In short, the guy was a nut case, but he was in it for the long haul and was dangling a big red carrot in front of enough people to garner their support and make him dangerous.

Five more things

1.   He was still trying to get the Sponsor to reinstate him. ("Still" … how many times had he tried?? Highlighted in pink)

2.   Anthony had run out of money and was riding high on the good faith of those who supported him. In return he was

320

relying on a significant cash settlement from the case to get him started in Qatar.

3.   If it went to court, his father, who was providing some of the financial support, would front up with the twenty grand (estimated) it would cost him to fight the case. From talking with Medani, I knew it would take at least three times that much. (highlighted in pink and green ... it would cost us just as much to defend it.)

4.   Immediately after the next court session, if no offer of settlement, then he would fly to Qatar and begin establishing the first clinic. Use income from Qatar to finance his case from there and pay back friends who were supporting him.

5.   Bring up associates from Zimbabwe. They were so desperate they would work for peanuts. (Highlighted in pink. Based on the conversations I'd had with the Chiros in Zim none of them liked or trusted Anthony so I couldn't see them working for him)

The "Still" in number 1 bothered me because he had written to George after I had specifically made it clear to Rashard that I wasn't having him back, (under any circumstances)

Still, with only five pages to go I was starting to breathe more easily. So far I hadn't found one single word to connect Rashard to Anthony's shenanigans. It was such a relief. The thought of my sponsor going behind my back fell into the category of the unthinkable.

Exhausted, but happy, I finished reading the entire hard copy of Anthony's e-mail account at 3.45 am and decided that if George and Linda wanted to help him open a clinic in Qatar, then they could go right ahead. They would be doing us a favor. I was confident, based on Medani's advice and Anthony's poor performance in the practice, that he would be unable to conduct a court case against us from that distance.

There was no more second guessing now or wondering what the hell Anthony was up to. No matter what happened the next day, I was getting rid of him. (I had it in writing!) Furthermore, Medani's advice to drive it into a "real court" would motivate him to go to Qatar sooner rather than later. For the first time in months I felt sure of what I was doing and was happy to go home and catch some zee's before the court at ten am. It had been another long day, but worth it and I made a mental note to give Naseem a special bonus for uncovering Anthony's e-mail trail. I was just finished rebinding all of the pages off the floor, to hide in my office, when I realized that I had failed to notice two things.

The first was a plate of cold food that Violi had delivered from Darling sometime after Medani's visit. It was a simple Middle Eastern dish of fresh hummus and taboulleh with a chicken salad wrap and a bottle of sparkling spring water. Fit for a king. I was suddenly ravenous and gobbled the lot in double quick time while I dealt with the second thing that had slipped my attention. The gift from Medani's father.

Wrapped in a piece of Egyptian cotton and bound by a length of cheap coarse string, I had little expectation of what I might find inside, so, was greatly surprised when a small bundle of gold fell onto my lap. On closer inspection it was an ornamental dhow (Arab sailing vessel) the size of a thumb nail with full set sail, attached to a very fine chain. Threaded through the chain was a piece of paper with an Arabic inscription that I could not read, but on the backside, Medani had been kind enough to write a translation.

"Do not forget this old Sea Dog that you helped to make human again. May God be with you on your journey!"
Hilal.

I was deeply touched. His English had been very poor and therefore a barrier to communicating. However, he "opened up" animatedly, when he discovered that I had sailed from the far side of the world with my wife and two children in a small boat. He had been a fisherman and a trader in his early years. So, as kindred spirits, we had several lively conversations about the size of waves fought, the size of fishes caught, whales seen and anything that could be gesticulated with two hands and a pair of wondrous eyebrows.

Being superstitious (never change the name of a boat and never sail on a Friday) I took the gift as a good omen and decided that I would have Darling wear it while I went to court.

15

'It will buy you lots of time!'

I returned to the practice at eight am with five manila envelopes under my arm. There, waiting as planned, was Abdullah with two of his minions, ready to take the folders of translated evidence from Anthony's wife to the relevant government departments. Abdullah was looking forward in particular to dealing directly with his contact in the police who had had made him look like an idiot. Whether or not (according to Medani) the evidence was enough for a separate action to be taken by the departments remained to be seen. The objective though was still the same. To cause maximum damage to his reputation so that no matter what happened after that, they all knew that they were dealing with a child molester.

How to confront our trusted PA and George without revealing our source still remained a question. I had decided it could wait until I had Anthony well and truly nailed, for which I was well and truly pumped. Noting a spike in Anthony's correspondence just before and after each court date, I had allowed enough time to log onto his e-mail (as he would be with ours) for any last clues as to his intentions. We could have changed our password, but had decided against it to make sure that he did not suspect anything.

Instead, I had "planted" an e-mail to Rashard letting him know we had lost our lawyer. That I was on my own, running scared and the evidence I had presented was insufficient legally to dismiss Anthony. That the thought of going to court was "terrifying" and therefore I was likely to have to re-instate him in order to avoid a costly settlement. Genius really! (It had been Darling's idea.) I wanted him and his lawyer to be caught totally off guard when I dropped the bomb provided by his wife in the form of notarized evidence against him.

Sure enough, he had picked up on my e-mail to Rashard and copied it to his father in Canada, George at the marina and even Saul in Zimbabwe. Noted at the bottom of my e-mail to Rashard was the following:

We have him on the run! See "terrified of court" on fourth line. Reinstatement serves us better and will solve immediate cash flow problems. I have found out through another source that my sponsor is broke. His other businesses have failed and he is desperate for money. He has agreed to replace him with me when his contract comes up for renewal in a few months' time. It will reduce overhead and give him a better deal. Reinstatement gives me a chance to reestablish myself in the clinic so that there will be no drop off in patients when he gets the boot!

It's the home straight guys, thanks for all of your support. It has been a challenge, but I knew that we could do it. Watch this space. I will fill you in on his humiliation when I get back from court!

It was the fifth sentence that blew me away.

The sponsor has agreed to replace him with me when his contract comes up for renewal in a few months' time.

I read it again

The sponsor has agreed to replace him (me) *with me* (Anthony) *when his* (my) *contract comes up for renewal in a few months' time.*

'The bastard!!!!'

Then the screen blinked and I lost the connection. It was likely that Anthony had come on line and was now reading my e-mails before he went off to court.

324

One Mississippi, two Mississippi, three Mississippi, four ... breathe in, breathe out, breathe in, breathe out ... 'you two faced whore!' I shouted at the ceiling.

My next reaction was to blow off the court and drive out and see Rashard at his workplace and have it out with him face to face. The idea though was stumped by the need to preserve my very valuable source of information. For the first time I was looking at a genuine case of unfair dismissal, but it was me who was staring down the barrel of a gun! Had Anthony been standing in front of me that very moment, I would have wrapped my hands around his scrawny neck and dismissed him for good!

'F&#k! Breathe in, breathe out, this is not happening, this is not happening ... except that it was. Then I thought about Edvina and George at the marina and it clicked why he was so motivated in helping Anthony. It had nothing to do with opening clinics. I'd heard stories of boats being confiscated because the expat owners had been unable to pay the marina fees. No practice, no money, no fees!

Then I remembered that Rashard's brother as Head of Ports had organized custom clearance for Edvina into Muscat and suddenly ... I felt *very* vulnerable. This was the sort of thing that happened to lots of other expats ... it didn't happen to us. I had a contract that protected me, but then I remembered that Medani had little faith in his own contract.

So why had he not already gotten rid of us?

The thought settled me down.

Because he didn't have any grounds to, that was why. The practice was a success, we had dotted our i's and crossed our t's and done everything right. "Better the devil he knew," until he had the guts to replace me. Reinstatement represented the softer option and would give Anthony the chance to transition and minimize the damage that would be caused by my otherwise sudden departure. Better therefore, to have patience, bide their time, then when my contract came up for renewal ... fuck us!

That was only if I reinstated the bastard, which was never going to happen on my watch.

"It will buy you lots of time!" was the last piece of advice that Medani had given me. More than ever I could see the importance of driving this thing into a real court and giving myself some thinking room.

I waited until the last minute, till I was sure that he had already left, then logged on to Anthony's e-mail account again. There were two new e-mails in his inbox. One from his father wishing him good luck and another from George arranging to meet later that day. However, when I logged onto his sent box, the e-mail that I had read less than fifteen minutes before had disappeared. I checked his deleted box, but it was now completely empty. 'F&#k!' It made sense then why it had been so hard to piece his e-mail history together. His inbox and sent box had reached maximum capacity (used to happen in those days) so he had been deleting as he went. 'F&#k!' I had hoped to print the e-mail off and hold it as evidence to use against Rashard, even if (a last resort) it meant revealing my source.

'Abdullah, are you at the Police yet?' I thanked the Gods for the "heads up" and mobile phones as I raced across Muscat, late for the court.

'No Docta, I go now.'

'Abdullah, wait. I have big problem with my sponsor. We need to have a meeting so that I can explain.'

'Okay Docta, I wait,' but then the line went dead.

To my great relief, ten minutes later, he was waiting at the main entrance to the Department of Labor when I arrived. I explained what was happening with Rashard.

'Wallah Docta, dis not surprise me. Dis big problem in Oman. You are my friend. I will stand with you in da court.' After his last knock-down drag-out with Anthony's lawyer I doubted that he could do anything to defend me, (or himself) but I was never in my life more grateful for a friend, as we climbed the stairs, shoulder to shoulder, to meet the enemy.

16

'Stop!'

Fortunately the proceedings were running late so we arrived in the judge's room just after Anthony and his lawyer had been seated.

'Where is your lawyer?' The judge, by now having grown used to my lack of Arabic, cut me some slack when she saw Abdullah sit beside me.

'He has withdrawn from the case.' I could see Anthony pass a smirking glance to his lawyer, who had already been notified by Medani's office.

'But you need someone to represent you!' She looked to Anthony's lawyer who had made a big scene about me not having proper legal representation at our first hearing.

'Anthony's lawyer can get fucked!' I didn't say it, but Abdullah and I gave him a look that conveyed our answer.

He held our stare momentarily, then nodded to the judge his acceptance of our position before launching into *round eight* with what he expected to be the killing argument that would win his client's case.

'*Arabic, Arabic, Arabic, Arabic, Allegations, allegations, allegations, allegations, Arabic, Arabic, Arabic, Arabic, no charges, no charges, no charges, no charges, Arabic, Arabic, Arabic, Arabic, defamation, defamation, defamation, defamation, Arabic, Arabic, Arabic, Arabic, nothing proven, nothing proven, nothing proven, nothing proven, Arabic, Arabic, Arabic, Arabic, Police okay, police okay, police okay, police okay, Arabic, Arabic, Arabic, Arabic, Department of Health okay, Department of Health okay, Department of Health okay, Arabic, Arabic, Arabic, Arabic, client deeply hurt and offended, Arabic, Arabic, Arabic, Arabic, compensation, compensation, compensation, Arabic, Arabic, Arabic, re-instate, re-instate, re-instate!'*

I knew enough *Arabic* by now to catch the gist of his award winning performance. It was the first time I have ever seen a black man rage enough to go red in the face!

Anthony, the victim, held up his end, with his head bowed, silent, hands folded on his knees, the picture of patience, waiting for justice to *finally* be served. The word "compensation" though proved too hard to resist. He nodded his head, lifted his chest and inhaled deeply in a silent alleluia! It was then that our eyes met for the first time since we had walked into the room. It was like looking into the face of evil.

'Stop!'

That look was enough to spur me to action. Anthony's lawyer was stunned by my outburst. I doubt that he had ever been cut off mid-sentence in his entire career. As for his client, he looked like I had slapped his face!

'You have said enough!' I handed one of the two envelopes of evidence from Abdullah to the judge. The other I threw at Anthony, so hard that his folded hands shot up to prevent it from hitting him square in his face.

'Arabic, Arabic, Arabic, Arabic!!' Anthony's lawyer shouted.

'I also object in the strongest possible terms! I suggest you read the evidence before you make a complete fool of yourself.'

Don't ask me where it was coming from, but even Abdullah was taken aback by my bravado. Anthony's lawyer hesitated for a moment then sat down. I thought he might try to get the judge to hold me in contempt. It might have been the word "suggestion" or "fool" that made him pull the translated sheets from the envelope, or the fact that the judge was already on page three and shaking her head.

'What is this?' he demanded of his client, when he finished page three. The two of them looked like they had been hit by a stun grenade. Anthony sat staring, wide eyed and mystified, stuttering in disbelief, not by the evidence I'm sure, but how I had managed to obtain it.

'It's ... I don't know ... I have never seen it before!' he stammered, incredulous. He looked to the judge that she might believe him, but she shot him a withering glance.

'You have ruined my case!' his lawyer admonished. 'I cannot argue against this!' He shook the evidence in front of Anthony's face. 'Look,' he thumbed the pages through his fingers, 'they are notarized by another lawyer. You said that they were only allegations!'

I caught sight of Abdullah out of the corner of my eye, smiling, as he relished his opponent's sudden loss of face. He would dine out for months on the telling of this story.

Anthony sat shaking his head, speechless, his face turning a whiter shade of pale when he heard his lawyer announce that *he* had ruined his case.

'Do you want to make an offer of settlement?' The judge, seeing Anthony on the ropes, seized the opportunity to end the proceedings. Her nod let me know that something small would be sufficient for closure. I just had to name a figure. *Why hadn't this question been asked at the start?*

'No!'

'Don't you want to negotiate a settlement?' She was confused. I held all of the cards. Even Anthony's lawyer was quick to change his tune at the mention of remuneration and looked across at me, hopeful that I might acquiesce.

'No!'

'No? Surely you must have something more to say?' The judge who had bound me to silence for so many months was finally giving me permission to speak my mind.

'Actually, yes, I do.' I changed my mind and leaned in towards Anthony so that he had no doubt as to whom I was talking to.

'Fuck you, you lying bastard!'

I stood up then and nodded to the judge (who couldn't believe her ears). The proceedings were over. 'I will see you in court!'

Abdullah, always the gentleman, quickly interceded and apologized to her for my bad language. He told her how stressed I had been, but also how grateful we were "for her patience and wisdom in resolving the matter!"

Before leaving the room, he reached into the pocket of his dish dash and, turning to Anthony's lawyer he handed him a one Rial note.

'What is this for?

'I pay you your fee. Dr Anthony has no money!'

'But it is only one Rial.' ($4 U.S)

'That is all you are worth. Had you done your job properly and ended this at the start, you would be holding dis now!' To everyone's surprise, my friend pulled a large wad of cash (at least a thousand Rial) from his other pocket and waved it in front of the lawyer's face. It was the best "up yours" I have ever seen!

We left the room immediately. Behind us, we could hear raised voices as Anthony's lawyer gave him an earful.

'Wallah Docta, now I understand this American saying "kicking ass!" We kicked ass! No?!' he laughed as we raced down the stairs to bring the evidence to the Police Headquarters.

Our victory though was short-lived as I explained the implications regarding the *rules*. 'Medani says that Rashard can still replace me if Anthony has no "official" charges against him.' Unable to counter with a solution, Abdullah drove us across the city in a stultified silence as the grim reality of my situation began to sink in.

Everything we had worked for, fought for and sacrificed boiled down to this moment. Of the three departments (Health, Police, Immigration) just one had to take sides with us and make a stand for what was right.

'Docta, I tell you now, this man, he will never work in Oman again.' Abdullah drove us into the Police headquarters. 'If these people do not break the rules to keep him out … then I will. Believe me! I do it before,' he confirmed as we got out of the car. 'It is not wrong when it is for the children!'

My bravado had abandoned me. When I leaned into a water fountain in the entrance hall of the building to try and quench my parched mouth, my hands shook. I knew that my friend was sincere in the heat of this moment, but I was too dizzy with the storm that was raging in my head to even consider such an option. Never before in my life had I come so *gut-churningly* close to losing everything.

Fifteen minutes later the secretary led us into see the Head of the Police who was on the phone. He whispered in his boss's ear (literally) showed him the evidence, (which Abdullah had made him read) then left us with an encouraging nod that we had a good chance of being taken seriously.

'He was here again the other day, this Mr. Anthony,' the head of Police finally said after he had read the evidence. 'He is *very* persuasive, very hard not to believe,' he shook his head. 'But this!' he pointed to the envelope. 'You are this close!' He held two fingers almost touching to indicate the cosmic void that still stopped him from taking decisive action. 'I have to have charges, you understand. Otherwise he can waste years of my life in court. But the Minister of Health…'

'We go to the Health Department now,' Abdullah chipped in, encouraged by his reference to our next stop.

'No, you must go to the Ministry. Ask to see his Excellency. You do this and "hallas" my friend … it will be finished!'

17

'Are you calling me a liar?!!'

'*Arabic, He, Arabic, should, Arabic, not Arabic, be here!*' the receptionist pointed at me, and shouted at Abdullah from behind the counter at the Ministry building.

'*Arabic, You, Arabic, should, Arabic, be Arabic, ashamed!*' Abdullah shouted back for the umpteenth time. They had been locked in a heated exchange for at least ten minutes about everything from "me being in the building," to "improper procedures" (we should be at the Department of health) to "it's the end of the week."

Done with propriety, Abdullah stood on his toes and leaned over the counter so that his face was almost touching the receptionist's. '*Arabic, Arabic, Arabic, Arabic!*'

A look of dread washed over the man's face. He looked left, then right to see if anyone had heard. '*Arabic, Arabic,*' he argued meekly, but then relented and picked up the phone. A minute later, he pointed through a plate glass doorway and pressed a button to allow us access to a huge staircase at the end of the hallway. '*Arabic, Arabic,*' he looked to the ceiling and showed four fingers. '*Arabic*, please, *Arabic, don't!*'

Abdullah dismissed him and then took me in tow towards the stairs.

'What did you say to him?' I had not been able to interpret the last few words.

'He say the Minister not here, but he say one of his deputy see us on fourth floor.'

'I know, but what did you say to get him to let us through?'

'I know something about his sister that he not want anyone else to know!' Abdullah smiled.

'Is there anybody you don't know in this country?' He was moving too fast to answer as he took the stairs two steps at a time ahead of me. By the third floor he was sweating profusely and out of breath. 'We only have ten minutes, then ministry close for weekend,' he gasped when I encouraged him to slow down. As luck would have it, Abdullah recognized the Deputy as a friend of his brother. Formalities dispensed with, we were quickly ushered into a fog of smoke that emanated from a fully laden ashtray on the Deputy's table. He lit up another cigarette, pushed back in his chair and silently read the evidence after Abdullah explained the urgency of the matter. He was halfway through his second cigarette before he placed the pages back on the table.

'What do you want me to do?' He took another long drag, his expression giving no hint or reaction to what he had read.

'Arabic, Arabic, Arabic!!!' Abdullah stated the obvious.

'I cannot do this!' the Deputy leaned forward looking directly at Abdullah. 'Please,' he lowered his voice, 'you must not speak like this, especially in this office.

'Arabic, Arabic, Arabic!!!'

'I understand. But it is not like the old days. The rules, we must obey them too!' He turned then and looked at me.

'He has been here, this Mr. Anthony. He sat in that seat, spun me all sorts of bullshit. You think I don't know?'

'Surely you can do something?' I tried very hard not to show the desperation that I felt. I didn't think that I should have to beg, but I was prepared to do so if necessary.

'This man,' the deputy pointed at the evidence, 'he knows the rules better than anyone, even the Head of the Police. His hands are as much tied as mine,' he gestured with clenched fists. 'That is why he has sent you here. I have seen this before. This Anthony is not afraid. He knows what he can do,' he was now shaking his hands in frustration. 'He came here and told *me* the rules. *Me,* in my own office! I wanted to take him outside … you know,' he made the shape of a gun with his right hand. 'He knows how to play this game!'

'I want a meeting with the Minister!' I saw no point in arguing any longer with the Deputy. He was as bound by the rules as we were.

'It's impossible, believe me. You might as well try for a meeting with God!' He looked up at the ceiling. The Minister's personal office was three floors above. 'His Excellency is a very busy man.' he shook his head. 'He deals with the hospital boards and the army and the navy and the air force. He is responsible to his Majesty for the health of everyone in this country. Something like this ... no way.'

'But!'

'Please,' he raised his hands in a stop. 'Please, don't beg me. I am one of *many* Deputies. Truly, it has to be life and death and even then I can only go to my superior. I could lose my job!'

'What should we do?' Knowing the difficult situation he had placed his brother's friend in, Abdullah had calmed down.

'I don't know, but don't do anything stupid, please. He has involved too many people, too many witnesses. If anything was to happen!' he trailed off. His silence underscored which side of the law he would have to come out on.

'You want to be sick Docta?' Abdullah was driving us back across Muscat in his new top of the range Lexus. I was leaning forward, elbows on my knees, head in my hands, eyes closed. '*This is not happening!*' I kept repeating over and over to myself, shaking my head to let Abdullah know that I wasn't going to throw up in the floor well of his new car.

It all made sense now, why Anthony had been so belligerent. He knew the rules, better than everyone else. He'd played me for a sucker and I had fallen into it, lock, stock and barrel. As for Rashard, I still could not believe it. We'd had our moments, from which, in all honesty, I had decided I did not especially like the guy, but business is not about liking people. It's supposed to be about service and profit and honor and loyalty (isn't it?) We had fulfilled the obligations of our contract right down to the last letter and cent. I was totally unaware of his problems with his businesses. Had he shared them with me instead of siding with Anthony, I could have channeled all of the legal fees and loss of business as a consequence in his direction to help him. It may not have been enough, but "*a bird in the hand is worth two in the bush.*" I couldn't imagine what sort of lies Anthony had suckered him with that he would fall for his false promises over the hard cash that we were generating in practice.

'You want I take you home Docta?'

'No, thank you.' I was so grateful for his support. 'I have a meeting at the practice with my sponsor at five o'clock. I need to go back and try to get my head together.'

'You want I meet with you? Tell this man how stupid he is?'

'Thank you, no.' I smiled at the thought of Abdullah punching Rashard's lights out. 'Later, maybe, I will meet you at the hotel or you come to my house. I have a bottle of rum with your name on it.' He had pulled so many strings of late that it was the least I could do. Getting drunk together was starting to look like a great idea.

It occurred to me to call Darling after Abdullah had dropped me off, but she was just as likely to want to come down and face off with Rashard in the same way as my friend. I had no idea what I was going to say, or how I would handle him when he appeared, but I figured it would be better dealt with one on one. That is, *if* the bastard showed. No doubt Anthony would be on to him the second he left court with the unexpected news of what had transpired. If he arrived at the arranged time, then he would have had about two hours to see Anthony and devise some sort of plan, but it would all depend on what I had to say. All sorts of expletives and profanity ran through my mind.

For once in his life, he didn't disappoint and showed up on time. I had calmed down enough to have coffee prepared and shake his hand when we came into the clinic. To pretend that all was good, and that the court had gone fine and that we were friends (still). That our working relationship was rock solid and we cared about each other's families and I suspected nothing. But I realized very quickly that I was way past pretending and cut Rashard's own B grade act short by placing a copy of the evidence in front of him and giving him the silent treatment until he read it.

It's amazing how the eyes give away what the face tries to hide. I knew within seconds of him opening the envelope that Anthony had already shown it to him. Everyone else had taken less than three minutes before they were shaking their head or making some sort of noise to express their disgust at the contents. Rashard sat in silence for a good ten minutes without so much as blinking an eye. If his face was expressionless, then the cogs of his mind echoed off the walls as they raced for something he could say to cover his sorry ass.

'I want to know what's going on between you and Anthony.' I'd had enough of waiting. It was time to call a spade a spade (or in this case a lying bastard).

'What do you mean?' He feigned surprise.

335

'You know what I f&%$#n mean. All of these meetings, walks on the beach, coffees at the marina. I want to know what's going on!'

'I have no idea what you are talking about!'

'You have sons, Rashard. Rami, your youngest, is the same age as *his* son! How could you possibly have anything to do with this prick?'

'You think that I would do such a thing after all we have been through?' He pointed to his right arm where the hospital had drawn blood for Molly's surgery.

'I don't know!' I was shouting. 'That's why I am asking you!'

'I have nothing to do with him!' A bead of perspiration had formed on his upper lip. 'I don't even have him in my phone!' He took his brand new mobile phone out of his pocket and waved it in front of me.

'Show me.' I continued shouting, to egg him on. I couldn't believe the opportunity he had just presented.

'What?'

'Give me your phone!' I reached out my hand. All I had to do was scroll through his Call History to prove that he was lying.

'Are you calling me a liar?' It was his turn to shout.

I answered him with silence.

'You make me so angry!' He took one step backwards, raised his hand high above his head and five hundred dollars of Motorola exploded on the ground between us. 'Now look what you made me do. I am telling you the truth!' He was just as quick to pick up the broken part that held his SIM card and place it back in his pocket.

In that very moment I realized that while I might be able to win the battle in the court, we would actually lose the war. Even if I had managed to secure proof by e-mail or off his phone, it would not have mattered. Our relationship had finally boiled down to nothing more than indentured labor. Short of a miracle occurring to save our sorry asses, it was now just a matter of time.

18

'I think I can help you.'

When I arrived home, I found Abdullah sitting outside in his car waiting with his most senior PRO who had just returned from the Department of Immigration. The news was the same. *The rules*!

I told him about Rashard. How he had ended our meeting immediately after smashing his phone, to dash off to another *important meeting* (no doubt with Anthony).

'I am sorry Docta,' Abdullah gestured to the house, 'does Madam know?'

'No.' I had yet to tell her. It wasn't the sort of news you gave by phone. 'Come and have some rum!'

'No Docta, I just wait see you are okay. Tomorrow we think of something.' He tapped his head. 'Allah Akbar believe me. God is good! He will not let us down!' They were brave words from a man who had professed to having "no religion" in a conversation months before.

As I opened the door to an empty house I was glad that he had turned down my invitation. What was I going to tell Darling? The last time we spoke, I was going to go and kick Anthony's ass in court. She was likely to bring home a celebration cake!

Five minutes later she arrived back from the Early Intervention Center with the kids and a bunch of their friends in tow, all rowdy. Sure enough, expectant of good news, I received a hero's welcome and there was a confectionary box (she is not usually this predictable) in amongst the shopping for our evening meal.

'It didn't go so well!' It was difficult to explain with tears of disappointment punctuating my sentences.

She ushered the kids into the TV room to watch a DVD then we stepped out onto the back porch for some privacy.

'Rashard is involved with Anthony!' It was all I had to say. She could tell by my defeated tone that we were now in serious trouble.

Ten minutes later, her interrogation over, we both sat arm in arm on the steps, dumbfounded, silent, broken hearted. We had come to Oman to provide a service. To teach our kids to try at least to give back as much as we received. Had we tried and failed, we could have handled it. But to try and succeed only to have it taken off of us? We had no contingencies for such an event.

'Dad, Hasan is on the phone!' Poppit disturbed us and handed me my mobile. 'Are you guys ok?' She could see that Darling's eyes were red and that she had mascara on her sleeve.

Anyone else, and I would have pressed the reject button and turned off the phone, but Hasan was the senior director of the Early Intervention Center and a good friend. It would have been rude of me to cut him off.

'Doctor, I have done it again!' Clearly his tone was one of pain. Hasan had one of the worst spines I had ever come across. 'I strained it lifting my granddaughter into the car.'

It was the last thing I wanted, but I had encouraged him to call me when he had a problem (about once a month) so was obliged to stick by my word. We had an adjusting table at the house for such emergencies.

Ten minutes later he pulled into our driveway.

'Doctor, you look terrible!'

I'd had a shower and a shave and thought that I looked presentable when I answered the front door.

'Is everything okay?'

'I have a serious problem with my sponsor.' The words just blurted out. Besides our lawyers (ex) and Scotty and Angel in the UK, no-one else knew of the problems we were having with Anthony. I had no intention in offloading my tale of woe on Hasan, but he was a good listener and encouraged me ... from the first day that Abdullah had warned me about Anthony, to talk, and sometimes falter, until I reached my meeting that day at the Ministry.

338

'No expatriate has ever gotten past the third floor of the ministry. Your friend must be very connected!' Hasan stood impressed.

I nodded, but he had failed to pull the rabbit out of the hat like I had grown used to.

'I think I can help you,' Hasan stated simply.

'No-one can help us, Hasan.' I was grateful that he would offer, but did not feel like listening to one more solution that would result in a dead end. 'My lawyers have quit, the police have fobbed me off, immigration are not interested and the Ministry of Health keeps quoting us the f&$#*n *rules*!' I hadn't meant to curse. Hasan was deeply religious, but he smiled at the tone of my Irish invective.

'You should have come to me before now!' he scolded.

'Hasan, unless you have a direct connection to God!' I was being derogatory because I felt that he was making fun of me.

'I can do better than that!' He laughed and pulled his mobile phone from his pocket.

'How?'

'My brother is the Minister for Health!'

Book 6

1

'There will be no appeal!'

'Jusef, *Arabic*, Hasan, *Arabic*, friend, *Arabic*, trouble, *Arabic*, ministry, *Arabic*, problem, *Arabic*, clowns, *Arabic*, *Arabic*, important you intervene!' A one-way conversation lasted at least ten minutes while Hasan explained our predicament to his eldest brother.

Silence followed, he listened, nodded, spoke some more, then turned to me. 'The evidence that you mentioned, can you give me a copy to bring to him now?'

It was my turn to nod enthusiastically.

Silence again, his eyes searched the room. He asked me for a piece of paper and a pen, wrote down some instructions and then hung up.

'He says that it is very important for me to make it clear to you that even though I am his brother ... he *cannot* promise you anything. You understand, it's those f&$#*n rules again.' he smiled. 'I have made the time for one o'clock tomorrow so that you can see your patients and then meet him. That way,' he tapped his nose with his index finger, 'your lovely secretary does not have to know.'

My lovely secretary indeed! The one half of me that wanted to go down and slap her up the side of her head was held back by the other half who saw George as the instigator and as such, much more dangerous. I had employed Linda based on his trusted

342

recommendation. She had done a good job, but it was her loyalty that had made it possible for him to take advantage of our ill-found trust. If it had been anyone else, I would have just fired her, but George had direct access to Edvina and therefore represented a greater possible threat than Anthony. An adjustable spanner and half a dozen well placed ball bearings could destroy her engine in seconds.

'What are we going to do about Linda?' Darling had always been good at reading my mind.

'We pray that Hasan's brother can help us!' Earlier that day we had been staring into the jaws of treachery and defeat. Now the Gods had intervened yet again and were offering us the possibility of a last minute reprieve. What that might be, only time would tell, but either way, Linda was the least of our problems.

Two hours later Hassan called. 'His Excellency will meet you tomorrow in his office with his three senior advisers. You will have twenty minutes, maybe half an hour, to present your case, then they will make a decision.'

I couldn't thank him enough.

'Doctor,' he stopped me so that I would catch the seriousness of his tone. 'Please, remember, that my brother cannot guarantee you anything. Their decision could take weeks, maybe longer. There may have to be an investigation. I advise you to make sure that you have an answer for every question and be prepared. There will be no appeal!'

Another sleepless night. I stripped the binder of evidence and laid the pages out on our living room floor in a sequence of events starting from day one. Hassan had given a copy of the same folder to his brother. I already knew all of the contents from back to front, but wanted to make sure that I could refer to or answer for any page at the drop of a hat.

It didn't take long, so I watched a movie, reviewed the pages some more and then went for a walk and tried to visualize myself presenting our case in front of his Excellency. My rehearsals took me down most of the streets in Shatti Al Qurum where we lived, past the shopping area and onto the beach where I found myself stopping and starting and gesticulating and pointing to an imaginary folder of evidence that I held in my left hand.

Every now and then, I was overcome by the question why? Not me, but why was this happening at all? We had such a good thing going here. We truly believed that we were doing the right thing with the practice and the Early Intervention Center and making the world a better place to live. What had we done to attract this evil?

The overwhelming question though was *how would we extricate ourselves if it all turned to shit?* It had taken two and a half years of hard graft to get to this point. It wasn't just a matter of driving to the airport and getting on a plane. For a start there was Edvina. We were several thousand miles from what could be considered the nearest 'friendly' territory. Getting her ready for an open water passage would take months of hard work. As for suitcases, unlike Scotty and Angel, we had brought a twenty-foot container of everything that we owned. Maybe they had been smarter than us, but we had committed, lock, stock and barrel and had no intention of leaving.

Too late to cancel the next morning, I went through the motions and avoided Linda as much as was possible. If she knew what had transpired in court with Anthony the previous day, she did not let on and I did not invite any conversation other than that which served my patients. Thankfully, I was spared the awkwardness of any further exchange when she had to rush off to meet George for lunch at midday, just as the last patient departed. This gave me time for one last rehearsal of my notes before Darling delivered a freshly ironed shirt with a 'serious' silk tie.

'Wallah Docta, I tell you God is good, no? This Minister he is very powerful!' Abdullah had volunteered to drive me to the Ministry. 'You make good de case, he make good de decision, you will see!' His well-meaning words of encouragement did little to dispel my fears. We drove the rest of the journey in silence knowing that his Excellency could just as easily find against us.

The receptionist at the Ministry this time was entirely different. He greeted us as old friends, offered us water while we waited (thankfully) and made a fuss when the Minister's secretary was slow to answer his call.

'He will see you now.' We had waited less than five minutes.

Abdullah and I stood up, expecting to be buzzed through the glass door. However, the receptionist pointed in the opposite direction. Leading the way to the other end of the hallway, he stopped in front of beautifully carved ornate slab of rectangular wood attached to the wall. There was a small green button beside it which he pressed. To our surprise, the slab swung open to reveal a lift big enough to carry half a dozen people.

'For his Excellency, please!' He gestured and waved me inside. There were mirrors on each side, encased by a dark hardwood and gold leaf trimming and an ornamental cornice that ran around the edges of the ceiling. The carpet was handmade, of intricate weave and soft underfoot compared to the marble floor in the hallway.

'No!' The receptionist blocked Abdullah when he tried to enter the lift. 'He must go alone.'

'But, my friend, he does not speak Arabic!'

'Please, it is the rule.' The receptionist apologized. 'His Excellency, he speak good English. It will be okay.' He reached in and pushed the only button on the wall.

'Allahu Akbar!' Abdullah cried out as the doors separated us and with that, I began the ride to the seventh floor.

2

'She is the boss, no?'

'First floor Mississippi, second floor Mississippi, third floor Mississippi.' By the fourth, I found myself taking deep breaths to steady my nerves. When the doors finally opened to the seventh, a bead of sweat trickled down my spine and washed away all of the confidence I'd worked so hard to build up for the meeting.

Before me stood a room big enough to park at least four large vehicles. It had a high walled cornice gilded ceiling from which hung three ridiculously large chandeliers. There were plush green velvet curtains draped over each window and the carpet looked the same as in the lift only twice as thick. Considering its size, the room was relatively bare save for a large ornate rosewood desk parked in the middle. A man sat behind it in official dress, head down, absorbed in paperwork. He failed to notice my arrival.

I stood for a moment, waiting to be acknowledged, but when he continued to ignore me I stepped into the room.

'Your Excellency!' I approached his desk with my hand extended. 'Thank you for the opportunity to meet with you.'

He ignored my hand. Instead, he grabbed a rubber stamp from its ink pad and hammered the piece of paper he had been working on three times. Then, with the biggest fountain pen I had ever seen, he signed it with a flourish before placing it carefully on a tray marked "out" beside him.

'I am not his Excellency.' He pushed his chair back, stood up and finally extended his hand. The guy was so short that I had to lean half way across the table to reach him. 'I am his secretary. You must be the doctor who has been causing all of the trouble!' His handshake was lame, his manner gruff. He gave me no chance to respond before he turned and led me to a set of doors that I only just noticed behind his desk. They stood at least ten feet from floor to ceiling.

He turned the handles and groaning with effort, he pushed open both doors at the same time. They were at least two inches thick and made of solid carved hardwood just like the lift. The carpet felt like I was walking on air as we stepped into a room as big as a tennis court. The ceiling was higher than the secretary's and had even bigger chandeliers. In the middle of the room, a solid cream, richly veined, marble table stood at least six feet wide with legs that had lion's paws for feet. It was long enough to seat ten red velvet armchairs comfortably on either side. The table was crowned at the far end by another chair the equivalent size of a throne.

'His Excellency will be with you shortly.' The secretary grunted as he closed the doors behind me. I was so awestruck by the room that it took me several moments to gather my senses and refocus on the purpose of my visit. From the reception I had received, I was now less than hopeful, but I tried to put it behind me as I came to grips with my surroundings. In the end, I decided it would be easiest for everyone if I laid out the evidence on the table in the same manner as I had done on our floor at home and then talk them through it page by page. By the time I finished, the A4 sheets covered almost the entire length of the table.

I was halfway through a silent rehearsal, when a white haired elderly bearded man, stooped in stature and dressed in a simple white dish dash entered the room through a side door. In his right hand, he carried a small tray with a traditional coffee pot, two small cups and a saucer laden with dates. In his left, he had a stick which he leaned on as he limped slowly towards me.

'Would you like some coffee?'

I nearly had a fit when he set the tray down on the table and came within a degree of spilling the contents of the coffee pot all over the evidence.

'No!' I caught myself from shouting. The last thing I needed was to have my presentation ruined by some old geezer who could barely do his job. When I pushed the tray back from the pages to the opposite side of the table I noticed that my hands were shaking. 'Please, I have a very important meeting with his Excellency!' I pointed to the pages. 'I don't want any coffee!' but he had already started to pour.

'I am Jusef.' He offered me a cup when he had finished. 'I can get my secretary to bring you some water instead, if you would prefer?'

'I,' (stutter) 'was,' (fuuck!) 'I'm sorry, I was expecting more people. Hasan said that three of your staff would be attending. I, I, I, I,' felt like an absolute dickhead.

'No, it will just be me.' He glanced at the evidence as he took a sip from his coffee.

Normally the meeting would have begun after pleasantries had been exchanged and the coffee finished, but I took his glance as my cue and decided not to waste the twenty minutes that Hassan said I had been allotted.

'Doctor Anthony first contacted me …' I pointed to the first page. By the third page we were in South Africa, the fifth … Scotty and Angel had gone back to the UK, the seventh … Anthony and I had an agreement in principal, the tenth … he had just visited Muscat. I was a third of the way down the table before my mind stopped skidding and I gained enough traction for my mouth to shift into top gear. The whole thing was surreal. It was like I was floating above two guys in a room, one speaking in muffled tones and flailing his arms as if he was drowning, the other standing disinterested on the shore.

When I reached page twenty he put his hand in the air.

'Stop, please!'

I couldn't believe it. I tried to pick up the next page (just this one!) sure that I was making an impression.

'Halas, it is finished!' He had both hands in the air now, like a police man halting heavy traffic.

'But you haven't listened to!' I pointed to my watch. 'Hassan said that you would give me twenty minutes at least!'

'I know, but it is out of my hands.' He shrugged. 'There is nothing more that I can do!'

Forewarned, I had gone into the meeting knowing that there would be no appeal, but it had done nothing to prepare me for such finality. It made sense then, why there were just the two of us in the room. The three senior members of his staff must have already voted against me.

'You look tired, Doctor.' He struggled as he pulled two chairs out from the table. 'Please.' He motioned for me to sit opposite him.

I was grateful, as wave upon wave of defeat washed over and numbed me. However, as the gravity of the situation pulled me back into my own being, I was not so desensitized as to fail to notice how he struggled to lower himself into his own chair, obviously in a great deal of pain.

'I have been up all night.' I reached forward instinctively to help him settle the last few inches.

'So have I.' He shook his head. 'I was shocked by the information that you sent with my brother. I realized after he left that it was pointless showing it to my staff.' He shuffled his body to find comfort. 'I decided instead that I had no other choice, but that I would have to show it to the Boss.'

'You took it to his Majesty the Sultan?' I was aghast. (The Sultan is often referred to as the Boss.)

'No.' He looked at me as if speaking to an idiot. 'I showed it to my wife!'

'Your wife?'

'Yes, my wife! You have a wife?

'Yes.'

'She is the boss, no?' He held his hands in submission.

'Well, yes, kind of, I suppose.' (Who did I think I was kidding!)

'We have been married almost sixty years now, since we were fifteen!' He was obviously proud of the achievement and spent the next five minutes telling me how many children, grandchildren and great grandchildren they had brought into the world. Any other time it would have made for great conversation, but my mind was bouncing off the walls, wondering where the hell he was going with this exchange.

'In all of this time I have never seen her cry the way that she did when I showed her the evidence. Big tears, she wailed, as if somebody in our family had died. Then she got angry. *Veeery angry*! Then, halas, it is over!'

I still didn't understand.

'He is gone!' He threw his hands in the air. 'My wife, wallah, you do not want to make her angry!' He shook his fist. 'She called the wives of the three directors who were supposed to be here today. She told them!' He punched the palm of his hand with his fist. 'They told their husbands! Then she called the wife of the Chief of Police. She told her! Then *she* told her husband! Then she called the wife of the Head of Immigration and she told her!' He was beginning to smile as

349

he regaled what had happened. 'He has three days.' He held up three fingers. 'Then this animal must leave!'

Excuse me for being thick, but I was still too numbed to fully understand what was going on.

'This morning.' He leaned forward and tapped my knee as he delivered the *"piece de resistance."* 'She called the wives of the Ministers of Health in the other G5 states. (Qatar, Saudi Arabia, Bahrain, The Emirates) 'He has been black-listed. This so called *Doctor* Anthony will never practice in The Middle East again!'

'But you just said that it was out of your hands, that there was nothing you could do?' My mind, still not fully realigned, struggled to understand what he had just told me.

'I wanted to take him out into the desert and show him old fashioned justice!' He made the shape of a gun in the same way as his deputy had done. 'But there was no need to once my wife got involved!' He laughed some more. 'Now, let us finish the coffee before you go.' He creaked forward and emptied the last of the jug into both cups. 'Did you know that Sinbad the Sailor came from Muscat?'

I did.

'I want to hear more about your sailing to Oman with your family!'

3

'luxuriant well of oblivion'

Twenty four hours before, I had been wondering what we had done to attract so much evil into our lives. Now, as the lift brought me back down to earth (literally) I was dumbfounded by the presence of goodness that had just altered our course yet again and pulled us from the rocks. When I thought about Anthony, it was no longer "f&#k you!" Rather, it was more like "what the f&#k just happened?" As I looked into the gilded mirrors, I found it hard to believe I was staring at the same face, who an hour before, had been preparing for the worst. When the bell pinged for the ground floor I wanted to press the button and ride to the top again, to see if it had all been just a dream.

'Are you okay?' His Excellency's receptionist called out to me from his desk when I failed to leave the lift after the door had swung open.

'I think so.' I was staring at my surroundings as if seeing them for the first time. It felt, I imagined, what a patient must feel like when awaking from major surgery to remove a life-threatening cancer.

'Docta, everything is good, no?' Abdullah was now standing in front of me, staring, as the first of several tears welled in my eyes.

'Allahu Akbar!' I declared and stared right back. Still I didn't move.

'Wallah Docta, I tell you he is de good man, no?' He took me by the elbow and led me, trancelike, from the building, down the stairs, between the cars and across the parking area. His driver opened the door to his Lexus and sat me in the rear passenger seat and buckled me in. We were half home before I was able to speak coherently.

'Abdullah.'

'Yes docta?'

'I need a rum!'

As a consequence, Darling had to call Linda and cancel my afternoon in practice. Call it divine intervention, call it dumb luck, call it as you see it. Perhaps I should have gone down to the Mosque and knelt prostrate in the direction of Mecca, but the shave that had saved our asses had been way too close for comfort and I had two bottles of Mount Gay waiting at home to prove it. By four that afternoon Abdullah, his driver and I were well on our way to being shitfaced.

Truth be told, I did not want to think about what had just happened. I did not want to weigh it up, or analyze it, or arrive at some inane conclusion that I would end up pontificating about later on. I wanted all thoughts, all emotions, all feelings to stop. I needed my brain to disengage and reset itself, so that my heart could slow down and beat normally for the first time in months, even if it only lasted a few moments. As I fell into that deep and luxuriant "well of oblivion" that all happy drunks fall into, I knew that I would have to resurface the next day to face a new and probably less desirable reality, but I didn't care. The night belonged to us and I was intent that we should spend it celebrating as champions.

The next three days were suspended in a "this is too good to be true" chronic (hung over) state of disbelief where we didn't know our ass from our elbows. It was not a case of mistrust, but more our experience of the Middle East where if you did not have an agreement in writing, then there is very little onus on the promissory to make good their word. Hindsight being what it was, it occurred to me that I should have asked his Excellency for a letter of proof, but it would have been the equivalent of calling him a liar. Not such a good move when someone promises to save your ass! We tried to log onto Anthony's e-mail to see what was going on, but were unable to gain access. Either he had changed his password or the ministry had shut him down. Without it we were blind to what was happening around us.

Still, regardless of not knowing if we were coming or going, the wheels of life required us to go through the motions. On the first day back in practice I left a large envelope of "fresh" evidence on Linda's desk. I gave no explanation to her other than a "recent development" had made me decide to "confide" in her and that it was important that she understood what was going on.

Did I think it would make any difference as to whose side she was on? Not really. We saw George as the instigator to whose good will she was ultimately beholden. However, she was a mother, and as such, I hoped that it might have some bearing, especially if His Excellency came through and Anthony ended up on the wrong side of the law. Our relationship now boiled down to one big pretense, in which we felt no remorse in faking it until we could make it clear that they were no longer welcome in our lives.

The spell was finally broken on the morning of the fourth day when Hassan called.

'The police escorted him to the airport this morning. Alone. They tell me that he has gone to Malawi.'

'Where?' I had never heard of the place.

'Malawi, it is one of the poorest states in Africa. He will have a very hard time making a living over there.'

'What about my sponsor? What did His Excellency say to him?'

'Nothing. He had one of his junior deputies at the Department of Health summon your sponsor to his office and warn him that if he tried to interfere he would revoke the clinic license and shut him down!'

'Really?' I had never considered it as an option.

'No, but I can guarantee that you will have no problems with him from now on!'

True to his word, His Excellency had come through, but not before we had started to have second thoughts about what the hell we were doing in the Middle East.

4

I hate when she does that!

'No, Docta, you cannot leave!' Abdullah banged his knife and fork on the table of his favorite restaurant. We had invited him and his wife Sada for dinner to thank them for all of their support. I was surprised by his angry outburst at the difficult decision that we had made to leave Oman. He was just as abrupt in dismissing the waiter who came over to our table to see what was wrong. Of all the people who had supported us, I had been sure that he would have understood our dilemma.

'You have won de case and you have shown de asshole Rashard who is in charge. If you leave now then truly, it will be them who have beaten you!'

It was three weeks since Anthony's deportation, but our heavy hearts had still not recovered from the treachery. Whatever about giving Anthony a beating, we had taken one in return and I was struggling to get out of bed in the mornings, let alone go through the motions. The practice, which had started out as a bright star of inspiration, had suddenly turned into a black hole that sucked all of the energy from my soul. As a consequence, the gloss had worn off sufficiently for us to see that the flip side of our success had been coated with too much good luck. That we were just as likely to land "heads down" the next time the Gods decided to toss the coin.

The decision to move on had not come easily. We were well into our third year of living in a country that had become deeply ingrained in our hearts. We loved the life that we had built in Oman. We loved our practice and the Early Intervention Center and all of the Omani and expatriate friends that we and our children had made. But to have it all rely on the good will of a sponsor who called two days after Anthony was kicked out to say that he had "engineered his deportation"? It was pretty much the last straw.

Had he been upfront about his losses and shown some form of contrition, we might have been able to forgive his desperation. His continued deception though had robbed us of any desire to continue the partnership.

To make matters worse, the value of the Omani Rial had plummeted by almost 30% on the international exchange. This and the "war torn" decline of the practice from dealing with Anthony, had effectively wiped out our entire profit margin. No profits meant no fun. No profit meant no fees for the kids' education, no funds to subsidize the Intervention Center, no savings for the future, no reserves for the next calamity (a foregone conclusion), no trips home and no Edvina. Pretty much no point in being there.

The more I crunched the numbers the more depressing it got. Our original three year plan stretched to five, then eight before ballooning out to a ceiling of ten years to make any of our originally hoped-for gains worthwhile. To have put in almost three years of hard work and have nothing to show for it in return was gutting. My confidence as a consequence was at an all-time low.

'What do we do about Rashard and Linda and George?' I pushed my plate away.

'Wallah, you do nothing!' Abdullah, oblivious to my loss of appetite, picked up his knife and fork and started to carve the last of his steak. 'Now you know ... this is de life. You have good life I tell you. The people in Oman, they are good people, but you have bad sponsor. In future, you give him his money, but you not be his friend. You don't trust him and you no bring other doctors from your country.' He pointed his knife at me, 'that way, he cannot fuck you!' He brought his hands together in an act of prayer and looked to Darling and Sada for forgiveness.

'This Linda and George, they are nothing without Dr Anthony so,' he hunched his shoulders, 'you treat him that way, but you *don't* fire the Linda! George, he like Mr Anthony. You don't want to go to the court again. He make big problem for you *and* your boat. Better you keep them close so that you can see what they are doing!'

I listened patiently to my friend's sober (for a change) advice, but my silence lacked any sense of commitment.

'Please Docta, think about it!' Abdullah pleaded one last time as we parted outside the restaurant after he had insisted on paying the bill. 'You try for six more months. If it good, you stay. If you don't like, then I will help you leave.'

Sada, whose English was worse than her husband's nodded in agreement and reached across and gave Darling's hand a reassuring squeeze, but still, we made no promises.

'What do you think?' Darling asked as we drove home. I was equally moved by Abdullah's impassioned plea and could sense her wavering (as I had). Added to the thought of uprooting Poppit and Jack and getting back on Edvina with their special needs sister further dampened my enthusiasm, but whatever luck we had left, I still felt (reluctantly) that we should be using it to punch our way up the Red Sea rather than wasting it on the good will of our sponsor.

'We would be Captain of our ship.'

'And Master of our souls, I know.' Darling finished my line. 'But after all of the crap we have been through in the last year, we really could do with a break from adventure right now! Maybe next year, when our confidence is up and Molly is bigger?'

It wasn't so much a suggestion. It was more like an appeal from the heart (I hate when she does that!) Hope hollowed out to an echo of its former self. Not enough to force my hand, but enough to let me know that I'd have a hard time getting everyone on board.

Before we had a chance to discuss it any further, we were distracted by a silver Dodge Suburban parked in our driveway and a seed that Darling had planted well over a year before.

When we entered the house, we were surprised by two couples from the Early Intervention Group sitting around our lounge sipping tea. Their leader, Barbara, was an American mother who had a son with Down Syndrome. Her husband, Salem, a local Omani, sat beside her. Sitting opposite was Zuwhail and Abdullah (another one) who had a four-year-old girl and had been active members of the group from the very beginning.

'You did it!' Barbara jumped up and danced several twirls around our lounge with her hands in the air, before grasping Darling's hand and pulling her into her groove. Darling had no idea what she was talking about.

'The licence!' Barbara sang again. 'Our contact from the Ministry just called. It will be announced on Monday!'

I didn't have a clue what they were talking about either and looked to Abdullah.

'World Down Syndrome Day is in three months' time,' he explained. 'It has taken almost a year of constant haggling with the Ministry, but they have given the Group a license to do a fund raiser under Darling's name!' The tone of his voice said I should be proud of her achieving the impossible.

'We just thought that we would come around and share the wonderful news in advance!' Barbara chimed, but just as quickly she stopped celebrating when we failed to join in.

Crunch time!

I looked at Darling, who should have been dancing for joy, but she was stilled instead by the knowledge of our decision.

One of us was going to have to make the announcement. Being the perpetrator, that responsibility weighed heavily on my shoulders.

'We have decided to leave Oman.'

'What?'

Consternation followed. Questions started flying, Barbara started crying, Zuwhail rushed into the bathroom to get her some tissue.

'Why?'

Caught in the collateral damage of the emotions that were going off left, right and center, I found myself unable to speak and could only purse my lips and hunch my shoulders in reply to their questions.

'We thought you were happy?'

Nods to the affirmative.

'Don't you like Oman?'

Smiles.

'Is it your children?'

Shaking of head.

'We don't understand!'

Darling now in tears as well.

'We will do all of the work!'

The least of our worries.

'Is the practice not a success?'

A "yes and no" wobble of my head.

'You have a problem with your sponsor?' It was Salem who guessed it.

I nodded in confirmation.

'He is making you leave?'

'No, but we think it is best.'

'Why?'

'We have had a lot of problems and no longer trust him.' It took me ten minutes of broad brush strokes to paint a picture of the ordeal that we had been through in the hope that they might understand.

They didn't.

'Before you came to Oman, nobody gave a shit about my son,' Abdullah stood to face me. 'They give him to me at the hospital and they tell me nothing. We know that he is not right, but we don't know what to do, how to raise him. Then you come and you give us hope. I begin to think, Inshallah, that someday, maybe, my son, he can go to school. I *believe* because of you. Now you want to leave?'

Compared to Abdullah's passionate plea at the restaurant, this Abdullah was pissed.

'But I explained …!'

'Everybody has a difficult time with their sponsor when they first come. It is normal!' He admonished me as if speaking to a wayward child. 'You have fixed the problem so why are you leaving?'

So much for broad brush strokes. The way he spoke made it sound like we no longer had a problem. For the second time that night I questioned the wisdom of our (my) decision.

Our uninvited guests pretty much refused to leave until they had extracted a promise from us that we would at least reconsider our position.

The following day, the jungle drums at full beat, Darling was inundated with phone calls and more visits from several mothers beseeching her to stay. By the end of the week, almost every family member of The Group had contacted us. All with the single intention of changing our minds.

'You see Docta, what I tell you!'

Several of the Group's fathers had invited myself and Abdullah to the Five Star Hyatt for lunch to speak to me personally about the matter.

It had never occurred to Darling or me that we were doing anything special. We had recognized a need and had started the Group as an extension of the new practice. It was no big deal. Nonetheless, their sudden outpouring of support was overwhelming and a stark contrast to the lonely months we had spent fighting for our survival. I now realized that somewhere in the isolation of keeping it all quiet, we had forgotten what it was that we had been fighting for. That the Group, above all else, was what brought meaning to our lives.

'Now you know de life you have. These people are de good people. You have looked after their children, they will look after you!'

I don't think I had ever seen my friend look so proud.

Between that, and the wine that they had just served for lunch, my resolve to get back on Edvina was quickly evaporating.

It was Darling though who finally persuaded me to give it one more try.

'If we stayed for another year, then you could use the time to work on 'The Christening'!' (Bloody tart!)

I had forgotten. About the promise that I had made to Lewis (again). About Kate and Paddy. The shit that they were going through made our own challenges pale in significance! The last time I worked on the manuscript, Paddy had been badly wounded in a big scrap with a squadron of Messerschmitts. I recalled vaguely that he had made it back to base, but six months was too far back to remember. It was hard to believe how far removed our lives had become from that which we had originally imagined.

It was time to get back to living the dream!

5

Reto

Permission to fundraise for the Group was less about the money and more about giving them a voice. Not just the Group, but every family in Oman who had a child with Down Syndrome. For the first time in their lives, they could speak out, be proud and make a stand for what mattered most, their children.

The door marked prejudice had finally been cracked. The Group was determined to make the most of it by pushing it open as wide as possible to let the light shine on a darkness that had prevailed for far too long. Electrified, every one of the parents took on the collective persona of a champion whose day had come. There would be no second place, no faulting the line and positively no excuses. This included Darling who, as their founder and leader, was expected to carry the banner and lead the charge.

Caught in the heat of their infectious enthusiasm, we crunched the numbers again and again *and* again until we found a way to make it possible to stay, at least till after the event. Beyond that, we would have to give up our villa and move into the apartment above the practice, home school the kids instead of private school, have no overseas holidays and spend what little cash there was to spare on getting Edvina ready to sail to Europe. If it all went well, then Darling and I agreed that we would give Oman another year and see how we got on. If things did not work out, then we would leave while the winds were still in our favor for the Red Sea.

Either way, as much as we loved her, Edvina would have to go north for resale in Europe as we could no longer afford to have her in our lives.

It was true, we were no longer living the life that we had imagined, but as Abdullah had said, it was a good life, one that had significant meaning. We had found a place where we were making a real difference and felt that we belonged. Provided Rashard continued to make it possible, then we were prepared to commit for the long term future.

It's a strange thing, this beast called commitment. I had forgotten about the quality of its power, but was to be reminded once again of its essence. *That the moment one definitely commits, then Providence moves too and all sorts of things occur to help that would never otherwise have occurred.* Twelve weeks was bugger-all time to organize a national fundraiser. We had our doubts that we would get much out of it, but Providence had different ideas.

The first dignitary to lend a hand was the Lord Mayor of Muscat. I knew nothing of the man other than as an occasional patient of the clinic. When word reached him about what we were doing, he called to offer his personal support and that of his office. The newspapers got wind of this, photo shoots were organized and suddenly we had a reporter assigned to us to write about the story as it unfolded.

The next to join in was the radio station. They counted down the days to National Down Syndrome Day every time they ran the "click clack, front and back" safety campaign.

At T minus nine weeks, a very discreet group of well-connected business women made contact out of left field and threw their hats in the ring. Suddenly we were leaping tall buildings with a single jump!

With the Lord Mayor on board and the newspapers behind us, Abdullah was able to persuade the Chief of Police to give us permission to set up tee-shirt stands and collection buckets outside the malls and shopping centers, a first ever for any fund raiser in the country.

Somehow, the publicity from the papers put the city in a good humor and everywhere we went, we were recognized and greeted with a willingness to forgo the rule of "Inshallah." People actually worked to make things happen on time and offered us substantial discounts instead of us having to bargain for a better price.

Unused to these type of events, it was as if, for the first time, the community had permission to give. To show grace and understanding. and bring out a better part of themselves. This included Oman Air and Emirates airlines. At T minus seven weeks they were persuaded by Darling to fly "Reto", South Africa's leading hair stylist (we had met on our trip) to host a hair and fashion event in Muscat in return for donations.

Eight hundred kilometers away, the retired Surgeon General of the army of Bahrain heard about us through the grapevine. He too had a child with Down syndrome and had recently opened a center for Early Intervention. "Would we like him to come and speak at a conference that we were organizing?" Gulf Airlines provided his ticket!

The upside of all the publicity being thrown around was that our clinic was being "name dropped" left right and center. The exposure, as a consequence, created an unexpected kickstart that put us back on the map and the dwindling patient numbers began a steady climb back to positive cashflow. One minute we were counting our cents, worrying about where the next dollar was going to come from, the next, I was running around like a blue-arsed fly, wishing that Scotty was still there to help.

It was hard to believe that eighteen months had passed since they had split the scene. Nothing much had changed in their lives. They were still living in the UK doing the same old thing. Scotty and I had yet to talk, but we were mellowing and sending messages to each other through the girls. It was as good as being in contact every week. Based on the jump in practice, I was gearing up to shout us a surprise "reunification" trip to Bahrain for the first Formula One Grand Prix in the Middle East.

As for Rashard? Well, Abdullah (number two) it seemed had been right. We had gotten over the hump and settled into an unspoken understanding that had pretty much laid waste to his original sham of establishing a practice to *provide a service for his people.* It was early days yet, but with his weekly stipend being paid by direct debit, the only time we heard from Rashard was by e-mail.

Not being friends, was a difficult thing to get used to. It was the same with Linda and George. They had been our first point of contact in the Middle East. Trusted, included, confided in and embraced. In hindsight we had been naive, to the point of oblivion almost, but Abdullah (number one) was right. We knew where we stood and maintained a certain vigilance. If all did not go as committed, then we were just as prepared to leave at the shortest of notice.

362

Happy, therefore, was not necessarily a word to describe us. Busy more like, with a renewed sense of hope for the future that we would not have to punch up the Red Sea. Waking in the morning was no longer a drag. The spring was back in my step, I was humming in the shower and the kids had stopped calling me Codfish! I practiced by day and wrote by night. Darling worked on her new idea to increase the potential for profits by stretching the fund raiser for National Down Syndrome Day out over an entire week.

Her goal, the heady sum of thirty thousand dollars, was way beyond the imagination of most of the families involved, but no-one questioned her cast iron belief that they could do it. Thirty thousand smackaroonies was enough to buy an entire year of the necessary resources *and* pay the therapists who were already giving their time at a discounted rate. Thirty thousand placed a value on each and every one of their children who before had been written off by society and seen as worthless.

'Next year, we will have more time. It will be fifty thousand!' I overheard one of the fathers.

'The following, a hundred!' another declared.

Still, nobody questioned it. If someone had said a million they all would have believed. There is no holding down the power of the human spirit once it is awakened.

T minus six had us believing in the unthinkable, that we might just pull it off, that we might stay in Oman and that our renewed hope was not without foundation.

6

'Captain of our ship!'

The letter was delivered to the practice by hand and required my signature before the bearer would release it. It was the strangest of encounters. Muscat had no postal service other than the P.O. boxes and he wasn't a courier, so the guy was out of his depth. Still, he made every attempt to be officious and it was only after he left and I saw him climb into his car, that I discovered that he was a taxi driver!

I was too busy seeing patients at the time to give it a second thought, so threw the letter on my office table and forgot about it until I had finished for the day. When I picked it up for the second time though, I was struck by a sense of foreboding. The handwriting, which I had not recognized earlier on, suddenly clicked. It was from Rashard.

I was in two minds to open it then, knowing in my heart that the contents meant only trouble. I turned it over several times, bounced it in my hands as if I could somehow measure the weight of pain that it contained, then threw it on the table thinking I might halve its effect if I waited to share it with Darling. I paced the room several times, walked out to reception to see if Linda had gone home (she had), then found myself back in my office. Hesitating, I picked it up again, decided that I was over reacting, then ripped it open, thinking either way that there was no point in delaying.

'Bollocks!'

It made sense then. The taxi driver was a witness. My signature was proof that I had in fact received the letter and been officially "notified".

I read it again.

'Rashard!!' My voice echoed off the concrete walls of my office. I picked up the phone and dialed his mobile. There was no answer, so I punched his home number, more forcefully, that it might connect. I was just about to give up when he finally answered.

'I have received your letter,' I was trying to keep the shock and anger out of my voice.

He replied with silence.

'I think we need to meet to discuss this, I ...'

He cut me off. 'It's a straightforward request. Just acknowledge that you are in agreement and I will organize for the lawyers to renew your contract.' He was matter-of-fact, rehearsed, like he had been preparing for this for a long time.

'Rashard, this is outrageous!'

'The letter is in line with our original expansion plans. That is all. I think that you have a strong incentive here to make them happen.'

'What plans?' For the life of me I had no idea what he was talking about.

'You promised me that you would have several doctors working for the clinic by now.'

'What do you think I have been trying to do for the last ....?!' I had never made any promises other than to hope out loud that it might go so well. Two-faced, lying, interfering back-stabber came to mind.

Silence again.

'We will have to negotiate.'

'No. I think that three years has been long enough. If you don't agree then I will not renew your contract.'

'Rashard, we are supposed to be business partners. We need to sit down and discuss this!'

'We just have.'

A half an hour later I gave strict instructions to the kids not to be disturbed, then sat in silence at the kitchen table while Darling read the letter.

'Five hundred percent!' She re-read the page again. 'He can't be serious!'

'You have it in writing!' I pointed to the page.

'After all he has done, he now expects us to raise his dividend by five hundred percent?'

'Kentucky Fried Chicken.' I shook my head.

'What?' Darling hates fast food.

'Remember at the beginning, how he spoke about franchising the practice once it was established?'

'One in every town!'

'Yes,' I nodded. 'Five in total. Three in Muscat, two outside, one of them in Salalah, a thousand kilometers south.' The logistics alone would be a nightmare. Based on our experience over the last two years, finding the right doctors to come to the Middle East would be nigh impossible. 'I thought that I had talked him out of it.'

'That's why he joined forces with Anthony,' Darling reasoned. 'You can bet *he* promised him that he could do it!'

Had he requested a meeting, allowed us to clarify the reality of *our* position, (the partnership) explained his own dire financial situation and squeezed us for a few dollars more, we might have worn it. Might. If we ever managed to reach profitability. But five hundred percent!

Our so-called "business relationship" had now broken down to haggling, the rule of which goes something like this

"They ask for ten
They are looking for eight
They will take six
You offer them two
They settle on four"

Using this rule as a guide, we would end up at a two hundred percent raise in dividend which, after all of the cutbacks we had agreed upon, we simply could not afford.

'What if we say no?' Darling was serious.

'Then it's over and we get on Edvina and go!'

Whether he realized it or not, Rashard had started a high stakes game that *we* were willing to walk away from. With no way of replacing us, he was the one who would end up the biggest loser.

The following morning, he again declined my request for a meeting, so we sent him a reply through our *new* lawyer offering a maximum one hundred percent increase in his dividend with a whole bunch of conditions attached.

Three days later, the end of T minus week six, our lawyer handed me a reply that stated that Rashard was *non-negotiable*.

'This is crazy!' It had taken Rashard three years of searching before serendipity had connected us with each other. There was no way he or I would find a replacement in seven weeks. Even if he did, no doctor in his right mind would take over a practice without at least speaking to the departing doctor.

'Don't worry, it is machismo. He is trying to show who is boss.' The lawyer was confident. 'You still have eight weeks to go on your contract. It is likely that he will play tough to the very last day and then do the deal.'

Likely or not, we were now caught between the devil and the deep blue sea as to whether we were staying or leaving. If it wasn't for Edvina then we could hang tough and play it down to the wire. However, the weather window for departure was growing narrower by the day. If we were going to be on board, then we had to think seriously about leaving with some margin for safety before it shut completely.

I was thinking this as I drove home from our lawyer's office. About how complex our life of adventure had turned out since we had become involved with Rashard. How the tides of men were far more complex and unpredictable than the tides of nature and that we'd always seemed to be pushing against them since our arrival in Oman. How the harder I tried to fulfill my promise to my mate Lewis, the more life seemed to throw bad weather our way to prevent us from reaching that elusive goal. So much so, that the idea of punching up the Red Sea was starting to look like a more attractive option to sticking around another year. I was thinking about this and sighing for the simplicity of being back at sea, when Darling called me on my mobile phone.

'Guess what?' She was in a much better mood.

'What?'

'Zuwhail just called. The Group has already received over thirty thousand in pledges!'

'Guess what?' I couldn't help but burst her bubble. 'Rashard is non-negotiable!'

Purse lipped, I could read Darling's mind as she stared at Rashard's letter.

'I'm way past the point of having our life manipulated and messed around by this greedy, conniving, two-faced bastard!' she declared. In spite of the heartbreak and hardship that it would bring, the Red Sea was back on the agenda.

'Are you serious?' I was surprised by my own relief.

'I have had enough of the (expletive)!' She scrunched up his letter and threw it at the bin.

'What about the Group?' After all of the encouragement and support that we had received in staying, I was concerned about how they would take it.

'The Group will be fine.' She sighed, reluctant to admit it. 'They are well organized now and already have the thirty thousand dollars. The last thing they need is another Mother Theresa to go along with it!' Still, I could see that the thought of leaving still upset her.

'It's T minus five to National Down Syndrome week. I think we should be ready to cast off two weeks after!'

'Captain of our ship!' She put on a brave face.

'Master of our souls!' I agreed. We stood and hugged, knowing too well what we were getting ourselves into, but our determination to live life on our own terms far outweighed the unsettling discomfort of what lay ahead.

Thankfully, while counting down the days to the big commitment, we had also maintained a sense of vigilance and made the preparations required on Edvina for the possibility of our departure as well hers. The kids had been briefed, an "exit" planner stuck to the wall to time-line the breakdown of camp (if necessary) and Violi put on notice that she should make tentative inquiries in finding a new boss. Based on our previous experiences we had just enough time to prepare for sea.

'When do we tell the kids?' Darling was all business as she scrawled down the departure planner with her finger to prioritize what would need to happen and when.

'We don't, at least not for the moment.'

'Why not?'

It was a good question that had a raft of moral, ethical and professional issues attached to it. Who to tell? Who not to tell? When? Where and eventually how to deal with the blame game that was bound to happen when it came to Rashard? In particular, I expected that there would be a list of financial issues at stake that depended on who was eventually held responsible for the demise of the practice.

Our legal agreement with Rashard was binding for both sides and originally designed to sustain and protect our longevity in Oman. As such, there were no clauses or contingencies to cover our eventual departure. In particular, I was not obliged to replace myself. I had written the contract that way so that a) it excluded Darling from any liability and b) we could, in an emergency (or dissatisfaction) leave without having to give any more than one month's notice as required by the labor laws. More importantly, if he wanted to ensure successful continuity with a new doctor, which he would be dependent on me to find, then he was obliged to make sure that we parted on good terms. Since that was unlikely to happen, we now had to be careful to cover our asses.

'We stick to the contract and the letter of the law and fulfill all of our obligations, which means one month's notice. When we tell Rashard, we tell the kids and anyone else who has not been told.'

'He's not going to like it!' Darling shook her head.

Like it or not, in T minus 48 days, it would be every man for himself.

7

He threw away his walking stick

By the end of the day we had attached six itemized sheets of A4 paper to the exit planner to help us plot the critical pathway necessary to reach our departure date on time. The sheets were headed Edvina, Practice, House, Kids (with a subheading for Molly), Legal and "Who to tell?" We were now looking at working sixteen hour days, seven days a week with no breaks until the day we cast off.

From day one, the list of "Who to tell?" boiled down to only those people absolutely necessary to help us achieve our goal. To begin with they were limited to Abdullah, family and friends overseas, some trusted friends in Muscat and His Excellency the Lord Mayor. He had not only helped kick off National Down Syndrome week, but was now talking enthusiastically about next year, and Darling's continued leadership of the Group. On top of this he had reignited our original plans to sponsor two Omani students to travel to the New Zealand College of Chiropractic to become doctors. Unfortunately, his infectious enthusiasm, which before had been a source of inspiration and an incentive to stay, now put us in a difficult position. Although we barely knew the man, he had put his reputation on the line to support the Group. If we left Oman without giving him notice, it would amount to a significant loss of face. This in turn would probably do more damage to the reputation of the Group and Chiropractic, than any progress made under his patronage.

By coincidence, or divine design, I no longer know which to call it, he arrived unexpectedly at the practice the day after we had made our decision to leave.

'I had a very disturbing dream last night.' He was face down on an adjusting table in the treatment room. 'A man from your country came to visit me. He had white hair.'

I was glad that he could not see my expression. If the eyes are the window to the soul then this guy had mine wide open. What the hell was Lewis doing in his dream?

'Do not worry Doctor, I have many dreams. They are important to me. But this one, it was very disturbing. He said that you are going to leave Oman!'

Holy f&*%$n shit multiplied by ten! A chill shot ramrod through my spine.

'Well? Do you have something to tell me?'

'We are having too many problems with our sponsor.' I was dry mouthed in admitting to his revelation. His Excellency persisted, so I told him our story, from the beginning, including Anthony and all of the shit that we had been through with Rashard.

'Do you want me to speak to your sponsor?' He had a determination to his voice that bordered on anger. A force that would make an impression.

'It would make a difference, I'm sure.' I did not want him to think that I did not appreciate his offer. 'But what about the next time, and the next time? You have better things in life to do than babysit us.

'It is a pity.'

I appreciated his respecting our need for self-reliance. 'When will you leave?'

'After the big event.' I informed him of our plans and asked him to keep them secret until the appropriate time. He agreed and so ended his visit.

Next on the list, was Abdullah over lunch, where I planned to break the news. I was dreading the encounter, and many more like it, where Darling and I would have to sever ties with other friends who had grown near and dear to us. I was just about to leave the practice after another busy morning, when Linda patched a call through to my office.

'It's His Excellency, the Lord Mayor. He says that the call is urgent!'

371

Unsuspecting, I answered, *expecting* that he wanted me to see his mother (again) for a chronic hip problem that had not responded to surgery. Unsuspecting, that is, because he was just about to blow my mind for the second time that day.

'I have been speaking to some people about the problems that you are having.' His tone was serious. 'Would you consider staying in Oman if we were to organize a release from your sponsor?'

I thought that I was hearing things. A voice from the part of my mind that believes in fantasy and echoes the dream of every expat who ever had a problem with their sponsor.

'Are you serious?' The mythical release would require his Majesty's signature. Once given it was beyond reproach.

'Of course, it involves special circumstances, but I'm sure his Majesty will agree.'

'Really?' It sounded too simple. I was too dumbfounded to think of anything else to say.

'Really.' He sounded annoyed, as if I somehow doubted that he had the power to make it happen. 'You haven't answered the question!'

'What about my sponsor?'

'If he knows what is good for him, then he will not object. It is important that you do not discuss this with him or anyone else. If he was to find out before the release is given, then he could take legal action against you which would make things very complicated. His Majesty is also bound by the law, so he might have to withdraw the release until the case is over, which could take years. If the sponsor does not know until after the release is given, then, as I said, he is up against his Majesty.

'I will have to talk to Darling.' It was the last thing we expected. 'What exactly do we have to do?'

'You will have to choose a new sponsor and come to an agreement. The rest I will do.'

'What about you as our sponsor?' It seemed like the logical choice.

'No, it would not look right. It needs to be someone completely separate who is willing to support you.'

My head still spins now when I think about it. One minute we are staying and making plans for the future. The next we are leaving and making plans to punch our way up one of the most dangerous patches of ocean in the world. The next … well, Lewis shows up out of the blue (in somebody else's head for a change) and lo and behold, it looks like we are staying again, with the opportunity to get out from under Rashard's thumb and start afresh with the support of his Majesty!

I cancelled lunch with Abdullah and went home to tell Darling about the possibility of the release (freaked) and His Excellency's dream about Lewis (double freaked). We were deeply affected by Lewis's appearance at a time when we were going through another major upheaval. For him to show up in one of *our* dreams we could handle. He had actually done it more times than I have dared to mention. But to show up in His Excellency's! It was really hard not to interpret it as anything less than "angelic intercession."

'Well, what do you think?' I felt that his Excellency was genuine and that it was worth exploring the possibility.

'Whatever happened to being Captain of our ship and Master of our souls?' Having had less time to consider it, Darling was a little more reluctant.

I understood her hesitation. Once steeled to go to sea, it is very hard to do anything else but follow through on the decision. 'Let's say that this thing is for real. What would it take to make you want to stay?'

We sat down, drew up a list of all of the conditions that we would want and after a couple of hours' discussion, arrived at the same conclusion. No Sponsor, at least none with a financial interest. We would require total freedom to run a new practice as we saw fit and donate the Sponsor's dividend to support the Group.

At first we thought of Abdullah. For a start, he did not need the money and as our "shaker and a mover" he could make things happen for the group at the drop of a hat. However, our decision to never again involve friends in our business ruled him out as quickly as he had crossed our mind.

Our second choice was a sixty-nine-year-old patient whose construction company had made him a massive fortune building roads throughout Oman. Papa Al Araimi had a four-year-old son (to his third wife) but had been having serious difficulty keeping up with him before he came to see us. Within three months of starting treatment he threw away his walking stick. By six months, he was talking about having another child! I'd like to be able to take the credit, but know too well from experience that the human body is the greatest miracle worker. That sometimes it just needs a helping hand.

Papa Al Araimi however thought differently and was forever trying to find a way to pay us back other than our fee. When I called to explain our situation, he was immediately sympathetic and enthusiastic about the idea of sponsoring us and being benefactor to the Group. It helped furthermore that he was an old friend to His Excellency and therefore could also be trusted.

'You must be seen to have made every effort to resolve this with your sponsor,' His Excellency advised when we met again to finalize the details of the release. 'Record everything in a diary. Phone calls, e-mails, letters from your lawyer, responses, dates, anything that can be used to show that he refused to offer reasonable terms for a resolution.'

If Anthony had taught me one thing, it was how to gather evidence that could be used in a court of law. By the same token I had already started a file on my most recent dealings with Rashard in expectation that it might come down to a legal battle.

So, two days after we had committed to leaving Oman, we recommitted to staying with a different agenda. The question remained. Could we pull it off without Rashard finding out?

8

In the "Free World"

'What's happening now? We need another installment!' It was Angel again, the second time in one week, calling to find out what was going on with Rashard. Our lives had turned into a drama that was being closely watched by family and trusted friends overseas, but none more so than Angel and Scotty who had decided to break out and change their mundane lives for the better. We were glad for them. After Oman, they'd had a difficult time settling back in the U.K. and had finally found the courage to do something more exciting. In their case, their new destination was a big surprise and they were not telling anyone about it (even us) so as not to jinx the outcome. We didn't mind. The world was their oyster and like us, they could go anywhere and build a new life. All it took was imagination. Still though, the questions kept coming about our ongoing issues, the answers to which were important to anyone in the Chiropractic community thinking of setting up in new territory.

What about giving your sponsor notice? The lease? Notifying the patients? Transferring the files? Legal implications? Linda? Would we be required to pay Rashard any form of compensation? What legal grounds did we have? Who else was involved besides the Lord Mayor? How were we going to deal with Rashard after the event? Who else had we told what was going on? Keep in touch!

For us, nothing had changed and everything had changed. There were a thousand details to be sorted out and lots of questions we had never expected to have to deal with.

Legally, I was no longer required to give notice. Our lawyer had advised us that Rashard's persistent stance of non-negotiation fell within the guidelines of the Labor Court's requirements for dismissal. Effectively, it could be interpreted that Rashard had given *me* notice and as the clock ticked down to the final day, I was just honoring my obligations as per our contract.

The question was how to go about creating a new center? Like everything else, the current practice lease belonged to Rashard and would expire six months after my contract was to be renewed. The loss of his dividend plus the lease payments would represent a massive dent in his income that he could ill afford. This would leave him with two options. Suffer the cost of carrying the practice and all of its overheads until he found a new doctor, which potentially could take years. (Meanwhile we would have set up down the road and taken all of our patients with us which meant a new doctor would have to start from scratch) Or ... wash his hands of it completely and walk away. The former represented a prohibitive financial burden that we hoped would make the latter plus a cash incentive the more attractive option.

The shoe was on the other foot now and it was very tempting to use it to kick Rashard's ass and leave him bruised with "extraordinary expenses" after what he had tried to do with Anthony. However, in a twisted kind of way, we owed him a significant debt in creating this opportunity for us, so we were determined to not treat him as a villain. Call it being magnanimous in victory, call it covering our own ass, our goal was a clean break with no loose ends that he could use to slap us around the head at a later date.

As T minus five ticked down to four and then three, Darling and her team went into high gear organizing the event. Dr Al Bashar's accommodation was sponsored by The Intercontinental Hotel who also offered a large conference room at no extra charge to go along with it. Reto and his assistant would stay with us.

In the meantime I was busy considering a crew and preparing Edvina for sea. I also had to find an alternative building if Rashard decided to dig his heels in and try to source another doctor. In doing so, I put Paddy and Kate back on the shelf for the umpteenth time, but with a promise to myself and them that I would complete their story once our situation had been secured.

If our future was beginning to look brighter, then it was also overcast with sleepless nights as we navigated our way through the smoke and mirrors of secrecy and uncertainty connected to gaining the release. We still could not believe what was happening and had to be very careful of what we said, especially in front of Linda. Her reward for disloyalty would be the loss of her job the day Edvina sailed for Europe and was no longer under threat from her lovely George.

In the Free World, none of this skullduggery would have been necessary, but we were not free until our release had been secured.

While the clock ticked down to zero hour I made (as instructed) over a dozen separate recorded attempts to get Rashard to sit down and negotiate, including phone calls, registered mail, e-mails and lawyer contact. Most he ignored, but in the few that he did reply to, he was still adamant that he was not budging on his demands. It was a relief, for his impatience and greed was like a permanent fault line that we could never hope to build a future on.

At T minus three weeks we received a worrying call from Angel. Our ten-year-old godson had developed an obsessive need to wash his hands every hour of the day and night. The news was disturbing, but we could relate to the stress that they were all under with their "Big Move" as Angel had labeled it. By T minus one week though, our concern was piqued when they were having to hide all of the sharp knives and objects around the house that he might use to self harm.

'When the fund raiser is over, I want to fly over and support them.' Darling was distressed on hearing the news. In a matter of weeks our lives would be back on an even keel which she could use to bring stability to Angel and Scotty's transition. It wasn't as good as my idea of going to Bahrain for the Formula One G.P.! However, having swallowed my pride, I was more than happy to build a bridge to sustain them in their hour of need in the same way they had helped us with Molly.

At T minus one week, Reto landed to great fanfare and immediately started weaving his magic among the packed waiting list of expat ladies who had signed up for a "personal transformation". More than impressed, I was amused also by how he charmed the pockets of his clients (and their husbands) to add to the fund that was going ballistic.

By T minus two days to World Down Syndrome day the Group had received or been pledged almost sixty thousand dollars with some big players waiting to write *bigger* checks on the day!

How did we feel? Like rock stars! Again, it was as if the Gods had been testing us all along to make sure that we were worthy of the task. Having proven ourselves, the Universe was now revolving around us with the *powers that be* intervening in a multitude of quirky ways to help us reach our goal. It was as if our lives had become entwined with a special grace, a *Divine Design* hidden behind the stars who held us in the palm of her hand. Of all the billions of people on earth, she was keeping an eye on *us* and maneuvering "just so" for our favor. After three years of continual challenges and hard work it was time to reach for the stars.

9

No hint or warning.

The morning of World Down Syndrome day kicked off with Dr Bashar giving an inspirational presentation to a packed auditorium. The audience included parents and supporters, the Lord Mayor, local dignitaries and reporters from the newspapers. It was standing room only as he spoke passionately about his own daughter and not just the desire, but the *necessity* for inclusion of children with Down Syndrome in our modern society. He was responded to favorably by a representative of the Ministry of Health. They promised financial support and the setting up of a committee that would research the next step of getting 'our children' (as he termed them) into the national schools. It was a long shot that we all knew would take years to reach its target, but the door had been opened and that was what mattered the most to every parent in the audience.

"Inclusion" was the catchword for the day and repeated over and over on the radio as I listened to Dr Bashar being interviewed while I delivered the last load of T-shirts. Darling's group of merry "activists" was set up outside the malls doing a roaring trade.

'It has a nice ring to it!' The radio presenter was delighted when Dr. Bashar gave her a gift of a T-shirt at the end of their interview. By midday the Fund had reached over eighty thousand dollars. We were on a roll. His Excellency had reassured us that very morning that we could expect the release in less than two weeks. All we had to do was keep our heads low till the day our contract expired. He flew to India that evening with his mother for further treatment for her hip. The day would end by the hotel pool with a grand finale where Reto, in front of two hundred and fifty champagne-imbibing women would transform another Cinderella into a beauty while fireworks flew overhead.

I had planned on taking the day off, but I was obliged to work a busy afternoon with patients. I had no reason therefore to think that anything was amiss until our busy afternoon ended with Rashard suddenly showing up in the waiting room. He was accompanied by four men. One had a tool box. The taxi driver stood beside him and the other two had the hardened expressions of bad boys up to no good. A quick glance at Linda gave me the first sign of what was about to happen. She made eye contact with Rashard then practically ran from the building. Without explanation, he started pointing and giving orders in Arabic. Mr. Tools opened his bag and withdrew a screwdriver and a brand new dead bolt and began changing the lock on the front entrance.

'Rashard, what the hell is going on?' I walked out from reception to confront him, but his two henchmen blocked my path.

'I hear that you are forming a new partnership with the Lord Mayor!' His eyes dared me to deny the accusation.

'What?' Caught off guard, there was no bluffing or time to feign surprise. We had been rumbled and I was momentarily too stunned and disoriented by the knowledge that we had an informer in our camp to argue.

'This is my business. I am changing the locks. You are to leave and not come back to this building without my permission!' His voice harsh, he pointed to the door, expecting the two gofers to remove me. Behind him, the taxi driver took a step backwards to avoid being caught in the melee he expected to follow.

However, my adrenalin started to kick in and I could sense a hesitance in my opponents who a minute before had tried to appear menacing. It occurred to me then that Rashard was too much of a cheapskate to hire real henchmen. Based on this hunch, I stepped forward and waved my fist in front of the guy closest to me and roared.

'You lay a finger on me and I will break your fuckin' neck!'

I don't know who was the more shocked, me or them. The taxi driver ran out the door! I could tell by the exchange of shaken looks between them that none of Rashard's minions had signed up for violence.

'This is my clinic!' Rashard shot back less convincingly, but he too kept his distance. 'You have to leave!'

'Fuck you!' I wanted so badly to shake him. To knock him around and beat some sense into his stupid brain for delivering this moment unto us all. Had he walked in and announced instead a desire for reconciliation and to recover our partnership, I would have gladly taken it, for in truth, we were sick of the treachery and the subterfuge that underpinned our lives. All we had wanted to do from the start was get on with our work and do the job that we thought we had been brought to Muscat to do. All he had done was fuck things up. Thumping him though, was out of the question. There were too many witnesses and with His Excellency in mind, it would make me look like the guilty party.

I was just about to pick up the phone and call Darling when she arrived to bring me to the hotel for the Grand Finale.

'What's going on here?' She bounced into the reception looking like a million dollars, totally unsuspecting. I left it to Rashard who mumbled an answer to her question, but the tension in the room explained everything. Now that I had my own witness, the two lackeys backed off completely and joined the taxi driver outside over hushed tones and a cigarette.

Darling, crestfallen, understood the reality of our situation when the carpenter started hammering at the door to fit the new locks. It was impossible to fathom at that moment how deep the shit we were in, but we both knew that we had to do something to save ourselves. She called the hotel and told them we had a "situation" and to go ahead without us. Then, rolling up her sleeves (literally) she went to the coffee stand and started dismantling the coffee maker.

'This is my business, you can't take that!' Rashard pulled a sheaf of invoices and receipts from his pocket and waved them in front of her in an attempt to claim possession.

'Show me the receipt for this!' She held up the coffee machine knowing that she had paid cash for it.

He ruffled through the sheets in an attempt to locate a receipt, but found instead that she had him stumped. 'You can take what is yours tomorrow.' He pointed again to the door, as if we could trust him to let us return, but we refused. Having somehow managed to gain the moral high ground, there was no way we were leaving without what belonged to us.

It was hard work. Hard, in the sense that we knew from Rashard's stance that there was no coming back. Hard in having to leave our most favorite place in the world, created from the distillation of our imagination and experience. Hard with his Excellency's warnings against discovery in mind, as we had no idea now where we were going or what lay ahead for us.

We worked in silence, under the equally resentful eye of Rashard who followed us everywhere in an attempt to tick off what he owned (very little) in comparison to the large mound of chattels and equipment that was building up on the street outside. His dismay at seeing the practice slowly whittle down to nothing was of some consolation, but it made me suspicious.

My biggest concern was the specialized handmade treatment tables that we had paid a small fortune to import from the States. Rashard tried to argue that they belonged to the business, but the receipts were in my name and with the two of us shouting him down we were able to claim them. His lackeys refused to be drawn into an argument with a woman! This represented a significant blow to whatever plans he had made for the future. They normally took four people to lift, but without any willing help on hand, we somehow managed to wrestle them out on to the street.

The rest I considered "replaceable," but Darling, her special outfit for the Finale now ruined from the heat, was madder than hell and determined to take every last thing that Rashard could not prove possession. Within an hour the practice was stripped bare save for the furniture in the waiting room and the reception desk that was screwed to the wall.

The changing of the locks was completed just as we had moved the last of our stuff out onto the street and with a final rattle of the door to make sure all was secure, Rashard left as just quickly as he had appeared.

'What now?' Darling sat heavily beside me on one of the treatment tables. Still stunned, we were exhausted from the exertion and numbed by what had just happened. There had been no parting words or "see you laters." No arrangements for the continued care of the patients who would show up after the weekend to an empty building and no doctor.

As we sat on the street under the stars a massive fireworks display started in the direction of the hotel. I didn't know what to say or do next. One of the greatest days of our life had just been spoiled by one of the worst.

Rashard was now in serious breach of our contract. Technically, this made us the innocent party, but in spite of the argument that we might make to support it, in reality we had been caught red handed. Given another couple of weeks, he was the one who would have been receiving his marching orders, although not in the same ignominious fashion. Possession being nine tenths of the law, it was our ass now sitting on the street, and knowing the law, we had a massive battle ahead to prove our innocence. How we would go about doing it was for another day. The more nagging question was "how had he found out?"

10

'It makes you wonder!'

Flush with success and too much champagne, Reto returned home hale and hearty sometime after midnight. He had a leftover bottle which he had "lifted" to continue the celebration with us at home.

'$120,000 man, can you believe it?' He announced the final figure raised by the Group as he stumbled through the entrance doors of our large hallway. His assistant let out a high pitched cheer of good spirits as she brought up the rear. 'Weeee are the chaaaampiiiiioons of the world!' He sang Queen and waved the champagne in the air, oblivious, as he danced his way towards us. 'Where were you guys?' He did his best to hide it, but there was a hint of disappointment in his tone. We had missed his Grand Finale. He was halfway across the room before he noticed the wreckage from the practice that was scattered everywhere. 'Shit man, what's going on here?' His hands slowly lowered, his shoulders slumped. 'Are you guys okay?'

I shook my head. Weighted down by the growing realization of what had just happened, it was impossible to rise above the deep shit that we now found ourselves in to celebrate anything.

Sensing this, Reto placed the bottle of champagne on the floor out of view. He sat down beside Darling, put his arm around her and gave her a hug to try and console her.

'Fuck man, can they do shit like this over here?'

We had not thought so until I heard Rashard turn the deadlock in the front door of the practice. Discovery of our plans, we had reasoned, would have strengthened our case and made Rashard more negotiable if he knew that we had the option of a Release from on high.

The more I thought about it, the more the stress started to build. Throwing us out on the road did not make any sense. Regardless of patient care, the practice had significant weekly expenses that *had* to be paid. The fact that I was not going to be there any longer begged the question ... *who was going to pay them*? Not Rashard, as we were sure from Anthony's e-mails that he was broke.

Once more, loyal to the core, my un-trusted PA Linda was party to what had taken place and I wondered what else she knew that we didn't. I'd heard through the grapevine that Rashard had made contact with an Australian Chiropractor, but nothing had come of it. At least that we knew. No Chiropractor in their right mind would attempt to take over a clinic without having at least spoken to the previous doctor. So what the hell was going on? We could only second guess what he planned to do next, but the question would have to wait. The following day was the weekend. His Excellency was away for a week and our lawyer was un-contactable (bloody typical) so there was nothing we could do but wait for his return to find out where we stood. Besides, it was Reto's last day in Oman and the Group was hosting a special lunch to thank him for his monumental support. As such, we had to go along too and pretend that everything was okay.

It was a horrible day that ended infinitely worse with a phone call from a friend at the marina just after we had said our goodbyes to Reto at the airport.

'Did you know that the police were on your boat yesterday?'

The drive from the airport to the marina normally took just over an hour. We made it in forty-eight minutes.

As we ran from the empty car park onto the floating pontoons, nothing seemed amiss. Edvina sat as she always did, stately and regal, the picture of perfection, until we noticed that something was out of place on the guard rail that ran down the side of the deck. As we got closer we could make out a piece of paper covered in a plastic insert. With the certainty of dread, I knew what it was before we reached it.

'Dad, what's this?' Poppit pointed to the cleat on the marina to which the bow of Edvina was secured. Around the rope were two thick plastic cable ties. I was so intent on the paper on the rail beside the cockpit that I had walked past the cleats unnoticed. Attached to each cable tie was a badge with Port Authorities stamped on either side that confirmed my greatest fear. The paper attached to the rail had the same heading. The writing was in Arabic, but I already knew what it said. *Impounded!*

'They can't do this!' Darling was beside herself. It was like finding our best friend had been slapped in irons. The notice forbade anyone from boarding, but it did not stop us. A furtive search below deck revealed that the cylinder head on the engine had been removed to prevent it from being used.

'Abdullah!' Thankfully he answered on my first call. 'We need to have a meeting!' An hour later we were sitting in the lounge of his house being served coffee by his wife.

'Wallah Docta, dis is very bad!' He must have said it a half dozen times. 'It is illegal, you understand, but his brother, he is the Head of the Ports so he can make dis.' He threw the notice on the table in disgust. 'You can get your lawyer and he will fix it, but his brother, he can keep doing it, around and around and around!' He gesticulated with his finger, like he was stirring his coffee. 'I know him. He is like Rashard and the Linda and the George. He has the black heart too!'

'What do we do?'

Abdullah sat back and thought for a few moments. 'Tomorrow morning first thing, *first thing!*' He tapped the arm of his chair. 'You go to the bank and take out all of your money!'

I was incredulous.

'Really, if he has the friend in the bank then they can make your money disappear, by the "mistake" you understand?' He tapped the side of his nose with his index finger. 'One month, maybe two before you get it back. They know the rules! They can cause you big problems! When you are finished with the bank you go to your lawyer and you sit in his office and wait until he sees you.'

'What about the release?' Darling reminded him. The release was supposed to have solved all of our problems. So long as we had not been discovered.

Abdullah shook his head. 'You pray to your God,' He pointed to the ceiling. 'I will pray to my God.' He pointed to his heart. 'I will make some inquiries and see what I can find out.'

'It makes you wonder!' Darling sat lifeless, staring into the distance, as we drove home for the first time within the legal speed limit that day.

'Wonder what?' I was caught up in my own little world.

'How he knows all of this stuff about the bank and impounding property.'

'You don't think he is involved as well do you?' I was disturbed by her train of thought.

'No, he is the only one I trust, but I wonder how many people he has done this to in his own company?'

The thought had crossed my mind several times before. I loved the guy dearly. We had a privileged relationship, but I had come to know that I would never want to get on the wrong side of him.

The following day, the shit just got deeper, when the bank teller, who knew me on a first name basis, couldn't find any trace of our account. He summoned his manager, who also knew me, but their mutual tapping of fingers on the key board and scratching of heads failed to find us anywhere in the system. The manager picked up the teller's phone, dialed a number and then pointed to the floor above. When he got an answer he reeled off our account details, then paused, nodded a couple of times, spoke in rapid Arabic, caught my eye, shook his head and then excused himself instructing the teller to follow him. Both shuffled out of the booth and headed for a stairs in the far corner of the bank. A half an hour later a different teller appeared and explained that his colleagues had to go to a meeting at another bank and asked me to return the next day. When I pressed for information, he blamed the computer.

It occurred to me there and then to stage a "sit-in" and shout the place down until someone gave me some answers. It occurred to me also that in spite of our freedom, we were in fact living in a police state and that they could be real bastards when they wanted to be. It was one more reason to go to our lawyer and stage a sit-in there until he made the time to see me. I waited almost two hours.

'I understand,' he sympathized. After a further half hour of questioning and listening to me, he had three foolscap pages of our tale of woe in front of him. 'First things first!' He pushed the pages to one side, when I finally stopped running my story. 'We will need to sort out payment of your account before we go any further.'

I was stunned. I was drowning in front of him, needed someone to throw me a rope and he wanted to talk about money?'

'You want me to help you? Okay, I can do that. I can already see where they have made some big mistakes so you have a good case, but I will have to stop all of my other work. So, we need to work out how you are going to pay for my services.'

'I will pay you!' That he would doubt me!?

Distrust was written all over his face.

'You have my word,' I found myself promising and suddenly realized that I probably wasn't the first wretched expatriate to cross his doorway.

'You have no job, you have no assets, you have no bank account.' He spelt it out by tapping each underlined point on his notes. 'For this sort of case, I can only work for payment in advance.'

'How much?' I knew then, that his empathy did not exclude the need to be brutal. It made me wonder if some of my patients had thought of me in the same manner.

'How much do you have?'

F&#k!

After three years of hard work and continual challenges that drained our resources we had very little to show in terms of financial gain. We ran a cash practice, some of which I kept in a biscuit tin under our bed (I kid you not) for the contingencies and emergencies that had become the norm in our everyday life. The rest was sitting in the bank somewhere yet to be found. By our estimation the previous night, we had enough to cover our expenses for a month so long as nothing else too untoward was to happen. That and two credit cards which thankfully were hovering around zero balance. I took one of them out of my wallet and threw it on the table in front of him.

'It has a ten thousand dollar limit!'

'That is enough to get started.' He smiled and picked up the phone. 'I will have my secretary take five thousand for now. I will want an imprint for the balance to hold in reserve. If you are in agreement, then we can get started.'

After all of the problems that I had with Anthony, I knew that it wouldn't be long before he came looking for the second card. After that we would be calling family overseas.

My head spun when I finally left his office later that afternoon. By the time he had finished we were looking at three months minimum to extricate ourselves and Edvina from Oman, so long as Rashard was cooperative. When he said three years if Rashard decided to be a bastard, I nearly threw up on his desk.

'How can you tell when an Al Abdesalam is lying?' He joked in mentioning that he had once had to deal with Rashard's brother in a similar situation.

'How?' I felt like a sucker.

'Their lips move!' He laughed as if it was the funniest thing.

How much worse could it get?

11

There is nothing worse

There were only three people in Oman who knew of our Release. Abdullah, His Excellency the Lord Mayor and a Kiwi family who had become close friends. All were trusted beyond question, all were discreet, all knew the stakes that were at play. So how the hell had Rashard found out? We finally decided that while it did not come from his Excellency, it was most likely someone in his office. Tribal by nature, all of Muscat was interconnected by vested interests rooted deeper than a job title or fear of a boss. The same wagging tongues that had built our practice through word of mouth were probably the same ones that had spread the word of our "golden release" until it somehow found its way to Rashard. The trouble is that thinking like this will eventually drive you crazy! With almost a million population living in the city, the likelihood of someone saying something to somebody until it reached Rashard had the same odds as him winning the lottery. We did not believe ourselves to be that unlucky.

The alternative though, was that he knew what our plans had been for some time and was therefore prepared to shut us down on every front. The question was how?

The next two days were spent at our lawyer's office building our case. In an early morning review session of the third day he "believed" that he had sufficient evidence to take Rashard to task and "hopefully" force an early settlement.

'You have the law,' the lawyer held up his right hand, 'and then you have the rules,' he held up his left. 'He has broken the law!' he squeezed his fist shut, 'eventually, we can make him pay for it. But he can use the rules to frustrate the law for long enough that you will eventually give up and go away!'

No shit Sherlock! I didn't say this. I was way past drama and just wanted him tell me something that I didn't know.

'I have made some inquiries and discovered that he has done this before to the manager at his factory that went broke. He blamed him for everything and threw him and his wife and two kids out on the street. The guy had not been paid for months. He had no money so there was nothing he could do to defend himself. Somehow he managed to scrape enough for tickets back to India and left within a matter of weeks.'

These were the kind of stories that happened to someone else, someone less fortunate, less prepared, less smart, less lithe, less lucky. They did not happen to us. Given a different terminology that included the word "genetics" ... he could have been talking about cancer.

'I am surprised though that he would do this to you. It is most unusual with an expatriate.' He didn't say it, but he was referring to the color of our skin. 'He is desperate, very desperate. Based on what I have found out and what you have told me, he needs you as much as you need him. While I think it is in his best interests to bring about a quick resolution, I think also that he is using this as a way to drive the hardest bargain!'

I didn't disagree, but I did not agree either. The way I had figured it, we were both going to be broke in about a month. Rashard could play hard ball all he wanted, but he could not make us stay. What we needed most was an "out". If his Excellency could not provide it then as far as we were concerned it was the lawyer's job to get us out of Oman.

'Unless there is something that you have not told me?'

'What?' he caught me off guard.

'My brother, he is a doctor at the hospital. He told me once that many times, the problem that people first present with is not the real problem. That he has to dig much deeper to find out what is really going on. It is what makes the practice of medicine and the law so difficult and expensive!' He eyed me suspiciously.

The only thing we had not told him about was the Release. When His Excellency returned from India we hoped and prayed to the Gods that he could weave his magic and make all of this go away (and save us a fortune). We prayed because we had been warned by His Excellency and Abdullah, that discovery before Release could destroy our chances altogether. As such, we would have to fight our own corner, hence the gunslinger who was sitting in front of me.

There is nothing worse than having to stand back and have someone else fight for your life and that of your wife and children. Nothing more terrible than having to give up your power to a complete stranger, when you know that it could still end in misery. Having done it successfully before with Molly's delivery and subsequent open heart surgery, did not make it any easier. If anything, it made it harder. We were now living on a knife edge that could just as easily turn our world to shreds.

With time on our hands we spent the rest of the week with the kids, pretending that everything would be okay, that we knew what we were doing (not) and that the risks and the short term pain we were taking was worth it for the long term gain. Anything we could think of to keep our spirits from sinking altogether. We were back in Limbo, neither coming nor going, so for the sake of economy we decided to order a container to send our belongings to New Zealand and downsize to a two-bedroomed apartment with the bare essentials.

By now word had gotten out that the practice was closed. I was inundated with phone calls on my mobile from patients in various stages of discomfort and sickness looking to continue their care. I saw no point in hiding it, so let people know what was happening. Most were understanding, "it happens a lot" being a frequent comment. For those who were irate and demanding, I gave them Rashard's personal mobile so that they could call him a bastard instead of me.

A week after we engaged the lawyer we were pleasantly surprised to begin receiving a return on our investment when he called me.

'We have a meeting with Rashard and his lawyer at the beginning of next week.'

I wondered out loud how he had managed to organize it so quickly.

'I called his lawyer and requested it.'

'That simple?'

'No, not usually. I did not have to barter or negotiate conditions. It makes me suspicious of what they are up to. Even more so, when they suggested we meet at my office!'

'So what do we do?'
'We meet them.'

12

'Whaaaaaaaaaaaaaaaaaat!!!'

'Are you not afraid of pirates or storms?' I recalled someone asking before we left on the boat. The idiot! By now we had come to know that there were more pirates and storms on land than you are ever likely to meet at sea. As for the lawyer we had engaged? I couldn't help but think that he lived up to the reputation of a *shark* when he used the money we had given him to go out and put a deposit on a brand new Porsche Cayenne.

I have never been so terrified as I was the morning of the meeting riding the lift to our lawyer's office on the fifth floor. My mouth was parched and my heart pounded so hard that I was sure I could hear it echo off the walls of the elevator. In spite of our previous experience in dealing with Anthony, I knew instinctively that we were out of our depth with Rashard. He knew the rules too well and had used them to outmaneuver us in the past. It was only the divine intervention of the Minister of Health that had saved our asses. This time Anthony was not the problem and I couldn't persuade His Excellency's wife to ship Rashard off to Malawi for bad behavior!

From the reception, I was led to a large meeting room where I discovered that our fee was also paying for an expansive view over Muscat to the distant ocean.

'You can watch the whales migrating down the coast,' our lawyer motioned when he entered. Standing in the opposite corner of the room was a tripod with a large white telescope pointing out to sea.

My desire to have a peek and lose myself through the looking glass of memories past was so strong that I dared not, for fear I lose also the purpose for being in the room.

'Anything can happen today. Anything!' Our lawyer warned. 'No matter what, try not to look too surprised. The meeting could last two minutes, or it might take hours. The longer the better, for it will mean that they are open to some sort of negotiation. You must be careful not to get drawn into any arguments or insults, especially at the beginning. I will do all of the talking. If I defer to you, it will be to answer yes or no, nothing else.'

I nodded.

'Poker face, okay?' He passed his hand over his face as if washing away any emotion.

I didn't have a clue how to play poker!

Rashard and his lawyer made their entrance a few minutes later. Hands were shaken, greetings took place in Arabic, resentful glances were exchanged, but thankfully, unlike the courts, it was agreed by the lawyers that the proceedings would take place in English. However, once seated, no-one seemed inclined to talk. It became a face off of sorts, a stare down where the two lawyers deferred to each other through friendly smiles and hand gestures across the table for the other side to begin. The loser would be the first to speak.

It didn't take long for me to lose my cool.

'What about the patients?' I addressed Rashard directly. 'I have them ringing me every day. You cannot just leave them hanging like this!'

His lawyer looked to his client for an answer.

He was sullen and acted superior to everyone in the room, including his own lawyer. Finally, he spoke in Arabic.

'The patients will be taken care of.' His lawyer relayed the message.

'By whom?' I saw no point in delaying the inevitable any longer. If, by some divine or devious intervention he had managed to organize a new doctor, then we needed to know about it. Rightly or wrongly I had assumed that we were geographically irreplaceable. "I" was all I had to negotiate with. If he had really managed to organize another doctor then "we" were f&#$*d!

Rashard spoke again, staring at me, stone faced as he delivered the news.

'Arrangements have been made.' His lawyer repeated in English

'You cannot do this to the patients, it is unethical and unprofessional!' I tried to sound indignant, but my words foundered on the table along with my sinking heart. Whatever about the rules of poker, I could tell that they were not bluffing. In that single moment I had been *replaced*. Whatever was going to happen now was out of my hands.

His lawyer reached into his briefcase which lay open on the chair beside him. He pulled out a sheaf of stapled headed paper and shoved it across the table.

Our lawyer had been expecting it. He pulled a similar document from a folder and slid it across to his opponent. They took out their pens and signed in receipt, tearing off the front pages of each document and exchanging them.

'Please contact us when you are ready to discuss this matter further.' Rashard stood abruptly. His lawyer followed suit. Hands were shaken (not mine) and before I knew it, they had left the room. When I turned for an explanation, my Lawyer was busy flicking through the document that ran about four or five pages.

'He is suing you for breach of contract and fraud.'

I could not believe what I was hearing.

'It says, among other things, that you have failed to make financial returns for the last two years and that you have siphoned off two hundred thousand dollars in undeclared fees!' He shook his head, smiling.

'Whaaaaaaaaaaaaaaaaaat!' I stood as if kicked up the ass and started pacing the room.

'You have a lot of explaining to do.' My lawyer placed the document on the table and pulled a packet of cigarettes from his jacket pocket.

'You don't believe this shit, do you? It was my turn to be surprised by his curious expression.

'I told you, the problem is never what it seems.' He pulled a cigarette from the packet and began tapping it on the table. 'If you can persuade me that they are lying, then I will have some chance against them. Sooner or later though, the truth will come out. If you are not telling the truth, then you have already lost your case and might as well take back what's left of the money that you have given me and leave.'

'What did you give him?' I had no intention of leaving the room.

'You are suing him for two hundred and fifty thousand dollars for breach of contract, eviction, assault, irreparable damage to your reputation and anything else I could think of to keep him awake at night!'

It was the beginning of a long and arduous journey. Not to mention expensive.

'You said that he could not replace you. How do we find out?'

I dialed my mobile phone. 'Abdullah, where are you?' He always seemed to be close by when I was in trouble. Sure enough he was having breakfast at The Hyatt. I asked him to do me a favor.

'So, why haven't you made financial returns?' He took a long drag while he waited for my reply.

I was starting to feel like an errant school boy who had failed to do his homework. 'It's a tax free country. No-one had ever told me!' Rashard, who had been obsessive about us sticking by the rules and abiding by the law from the very start, had never mentioned there was such an obligation. 'Honestly, there is no such stipulation in my contract!'

'So where did he come up with the two hundred thousand dollars?'

I shrugged my shoulders.

'You do keep books?'

'I have an appointment book.' It was scribbled on in pencil and covered in eraser marks and white-out over reschedules and cancellations. He looked at me like I was the village idiot.

'How do you work out the profit share?'

'Profits?' I was suddenly ashamed to admit after three years of busting my ass and having our asses busted, that we had yet to turn any sort of real profit. It was always next week, or next month or next year when the dust had settled and we finally, FINALLY, got our shit together! I explained instead how Rashard received a monthly dividend regardless of whether we made a profit or loss.

'This is like with your friend Doctor Anthony!' He held the lawsuit and the cigarette in the same hand. 'These are very serious allegations. They make you look guilty until you can prove your innocence. Mr. Rashard knows this. Unlike you and me, he is not interested in the truth. What he means to do is make you pay for your stupidity.

The realization alone was bad enough, but having to pay the guy who was telling me made it ten times worse!

My mobile rang then and I used it as an excuse to turn my back to my lawyer and save any further loss of face by looking out the window.

It was Abdullah.

'Docta, I have very bad news.'

'I'm listening.'

'Doctor Anthony is in the clinic!'

'Whaaaaaaaaaaaaaaaaaat!'

'Really, I have seen it with my own eyes.'

13

'I will take care of it'

The pieces began to fall into place as I drove to the clinic to see for *my* own eyes. They started with the look that Linda had given Rashard on the night of our eviction. She had known all along of their plans which, with all of our second guessing, would never have included Anthony. We had taken it for granted that he was out of the picture permanently and therefore no longer posed a threat. I could only speculate that somehow, they had gotten hold of our new e-mail address off the practice computer and hacked into our every movement. As I drove into the central business district, I cursed myself several times for my lack of vigilance and failure to fire the *bitch* at the same time that we had gotten rid of Anthony.

I parked a street away from the practice and walked down a laneway between two large villas. From there, it was possible, behind a row of bushes that ran parallel to the side of the building, to get a clear view through the front windows without being seen. Sure enough, there were Rashard and Anthony, sitting on the sofa in the waiting room, locked in meaningful conversation. Between them they shared some papers. I was sure that it was the lawsuit and that he was explaining what had just happened at our lawyer's office. It was no wonder now that he had been so arrogant at our meeting, for he already knew that he had us on the ropes. After a few moments, Linda appeared from the reception area and served them coffee.

Confirmed of the knowledge, I had just stepped back into the cover of the bush and was about to leave, when lo and behold, good old George arrived in his metallic turquoise Jaguar and parked outside. When he entered the clinic there were smiles all around. He shook hands with Rashard first, then Anthony, who held onto him with both hands like a long lost brother. It looked like this might be the first time they were seeing each other since he had returned from deepest darkest Africa. Someone made a joke, laughter carried out an open window, then George finally kissed Linda on the cheek before they all sat down together. One big happy family!

Then it hit me. Two plus two equals Edvina! The two hundred thousand dollar lawsuit had nothing to do with the practice. Now effectively under his control, George had first claim on our beloved. If we fell into arrears with our lease on the marina berth, or the courts found in favor of Rashard, or both (probably) he was in a position to seize the "cruising boat of his dreams" on behalf of the marina or Rashard and sell her at a massive discount to *himself* to pay her expenses. That thought alone made me want to go in with a baseball bat and show them there and then who was her captain ... except for one thing!

At the very same moment, it occurred to me that their plan suffered from a serious imperfection and I felt the first wave of hope in weeks wash over me. That their evil machinations had a serious flaw and he was sitting between George and Rashard. Not only had Rashard broken the law in having us evicted, but I was now sure that bringing Anthony back into Oman constituted some sort of offence. With hope renewed, I returned to the car and called our lawyer to explain what was happening.

'If he has been black-listed then your sponsor has indeed broken the law, on several counts. Not to mention Mr. Anthony himself, who must have crossed the border illegally. Go to The Ministry of Labor and report him. They will have to investigate. It will take a time, but they *will* stop him from working, which will cut off the cash flow that Rashard needs to support his case. This puts you back into a stronger negotiating position!'

With the winds of favor now blowing in our direction, I had a better idea and told him not to do anything more on the case until I gave him further instructions. Still active with the Group and the Early Intervention Center, we had just had a meeting two days before to discuss how their cash rich coffers would be spent over the coming year. Because we had been missing at the Grand Finale, it was inevitable that our precarious circumstances came up for discussion. The members of the Group in return had reassured us that they would do whatever they could to support us. In particular our friend Hassan, whose brother, you will recall, was the Minister for Health. I dialed his number which he answered on the second ring.

'Hassan! Guess who is back in town!'

'I will take care of it.' He took it personally that Anthony had somehow managed to get back into Oman.

It took a little longer than expected. Somewhere between finishing packing our container and moving into our apartment, Anthony was "apprehended," and ignominiously marched through Muscat airport by the police for the second time to be put on a plane back to Malawi. The news was relayed to us by Abdullah, from the airport, where he had a V.I.P. pass that gave him access to almost any part of the facility. This included a holding room with a one-way mirror, behind which his cronies allowed him to observe Anthony being processed by immigration.

'Docta, I wait till I see him get on the plane. He is gone!' The tone of finality in his voice was a cause for a major celebration that would begin as soon as His Excellency the Lord Mayor returned from India and delivered the *coup de grace!*

14

'I have prayed for this for a long time'

His Excellency was a humble man who was grateful for the position that life had bestowed upon him. He would discuss anything but himself and, through the unique culture that he had established in his office, was always looking for ways in which to help his fellow citizens. However, it was on my first visit to said office when he had offered to help us, that I discovered that it was his rooms, inherited from his predecessor, that did all of the talking! More palatial and ornate than the Minister for Health, I was left with the reassuring impression that this guy could pull all sorts of strings. Therefore, unlike our lawyer, putting our life into the hands of His Excellency's was an easy choice, for we felt that they reached all the way up to his Majesty.

Our faith was further reinforced by the fact that on his first day back on the job after his time away in India, he had given Darling and me the very first appointment ahead of everyone else to begin processing our Release.

To honor the occasion I'd had our car cleaned and polished, my hair cut and bought a brand new pair of shoes to match the "glad rags" hanging in my wardrobe that I only wore on very special occasion. Darling likewise, wore a designer suit with subtle heels and a matching briefcase that had business written all over it. Rashard had made his play and been sidelined by the Minister for Health. All going well, His Excellency would help us to knock his ass out of the park.

After all we had been through, I can't tell you how good it felt to have the biggest guns in the country on our side to help us finish off our enemies once and for all. Of course we both knew that it wasn't going to be *that* easy. His Excellency had warned us that Rashard might be motivated in settling of scores afterwards, but we had devised a plan that we believed would appeal to him as a better option.

If he was in agreement, then the lawsuits would be dropped and we would buy him out of his share of the business instead. With terms by installment, he would continue to receive his same dividend for the next year. It wasn't part of the original plan, but we could see the value of spending our money this way, rather than on a lengthy legal battle where the only winners would be the lawyers. In addition to this appease, we would give him the right to bring any number of doctors into Oman and open as many Chiropractic Centers as he wished, without interference from us.

Suitably attired, we were just about to leave our apartment when Violi, totally out of character, stopped us at the front door. She proceeded then, like mother hen, to fuss over us, by making sure that my tie was straight and brushing imaginary lint off of Darling's jacket. Her fortunes now were tied with ours. Just the night before we had told her of what we were doing and that His Excellency had agreed to include her in the Release.

'I have prayed for this for a long time,' she whispered, as she fixed my tie for a second time, 'that God would be kind and keep us together.' Her eyes welled then, as she gently patted my chest. 'I'm sorry, you know, life can be very difficult here,' she reminded us of all that we had been through together. Of the injustices that she and many of her Filipina friends had endured under different sponsors. 'I am not sad, really, I am happy!' She wiped her tears when Darling gave her a consolation hug. 'This is my prayer being answered. It is my dream come true as well!'

In the briefcase were all of our passports and a folder that Abdullah had assembled with copies of every piece of documentation. Our visas could be renewed that day if His Excellency was so inclined. Furthermore, Abdullah had placed himself on standby at a hotel around the corner from His Excellency's office with one of his PRO's.

'One phone call, one minute, I will be there! He had promised the previous night over a preemptive rum while he explained the contents of the folder. 'Annnnnything he wants, I will get. You will see, or my name is not Abdullah Al Kyumi!'

From rock stars to paupers to now somewhere in between, Darling and I held hands and comforted each other as we drove through the Central Business District. I pressed play on the CD to try and relieve the tension, but she turned it off again, too wired to listen. My guts churned along in harmony as she tapped the fingers of her other hand on the armrest of her door. Short of kissing her for the first time many years before, I have never in my life felt such exquisite nervousness. Now, as then, we both knew that we were taking a leap of faith and that nothing was guaranteed. It was only what would follow afterwards that would prove the right decision.

I stopped at a T junction opposite the entrance to the Intercontinental Hotel where we had been members for the last three years. I was about to turn right when a car pulled up at the stop sign outside the entrance and indicated that they were turning in the same direction. Lost in thought, I subconsciously waved the driver to make his turn. He hesitated, so I waved again. Then something caught my eye. I glanced at Darling, to see if it was me, or if we were both seeing the same person in the opposite car. Her look of disbelief confirmed it.

Scotty was the driver!

15

What could possibly be worse?

I don't know who was more stunned, but he was the faster to recover. Instead of stopping, or waving or flashing his headlights to pull over and talk to us, he dropped the clutch, shot across the road and raced off in the opposite direction. Without a shadow of a doubt, we knew there and then that he was up to no good. It was in the determination of his jaw and the look of his eyes that refused to acknowledge us as he drove by. It was in the profane words that other Chiropractors had used to describe him when they heard that he had once worked with us. It was in the knowledge that we had been deceived by Angel, when she told us that their next move was to be a *big surprise*. It was in the realization that it wasn't Anthony after all who had been reading our e-mails, but Scotty and Angel who we had opened our hearts to again and trusted with our lives … and that they in turn had passed all of this information on to Rashard.

Keep up with me here!

It was the discovery of a thousand different things in one split second that would take hours, if not weeks to distill and toxify our minds.

I pulled over to the side of the road and called to cancel our appointment, then turned around and drove back to our apartment. There was no point in going to see His Excellency if Scotty and Angel had indeed done the dirty and taken over the practice. It had yet to be confirmed, but there was no way that Rashard would come to an agreement when he knew that he had Scotty's back.

'Abdullah, we have a problem!'

'No problem, I fix anything Docta. Tell me, I will come!'

'Dr Scotty is back in town. I'm pretty sure that he has done a deal with Rashard over the practice.'

'My God!'

Fifteen minutes later he met us at the apartment. 'Why he do this? He is your friend! His wife and Madam!' He pointed to Darling who was sitting at the phone trying to contact Angel in the UK. 'They are like the sisters!'

"Vigilance!" Captain Keith had advised us, 'Vigilance!" but nothing like this had ever hit us at sea. I cursed myself *again* for having defended Scotty a hundred times against all of our other colleagues who had spoken badly of him. Cursed myself for *not* believing, but choosing instead, to see him as I had wanted to see him. I shook my head that it might erase this growing abomination.

'I will go to the airport and I will check with the Immigration. They will tell me what he is doing here. After, I will call you!'

Darling managed to get through to Angel just after Abdullah left our apartment. There were no formalities, no how's the kids, no terms of endearment or affection.

'Scotty has just driven past us. What's he doing here in Muscat?' She sat cross legged and squeezed her thigh and dug her nails into her knee to try and ward off the numbness that was quickly overwhelming us. Sitting on the table in front of her was a framed picture of them both, cheek to cheek in the cockpit of Edvina, laughing, with two glasses of champagne raised to the camera. Scribbled on a writing pad in front of the photo were the dates and times of the flights that she had booked to fly back and support Angel after we had secured our lease. She couldn't take her eyes off it.

We had no speaker phone, so all I could do was grit my teeth and sit on the sofa opposite and observe Darling's body language. At first it seemed hopeful, like there was indeed a huge surprise that we could never have imagined. A thing of beauty and excitement that would make us regret the day that we had ever jumped to such terrible conclusions. Something amazing and full of joy and abundance, that could not wait to be shared with best friends, like winning the lottery or finding buried treasure.

Hope though, quickly turned to devastation. It was as if the phone receiver was connected to some dastardly living thing whose tentacles ran directly to Darling's heart. All I could do was watch in horror as it delivered its deadly poison, then begin to suck every last ounce of dignity from her being. Caught on the sofa in the same web of deceit, I was unable to save her as I struggled against the very same evil. She began to crumble, slowly at first, every muscle in her body fighting a losing battle against the invisible forces that had been premeditated against her. By the time I struggled free and reached her, she had withered completely. The phone hung by her side, her face was buried in both hands. Beside her the photo was turned upside down on the table.

I picked up the receiver in an attempt to fire off a parting volley, but the line, like our friendship was dead.

'So much for the story that she gave you about having to hide the sharp knives!' I stood beside Darling and laid my hand on her shoulder to console her for her loss as I placed the phone back on its cradle.

'She said that Scotty took the knives to the airport and left them in the car!'

'Christ!' I couldn't think of what sort of a madness we were dealing with that he would leave his son in such a perilous state.

'She said that as far as he is concerned, they have done their two years. That they have every right to be here and that Rashard is dealing with them!' Angel's twisted logic was a poor justification for what they were now doing.

The two year rule that had prevented them from returning had just passed its expiration date. Any time before and we could have objected as part of our contract. The stupid thing was that if they had expressed a genuine desire to come back, then we could just as easily not objected and they would have had the right to return any time in those two years. But they hadn't. It would have meant them starting from scratch and investing their own money and doing the hard yards that we had done. That had never been their intention!

With Edvina in lock-down and our bank accounts still missing, I was beginning to wonder what else they intended when Abdullah called from the airport.

'Docta, I have the very bad news for you. Rashard processed Dr Scotty visa six weeks ago with Dr Anthony. He was not supposed to come for another month, but when you got rid of Dr Anthony, he make emergency flight and come last night. He will stay for three days, then he go back to UK. Next week, he will come back again. Rashard is trying to make their visa sooner so that he can bring his family. Maybe two weeks, maybe three they will all come!'

I couldn't believe it. Six weeks and who knew how much longer that they had been playing us along. I was further shocked by his association with Anthony. He knew everything about Anthony's history and what had happened between us. So did Angel. It was one thing for them to do a deal behind our backs and steal our practice, but to stoop so low as to become associated with a pedophile? My only consolation was that we had gotten rid of the bastard before they had arrived. God only knows what hell we would be in if he was still around.

'Docta, this is not the bad news!' He interrupted my thought processes.

What could possibly be worse?

'They have blocked your passport!'

'I don't understand.' But I had an idea. It's amazing how many horror stories come out of the woodwork when you start sharing your own.

'Mr. Rashard, he put the block on your passport at the airport and at the borders and at the port. He make it part of the case in the court. You cannot leave Oman until the case is fixed.'

'Can he do that?'

'Wallah Docta, this man, he like your friend. He have very black heart. He make the case look very bad so he can keep you in Oman.'

'What about Darling and the children?' The last thing we needed was them getting caught up in the collateral damage.

'No, their name it is not on the contract, so he cannot hold them.' Rashard had tried very hard to persuade Darling to take ownership of our so called "partnership" by putting her signature alongside his wife Salwa's on our agreement at the start. I let out a deep sigh of relief that we had stuck to our decision to not do so.

'What do I do?' Edvina had always been our back door escape if things turned bad in Oman. It would have still been possible, if it had not been for our other "dear friends" George and Linda who now had an equal interest (not) in our welfare.

'Call his Excellency, tell him what they have done. He will help you, no?' He didn't sound half as confident as he had that morning.

'What if he can't?'

'Then you will have to go to the court and fight the case.'

With no job, no assets and no money other than what would burn out in a matter of weeks, I felt sick at the thought of the nightmare scenario being dragged out over who knew how many years. Short of escape, which now seemed impossible, His Excellency was our last resort.

I called to rebook an appointment later that afternoon, but was surprised when his office answered that he was not yet back from India. In spite of the fact that we'd had the first appointment that morning, I accepted the excuse. He had a habit of not showing up when he was supposed to, but they promised to call me with the first appointment on the day that he returned.

Two days later Scotty flew back out to the UK. I still had no word, but when I saw His Excellency in his chauffeur-driven BMW pass me on the highway traveling in the opposite direction I knew that something was up. Confronted with this, his office changed their tune.

"He is busy with his mother. He is busy with his Majesty. Sorry, he is out of the country … yes again. Yes, yes, yes, yes, yes, yes, yes, yes, yes, yes, yes, yes, yes, yeeeeeesssss we gave him your message!' By this time another week had gone by and Scotty had returned to do a three day intensive clinic. The day he flew back out to the UK, His Excellency's office told me that his brother was sick and that he would have to travel to his village in the far south for "who knows how long?" I'd had enough of the "no's" at that stage and slammed down the phone. F#$@^&%$#@*&^%$#!!!!

What the hell was going on? The week before we had been like the best of pals, there was nothing he would not do. "It's all for the children," he kept answering, whenever I tried to thank him for how much trouble he was going to in supporting us.

'Maybe Rashard he get to him … maybe his brother from the Port he call him and make trouble … Wallah Docta, maybe his brother he really sick!' Embarrassed, Abdullah made all sorts of excuses for his esteemed countryman. Seventeen unreturned phone messages in my diary and two further sightings of his BMW around Muscat were enough to prove otherwise. Save for our lawyer, who had just cashed our second check, we were now well and truly on our own.

15

You will have an Alibi

Devastated, disoriented, disenchanted, disgusted and disbelieving were just a few of the emotions that washed over and threatened to drown us that first week. For the first time I truly understood how our good mate Lewis felt when his cancer returned. He had fought the good fight and done everything right, only to have it revisit him in a more aggressive form.

'Where's the justice?' I could not help but cry out when our lawyer announced that we had no other choice but to go down the court route. We had come to Oman in good faith and tried to do the right thing. When the going got tough, we dug in and fought what we thought to be the good fight. In doing so, Anthony, Rashard, George and Linda had shown their hands, but we were still struggling to believe that our best friends had used theirs to stab us in the back.

'Greed!' Our lawyer answered to my cry of frustration. 'Still.' He paused to light one of his hideous cigarettes. 'It has no friends either! When you are here long enough, you will see. Greed will work in your favor. They will be allies so long as they think that they can profit from you. But as soon as it starts to cost them, and believe me it will, you can be sure that their so-called *friendships* will fall by the wayside.'

He must have read my doubtful expression.

'Families are the worst. I have seen families, good families, with a thousand times more money than you or I will ever have, devote it entirely to tearing each other apart. This is a very dangerous time. You must be *very* careful!' He pointed his finger directly at me. 'Don't … do … anything … stupid! You may already be thinking certain things or have friends telling you what to do.' He wagged his finger. 'You will get the opportunity, believe me! You must promise me that whatever you do outside this office, that you don't do anything illegal. *Please.* You have already given them enough. Don't give them any more reason than they already have!'

I nodded, but unable to hold eye contact, I looked away and feigned a sudden interest in the telescope on the far side of the room. It was like he had been reading my mind!

It wasn't long before the waves of devastation, disorientation, disenchantment and disgust had soon given way to a counter surge of anger, bitterness, resentment, recrimination and finally, with the encouragement of those who supported us … retaliation. As word of our true predicament spread, we were overwhelmed (like our lawyer had suggested) by people offering us all sorts of help. Commiserations and empathy flowed like a river. Food was delivered with the promise of more. Long term accommodation was offered at no cost. The legal opinion of many was given freely and while it might have reached the same conclusion as our own lawyer, all offered hope, all held a torch and many promised to stand beside us until justice prevailed. But there were some, as the lawyer was now warning me, who offered a different kind of justice. Some who had suggested that the scales be balanced in a different manner.

The most extreme measure of assistance was offered two days after our eviction by Hamish (not his real name) a patient who had become a friend. A former member of the British Special Air Services, he held the title of 'consultant' to a U.K. security firm that operated in the Middle East. He had started care almost a year before for several traumatic injuries sustained in 'the line of duty.' In particular, a failed parachute jump at low level that had broken both legs, fractured his spine in three places and put him in a wheelchair for six months causing him early retirement at forty. A spinal fusion had sorted out most of the mess, but he still suffered debilitating pain from time to time. In spite of his injuries, he made a remarkable recovery under Chiropractic care to the point that in the summer months we played squash together in an air conditioned court and ran on the beach in the cooler winter months to try to maintain our fitness. I enjoyed his company for the war stories that he shared and he became one of the few people I had confided in after all of the problems we'd had with Anthony.

Pissed would be a mild word to describe his reaction when he found out that our eviction from the clinic meant he could no longer get the adjustments he needed to maintain his spine. (All of our equipment was in storage in our container).

'Can you meet me on the beach?' I was coming back from the marina after checking on Edvina when he made contact.

'Sure.' I thought it a little strange, with the heat that was in the day, but there was something in his request that required seclusion. Fifteen minutes later we met at the beach that we used for training. The tide had receded far out to sea. As we walked away from our cars, he made small talk about how sorry he was that this 'hideous thing' had happened to us. When we were well out of earshot his attitude changed dramatically.

'Look, I have been giving your situation a great deal of thought. I know from what you have told me that you have been receiving all sorts of advice, but I have an option for you that no-one will have suggested.'

He glanced back over his shoulder before continuing.

'The company that I work for has a number of divisions.' He explained it slowly, so that I would catch his meaning. 'One of them provides security. Under normal circumstance this is a defensive role. We protect our clients. Whatever it takes, depending on the customer's requirements and our assessment of the situation.'

'Go on.' I said when he paused.

'We provide an offensive service as well.'

He stopped walking to allow the revelation to sink in.

'We are not having this conversation. Are we?' When he nodded, I knew it was my turn to look over our shoulders.

'You solved your last problem by getting rid of Dr Anthony. We can solve your new problem by getting rid of that other bastard!'

'You need to define getting rid of!' I was amazed by the words that spilt out of my suddenly dry mouth. ' "Kill the fucker!" was the first suggestion from everyone else who had heard our news.' My voice descended to a whisper.

'From time to time we take on new recruits that need to be tested to measure their competency and ability to deliver on whatever it is we request. We have two such recruits at present. South Africans, former

412

military. I have discussed it with my boss and he is open to you using our services.

'What services exactly are you suggesting?'

'Depends on what you want. We can make it look like a robbery gone wrong. By the time we are finished though, he will never practice again. On the other hand, we can crucify and fuck him up so badly that his wife will leave him and his kids will claim that they have no father.'

My stomach heaved at his description of the process.

'It only takes a matter of minutes!'

In spite of what he had done, this was my best friend that he was talking about.

'The first job is always expenses only, an opportunity for the service providers to show that they can follow orders.' he explained the arrangements. 'A couple of K at the most. Petrol money, a motel for as many days as it takes to set it up. A weekend in Paris afterwards if they have done a good job. If it is a robbery, then whatever money they find on the premises can be offset against expenses. The balance remaining can be deducted from my fees for your continued care here in Muscat!' He smiled.

I was struck by the irony of Scotty paying for his own demise. I doubted if there would be any invoices or receipts.

'The thing is, you will have to act quickly. He is in the U.K. at present which makes it easy. It is only a matter of a long drive and an overnight stay in a motel. All of the hardware that is needed is already in place. You say the word and your problems will be solved. The only thing we will need from you is his address and a recent photograph to make a proper I.D. I can have the job finished by the end of the week.'

He was matter of fact. Like a builder quoting for a job, he made it sound like I was getting a bargain.

'This is not the first or fifth time that we have provided this service,' Hamish advised 'There will be no down side. You will have an alibi. He will be in the UK and you in Oman.'

To have all of our problems solved in one foul swoop was sorely tempting. *Rashard would become compliant. We could get to stay in Oman, keep the practice, get Edvina back and continue with the work that we had started. George and Linda would be shitting themselves thereafter. I wondered how much extra I would have to pay to have Anthony included in the bargain!* I could hardly believe that I had been offered such an attractive option, or that I was even daring to consider yielding to the temptation.

'You must promise *me*!' My lawyer could see that I was wrestling with my conscience. He pulled open a drawer in his desk and withdrew an ancient copy of the Koran and placed the Holy book in front of me. 'Place your hand on the book,' he urged.

Easier said than done. I hesitated.

He reached across the table and grabbed my wrist. 'Do it!' His face was so close that I was struck by the smell of cigarettes on his breath, but more so, by the sense of fear in his voice.

'Too many times I have seen people take matters into their own hands. Your friend, he has sold his soul and that of his wife and children! For what?' He raised his empty palms in front of me. 'Don't you do the same! You will make your situation infinitely worse and spend the next ten years in jail. Is that why you came to Oman?'

My entire body shook with rage. To make such a promise was to give up the last vestige of power that I still possessed. Every fiber of my being rebelled as I held onto the armrests of the chair, preferring instead to "damn the torpedoes" and go on the offensive. To wage war instead of peace and deliver hell upon those who had delivered it to us.

When I refused to move, he leaned forward to retrieve the book. 'Forget about God, then, but some day, you will have to answer to your children!'

'Stop!'

He hesitated.

'What am I supposed to do? Just sit here while they take everything?' It felt like the walls were closing in. That we were being caged like animals.

'You must have faith and be strong, like on your boat.' He reminded me of the storm I had told him about. 'So long as you have this,' he thumped his heart with his fist, 'the waves are nothing, these people, *they* are nothing! You don't rage against the storm, you hold on and *have faith*. You told me this when I asked. You!' he pointed. 'Captain of my ship and master of my soul. *You* told me this!'

I had forgotten and felt all the more ashamed, for he had struck a chord when he mentioned my children.

'What have you brought up your son to do?' He knew then that he had me.

My hand found its way to the Koran.

'Halas!' (It is finished.) He waved his hand through the air in a single wiping motion, as if the hurt that had been committed against us could just as easily be erased. Then he took the Koran and held it in his right hand. 'I too promise, that when your money runs out, that I will continue to fight for you and your family until justice is served. But I promise too,' he pointed his finger at me one last time, 'that if you break the law, in any form, you will never set foot in my office again. Are we agreed?'

'Fuck the lawyer!' Hamish spat down the phone. Having been brought to my senses, I was now standing outside my lawyer's office anxious to follow through on my word. 'You have worked too hard and sacrificed too much just to walk away from it.' I was touched by his passionate support, but somehow felt reassured, even if only temporarily, that I was doing the right thing.

'I'll get over it, really. There are worse things as my grandmother used to say.' I was trying to sound braver than I felt.

'I have seen this a hundred times in this business.' He was determined. 'You can try all sorts of therapies until they are coming out your ass. Ashrams and Wise fucking men and Prozac and Holy God for forgiveness, but there is only ever one thing that will really cure the pain you are going through right now.'

'What's that?' I asked hoping for a short cut to enlightenment.

'Revenge!'

16

'Bring me the bag.'

Somehow I had changed my mind. Somehow I found myself sitting in a car next to Hamish. Behind us were two guys Peter and Jahns (not their real names). We were all heavily disguised.

'Here, take this,' Peter reached across the front seat and handed me a small white pill.

'What is it?'

'It is for your nerves.'

'I'm not scared,' I overstated in an effort to assure him that I could handle the next half hour.

'It is okay. It is good to be scared.'

'It sharpens the senses for going into battle,' Jahn smiled. A strange sort of madness from which to get high. I could sense that this was what they thrived upon. The drive from the hotel to the practice took no more than four minutes. Our surveillance phoned to tell us that Linda was leaving. We passed her as we turned down the street the clinic was situated on. In spite of the medication, my heart was pounding, and I found myself rubbing the palms of my hands on my dish dash to wipe away the sweat. I took several deep breaths to steady myself when Peter pulled up beside a white windowless van outside the clinic. This was it. There was no turning back. As we got out of the car a sliding door opened on the side of the van and two men stepped out to meet us.

'It's clear,' one of them nodded to Peter. The other was carrying a bag. It was almost a meter in length. Peter took it and handed it to me. It was heavy.

'Tools of the trade. Don't drop them.'

Without hesitation the five of us made our way through the gateway to the front entrance of the clinic. The two from the white van peeled off. One closed the double gates to the driveway and then sat on the front entrance porch to guard. The other slipped around the back of the villa to perform the same duty. Peter, Jahn and I stepped in through the front door to the waiting room.

'Hello,' Peter called out in a hopeful voice as we passed a large hole in the wall that was the opening to the reception area. It was empty. Jahn followed behind him, dragging his left hip as if in serious pain. 'Are you there Doctor?' Peter called out again.

'Just a second!' Scotty's friendly voice echoed off the walls, but we kept going to get as deep into the building as possible.

We heard a shuffling of papers and a slamming of drawers. By the time he had finished securing the takings for the week we had cleared the middle waiting room and almost bumped into him as he came through the door to the back room of the house. Behind Scotty each window was ornately barred to keep intruders out. All we had to do was get him in to the room and he would be beyond escape.

'Doctor,' Peter recognized him from the photos I had provided. 'It is my friend, he is very bad.' He pointed back to Jahn. 'We have heard that you are very good.' He used an endearing tone that was disarming and begged understanding for the inconvenience caused by our visiting outside of hours. I made a point of standing behind my two associates out of sight as Peter had instructed. It no longer mattered. Without warning, Peter floored Scotty with a vicious punch to the solar plexus that dropped him to his knees gasping for air. Jahn made a miraculous recovery and ran to assist. He grabbed Scotty by the opposite shoulder to Peter and they dragged their victim into the room. I followed close behind with the bag of tools and closed the solid mahogany door behind us.

Too stunned to resist, it only took a matter of seconds for my two associates to manhandle a disoriented Scotty into a seated position on the floor against the solid concrete wall that separated the back room from the kitchen.

'Listen to me very carefully.' Peter knelt down by Scotty's right side and grabbed his lower jaw and squeezed so that it made him look directly up in to his face. 'You do not resist. If you do, then we will do this to your son. Do you understand?'

Scotty was wild eyed and hyperventilating. 'Do you understand?' Peter shouted and rammed the back of Scotty's head against the wall when he failed to give an immediate reply.

In that moment of terror Scotty realized that whatever dream he might have been living, it was about to turn into a nightmare.

'Yes.' He winced through the nausea and pain. Tears flowed freely down his cheeks

'I am going to let go. If you make any attempt to move I will crush your skull. Do you understand?'

Scotty nodded as best he could.

Slowly, Peter released his grip and allowed Scotty to relax.

His eyes darted around the room, knowing that he was at the mercy of a force that he had brought upon himself, but was yet to fully comprehend.

'Bring me the bag.' Peter was all business.

I placed it down beside him and then sat on the end of a treatment table in the center of the room with a full view of what was about to happen. Scotty noticed my presence for the first time. I had not laid a finger on him which made me the good guy. His eyes searched mine for explanation and understanding and pleaded for my intervention in the "terrible mistake".

Any attempt to engage or recognize me was distracted by the noise of Peter unzipping the bag. He drew out several strips of thick, galvanized metal band cut to various lengths, each with the ends bent back at right angles. Selecting the one he needed, he gave the rest to Jahn to hold. He reached back into the bag and pulled out a masonry gun with a full magazine of sixty-millimeter hardened nails and high explosive charges. Taking the end of the first metal strip, he positioned it firmly where the wall met the floor beside Scotty's left hip. He placed the barrel of the gun on top, and with practiced precision, he pulled the trigger. There was a deafening bang. Scotty recoiled as the gun drove the first nail deep into the concrete. Jahn held him firm. Bending the metal strip around Scotty's waistline just below his belt, Peter handed the gun to his partner. Jahn positioned the strip tight to the floor on the other side, and pulled the trigger. Any hope of escape would now require bolt cutters.

'Please straighten your legs flat on the floor.' Peter placed his left arm gently on Scotty's shoulder and used his right to push down on his knees to show him what he wanted.

Scotty looked at me again, his eyes pleading.

'Relax, it won't hurt, Peter reassured in the same way that a doctor reassures a child he is about to inject. He bent a second metal strap over Scotty's legs just above his knees and drove two more nails either side into the floor. My ears started to ring from the explosions. Peter took the third strip and bent it around Scotty's ankles just above his feet. Scotty flinched as his assailant fired two more nails through the metal strip into the floor. At the same time Jahn took a surgical collar with thick foam and a hard plastic casing from the bag and placed it firmly around Scotty's neck. The final strip of metal was bent around the collar. Two more explosions and Scotty's head was held in a trussed-up position tight against the wall. Only his arms were left free to move.

Peter's hand went back to the bag. The next item of business was a small case that contained two pre-primed syringes with hypodermic needles.

'What are you going to do?' The blood drained from Scotty's face and he began to perspire in white hot terror.

'Shhh, it is okay.' Peter reassured in a soothing voice. 'This will help you to relax.' He inverted the syringe in full view of Scotty's eyes and squirted some of the solution out to clear any rogue air bubbles. 'Please, don't fight or my friend will hurt you more than the needle.'

'Think about your son,' Jahn took Scotty by the right elbow and wrist and bent his arm back against the wall to stop him flailing. Peter took his left arm and extended it across his knee, gripping the wrist under his own arm so that the skin exposed the vein that he wanted, just below the left bicep.

'No, no please don't, please!' Scotty begged, his head shaking as much as it could from side to side in the confines of the neck brace. His terror-filled gaze settled on mine in one last pleading. His soon to be tortured body beseeching me to show him mercy. It was then that he finally recognized me.

I had imagined making a speech. To let him know that he had been weighed, measured and found wanting. That he had been judged and found guilty and as such, I was now due my pound of flesh. But the *real deal* is nothing like the movies. The clock was ticking and every second counted. I had no problems with this. Actions always speak louder than words.

419

'You fucking bastard, I'll get you for this!' he screamed when he realized no mercy was forthcoming. He wanted to tell me that his would be the final revenge. That he could wait a thousand years if needed. That I would be the object of all his hate until the day it was spent in retribution, but Peter cut him off with a vicious backhand slap that broke at least two of his front teeth. He gripped his face vice-like again and prevented him from uttering any sound other than a sniveling grunt.

Jahn forced his arm and elbow further into extension so that the pain made Scotty's left shoulder rise up in search of relief. Scotty let out a muffled cry then another when Peter inserted the needle and injected the clear fluid into his body. The effect was instantaneous. The serum shot up his arm and into his head and turned his brain to mush. Scotty's eyes glazed over and he relaxed with a deep sigh as his muscles no longer cared to resist.

Peter withdrew the needle.

'See, it is not so bad,' Jahn said as he released his grip on Scotty's other arm. 'You make it hard on yourself when we are just trying to make it easy.' He patted Scotty gently on his left cheek, which to my surprise elicited a faint smile. His body relaxed further, arms flopping freely by his side, and his head bobbed to the left where he could see Peter preparing the second syringe.

'What's that for?' he asked softly in a faraway voice as blood and saliva oozed freely from the sockets of his broken teeth and dribbled down his shirt.

'It is morphine,' Peter answered. 'For the pain.' He inserted the second needle into Scotty's arm and pushed the plunger home. Scotty winced and drew in a deep breath, but relaxed almost immediately. 'That wasn't so bad.'

I was surprised to see him smile.

Peter put the used syringes back in the bag and took out a small spray can. 'Please open your mouth.' He waved the nozzle in front of Scotty's eyes. 'It won't hurt, I promise. It is like the morphine. It will help you to feel better,' he lied. When Scotty complied, Peter pressed the nozzle to release a long blast of gas down his throat. Scotty swallowed several times to try to void the taste from his mouth.

'Tell me the names of your children,' Peter requested.

Whatever false sense of detachment or wellbeing Scotty had enjoyed from the serum, it was suddenly shattered at the mention of his children. He struggled against his restraints, tried to shout, but the only thing that fell from his mouth was silence. The canister contained a neuromuscular suppressant designed to paralyze the vocal chords during surgical procedures. His gaze returned to me, fully cognizant of what was happening, fully aware that no matter how hard he screamed, no one would hear him.

Peter picked up the nail gun once more. He placed a large washer over the head of the next nail and nodded at Jahn. If Scotty was hyper relaxed before, he was now hyper alert and hyper reflexive when he sensed that he was in imminent danger. His arms flailed in immediate defense and he snorted and punched at his assailants to try to prevent them grabbing hold of his wrists.

'Don't!' I shouted when Jahn stood to kick him into submission. 'Don't hurt him. Just take him by the arms and stretch them out as we rehearsed and finish the job as planned.' My intervention saved Scotty a shattered rib cage and probable death from asphyxiation. It also relaxed him momentarily which was sufficient for them to grab each arm. Peter was beginning to perspire from the exertion as he used his left hip to hold Scotty's elbow against the wall. He stretched out his hand as far as possible, but Scotty, knowing full well what was going to happen, forgot about his son and put every ounce of his musclebound arm into resistance.

'I need help!' Peter struggled to extend Scotty's arm.

Time was running out. I abandoned my ringside seat to keep the game going. I grabbed the gun off the floor, forced Scotty's clenched fist back against the wall and rammed the gun into it. Scotty's entire body shook as the tip of the nail tore the flesh off his palm. I put my shoulder behind the gun to get the maximum purchase needed and then pulled the trigger. There was another deafening roar.

A bolt of red hot lightning shot up Scotty's arm and into his head. His mushy brain turned into a Molotov cocktail. Had the washer not been around the nail, it would have gone clean through and disappeared into the wall. As it was, the entire washer was imbedded at least a quarter of an inch into his skin so that the tendons that moved his fingers were exposed.

With the adrenalin now flowing freely through my own veins, I sprang across to the opposite side where Jahn had a better hold on Scotty's right arm. In spite of the fire that now raged within him, Scotty's sweat-filled eyes followed my every move as I knelt down to do my duty. His head shook and his eyes pleaded, but his scream was nothing more than a rasp as it blew blood and saliva all over the front of his white linen shirt.

I rammed the gun again into his clenched right fist. His head shook violently and his chest heaved in spite of the restraint. Had he been able to say anything it might have been to plead for mercy, or negotiate a deal or maybe, just maybe, having seen the light and the error of his ways that he might have begged for forgiveness. He seemed to nod his head in answer to all three. By this stage though, I didn't give a fuck. The feeling of release was glorious as I put my shoulder behind the gun and once again emptied all of my rage into the trigger.

The cordite from the explosive charges that fired the nails failed to mask the distinct smell of urine and shit as I stood up to survey the damage. So far, we had done little to harm him other than ruin his hands and maybe his career. So far though, was just the beginning. The damage from now on would become exponential.

Peter pulled two aluminum baseball bats from the bag and for the next thirty seconds we took it in turns to beat and smash Scotty's bare feet and knees to a pulp. He passed out halfway through the frenzy.

'Enough!' Jahn pulled the bat from my hands. It was lucky, for he must have sensed that the next place I intended smashing was the top of Scotty's head. 'Sit down' he ordered. 'We must finish as per orders. We do not have much time.'

Peter took a small case from the bag and opened it to reveal a selection of scalpels. Choosing the instrument he felt most suited to the job, he pushed the eyebrow over Scotty's left eye as far up his forehead as he could, then made a tiny incision into the brow.

Jahn pulled a Black and Decker cordless drill from the bag with a four millimeter drill already in the chuck and handed it to his partner. Inserting it into the tiny incision, Peter squeezed the trigger and the drill shot through three millimeters of bone into Scotty's frontal cortex.

Scotty shook involuntarily when the drill broke through and pierced his brain.

Peter withdrew the drill and changed it for another that sat in the scalpel box. It was entirely different, with flush sides and no cutting edge. When he pulled the trigger, the centrifugal force made two small arms at the top of the rod shoot out like a tiny propeller.

'Hold him steady.' He placed the tool into the small hole in Scotty's eye brow and pushed it the full length into his head.

Placing his hands on the top of Scotty's motionless head, Jahn pushed down with most of his body weight to insure that his victim was securely held in the cervical collar.

Peter pulled the trigger, and using circular motions in and out and in and out and in and out, he obliterated the frontal cortex of my best friend's brain and any thoughts that he might have had about revenge.

I was surprised how little blood loss there was when he finally withdrew the drill.

He placed a cotton-wool compress over the wound and had Jahn hold it in place. Reaching into the bag he took out the final tool for the job. It had a handle on it just like a gun, but the barrel was a narrow tube with a very fine filament sticking from the end. Peter squeezed the trigger and the filament immediately lit up red hot which he then used to cauterize the small wound. When he was finished he let the eyebrow drop back into place to completely hide the point of entry. Save for the slightest of swelling there was no visible sign of the destruction that had been wrought. Scotty was barely breathing.

'Finished!' Peter announced and my two new best friends stood up to admire their handiwork.

From spectator to villain back to spectator again, I was overcome by a wave of nausea and ran from the room to throw up in the downstairs toilet.

17

'The whole world has gone crazy!'

I woke up a few hours later on the bathroom floor with ringing in my ears. My entire left side was numb. Pins and needles pulsated like a river of fire down into my fingers. There was a pillow under my head. Somewhere in the background, I could hear the sound of muffled voices and laughter from children playing. A set of footsteps approached, light at first, but they grew heavier on the tiles until they reached a crescendo beside my ear.

'Are you awake, Captain Codfish?' It was Darling. She placed a mug of warm tea in front of my face. 'Abdullah just called to see if you were okay. He didn't sound so good!' She laughed and ruffled my hair. 'Breakfast in half an hour, okay?'

No, not okay, but I did not say it as she walked back out to the kitchen. How do you tell your wife that you have just completely fucked up your best friend's life? That you have crossed the line and joined the ranks of the *Coalition of the Willing* who proclaim to fight the good fight and are prepared to accept whatever collateral damage it takes to reach their objective. For the first time I understood the fear in our lawyer's voice when he had warned me not to do anything stupid.

And yet, something was not right. What was I doing on our apartment bathroom floor? The last thing I remembered was throwing up into the toilet at the office. And why was Abdullah calling to see how I was at this time of the morning?

I tried to sit up, but my head wouldn't have it. I eventually gave up and lay on my back. In the process, I noticed that Darling had placed my mobile phone beside the mug of tea. When I managed to retrieve it, I found eight missed calls, six from Darling the previous night and two from Abdullah. The most recent was five minutes before and I guessed that was the ringing that had woken me.

'Abdullah!' He answered almost immediately.

'Docta, you are still alive.' He sounded equally sick, but just as pleased to hear my voice.

'What happened?' I sipped on my tea, but got the distinct smell of stale rum from the mouthpiece of my mobile phone.

'Wallah, you come to my house yesterday after you see the lawyer. You bring the rum. We drink and we curse your friend. Then we make the plan for you to work in Dubai. Then we drink some more. Then you send my driver to your house and he get more rum. When my friend from the immigration come to visit, then we drink until we finish all the rum!'

The messier it got the more hopeful I became. I recalled having two full bottles stashed in one of the kitchen cabinets. 'What time did I leave?'

'I don't know. Two o'clock, maybe three. My driver, he bring my friend home first, then he come back and he bring you. My son, he had to help you walk to the car in his, how you say … pyjamas!' He laughed. 'How is Madam?'

I looked at my shirt. There was no sign of blood. I raised my legs one at a time to inspect my trousers. Save for some food stains probably caused after things had gotten messy, they were both clean.

'I will call you back later, okay.'

Hyper-motivated by a sudden flashback to what must have been an alcohol-induced nightmare, I just managed to get my head into the toilet before my stomach heaved. Again and again and again. Each barf was colored by its own flash back of exploding nail guns and flailing baseball bats and the drill plunging repeatedly into Scotty's skull. Somehow my mind must have latched onto Hamish's description on the beach of the crucifixion and turned it into a nightmare. The last heave brought tears to my eyes. Tears of shame for having had such terrible thoughts, but tears also of overwhelming gratitude, for I had not allowed myself to be persuaded by Hamish's beseeching.

As the waves of nausea and turmoil slowly receded, they were replaced by an unexpected inner calm.

Order had been restored.

Our twisted lives seemed slightly less bent.

I had, through the entreaty of our lawyer, stepped back from the edge and chosen life over the Devil knows what. The decision brought with it the gift of a renewed sense of faith in the future. I knew that it was as fragile as I felt there and then, but like a new spring shoot that dares to push its hope above the ground, the future was suddenly looking brighter than it had been for some time.

It was to be the defining moment of my life. The one that will forever save me. On our journey so far, I had learned that it is not God, but ourselves who decides if we live in Heaven or Hell. In this case my 'good friend' Hamish had been prepared to hand me my best friend's head on a platter. All I had to do was play Judas.

I could have justified it in a movie or a bestselling novel, but we'd had too much luck and love and experience of life by this stage to make any other choice. If balancing the books meant that we had to go through the nightmare of losing everything and starting all over again, then so be it. We were neither crusaders nor colonialists, soldiers of God nor mercenaries. North of us, the Americans were bombing the crap out of Saddam Hussein in the name of "weapons of mass destruction" when the only real weapons that existed were the ones that the US were dropping on the innocent Iraqi people. West of us, the Israelis and the Palestinians were trading punches over a piece of dirt that had seen more blood spilt on it in the name of God than any other part of the planet.

'I think that we should leave the Middle East,' Darling announced when I finally sat down at the kitchen table to fill my empty stomach. It was as if she had been reading my mind.

'What about working in Dubai?' A cold shower had cleared my foggy brain and I remembered telling her about Abdullah's plan to smuggle me across the border in order to support ourselves.

'I think that working in Dubai is clutching at straws. If you get caught you could end up in jail.' The stories that we had heard were chilling. I could see it in her eyes then, how she weighed the next sentence as if our whole future depended on it, 'I think that we should follow the lawyer's advice and have faith that justice will be served.'

'I think so too.'

'The whole world has gone crazy.' She continued breathlessly in an attempt to persuade me of her determination. 'There is a war up North and a war in the West and after what Scotty and Angel have done and the state you came home in last night who knows what might happen next?' She was obviously distressed and had not heard me. I stopped her by raising my hand.

'I agree!' The decision had been made, simple as that. I didn't need any persuading. It was unlikely that I would ever tell her about my meeting with Hamish or the nightmare that had followed. We were both singing from the same hymn sheet now and that was all that mattered.

'What about Edvina?'

'I will find a crew and take her to the Maldives. You can fly over and meet me there and we will wait for the next cruising season to come through.' Getting her out of the marina under George's watchful nose would be one thing. To leave Oman without clearing customs in a boat that had been impounded by the court was, our lawyer had advised us, an offence punishable under the laws of piracy.

'It's hurricane season!' Darling reminded me. There wasn't a year had gone by since our arrival in Muscat, that at least half a dozen fishing vessels bigger than Edvina had gone missing in storms across the Indian Ocean at this time of the year.

'There's a million square miles between us and the Maldives. We'll find some way to make it through.' The degree of risk we were willing to take to gain our freedom was growing exponentially by the day.

How we were going to pull the whole thing off, I didn't have a clue. The thought of the risks, combined with my present fragile state, was enough to make me want to throw up again on the spot. However, I was encouraged by the fact that if we managed to escape the marina, and get far enough offshore into international waters, then we would be truly free. The trip would only take three weeks at most. Once reunited, we would be back in control of our own destiny.

'Here's to living the dream ... again!' Darling tipped mugs trying to sound brave.

18

'Ye still don't know who I am, do ye?'

We decided that the best place for our container was Ireland. Once there, my family could flog off its contents and send us the money to support our trip, when we needed it. If things weren't bad enough, it was another bitter pill to swallow, to realize that we would be lucky to a get a third of the estimated seventy thousand dollar contents. The price for freedom can sometimes be f$#@&n expensive! The paperwork itself should have been just a formality, until we got to page six of the documents. Printed in bold at the bottom of the page was a space for the *Sponsor's signature*.

'You have to have your Sponsor sign this.' The Indian clerk behind the desk wobbled his head when he saw my hesitance.

'But it is our stuff, it has nothing to do with our sponsor!'

'It is the rules!'

'There must be some other way we can do it. What about my lawyer? Surely he can provide a letter of ownership?'

'It is the rules, the sponsor *must* sign it!' His finger was non-negotiable as he tapped the signature line.

Frustrated it seemed, at every corner, there was no way that Rashard would sign the damn form. I was tempted to punch all four foot of the poor guy. He stepped back and was relieved when I asked politely to see his manager.

'I'm sorry.' He looked behind him to a corner in the warehouse. There was an office with a mirrored window. 'He has gone to lunch.'

'It's ten o'clock in the morning!' I raised my voice so that the shadow behind the reflective glass could hear me.

'That is not the manager. He is just like me.' A mirror image appeared at the doorway of the office in support of his colleague.

I scanned the warehouse. There was no-one else about. 'What if we come to some sort of an agreement?' I nodded my head and rubbed my thumb and index finger together.

'No, you must not, please!' The clerk stepped forward and covered my hand with both of his and pushed it gently down. 'We will lose our jobs!' The two of them looked around to make sure that we had not been seen. 'I am sorry, really. I have a wife and three children in India. He has two girls.' His friend was now standing beside him in support. We cannot afford to lose our jobs!'

'I want to see your boss.'

'He has gone to lunch. He started at work at four this morning.' The other clerk beseeched for understanding. 'Even he cannot do this thing that you ask!'

I was in two minds as to whether to stage a sit-in until he returned or to come back later. Knowing how the Middle East worked, he was just as likely not to appear for the day. I decided instead to call Abdullah.

A half hour later he slammed his fist on the same counter several times, shoved their order book so that it almost fell on the floor and threw their pencils at them while I looked on, mortified, but equally desperate. When they ignored the billfold that he finally threw in front of them ($500) I knew that all was lost. He knew it too, but to save face, he stormed out of the warehouse and threatened to bring back reinforcements.

I followed, but not before I had made profuse apologies to the two clerks who were really just doing their jobs. I had never intended it to get that ugly.

In the car park outside Abdullah made a big show of being furious, but quickly calmed down when I absolved him of any shortcomings. Another customer parked and disappeared into the building while we discussed what other options I had (none). We were just about to leave, when he came back out again.

'Hey!' He waved some papers in the air and called out my name to attract my attention.

'F%#k! I thought. He must be the manager. I braced myself for the bollocking that I rightly deserved.

'It's me, Peter!' He extended his hand as he approached. 'I met you at your clinic.' There was something about his Scottish accent that struck a chord. His handshake was more than friendly.

'We were wondering what had happened to ya. So, ye are having trouble with yer sponsor eh!?'

I still could not place his face.

'Bastards, they are all the same!' He placed the sheets of paper he had been holding on the roof of my car and flicked through them until he got to the sixth page.

I recognized them as the shipping papers I had been filling out.

'Who's your friend?' He nodded back to the warehouse where Abdullah had just given his clerks a verbal hiding. 'I have never seen a pale skinned Indian before in my life, until now!' he laughed. He took a pen from his breast pocket and signed over the Sponsor's line with a flourish. 'Take this to the office in the front over there.' He pointed to a two story building. 'There is a ship leaving in two days' time. If you can pay the account today, then I will see to it that your container is on board.'

I was too stunned to answer.

'You still don't know who I am, do ye?'

I shook my head.

'I'm Maggie's husband. Remember? She had the car accident, then she came to you and she had the baby!'

His eyes welled up. The good nature he had shown just before was all of a sudden choked and he was lost for words. He extended his hand again, but this time it was shaking.

When I took it, he squeezed hard and held on for the longest time. 'Thank you!' He handed me the papers to release our container.

19

God this, God that, God the other!

If the saying is true ... that the Gods help those who help themselves, then it is even truer for those who help others. You can be surrounded by a whole bunch of self-righteous dickheads thinking that they deserve a piece of you, but the rest of the world looking on thinks differently. Having our container released therefore, was as much a moral victory as it was financial. We could have managed without it, somehow, but to know that our most personal possessions had been saved from falling into the hands of thieves by friends we never knew that we had! Well, you can make your own judgment on that one.

The following day we received a call out of the blue from Naidoo who was the manager of the workshop at the marina.

'I have your cylinder head taking up space here on my bench. Do you not think that it would be better if it was sitting on your engine?!'

'*You* have it? I thought that the police had taken it away.'

'They told us to take it off, but they did not tell us what to with it after that!' He laughed at their incompetence. 'It belongs to you, so if you want it back on, then I will do it myself today.'

'What about George?' I had received a strongly worded letter from the marina management (George) warning us that we were only allowed on board Edvina with written permission from the Port's authority. To do so without it would constitute trespassing.

431

'Don't worry about him. Everybody here is looking after your boat. He is away in Qatar for the next week. It would be a good time to come down and get any work done that needs doing. You never know when you might want to go back to sea!'

Naidoo had fifteen skilled and unskilled workers ranging from mechanics to painters and general laborers. Three were working illegally under false papers that everyone knew about, including George who had hired them at a fraction of the normal wage. The balance he lined his own pocket with after billing customers the full amount. It was recognized as a fair trade and a way in which a worker could get a foothold into the country before gaining a proper sponsor (usually within a matter of months). Some however, like these three workers, were still with the marina after three years because George had blocked any attempts by them to move on.

Free to come and go otherwise, two had ended up in a bad car smash four hours south of Muscat on a sightseeing trip the year before. To help out, one of the other yachties had organized a "whip around" to which we had donated a couple of hundred dollars to get the two workers back to Muscat once they had been discharged from hospital. They were in such bad shape that George wanted to send them back to India, but after several weeks of free treatment at our clinic, they were able to return to work.

When I arrived at the marina that evening, Naidoo was waiting with my two patients Chandra and Heston. The cylinder head was already back in place, the engine had been serviced and tested and I noticed that Edvina had been cleaned inside and out.

'I can't afford all of these workers.' I explained to Naidoo about the practice and that I no longer had any work.

'When they had no work, you looked after them, no? So now, it is God's wish. We will look after you!'

God this, God that, God the other! I still had not reconciled what the Gods were up to, but before I had a chance to argue, he took a three page foolscap list of jobs to be done from my hand and started reading down through it.

'Chandra was a fisherman. He used to work on a commercial boat off of India. He says that you must leave as soon as possible.' He took the first two pages and called to Heston. They spoke animatedly for a couple of minutes while I wondered how the hell they knew that we were planning on leaving. 'George will be back on Saturday. We will have her ready by Friday night. Then you must go!'

'How did you know, about us leaving?' We had not told a soul.

'George, he told the marina security to watch out for *his* boat. That you might come and try to steal it! They tell me, so I tell you. Now you must do it before he gets back.' He laughed.

'What about your jobs?' Knowing George, heads would roll.

'Chandra and Heston have had enough of this place. They said that they will crew for you if you promise to fly them back to India from the Maldives.'

I was delighted by the prospect. To bring in a professional crew from overseas who was willing to do a delivery during Hurricane season would have cost us a fortune. Having an experienced crew instead, who knew the waters, would be a Godsend (there I go again with the God thing).

'My contract ends here in two months and then I go home as well, so it does not matter.' Naidoo shrugged, 'so long as he does not get your boat!'

The opportunity that we had been presented with was unbelievable. My original plan was to make a midnight dash from the marina and charter a local fishing boat to meet us as far as possible outside the twelve mile limit with provisions and diesel for the journey. All sorts of things could go wrong, especially if the weather was bad, but this would make it so much easier.

Five days though was a shock to the system. It had been three years since our last ocean passage. Darling had been looking forward to a month at least to psych herself up for our forced separation. With Edvina in hand and our container on its way, that was at least what we had expected … but … you guessed it. There were forces acting on our behalf that had entirely different plans.

20

'That's why it is called *faith*!'

'H.R.H. called. He wants you to call him straight away,' Darling handed me my mobile phone which I had forgotten when I went to the marina.

'What did he want?'

'Don't know. He has just come back from the U.S. and heard that we were having problems.'

An hour later, summoned to the lobby of the Intercontinental Hotel, we found ourselves waiting for him to finish a meeting.

'What are you thinking?' Darling was curious. I was staring into space, worn out from a full day of planning and organizing.

'Do you remember, how H.R.H. started as our first patient and saved the practice and our asses when we were just about broke?'

'Yes, but you saved him from having to fly all the way to Harley Street in London!'

'I know, but I was thinking about what the lawyer said … about faith and justice and what has happened in the last two days, with our container and the guys at the marina and Edvina.'

'You mean God closing doors and opening windows!'

'No, not God. Justice. How some sort of support always seems to show up when we are challenged. The scales tipping,' I mimicked with my hands, one up and one down. 'It has a long way to go before we get back to balance, but I'm just saying, that's all.'

'That's why it is called *faith*!' Darling condescended, but before we had a chance to get into some deep, meaningful philosophical argument, H.R.H. appeared at the far side of the lobby and waved for us to join him in a private room.

To be honest, as we went through the traditional formalities that included coffee and dates, (I would have killed for a rum) I wondered why we were there. While he and most of his extended family had become patients at the clinic, I would have classed them as friendly, but not friends. At least not the barbequing type. Still, when one of the highest ranking members of the Royal Family asks you to come and see him, you make a point of being there!

Taking one last sip of his coffee, H.R.H. finally got down to business. 'I went to the clinic today and they told me that you were not there any longer. I had to see Dr Scotty instead. He told me that you had been dismissed over some irregularity?' He left the statement hanging, along with its loaded accusation.

It was a question that begged to be answered, but neither of us was inclined. Embarrassed by the word "irregularity," Darling and I sat silent. Not only had Scotty stolen our practice, but he was now doing a hatchet job on our reputation.

'I don't like your sponsor, especially after what he tried to do with that fellow Anthony and I don't like Dr. Scotty either!' He looked directly at Darling. 'However,' he fidgeted in his chair, 'I cannot fly to England every time I have a back problem! Please, tell me what has happened. I might be able to help.'

I was still reluctant to talk. We knew well enough by now that even if he was a member of the Royal Family, short of breaking the law, there was nothing that he could do. With plans afoot to leave Oman in four days' time, I did not want him doing anything that might interfere with the window of opportunity that we had been presented.

'He kicked us out of the practice and he has impounded Edvina.' Overwhelmed by the need to unburden the weight of some of what had happened and perhaps what lay ahead, Darling spoke up.

'Who is Edvina?'

Darling now had his undivided attention.

I was annoyed at first, thinking that it might spoil our chance of escape. But the more Darling answered his questions, the more I joined in, until it became a competition to see who could vomit the most toxicity. Halfway through he stopped us and made a quick call on his mobile and spoke in Arabic. An hour later, our spleens were empty.

'If I get you a Release, will you stay?'

I felt so good after "letting it all out" that I almost laughed at his offer. We had made a point of being discreet and not mentioning our failed attempt with His Excellency the Lord Mayor, but I was obliged now to fill H.R.H. in on the rest of the details.

'I am not His Excellency!' He was neither admonishing me for disbelieving, nor bragging about his position, but his statement left us with no doubt that *he* could pull it off.

After the debacle with His Excellency the mayor, I wasn't so convinced.

'It's not that simple.' We had already had this conversation in the car on the way to the hotel. A half joking "what if" he made us such an offer. 'Our hearts are just not in it anymore.' Darling reaffirmed the conclusion that we had come to in the car. Even if we got the release, we would still have to deal with Rashard and the courts and be seen to be competing against Scotty and have Angel and their kids living down the road and on and on and on. 'Too messy!'

'I understand, but it is a shame. This country needs people with vision.' He pushed back his chair and stood to extend his hand after giving us almost an hour and a half of his time. 'Please.' He took Darling's hand in both of his. 'Don't think badly of the people of Oman because of those few who have no vision for the future.'

'We have made more friends than we have lost!' She reassured him.

I felt bad that we were saying goodbye without him knowing it. I was about to offer him my sincere thanks for his years of support as a patient, but was interrupted when he excused himself to answer his phone.

He nodded, then looked at me, nodded again then looked at Darling. Something in the conversation needed confirmation, a fact or figure of some sort, which left us all hanging in that awkward state of tension between urgency and rudeness. Finally, he finished. When he put down the phone he was smiling.

'Edvina is free to go!'

What I remember most is the silence.

The stunned looks that Darling and I exchanged. The sense of disbelief that maybe, just maybe, the world had shifted on its axis and returned to a more stable equilibrium.

'I'm not sure that we understand.' The word "free" conjured up a whole set of different possibilities.

'Your boat is in the water, yes?'

'Yes,' I confirmed.

'So long as it is in the water it is free!'

'How?' I was still feeling as thick as two planks.

'You have been to my office?'

'Yes.'

'I am the head of the Navy!'

'Yes?'

'In Oman, His Majesty the Sultan rules the land, but I rule the seas that surround it. So long as your boat is in the water, it is *I*, not Customs, or the Port Authority or the Police or your sponsor, but *I* who decides what happens to her. So! She is free to stay for as long as you wish, or she is free to go. As her captain you get to make that decision!'

I was going to hug the guy, but Darling beat me to it!

'It is nothing, really!' Unused to such a breach of protocol it was his turn to be embarrassed. 'Think of it as a small gift from the people of Oman for all that you have done for our special children.'

Now it was our turn to be self-conscious, for we had done so without expectation.

'Ma Salamah (God be with you) Doctor.'

'I think so. Maybe!'

I was still sitting on the fence, but I was getting pretty close to believing as we danced across the lobby to the bar for a celebration rum to welcome Edvina back into the family!

21

'You are crazy!'

'You are still here Doctor?'

I was in a meeting with our lawyer the next morning updating him on the latest developments. Our conversation had turned into a philosophical discussion on the true meaning of justice when his barrister walked into the room to have a document signed. He did a double-take on seeing me still there.

'His passport is blocked, he cannot get out, remember?' Our lawyer scribbled his signature impatiently across the page.

'Why did he not use the Medical Emergency clause?' the barrister inquired casually as he picked up the papers.

'Because there is no medical emergency!' My lawyer blustered.

'So make one up!' the barrister called over his shoulder as he left the room.

I gave our lawyer "the look." Like he had a lot of explaining to do.

When he reached across the table instead for his cigarette packet, I got there first and confiscated them.

'What?' He threw his hands in the air, suddenly defensive. Before I had a chance, he pulled open a drawer and retrieved another packet.

'What's this Medical Emergency clause?'

'It is nothing. You are a doctor, your family is healthy. There is no Medical Emergency!' When he struck the match I could see that his hand was shaking.

'My daughter had open heart surgery in the Royal Hospital here in Muscat when she was ten months old. Does that constitute an emergency?'

'Well, yes, of course.' His face had turned a crimson brown.

'Why didn't you fucking tell me about the Emergency clause?'

The barrister dashed back into the room to calm the shouting.

'Because you did not tell me about your daughter!' He stood up and started pacing the room. Taking a long drag from his cigarette, he gestured to his colleague to stick around. 'You had me believe that you wanted to stay and fight the case!'

'You had me believe that I could not get out!' It was the first time in my life that I wished I smoked!

'It's not that easy,' the barrister interjected. 'You will need reports and paperwork signed off by a surgeon. They will have to be on hospital paper and he must be prepared to testify if he is summoned to the court. It can be a very expensive exercise.' He made the money sign with his fingers.

'I'm sorry, truly. Had I known that you would have considered this, I would have suggested it. We will do it for free.' He looked at the barrister to back him up.

It's not often you see a lawyer fuck up or lose face, but it did not matter. A new door had opened and I was determined to jam both feet in it.

'I will have everything you need here first thing tomorrow morning. How long will it take after that?'

'Medical emergencies take one day,' the barrister answered, but I could tell that he doubted my determination.

'What time does the court open?

'Nine o'clock.'

'I will be here at eight!'

Six months after Molly's operation, we'd thrown a thank you party for the entire heart surgical team in the back garden of the home of the Head of Department. To help celebrate, we brought in a caterer who specialized in Indian food and I blew my alcohol license along with Abdullah's and a friend of ours who was glad to assist. The doctors all showed up in freshly pressed white shirts, new haircuts and trimmed moustaches that reminded me of Errol Flynn. The nurses in their traditional colorful saris looked stunning compared to the drab uniforms that they were required to wear on duty. Any other part of the world and it would have gotten messy, but in this case, "subdued" would be the best way to describe the night. Everybody was polite, they all shook our hands and thanked us, but then retreated to the opposite end of the garden and talked quietly among themselves. I thought at first that we might have made a mistake. That they were probably sick of attending social functions and endless parties being thrown by families to celebrate the miraculous work which they, in their humble way, had come to take for granted.

'Quite the opposite,' the Head of Department explained. 'You are the first family ever to thank them like this!'

I was aghast. As far as we were concerned, they had not just saved Molly's life, but ours as well. It was impossible to imagine how such selfless work could go unappreciated!

'Really,' the senior nurse confirmed. 'They are not too sure how to act because this has never happened before!'

It was then that we realized, our presence was wrecking their buzz! Still raw from our own experience, I tried to make a speech of gratitude to set the scene and get the party started. When I realized that my show of emotion made them even more uncomfortable, I cut it to half of what I had wanted to say. When I finished, Darling and I bade them good night and departed swiftly by the side entrance through which they had all come. It was only eight o'clock. Sure enough, by the time we reached our car we could hear a collective laughter as the party started in earnest and continued till two the next morning. Luckily no surgery was scheduled the following day!

When I called the Head of Department and explained our predicament he was more than happy to support us. By eight the following morning I had not one, but three of the most creatively written medical reports you have ever seen. One from the Boss himself, one from his second in command and one from the chief anesthetist! All were prepared to front up at the court where they would declare that ...

"The life of the child was in imminent danger!"

"The necessary operation could *not* be carried out in Oman!"

"*The mortality rate was so high, it was essential that the father (me) be allowed to travel with the child!*"

"And ..."

"On the head of the judge be it who blocked us!"

Or words to that effect.

The Head of Department also specifically recommended which judge I should take it to!

Bam, kapow, body blow followed by complete and utter knock out!

With Edvina now secure and under the protection of the Navy, we had come to realize that we no longer had to risk escape by sea. She could wait out the hurricane season in safety. If we could get out and re-establish ourselves somewhere else, then we could come back and get her at a later and safer date.

Imagine how confident I was when I walked into my lawyer's office the following morning!

'How much did this cost you?' The barrister whistled as he tested the weight of the folder containing the three reports with both of his hands. He flicked through each page, making notes on a foolscap binder as he went. The more he nodded and raised his eyebrows, the more impressed I could tell he was by the contents. 'Excellent, excellent, excellent!' His expression changed when he got to the last page.

I was shocked to see him turn pale, as the blood slowly drained from his face.

'No!' He flicked back to the front page. 'No!' His finger underlined the name of the judge to whom all of the correspondence was addressed. '#$@&^%#!' he spat in Arabic. He leaned across the table to his boss and pointed to the judge's name.

'#$@&^%#!' they exchanged glances and looked at me, both shaking their heads.

'What?' The news sounded grim.

'This judge, Al Karoobi, he is known as the Executioner!' Our lawyer, who minutes before had displayed the first signs of hope he had ever shown in my case, threw the pages on the table as if they were worthless. 'When the death sentence is passed in Oman, this is the judge who passes it!'

'So, what does it have to do with my case?'

'He has never given a reprieve. Ever. The man is ruthless. Getting a meeting with him could take weeks, maybe never!'

'You will have to go back to the hospital and get the doctors to address the letters to a different judge.' The barrister urged. 'It doesn't matter who or how long it takes, anyone is better than this man!'

441

'But the Head of Department specifically said that we should deal with *this* judge!' I had no reason to doubt his guidance. What's more, said Head and his team had just flown to India for a week to fulfill a training program in Mumbai.

'Not this one. He has no soul! I would not send my worst enemy to this man.' They spent the next half hour grinding me down with example after example of why I should follow their counsel. My lawyer was as adamant as his colleague that I change judges. What little confidence I'd had in having my passport unblocked was shredded by the time they were finished.

'What am I supposed to do?' I was at my wits end and exhausted from riding the roller coaster of emotion that had slowly been taking its toll on our lives.

'You only get one chance. You cannot appeal the decision or go to a different judge. Especially if *he* turns you down!' The barrister could tell that I was caving in.

'If!' was the strongest line of reasoning I could think of to shore up my position.

'He will, believe me! Then what?' My lawyer persisted. Despite his promise to the contrary, he knew that we could not sustain the fight indefinitely.

Any man with half a brain would have given in to their passionate arguments. A gambler even, would have followed their advice. Torn between the two, I still did not know which way to turn. If we delayed going to the court by a few weeks it might increase our chances of success, but we were just about down to living off of our money jars!

Then it came to me, as I thumped my sternum to stop a fit of choking brought on by swallowing a nervous glass of water and too much cigarette smoke.

'We go with Al Karoobi!'

'You are crazy!' The barrister threw the doctors' reports on the table.

'Maybe.' I couldn't explain, but as I held my hand to my chest, I realized the significance of the moment. I had no choice but to believe in the man who had held our baby's heart in his hands and saved her life by fixing what needed mending. If anything, my hour of need was now greater and if we could not have faith in him, then who could I trust with my own life?

'You remember that conversation that we were having about justice and the universe balancing things out?' My lawyer exhaled loudly then stubbed out his cigarette.

I nodded.

'Forget about it!'

22

'Don't worry about Mr. Asshole!'

It is one thing to profess "having faith." It was another to act upon it, I discovered, as we drove to the courts through the heavy traffic the following morning. It took all of my strength to stop myself from hyperventilating in front of the barrister who sat brooding over what he had labeled "madness." Twice, he had called me to try and change my mind. Twice, I had rebuffed him, the second time rudely. After discussion with Darling my mind was more firm, but it was only the strength of her own faith that was keeping me together. I have to admit though, as I parked among a sea of cars outside a formidable building that looked more like a fortress than a Court, it was me who was now doing the shaking.

'It would be better that you wait over there.' The barrister pointed to The Radisson Hotel on the far side of the road. 'I will visit the judge's office and lodge a request for a meeting with his secretary. After that, I will go and do some other business and keep going back until the secretary sees me. It could take weeks!' It wasn't the first time that he reminded me.

Memories of the Labor Court where I had sat among the sweat and stench of wall-to-wall people were enough to drive me across the road to the lobby of the Hotel. I ordered a coffee and a copy of the newspaper and sat where I could watch the front entrance to the court.

With grim determination, I was prepared to hold vigil for as many days or weeks as it took for the lawyer to exit and bring me news of my fate.

You can imagine my surprise then, halfway through the lifestyle section, I came across an advertorial for the 1st Chiropractic Center with a mug shot of Scotty mocking me from the top left hand corner of the page. Photogenic, everything about his smile said "trust me" and caused the bitter taste of coffee to regurgitate in my mouth

If that wasn't bad enough, I sat up, suddenly aware of a Kiwi voice booming over the radio speakers in the lobby. "Click clack, front and back!" just about setting my blood to boil. It was Scotty, the "new manager of the Chiropractic Center" carrying on like he owned the place and preaching about the importance of wearing a seatbelt. Like he really cared. I wondered if I had sounded so slimy. It was galling to think that he had picked up so easily where we had left off.

If it wasn't Scotty, then the Gods were mocking me as I remembered my lawyer telling me to forget about "justice." I had never in my life felt so lonely and vulnerable and angry and impotent, and stupid.

I stood up to pace the room, thinking *'how the hell are we going to get ourselves out of this mess?'* when I spotted the barrister. He was standing, agitated, on the traffic island on the center of the road between the hotel and the court. Twice he tried to dash between cars. Twice he failed and had to return to the safety of the island, each time waving a sheet of papers angrily at the drivers who had almost killed him. Finally, the gap big enough, he made another attempt, and waving both hands in the air as if possessed by some kind of madness, he made it across.

By the time I met him at the entranceway, he was lathered in sweat and leaning against the wall with his hands on his knees, gasping.

'What's happened?' I expected the worst.

'Who are you to God?' was the first thing he said when he finally caught his breath.

'Wha ..?'

'I want to know which God you pray to!' He shook the papers in front of me.

I looked around, as if he was speaking to someone else, but I did not get a chance to question him.

'I go into the court!' He pointed across the road with the same papers, 'and they are expecting me. *Me!*' He made it sound like some sort of mistake. 'The secretary, he greets me and sits me down in his office and gives me coffee. He asks about my family. *My* family. I don't even know this man! We talk. He talks, like I am some long-lost friend. When we are finished the coffee, he brings me into the judge's office. *He* greets me! It is like I am his brother or his cousin or something. He sits me down, gives me more coffee and we talk!' By now the barrister has caught his breath and he is on a roll. 'Twenty years of going to this court and I have never, ever had coffee with any judge. Imagine, twenty years and never so much as a greeting in the hallway or an acknowledgement in court other than formalities and curses and believe me, this man can curse! And now, here I am today, sitting in his rooms drinking coffee and he tells me all about his family!' He nodded as if the twenty years had been worth the wait.

I raised the palms of my hands in the air. He still had not answered my question.

'Here!' He handed me the sheet of papers which by now were half crumpled from all of the excitement.

'What is it?'

'It is your release!'

'???!!!!!!!!??????!!!!!!!!!'

'You are free to go!'

'Bu …!'

'I know! I did not have to state your case or plead with him. He just signed the papers while we were having the coffee!'

I should have said holy F#@% or what the F#@% or words to that effect, but I was too stunned to know how to respond.

'Aisha, his granddaughter?' The barrister was unsure. 'He said that she had been to some Group that your wife started? That you have a daughter, also, like her, no?'

I nodded.

'He said that she sits on his lap now and calls him "Baba" and that she is learning to read. That it is a miracle because she could not do that before.'

Every cloud has a silver lining … it's not what you know, but who you know … the Gods help those who help themselves … He who dares wins … God does not close a door but he opens another … perhaps, just perhaps there is a form of justice in the universe …

My eyes scanned the sheets, all printed in Arabic, but my incoherent mind was spinning, trying to connect all of the dots.

'His family, they have hope now. They are *very* happy. He told me to tell you that God is good!'

Who was I to argue?

'It is a shame!' The barrister spoke, humbled. 'Nobody knows him like this. Really, he is a good man!'

'When can we leave?' That much was obvious, but I was suspicious that there might be a catch.

'He said to be very careful,' the barrister warned, returning to business. 'Your sponsor's lawyer will be notified as soon as the release is lodged. It will be up to him to notify your sponsor who has the right to object. However, because he works at the airport, he might find out earlier. So, make your travel plans and then let me know when you are leaving. The sooner the better!' he encouraged. 'We will lodge the release on the day that you travel and Inshallah. You will be free to go!'

It was important to me to leave as we had arrived. A *free man*, and not like some criminal being stolen across the border in the boot of Abdullah's car. It was important also, to have the time to say proper goodbyes. To be able to show our appreciation for all of the help that we had received from our *other* best friends and members of the Group who had stood by us in this test of time.

To help us get organized, I met with my *bestest* friend of all that afternoon who had already made the arrangements for our departure.

'Docta, I book de tickets in my company name for this Friday afternoon, last flight. I will give the airline your names one hour before you travel. I will bring you to the airport and lodge the release with immigration myself so that nobody can stop you!'

'What about Rashard?' One whiff of what we were doing and he'd be onto us like a dog's dinner.

'Don't worry about Mr. Asshole. Remember the manager from India he fired without paying off? My friend from de Ministry of Labor have meeting with Rashard on Friday afternoon to question him about the case. He will have big headache by the time my friend is finished. Believe me, he will not want to hear from his lawyer!' Abdullah smiled. Of all our friends, I was beginning to think that this rogue had been our biggest Angel and that I would miss him the most.

There was an impossible number of people to get through, but somehow, by chunking them into groups and making lots of phone calls, we managed, through laughter and a few tears, to say goodbye to everyone. The hardest goodbye though was Violi who had become an important member of our family. To the bitter end she had been loyal to us, but she too had lost the gamble for a better life. Still bound to

Rashard through sponsorship, she would be at his mercy after we departed. This was the part that really sucked, but she still put on a brave face. Had we had a more secure future, we would have gladly taken her with us. Instead, we had no choice but to pay her off with what little money we had left. We gave her a bonus which she tried to refuse, but eventually accepted, knowing that she was going to need it more than us.

By Wednesday evening our physical, mental, emotional and spiritual lives had been deconstructed and dumbed down to five suitcases, four carry bags and a push chair. It was a somber affair as the clock slowly ticked away the end of our life in Oman to the inevitable departure the following day. We tried to act like a normal family by ordering pizza and watching a movie on DVD, but each of us was, in one way or another, caught up in our separate thoughts of betrayal and loss. Then suddenly the room erupted.

'Dad, look!' Poppit screamed.

'Mam!' Jack shouted as if a ghost had suddenly appeared in the room.

I sat up so fast that I almost fell off the sofa that I had been lying upon.

'Oh my God!' Darling's face was beaming.

In the center of the room Molly, now almost three years old, was standing unaided for the very first time in her life and daring to take her first step. By the time a third child reaches this point of development, most parents are pretty much over the thrill, but not this family! You'd think it was the Olympic Games the way we cheered her on.

'You can do it! ... Rah rah! ... Come on Molly! Yeah yeah! ... You are the champion of the world! ... Yee har!' ... or words to that effect! One step, then another, but then she stumbled and fell and we all wondered if we had been seeing things. Unperturbed, she got back on her hunkers and stuck her arse in the air and lifted herself back to a standing position again. Then, with her two hands raised above her head like the winner crossing the finish line, she took three more phenomenal, fantastic, ground-breaking, life-changing *unsteady* steps forward. When we all cheered for the second time, she sat down again wondering what all of the fuss was about!

If Darling and I took it as a good omen for our future we did not say it. Instead, when the kids were safely asleep we walked the two blocks it took to reach the Grand Hyatt Hotel, determined that we would leave on a celebration.

23

'I don't give a damn about you!'

For Molly, the rug rat, whose only means of locomotion had been to roll wherever she wanted to go … it was one small step. If she could walk, then maybe she could learn to talk. If she could talk then maybe, someday, she would go to school and learn to drive a car. The possibilities were endless.

For us, we saw ourselves as taking a giant leap of faith. That we were gaining as much as we perceived we were losing and that for every door that closed behind us, the possibilities for our future were also endless. As we walked hand in hand to the hotel, each step connected the dots between our successes and failures, the happy days and not so happy and the highs and the lows since we had set sail from New Zealand. The more positives we added to the negatives, the more coincidences we could recall that had swung in our favor and all of the heroes who had supported us, the closer we came to balance. By the time we reached the hotel we were cheerful, our life back on a more even keel.

The lawyer had been more right about justice than he realized. We had been challenged, but at the same time, there had always been a presence or someone to help us. There was a certain irony in the fact that the worst day of our life was the one that would eventually save us. Had Molly not needed heart surgery, then we would not have had the support of her surgeons to get out of Oman. More importantly, during the toughest of times, we had found within ourselves the resources that we had never imagined we possessed. *This one fact alone made us richer for the future.* Fair exchange had taken place and while it may not have seemed obvious at the time, we had faith that we were graduating from the University of Hard Knocks with a degree that would pay dividends for the rest of our lives.

It was a philosophy that had yet to be tested. How we would be served might take years to find out, but we were comfortable with the discomfort of not knowing. There would be darkness, no doubt. There is always darkness before the light, but as we entered the lobby of the hotel, we were determined to celebrate our *ending* in Oman as a new beginning and bid a fond farewell to a country whose people we had grown to love.

Sitting as a centerpiece in the grand entranceway was a large gold leaf table with a solid malachite stone top. A fresh flower arrangement worth at least five hundred dollars adorned the edifice. (The table was reputed to be worth half a million dollars). It got bigger, bolder and golder as we walked from the solid marble lobby into the grand reception area which was cavernous and full of majesty. It had full-sized desert tents, a fountain in which you could float Edvina, bronzed statues of wild animals grazing lazily and life-sized date palms whose fronds seemed to wave in an imaginary breeze. The dome ceiling, six stories above us, was etched out with star lights that twinkled the constellations.

It seemed fitting then, when the waiter served us Dilmah tea, that we should spend our last hour or so reminiscing about Merrill and Lewis and all of the other great people who had inspired us on our journey. While doing so, the lounge slowly emptied, the world fell asleep and our souls found peace as we sat silent, holding hands and watching the fountain do its dance.

Satisfied, we were just about to leave when our calm was disturbed from behind. Someone in a good mood had just made an entrance. Brash and loud, the door man and porter joined in the laughter. The person obviously had the same colored skin. Our ears followed footsteps to the reception. There was a tinkling of keys, another jolly conversation. Somewhere in the mix we thought that we could hear a Kiwi accent. The voice made its way across the lobby directly behind us, faltered, hesitated, made a decision. Then Scotty appeared in front of us.

'Hi guys!' He acted like we were long-lost friends who had not seen each other for years (two to be exact). We were equally surprised when he leaned in across the coffee table and kissed Darling on the cheek. It was unreal. He extended his hand and shook mine with enthusiasm. Thick skinned, the Rhino sat down uninvited, about as welcome as Anthony at a child care center! His eyes were wide, his nostrils flared, his tusks set to deflect any torpedoes that we might attempt to fire back at him.

'How are you, how's the kids?' Enjoying our obvious discomfort, he was charged for a confrontation.

We fielded his questions with some of our own.

He confirmed "indeed" that he had concerns for his son. Just to be sure, he had all of the knives in the glove compartment of his car at the airport.

Not all, I thought, as he searched for a chink in our armor. He was one word away from starting a war.

Whatever movie he had going on in his head though, we weren't buying it. We had made our peace with life and while momentarily disturbed, we were not going to waste it listening to him use us as an excuse for what he had done. The crime had been committed, the deed had been done. We were determined not to give him the pleasure of an argument. Nevertheless, he had us cornered and through sufficient goading, a "why" finally slipped out.

'Why?' he scolded in an impatient voice, like a teacher being asked a stupid question. 'Why?' (Was it not obvious?) 'Because I don't give a damn about you, that's why!' He squatted within a metre of Darling, but spat directly at me as if she did not exist.

If he said "I don't give a damn" once, then he said it a hundred times, each word aimed at our hearts, each sentence, a body blow that he had been practicing for years. 'I don't give a damn about your wife! I don't give a damn about your children! I don't give a damn about your life!' It was *surreal*. 'I don't give a damn about how hard you have worked! I don't give a damn about how much you have sacrificed! I don't give a damn how much it has cost you! I don't give a damn about Molly or the Group! I don't give a damn about your boat or all of your belongings!' On and on and on. His eyes were like daggers trying to bore into our souls!

When he finished ranting on about how much he didn't give a damn, he switched to how *he* couldn't believe how *I* had treated Angel. "How *she* had come to Oman (uninvited) and all that *they* had done for us when Molly was born!'

451

I can't imagine how many times he had rehearsed, but someone else had written his script.

'I hear you are telling stories about us back home. Making it look like we are the reason you are in the shit!'

Sitting there listening to his angry outburst, I finally understood for the first time that a *castle does not maketh a king nor a suit of armor maketh a knight.* The more he lied and twisted his version of the reality, the more he sounded like Humpy Dumpty!

"Hold!" I could hear my lawyer warn.

"Hold!" H.R.H. had counseled me from doing anything stupid.

They need not have worried. The adrenalin may have been flowing, but the more illogical Scotty's version of the truth became, the more I focused my anger on tuning out. He might have been giving the performance of his life, but it was like watching a B grade movie with the mute turned on.

Unmoved by his claims, the part of me that had wanted to rip his head off only a few short weeks before, sat silent in the knowledge that tomorrow we would escape from his madness. That our container was gone and Edvina was free to follow. That the suffering he intended had already faded to nothing. That the only thing he was spoiling now was our cup of tea!

Darling could have taken to the phone and humiliated Angel with all that *we* had done for *them* when *their* lives had turned to a shambles. But *he* had stood by Angel then, after *her* affair with Tollison and I knew that *she* would have to do the same while he fucked her two best friends.

The tears that ran silently down Darling's cheeks finally gave me the word that I was looking for. Pity. His looks would have made him a Hollywood movie star. His singing voice a Motown hit. With all of the talents and brains and charisma that he possessed, he could have made any dream come true. Pity. He had so little faith in his own imagination that he had to steal someone else's dream to act as a crutch to his handicapped soul.

My sorrow extended to Angel, whose crime of passion had gone unforgiven and cost her very soul. I hoped, truly, that she would think it worth it. His spleen vented from one long broadside without retaliation, he had no choice but to sit and wait, hopeful, that we might reprise and offer him an excuse to hit us again.

He soon realized that he had been firing blanks. Unscathed, our calm disarmed him and left him unnerved. We were conceding without

452

giving him the fight for which he had obviously prepared. The longer we sat in silence, the more his lies dissolved and crumbled around him.

'Leave now.' I finally reached across the table and offered my hand in peace, saddened by the loss of my best friend. 'This place is not what you think it is!'

'Don't bring Angel and the children here!' Darling shook her head.

Seeing no point in any further conversation, we huddled together and ignored our uninvited guest. Darling looking for a tissue in her handbag, me offering her an unsoiled napkin, our gesture one of muted dismissal.

Scotty shook his head and feigned the smile born of one who knows that his victory is hollow. You could tell by how he stood and faltered. As we watched him walk away, *slapped face*, I wondered what sort of lies he was going to tell Angel.

'Two years Docta, you come back. Two years … it nothing in a man's life!' Abdullah held me by the shoulder and shook my hand over and over. We were one minute from stepping on board our flight to Ireland, but he kept blocking my way until we made a deal. 'We make new clinic, bigger, better! Madam, she run the Group. Your children, they will be happy again!' With Abdullah, nothing had ever been a problem, but we both knew that this was one deal he was never likely to pull off.

We had just spent two of the most nerve-wracking hours of our life clearing immigration and customs. Any other judge and they would have challenged his ruling, but Al Marooki's name combined with Abdullah's threats were enough to get us through. We could see why the surgeon had insisted that we use him.

'Madam, you tell him, please!'

Darling hugged him instead.

Facing off with Scotty had rattled us more than we had been willing to let on. It is only when you step from the lifeboat into the ship that saves you, that you realize how close you have come to being shark meat.

The ground crew signaled.

We were the last to board.

'Brother!' Abdullah gave my hand one last squeeze. 'You come back some day.'

'Masalama!' (God be with you) I could not help but hug him.

'Alahakbar!' (God is great) He stood at the bottom of the stairs until we disappeared through the door of the aircraft. I was glad that our seats were on the opposite side so that he would not have to wait and wave goodbye.

Twenty minutes later the wheels left the tarmac. It was only then that we felt free from the clutches of madness that had gripped us for so long.

24

'Do you want me to call an ambulance?!'

Landing in Ireland was a bitterly cold and wet affair. Our one consolation was the warmth of the welcome that we received from our family at the airport who cheered and hugged us like warriors returning from a lengthy campaign. There was no mention of defeat, or judgment or shame. The tissues offered were only for the rain that ran down our faces. They bundled us and our luggage into several cars and took us home where food had been prepared and enough soft words and kindness to console us for our loss.

The following morning I woke early with what you might call three "significant" problems. No job, no house and no money. Necessity being the mother of all motivation, I borrowed my father's car and spent the morning driving around the area in search of a house to live in and open a practice. Call it sobering, it was the first glimpse of the mountain we had to climb to get back on our feet again.

Three hours and two strong coffees later, I was feeling no better when I came across a bungalow with a "For Rent" sign. It was in an ideal location. Main road, busy intersection and vibrant shopping area directly across from a bank. As luck would have it, I came across a Real Estate agency a short distance away.

'I'm inquiring about the house for rent up the road?' I described the location, but my eyes were searching for a bathroom. For some strange reason I was starting to feel queasy and put it down to jet lag.

'Sorry, that's a private house. You will have to contact the owner directly.' The agent was more than helpful. 'We have some similar houses on our books if you would like to take a look?'

My heart was set, but before I knew it, he had a folder in front of me and started leafing through the pages and pointing at other houses.

'How much would the house up the road cost?' I was determined not to be swayed.

He flicked through half a dozen pages and settled on a house that was not too dissimilar. 'A thousand Euros.'

'A *thousand*!' I almost choked. By the time we had finished paying for our airlines tickets and stepped aboard our plane, we had five hundred Euros left to our name.

'It has four bedrooms *and* a patio. Great for barbeques!' His tone changed though when he followed my eyes to the rain that was pelting against his shop window.

'What would it cost for a three bedroomed house?' If we could live in the tight confines of a relatively small boat through some of the most appalling weather, then I reasoned that we could start out smaller and upscale when our circumstances improved.

The agent took a sizeable chunk of pages and folded them all over at the one time, landing about half way through the folder. He rustled through several individual listings, couldn't find what he was looking for, then took another chunk and landed closer to the back.

'There, that would do you!' He pointed to a terraced house at on a dead end street.

I began to feel the life drain from me. 'How much?' I was forced to inquire. None of the pages had any prices on them.

'Six hundred!' He made it sound like the bargain.

'For that?' There was no driveway, hardly any parking on the road and the property backed onto an industrial estate.

'You are not from around here are you?' He pointed to my suntanned hands which were starting to shiver. 'It's the Celtic Tiger. Things are mad! How much have you got and I'll see what we can do for you?'

'Four hundred!' I remembered that Darling had taken a hundred to bring the kids to the city on a consolation outing.

'Right.' He stalled, trying to maintain his composure. 'Let's see what we have here at the back!' I don't know who was the more hopeless, me or the agent, but he stopped trying to sound upbeat when he landed on the last page.

It was there, for the first time, that the *truth* of our situation hit me with a photo of a two bedroomed mobile home on a site twenty miles north of Dublin.

'Are you okay?' The agent reached across the table to steady me. 'Mary, bring me a glass of water. Quick!' He shouted at his receptionist.

Two bedrooms, mains connections, running water, a built in shower and a view of the Irish Sea from the deck … the advert went on to enthuse about … *friendly neighbors (five metres either side) and an ablutions block where communal laundry could be accessed for a small fee …* whoopee!

My diaphragm seized, my heart stopped beating. It was like somebody had punched me in the guts. Already drowning, I refused the glass of water and stumbled headlong towards the front doorway like a deep sea diver who had run out of air.

'Do you want me to call an ambulance?!' The agent, now terrified that I might die on his premises, followed behind, but stopped short of the front steps where the rain gave us both a hammering.

'I'm fine, I'm fine!' The sting from the drops soaked through my shirt and helped me to catch my breath. 'Go back inside!' I waved him away like some drunkard, that he might see my shame.

He retreated, but kept a nervous eye on me as I leaned my back against the shop window to steady myself.

From there, the entire weight of the world slowly took over until my ass hit the wet ground and my head rested between my knees with my arms wrapped around my legs.

Call it post-traumatic stress disorder, call it feeling sorry for yourself, call it whatever you want, but there is nothing more pathetic than a man wailing like a child!

'Are you sure you are okay?' It was the agent again, in spite of the downpour. He handed me an umbrella when I refused to go back inside.

Embarrassed and not wanting to be any further nuisance, I managed to creak to an upright position and limp down the road. Oblivious to my surroundings and the people that stared, I passed the last shop and kept on walking.

Sometime later, I found myself leaning against a solid marble wall that seemed to reach beyond the rain to the heavens. It was there that I finally resorted to religion.

'Give me a sign, please, God, give me a sign, a whisper, a crumb of your presence and infinite wisdom,' I begged, 'that we might get through the ordeal!' I dropped the umbrella and looked up with blinking eyes through the clouds. In that instant, the rain got heavier!

'Give me something!' I was desperate. 'Anything!' I had lost all faith in myself and was prepared to offer up my soul in return for salvation.

Still, nothing. No sudden apparition or bolt of lightning.

I dropped my gaze to wipe the rain from my face with the sleeve of my sodden shirt so that I might see better. When my eyes came back into focus, I was looking at a billboard across the road. It was ten feet high and twenty feet long. On it was an advertisement for a famous brand vacuum cleaner, but it was the caption below the machine that caught my eye. *"Does your life suck?"* I looked at the board, then up to the heavens, looked at the board again and suddenly recognized. It was the same billboard which had persuaded me to go to Australia at the start of my journey.

Then I realized that I was standing beside the granite bridge that had almost ended my adventure before it had begun! F%$@#$#$#$@!!!!! It was the equivalent of being struck by lightning!

Call me a Mental Defective. Call me soggy on the brain, but I took it as a sign. That God exists? I don't know, but if she does, she has a wicked sense of humor. I could imagine Lewis sitting beside her, the two of them having a good old laugh at my expense! More importantly though, I realized that we were going to be okay. I may not have managed to sail all of the way around the world, but somehow I had come full circle and *survived!* If I had done it before, then I reasoned that I or we could do it again.

The pirates had taken our lifestyle, but they had not taken our lives. They had taken everything we had worked for, but not what I valued most, which was my wife and my children. Just as importantly though, they had not taken my dreams. If it meant starting from scratch again then so be it. I had met too many fantastic people and had too many fantastic times along the way not to give it another try.

But this wasn't just about me. As much as we tried to shield them, our children had lived through the same drama and suffered the indignity of losing their lives to a bunch of thieves who had professed to being closest to their hearts. What was I supposed to tell them? What words of compensation could I use to make up for the friends that they had lost? For the great life that they had won by daring that first day to step on to Edvina, only to have it taken by a bunch of Land Lubbing Pirates. As the Captain of their souls I felt responsible for their suffering. "Harden up" was just a little too hard to expect of them when they had stood by me so faithfully for so long. As the master of our disaster I considered it my duty to rally the troops and give them some sort of encouragement for the future.

I knew under the bridge that I needed to go home. To talk to them and give them some sort of inspiration. That we would be better off and not *bitter* as a consequence of this experience. That we had been blessed, not cursed, and while it may not seem obvious at the time, I was sure that there was justice in the world and that we would look back with gratitude for their *seeming* betrayal. A lofty idea when you are standing soaked to your bollocks in the rain with no job or a place to call your own.

I arrived home to an empty house and a note from Darling stating that they would return in the early afternoon. It gave me time to clean myself up and think about my speech. To refine my lines and color my verse so that our situation would appear the furthest thing from bleak.

When they returned, loaded with bargains, I ignored their good humor and marched them all to the kitchen table and sat them down for the collective uplifting that I was sure they needed. I'd had hours to rehearse, notes for back up and two strong cups of Dilmah to fortify my resolve. As Captain of the ship, I was determined that by the time I was finished, they would all be on board.

Nothing could have been further from the truth. My new-found resolve cracked the moment I started. The rally call I intended turned to blubbering and the prayers that I had meant to heal turned to blasphemy. What I'd had in mind was "I have a dream" by Martin Luther King mixed with "From the ashes of disaster grow the roses of success" from our favorite movie Chitty Chitty Bang Bang. "Grow the roses, those rosey roses!" Our future looked so bright, we were going to have to wear sunglasses!

Instead, the words I had planned ended in curses. 'Those f$%@&n b#@$&%@s!'

It was still too raw, too close to the heart.

'Our best friends … *Our best friends!*'

I cursed them and myself, over and over, guilty for having led my family into such a trap in the first place. Humiliated to find that I was in tears *again* for a second time that day.

'STOP!!!! Poppit yelled. 'Stop!' She held the palms of both her hands in front of her to prevent any further profanity. 'Don't say another word. Just listen!' She looked to her younger brother for support. 'Jack and I have come to a decision!'

'Wha …?'

'Just listen, okay. Stay quiet and listen!' My eleven-year-old son took command.

Poppit reached into one of the shopping bags and withdrew a rolled up poster.

'Dad.'

I searched Darling's eyes for an explanation. When none was forthcoming, I turned to Jack, but he was too busy helping his sister.

'Dad!' *Drum roll…* they looked at each other and then unfolded the poster. 'SHIT HAPPENS!' they announced at the same time. They were both nervous as hell, but equally determined that I should hear them out. 'When shit happens you have two choices!' This, from a fourteen-year-old lecturing her father!

'What are they?' I looked at Darling again, but she feigned ignorance.

'The first choice is to go around complaining to everyone who will listen that life stinks!' Their posture let me know, in no uncertain terms, that this would be a *bad* idea.

'What's the second?'

'You can do what Granddad does with the shit.'

'What's that?'

'He grows championship roses!'

'We think that's what you should do,' Jack chimed in.

'Dada!'

When I looked at Molly, she too was smiling, like the whole thing had been her big idea!

There was no guilt or blame attached, but rather a deeper understanding than I could ever have hoped to convey with my blubbering.

I cannot say that it was one of the happiest moments of my life … but it was certainly one of the proudest. In the school of hard knocks this is *Honors Degree* kind of stuff and here were my two young teenage children telling me that they had gotten the lesson. While it did not solve our problems, the burden of guilt was lifted and life suddenly became a whole lot easier. I began to believe for the first time that maybe we had not lost everything. That the wisdom our children had gained from the experience was worth far more than the price that had been paid or any education they might eventually receive at a university.

I knew then that somehow, given time and a chance to heal, that we were truly going to be okay.

THE BEGINNING!

Epilogue

Wait, there's more!

The importance of the Villain

It's been over thirty years since that fateful day under the bridge in Dublin. Half that, since I made my promise to Lewis. Less again since I met the Devil on a beach in Oman who had the best of intentions when he suggested we crucify my best friend.

What a journey. I do hope that you have enjoyed it! It started out with me, but now it's we and that includes Darling, Poppit, Jack, Molly and you our faithful reader! You will recall that when I made my promise to Lewis I was working on an idea called The Power of Story.

Ultimately, I believe that it is stories that save us. Stories of love, stories of adventure, of adversity, of great deeds done, of hardship overcome, difficulty, danger and misfortune … for contained within each and every story is a "silver lining" that lifts us when we are down, strengthens us when we are weak, acts as a balm to sooth our suffering and offers us hope when all else seems lost.

Who we are then, is not a matter of our circumstances, but the story that we chose to tell and act out as a consequence. Having told you my story, it would be remiss of me then to not ask you about your story. I'd like also to share some insights that you might find helpful. Then, all going well, I would like to invite you on the next stage of our adventure!

So ... when you wake up in the morning, do you see yourself as a success or a failure? Is your story empowered or disempowered? Are you the hero … or do you play the role of a victim? Are you running away or are you running towards your dream?

When the shit hit the fan for us, Poppit and Jack gave me two choices. I could play the victim and complain that life stinks, or go out and grow roses with the shit that life had given us.

What sort of a story do you tell when you are challenged?

More importantly, what do you tell your children?

You don't have any?

Then what do you tell the child inside of you?

"Wha …?" I hear you say.

Again, what do you tell the child inside of you?

Every one of us has a child inside. Stick with me here, I'm not being all new agey! It doesn't matter whether you are nine or ninety, every one of us has a child inside looking to tell their story. If you don't believe me, then this is how your story started.

"When I grow up I'm gonna be!

Do you remember? A rock star, an All Black, a famous scientist, a mega movie star, a racing car driver, an Olympic champion, climb Everest!

At the beginning of the book, it states that life is a diary in which we mean to write one story, but write another, and our humblest hour is when we compares the volume as it is with what we vowed to make it.

Ask your Self these questions.

Is the child inside happy with the story you are telling right now?

Is the child inside you happy with the adult that you have become?

Does the child inside you have Down Syndrome?

No?

Then what's your excuse?

I know that you have a dream sitting on a shelf collecting dust just like my manuscript The Christening was for a long time. It's a dream about your family or your relationship with your partner or your children or your business or a big hairy scary audacious goal that you have. You have made a promise to yourself. "You are gonna do it," but you are waiting for the right time and the right place. You are waiting for the stars to align, your ship to come in, lightning to strike, that perfect moment when all of the forces that prevail against you have been dealt to ... and then ... da da daaaaaaa ... you will be all that you can possibly be and deliver your masterpiece!

"Now hear this!"

It doesn't happen that way!! I learnt this from my good friend Lewis. The road to success is not linear. There is no A, B, C or 1, 2, 3 steps. It looks more like A for adventure, B for Best Friend, C for being crucified by your BF, D for depression, E for escape, F for being f$%#@d, G for gobshite (you). What you find then is that K is for knob on a door and O is for opening said door as a consequence of A, B, C, D, E, F, G, that would have never have opened otherwise. That R is for resurrection and S for seeing the light until you find out over time that A was actually for appreciation, B was for your brother, C was for Crap (you were full of it) D was for Divine intervention, F was for a brand new Future and R for rejection, over and over. It is also for Rewrites and Redrafts and Really sore head from hangovers brought on by said rejections until you find that G is for gratitude ... because ... if it had not been for my BF Scotty, I would never have discovered the grit and determination within me to push on through until I was a published author. (You might want to read this again!)

I had wanted to be a writer for the longest time, but I know now that I wouldn't have become one without my Best Friend Scotty. When he stole everything, he also took all of my excuses ... like waiting for the perfect time or the perfect place or the stars to align, or to be financially independent or for everyone to row in behind and give permission. Instead, he made me dare my genius, every day, until The Christening was finally published. There is a certain irony to this. That your nemesis ends up being your saviour. That living the dream can sometimes be a nightmare. That you sometimes have to go through hell to find your soul!

What I have discovered along the way is that all great stories require a Villain, for it is the villain who makes the ordinary person rise up to do the extraordinary.

Luke Skywalker would be nothing without Darth Vader.
Nelson Mandela would be a nobody without apartheid.
Who would Gandhi be without Colonialism?
Merrill Fernando and the Multinationals Tea Giants.
Edvina and the Storm.

464

The patient and cancer.
The child and the parent.
The list is endless.

Can you imagine how boring your story would be if you did not have some form of internal or external conflict to keep you motivated? I know now, that there is no such thing as being the Good Guy, that I too have played the Villain in Scotty's and many other people's stories.

What I have discovered also is that all great stories don't start with "when I grow up" or "once upon a time." They start instead with "What if?"

What if I listen to the voice inside and go to Australia? What then, if I go to America? What if I hand Darling the second verse of a Simon and Garfunkel song? What if, after all of our hard work, we decide to sell up and follow a bucket list that was made as a promise to a dying friend?

Does that mean that you dear reader have to do the same? Not necessarily!

But what if, you choose to be mentally defective and listen to the voice inside of your head instead of all of those voices who think that they know what is best for you?

What if, you dare your genius to walk the wildest unknown way to where you have never been before? To dream up a destination, a path to follow, a wildest unknown way, over rocks and crags, across high hills where the wind bites cold with malice, through deep mysterious valleys where the wild things echo and roar and rumble and stamp and hiss great clouds of steam from their terrible huffing ways. What if you dream the impossible dream and start walking towards it?

On the way you will be beaten up, chewed, spat out, mauled, ripped apart, double-crossed by Villains and given up for lost. Soon enough you'll learn what it feels like to be beaten up, chewed, spat out, mauled, ripped apart, double crossed and given up for lost. This is called experience and it's very valuable in life, because what you mostly learn from it is that you were more afraid of what might happen than what did happen. Most successful outcomes are caused by calling a series of conventional bluffs.

If you dare your genius, then one bright sunny morning you will discover that the wild and unknown way that you took is carpeted with moss and strewn with tiny flowers. It has become a familiar path, a well-trodden direction which, with the help of the Villain, has put you miles ahead of anyone else and much, much closer to achieving your impossible dream.

For us, it was only by daring our genius that we sailed around the world and produced the Christening. The next 'what if' is to make the Movie. We have been very fortunate to partner with Guinness New Zealand to publish The Christening.

The reviews have been great. To date, we have sold almost three thousand copies and raised over ten thousand dollars for worthy causes including the UpsideDowns Education Trust. A percentage of the profits from Wild Rover and The Christening will continue to be donated to help children with Down Syndrome in New Zealand.

My big challenge in fulfilling my final promise to Lewis is that I know nothing about making movies. I know that you have your own bucket list to work on, but instead of going our separate ways after the next page, perhaps you might consider joining us for a new beginning?

I would love to invite you to come on board our adventure in making the movie. You don't have to give up your day job or sell your house, but there are a few small things that you could do that would be a huge help.

Please purchase a copy of The Christening on Amazon. I promise you (cross my heart) that you will enjoy the trials and tribulations of another great adventure with Kate and Paddy. By doing so you will also help bring The Christening one step closer to becoming a movie.

Also, please go bananas and recommend Wild Rover and The Christening to your family and close friends on e-mail and social media and invite them to share in this adventure. It will be their contribution that will make the movie possible.

You can sign up to my blog at www.trysoftaproductions.com for weekly updates and inspirations to help you make your own dream come true.

You can also contact me on gary@trysoftaproductions.com and share your story. With enough support, I will let you know when and where it is time for casting. Who knows, there might even be a part in the movie for you!

Whatever you decide

Thank you so much for sharing this journey.

May all of your dreams come true.

Gary

The Connection

I write on the North shore of Auckland and practice at Connected Families Chiropractic with my Darling wife Lorene. Inspired by our experiences she founded The Connection, a Holistic health center dedicated to family health care and children with special needs. You can view The Connection and her specialist team at www.theconnection.co.nz. Our daughter Poppit is now a graduate doctor from the New Zealand College of Chiropractic. Jack qualified from Massey University as a photographer and designer. Among her many talents, our unsinkable Molly is a professional belly dancer! The last we heard of our beloved Edvina, she was free and easy sailing off the coast of South America!

With Thanks

Writing is a solo venture, but no writer can do it alone. I owe a deep depth of gratitude to my family and friends for their unfailing support and encouragement.

To my beta readers who were kind enough to suffer through the early drafts and still give me feedback. It meant more work, but this story is the better for your reflection.

Dare your genius has been adapted and rewritten with kind permission from my mentor Bryce Courtenay. His first novel *The Power of One* inspired me to dare my genius and start writing. I have since been fortunate to come full circle and spend time in Bryce's writing class before he passed away.

Cover photo and design by JD photography and design.

Manuscript assessment by Steven Stratford of Write Right

Copy editing and digital upload by Bev Robitai
at www.thebookcoach.weebly.com

Legal advice from Steve Barter and Associates